# Walter Benjamin and Political Theology

## Walter Benjamin Studies

In this series devoted to the writings of Walter Benjamin each volume will focus on a theme central to contemporary work on Benjamin. The series aims to set new standards of work on Benjamin available in English for students and researchers in Philosophy, Cultural Studies and Literary Studies.

Series Editor: Andrew Benjamin, Anniversary Professor of Philosophy and the Humanities at Kingston University London and Distinguished Professor of Architectural Theory at the University of Technology, Sydney.

### Editorial Board:

Howard Caygill, Kingston University, UK
Rebecca Comay, University of Toronto, Canada
Ilit Ferber, Tel Aviv University, Israel
Werner Hamacher, University of Frankfurt, Germany
Julia Ng, Goldsmiths College, University of London, UK
Gerhard Richter, Brown University, USA

### Other titles in the series

*Benjamin on Fashion*, Philipp Ekardt
*Modernism Between Benjamin and Goethe,* Matthew Charles
*Inheriting Walter Benjamin,* Gerhard Richter
*Forces of Education*, Dennis Johannßen and Dominik Zechner

# Walter Benjamin and Political Theology

*Edited by*
Brendan Moran and Paula Schwebel

BLOOMSBURY ACADEMIC
LONDON • NEW YORK • OXFORD • NEW DELHI • SYDNEY

BLOOMSBURY ACADEMIC
Bloomsbury Publishing Plc
50 Bedford Square, London, WC1B 3DP, UK
1385 Broadway, New York, NY 10018, USA
29 Earlsfort Terrace, Dublin 2, Ireland

BLOOMSBURY, BLOOMSBURY ACADEMIC and the Diana logo are trademarks of
Bloomsbury Publishing Plc

First published in Great Britain 2024

Copyright © Brendan Moran and Paula Schwebel, and Contributors, 2024

Brendan Moran and Paula Schwebel have asserted their right under the Copyright,
Designs and Patents Act, 1988, to be identified as Editors of this work.

For legal purposes the Acknowledgements on p. vi constitute an extension
of this copyright page.

Series design by Charlotte Daniels
Cover image: Eugene Fink, 1930 (© Imagno Brandstatter / Getty Images)

All rights reserved. No part of this publication may be reproduced or transmitted
in any form or by any means, electronic or mechanical, including photocopying,
recording, or any information storage or retrieval system, without prior permission
in writing from the publishers.

Bloomsbury Publishing Plc does not have any control over, or responsibility for, any third-
party websites referred to or in this book. All internet addresses given in this book were
correct at the time of going to press. The author and publisher regret any inconvenience
caused if addresses have changed or sites have ceased to exist, but can accept no
responsibility for any such changes.

A catalogue record for this book is available from the British Library.

Library of Congress Cataloging-in-Publication Data

Names: Moran, Brendan P., editor. | Schwebel, Paula, 1981- editor.
Title: Walter Benjamin and political theology / edited by Brendan Moran and
Paula Schwebel.
Description: London: Bloomsbury Academic, 2024. | Series: Walter Benjamin studies |
Includes bibliographical references and index.
Identifiers: LCCN 2023053468 (print) | LCCN 2023053469 (ebook) | ISBN 9781350284340
(hardback) | ISBN 9781350284388 (paperback) | ISBN 9781350284364 (epub) |
ISBN 9781350284357 (ebook)
Subjects: LCSH: Benjamin, Walter, 1892-1940. | Political theology.
Classification: LCC B3209.B584 W336 2024 (print) | LCC B3209.B584 (ebook) |
DDC 320.01–dc23/eng/20231226
LC record available at https://lccn.loc.gov/2023053468
LC ebook record available at https://lccn.loc.gov/2023053469

ISBN: HB: 978-1-3502-8434-0
PB: 978-1-3502-8438-8
ePDF: 978-1-3502-8435-7
eBook: 978-1-3502-8436-4

Series: Walter Benjamin Studies

Typeset by Deanta Global Publishing Services, Chennai, India

To find out more about our authors and books visit www.bloomsbury.com
and sign up for our newsletters.

# Contents

| | |
|---|---:|
| Acknowledgments | vi |
| List of Abbreviations | vii |
| Introduction  *Brendan Moran and Paula Schwebel* | 1 |

### Part I  Contra Schmitt: On Sovereignty and Political Theology

| | | |
|---|---|---:|
| 1 | Melancholy Sovereignty and the Politics of Sin  *Paula Schwebel* | 27 |
| 2 | Sovereignty and Revolutionary Astropolitics: Benjamin, Baroque Trauerspiel, and Calderón's *Life Is a Dream*  *Miguel Vatter* | 50 |
| 3 | Contra Schmitt: Leo Strauss, Walter Benjamin, and Jewish Political Theology  *Leora Batnitzky and Vivian Liska* | 73 |

### Part II  Critique of Law and Theocracy: Nihilism, Anarchism, and the Justice of Study

| | | |
|---|---|---:|
| 4 | Nihilism as World Politics: Benjamin's Theology of Entropy  *Agata Bielik-Robson* | 93 |
| 5 | My Kingdom for a Shirt: Untrammeled Atheism and Anarchism in Benjamin and Kafka  *James Martel* | 117 |
| 6 | Study, Sovereignty, and Justice: Benjamin, Scholem, and Agamben  *Brendan Moran* | 133 |

### Part III  Fate, Messianic Time, and Messianic Adjustment

| | | |
|---|---|---:|
| 7 | Benjamin's Concept of Fate  *Howard Eiland* | 157 |
| 8 | Fulfilled Time: Benjamin's Reception of Hermann Cohen's Idea of Messianism  *Tamara Tagliacozzo* | 174 |
| 9 | Beyond Mysticism and the Apocalypse: Benjamin's Dislocation of the Messianic  *Sami Khatib* | 195 |
| 10 | A Hunchbacked Political Theology: Creaturely Biopolitics as the Self-Sublation of Distorted Life  *Carlo Salzani* | 212 |

| | |
|---|---:|
| List of Contributors | 229 |
| Index | 231 |

# Acknowledgments

*Walter Benjamin and Political Theology* is the result of a fruitful collaboration, not only between us, the editors, but among several friends and colleagues, without whom the publication of this book would not have been possible. First and foremost, we would like to thank Andrew Benjamin, who has been a supporter of this project from the beginning. Andrew participated on a panel on "Walter Benjamin and Political Theology" at SPEP 2019, which sparked the initial idea for this volume. As the Series Editor of "Walter Benjamin Studies," he also provided guidance and advice, which informed the final shape of this project. We are grateful to our editors at Bloomsbury, Liza Thompson, Lucy Harper, and Katrina Calsado for their professionalism and support throughout the production of this volume. Heartfelt thanks are due to our contributors for their patient and engaged responses to our queries and suggestions. We also thank Will Best and Jacob Levy for their valuable assistance at crucial stages in the preparation of the book.

Brendan Moran thanks the Faculty of Arts at the University of Calgary for a sabbatical in 2023 that provided indispensable time for work on the final stages of this volume.

Paula Schwebel thanks the Faculty of Arts at Toronto Metropolitan University for a sabbatical in 2020–1, which provided crucial time for initial work on this volume. As much of the work on this project coincided with the Covid-19 pandemic, she is grateful to those who helped with childcare when schools were closed. Above all, she thanks Aaron and Carina.

Brendan Moran and Paula Schwebel

# Abbreviations

The following list contains references for all works in this volume keyed to abbreviations. For multivolume works, the abbreviation in the text is immediately followed by a numeral to indicate which volume is being referenced (e.g., *SW1*, *GSI*, etc.).

AP     *The Arcades Project*. Trans. Howard Eiland and Kevin McLaughlin. Cambridge MA: Belknap Press of Harvard University Press, 1999.

BS     Walter Benjamin and Gerhsom Scholem, *Briefwechsel 1933-1940*. Ed. Gershom Scholem Frankfurt/M.: Suhrkamp, 1985.

C     *The Correspondence of Walter Benjamin 1910-1940*. Eds. Gershom Scholem and Theodor W. Adorno, trans. Manfred R. Jacobson and Evelyn M. Jacobson. Chicago IL: University of Chicago Press, 1994.

CS     Walter Benjamin and Gershom Scholem, *The Correspondence of Walter Benjamin and Gershom Scholem*. Ed. Gershom Scholem. Trans. Gary Smith and Andre Lefevre. New York NY: Schocken Books, 1989.

EW     *Early Writings 1910-1917*. Trans. Howard Eiland and others. Cambridge MA: Harvard University Press, 2011.

GB     *Gesammelte Briefe*, 6 vols. Eds. Christoph Gödde and Henri Lonitz. Frankfurt/M.: Suhrkamp, 1995-2000.

GS     *Gesammelte Schriften*. Vols I-VII, and Supplements I, II, III. Eds. Rolf Tiedemann, Hermann Schweppenhäuser et al. Frankfurt/M: Suhrkamp, 1974-1999.

OT     *Origin of the German Trauerspiel*. Trans. Howard Eiland. Cambridge MA: Harvard University Press, 2019.

OGT     *The Origin of German Tragic Drama*. Trans. John Osborne. London: Verso, 1998.

SW     *Selected Writings*, Vols. 1-4. Eds. Michael Jennings et al. Cambridge MA: Belknap Press of Harvard University Press, 1996, 1999, 2000, 2003.

TC     *Toward the Critique of Violence: A Critical Edition*. Eds. Peter Fenves and Julia Ng. Stanford: Stanford University Press, 2021.

WuN     *Werke und Nachlaß*. Eds. Christoph Gödde and Henri Lonitz with the Walter Benjamin Archive. Frankfurt/M. or Berlin: Suhrkamp, 2008-.

# Introduction

Brendan Moran and Paula Schwebel[1]

1

In a broad sense, the term "political theology" refers to the interpenetration of religion and politics, and the specific ways in which theological concepts underpin, shape, or otherwise influence political concepts (cf. Newman 2019: 4–5). The concept of political or "civil" theology has a long history.[2] The usage of the term "political theology" in contemporary theory is, however, most readily associated with Carl Schmitt, and his pithy claim that "all significant concepts of the modern theory of the state are secularized theological concepts" (Schmitt 2005: 36). In the first place, Schmitt's claim is genealogical: he looks at the emergence of the modern sovereign state, and the legitimizing work performed by a set of systematic juridical-theological analogies that support political absolutism (for instance, between God and the sovereign, commandment and law, and miracle and the state of exception). More provocatively, Schmitt's claim is also critical and normative: he contends that liberalism, which attempts to put limits on sovereign power through a system of checks and balances, has its condition of possibility in unlimited, authoritative power. In other words, a normal legal order can neither found nor preserve itself without continuous recourse to a transcendent authority, whose task is to decide on what constitutes the "normal" situation, and what must be done to preserve it in a state of emergency. While the question of sovereignty is to varying degrees concealed or repressed by constitutional liberalism, Schmitt maintains that, in the extreme case, liberal democracy's illiberal foundations stand revealed. This was the case in 1932, when, with recourse to Article 48(1) and (2) of the Weimar Constitution, Reich President Hindenburg ruled by presidential emergency decree.[3] Contemporary history furnishes examples which seem to prove, once again, the currency of Schmitt's analysis: for instance, the government of President Emmanuel Macron and Prime Minister Élisabeth Borne recently passed significant socio-economic legislation by exploiting article 49.3 in the French Constitution, a clause that permits the passage of laws without a legislative majority. While such moves on the part of government may be considered threatening to the fabric of democracy, Schmitt, for his part, considers his theory of sovereignty to lay the conceptual foundations for supporting regimes that are even more authoritarian, including the Nazi regime, for which he provided intellectual and political support.[4]

Walter Benjamin is a significant interlocutor for Schmitt and represents a distinctive voice in the field of political theology, broadly conceived. As chapters in this volume show, Benjamin was a close reader of Schmitt, and took seriously the notion of a concealed but continued presence of theology in modern "secular" politics and culture.[5] Yet Benjamin arguably interrogates the political-theological complex from an opposing vantage point. Whereas Schmitt excavates the theological elements in modernity in order to shore up liberalism's illiberal inheritance and to support authoritarianism more generally, Benjamin seems to root out these latent structures in order to dissolve them and liberate us from their oppressive legacy. Benjamin's thought has thus become a touchstone, explicitly or implicitly, in efforts to conceive of a "new" political theology, not anchored in legitimizing and preserving power, but in justice and liberation of the oppressed. Johann Baptist Metz—a clear example of this tendency— refers to Benjamin in his development of a so-called "new political theology," which is explicitly opposed to the political theology of Schmitt.[6] Some have observed an affinity, moreover, between Benjamin and liberation theologies of the left.[7] Still others have used Benjamin's short text "Capitalism as Religion" to articulate and critique political-theological presuppositions of capitalism.[8] To explore why Benjamin has been a fertile source for thinking about political theology beyond—and often against—Schmitt, the chapters in this volume endeavor to address what is distinctive in Benjamin's thinking of the political-theological. While no volume can claim to explore every significant and relevant nuance, the ten original chapters in this volume address some of the most central and vexing issues for any consideration of Benjamin's rapport with political theology. Taken together, the chapters shed light on why Benjamin's work has come to play a significant role in contemporary endeavors to think through the explosive configurations of theology, politics, power, and justice in today's crisis-laden world.

Contemporary and recent philosophies have often been fed by Benjamin's writing in this regard. In his later decades, Jacques Derrida regularly referred to Benjamin— including in a very focused way in his much discussed and controversial essay "Force of Law: The 'mystical foundation of authority,'" which is an analysis of Benjamin's "Critique of Violence" (Derrida 1990). In *Spectres of Marx*, Derrida was also influenced by, and gently transformed, Benjamin's theological-political view (in "On the Concept of History") that—in the incompleteness of which theology reminds us—history has an ongoing and open-ended claim on us. If Benjamin refers to the past's "claim" (*Anspruch*) on us, Derrida reformulates this as its "injunction" (*injonction*), noting that the past interpellates us—practically questions us—with an injunction to consider it in ways we might not otherwise. Derrida refers to Benjamin's "messianism without messianism," or—in Benjamin's words—"'a weak messianic power'" that secretly, spectrally, and in a way that is never univocal, speaks against settling cheaply, superficially, our rapport with the past and indeed with the present and the future (Derrida 1994: 180–1 n21; also see xviii).[9]

Perhaps no prominent contemporary philosophy is more impacted by Benjamin's work than that of Giorgio Agamben, who is sometimes accused of misconstruing Benjamin in various ways. The influence of Benjamin on Agamben is enormous, multifaceted, and in continual development. To mention just one feature: Agamben's pervasive and critical conception of "*nuda vita*" (bare life) is a translation of Benjamin's comparably critical conception of "*bloßes Leben*" (mere life). Much of Agamben's work has adapted Benjamin's critique of "mere life" and its pliancy before institutional control in order to address a form of life that is not the subordination and acquiescence of "bare life" (Salzani 2015). Theological-political motifs with a Benjaminian inflection in Agamben's work are discussed by chapters in this volume and include: the contrast of Schmitt and Benjamin on the state of exception, approaches to questions of eschatology and questions of cosmology, opposition to Christian triumphalism, development of a non-Schmittian conception of decision, exploration of nihilism and anarchism, drawing on Kafka for conceptions of law and study of law, and interest in messianism and messianic time.

There are of course other prominent contemporary philosophies influenced by the way in which Benjamin constellates the political and the theological. Judith Butler's work has become increasingly concerned with Benjaminian motifs. Butler engages significantly with Benjamin's thought on questions of violence, messianic politics, and the theological-political more broadly (Butler 2020, 2016, 2012, especially chapters 3 and 4).[10] Other "contemporaries" of note in this regard include Slavoj Žižek (see Khatib in this volume) and Jacob Taubes (1923–87). The latter has, in turn, posthumously influenced recent receptions of Benjamin's work—as is particularly evident in Agamben's reading of Benjamin and Paul (Agamben 2005b). Taubes will be of concern in a few of the chapters in our volume (particularly that by Bielik-Robson).

There has recently been a veritable upsurge of books concerned with political theology. These run the gamut from studies of the political theologies at work in numerous philosophical figures and traditions (such as F.W.J. Schelling, German Idealism, Kant, Liberalism),[11] to attempts to develop a political theology beyond (and often against) Schmitt,[12] to projects that seek to develop radical democratic political theologies.[13] There have also been studies that seek to expand political theology beyond its Western—especially Christian—roots.[14] In this respect, a volume on Benjamin and political theology is timely. It is also of critical importance, since many of the attempts to take political theology in a non-Schmittian and emancipatory direction do, in fact, already draw on Benjamin, whether overtly or implicitly. If Benjamin plays an often pivotal role in contemporary political theologies, a focused study of this topic in Benjamin's thought is arguably overdue and would have a significance that exceeds the confines of Benjamin scholarship. While there are books that concern themselves with political-theological resonances in Benjamin's work (such as the 2016-volume edited by Dickinson and Symons on Benjamin and theology, and Andrew Benjamin's 2013 book, *Working with Walter Benjamin: Recovering a Political Philosophy*), to date there has (to our knowledge) been no book in English that centers on the political-theological in Benjamin's thought. In our volume, the authors endeavor to take a step in the direction of providing that focus. This step has, of course, been complemented and facilitated by an array of notable books that overlap with the concerns of this volume.[15] Our volume distinguishes itself from these previous studies by addressing quite distinct topics—such as the Reformation and the Counter-Reformation, Benjamin and Leo Strauss, theological entropy, anarchism, the relationship of justice and study, fate, Benjamin and Hermann Cohen on messianic time, and the role of theology in Benjamin's philosophy of history.

Our volume attempts to disentangle Benjamin's thinking of the theological and the political from Schmitt's political theology. At the same time, it asks whether there is something like a uniquely Benjaminian political theology. Benjamin did not explicitly use this term to describe his work, and even if we expand the notion of "political theology" to include sources much broader in philosophical nuance and political orientation than Schmitt, it is not clear that there is a straightforward approach to the topic of political theology in Benjamin's work. Positions on the question of whether Benjamin could be said to have a political theology diverge considerably in the literature, and this diversity is also reflected in the contributions to this volume. On one side, it has been suggested that there is in Benjamin's so-called "Theological-Political Fragment" not only no "salvific history" (*Heilsgeschichte*) but also no "political theology," let alone a "'theological politics'" (Steiner 2016: 51 critically quoting Jennings 2012: 43). In this view, Benjamin's interest is not in "what theology and politics have in common" but in "what separates them from one another" (Steiner 2016: 51). Sami Khatib's chapter in this volume offers a similar line of argumentation with respect to Benjamin's figure of the messianic in the theses "On the Concept of History." Representing what might be construed as the other side, Agata Bielik-Robson suggests, in her contribution to this volume, "that there is a consistent project of a political theology in Benjamin's whole *œuvre* and that it takes the form of 'nihilism as world politics.'" Most of the chapters in this volume suggest at least that there is indeed something distinctive at stake in Benjamin's inter-articulation of the theological and the political, which may be "political-theological," albeit not in a Schmittian sense. Because Benjamin himself advanced no explicit or systematic statement of his own in this regard, our volume does not seek to impose homogeneity where there might be none. Rather, the project that takes form in this volume brings together disparate elements into a unity, which does not expunge plurality. Central themes which emerge in this project are: (a) a consistently critical approach to an oppressive use of power, and the various "myths" that endeavor to elevate such power to a transcendent status; (b) attention to time and transience, as undermining the claim of any given power or state of affairs to be absolute or necessary, as opposed to contingent and changeable; and (c) an abiding concern with justice, and with the ways in which justice has not yet been realized in the present world, revealing it to be *unredeemed*, in contrast to the claim, put forward on some versions of Christianity, that the redemption has already occurred (or, in a secularized form, that the "end" of history has arrived).

These three themes differentiate Benjamin's thinking, in emphasis and orientation, from Schmitt's. It has been argued that Schmitt's intellectual project coalesces around an idea and an ideology of order (Hererro 2015; Meierhenrich and Simons 2016: 3–70; cf. Schneider 1957: 294; Pasquino 1986). Schmitt justifies the use of extra-legal means for the preservation of "law and order," and this reflects his palpable fear of the "other of order": disorder, chaos, anarchy, and disintegration, which for him are the antipodes of the strong, centralized state.[16] At least in *Political Theology* (a work of Schmitt's with which Benjamin was engaged), Schmitt's juridical-political idea of order bears structural similarity to the nominalist conception of order in voluntaristic theologies, according to which the order of creation is imposed, *ex nihilo*, by God's transcendent will. The order that emanates from this sovereign will contains no grounding outside of itself and is therefore not transparent to reason. The significance of the concept of the "state of exception" in modern theories of state, for Schmitt, is that it shows how the juridical order rests on the fiat of authority, rather than a system of normative laws. The "state of exception" reveals that the paradigm of juridical law is command rather than norm.

Benjamin repudiates the voluntaristic conception of order, which he regards as an exercise of power that is, at its basis, arbitrary. Unlike Schmitt, Benjamin does not shun the disintegration of such an order; rather, he conceives of its disintegration as making possible the arrival a more just mode of life. In her contribution to this volume, Schwebel argues that some of Benjamin's early writings, such as "On Language as Such and on the Language of the Human" (1916) and the "Epistemo-Critical Foreword" to the *Origin of the German Trauerspiel* (1925–8), imply an *immanent* order in connection with an eidetic conception of the name. This happens, however, in conjunction with an emphasis on a nature that "mourns" the *imposition* of any order. Benjamin's attempt to call attention to the ways in which imposed orders suppress or deny that which they exclude is complemented by his critical tendency, which aims at dismantling orders, the falsity of which are evident in their reliance on force or coercion. The crisis felt in relation to these orders is a critical opportunity open to a freedom that never abides forcing. Both Schmitt and Benjamin are critics of the inadequacy of the general and the normative, but their critiques come from divergent perspectives. Whereas Schmitt's critique of norms is that they are applied or suspended in relation to the decision of a sovereign, commanding will, which transcends principles, Benjamin's critique of norms is almost always that they do not do justice to the individual, or indeed any particularity, in its singularity.

A similar divergence of perspective is evident in Schmitt's and Benjamin's approaches to history. The linkages between political theology and the representations of history are somewhat under-thematized in Schmitt's early work.[17] In his post-war work, however, Schmitt articulates his own political theology of history, introducing the ambivalent figure of the *Katechon*, the restrainer of the apocalypse.[18] Schmitt sides with this ambivalent figure who holds back the forces of disintegration and chaos, but who—in delaying the apocalypse—forestalls justice (or at least the Last Judgment). Schmitt appears thus to side with order against justice, and accordingly regards law as an instrument of order rather than as an exercise of justice. If Schmitt seeks to restrain the forces of disintegration, Benjamin seeks to amplify transience and to redeem history and nature on this basis. Benjamin's most overt statement on the redemptive quality of transience may be found in his "Theological-Political Fragment," which is discussed in several of the chapters in this volume (Bielik-Robson, Khatib, Moran, and others). In this text and others, Benjamin redeems time against attempts at order that seek to deny it. Part of this redemption involves an endeavor to do justice to injustices and missed possibilities which continue to lay claim on us from the past. These are often suppressed or prematurely "reconciled" in the name of restoring or maintaining order, or instrumentalized as the suffering necessitated by "progress." Prescient of the current urgency with which we are now confronting questions of historical injustice, Benjamin proposes an ethics and politics of anamnestic solidarity, according to which each present generation is called upon to take up the missed possibilities of what has been, both for the sake of the past and for its own sake, as an antidote to the crushing neutralization of the subversive energies that we inherit from the struggles of the past. These are the teachings of what Benjamin calls "the tradition of the oppressed."

## 2

The volume is divided into three parts, reflecting distinct thematic clusters. Part I, "Contra Schmitt: On Sovereignty and Political Theology," debates various aspects of the relationship of Benjamin's work with the explicit political theology of Carl Schmitt and offers indications of how Benjamin parts ways with Schmitt, particularly regarding the concepts of sovereignty, decisionism, the state of exception, and Benjamin's insistence (in some ways similar to Leo Strauss) on the "unredeemed" quality of the world, in marked distinction from Schmitt's "Christian triumphalism." Part II, "Critique of Law and Theocracy: Nihilism, Anarchism, and the Justice of Study," focuses on concepts associated with Benjamin's attempts to develop what could be construed as a political philosophy. In particular, this section discusses Benjamin's concepts of nihilism, anarchism, and the justice of study. These chapters suggest that—in opposing the "mythic" necessity of the given—the critical, negative, and even destructive implications of nihilism, anarchism, and the refusal to settle that is inherent in study, may be understood as furthering justice. Part III, "Fate, Messianic Time, and Messianic Adjustment," takes up Benjamin's longstanding concern with time, and in particular with messianic time. The chapters in this section anchor an understanding of the central importance of the notion of a liberating—as opposed to a fate-propagating— time for a Benjaminian political-theological orientation.

Part I grapples with Benjamin's controversial relationship with Schmitt and the manifold ways in which Benjamin diverges from Schmitt's political theology. Benjamin's references to and adaptations of Schmitt are evident in various texts, including the *Trauerspiel* book and "On the Concept of History." According to Agamben, Benjamin and Schmitt were engaged in a subliminal dialogue, consisting of several cross-references between the two (Agamben 2005a: 52). As Leora Batnitzky and Vivian Liska discuss in their jointly authored chapter, "Contra Schmitt: Leo Strauss, Walter Benjamin and Jewish Political Theology," Schmitt has enjoyed a renaissance among both right-wing and left-wing thinkers. Given the current vogue for Schmitt, and the temptation to read Benjamin's affiliation of theological and political concepts within a Schmittian framework, they argue that it is all the more important to disentangle Benjamin's ideas from Schmitt's thought. The chapters in this section each contribute to this task. Chapters in this section take up key concepts in Schmitt's political theology—including sovereignty, decisionism, and the state of exception—and show how Benjamin was both influenced by Schmitt, while also developing his own, quite distinctive thinking on these topics, often in opposition to Schmitt.

Benjamin's 1928 book on the *Origin of the German Trauerspiel* (a slightly elaborated version of his 1925 *Habilitation* thesis) is a key text for assessing his relationship with Schmitt's thought. Following the publication of his *Trauerspiel* book, Benjamin wrote a now infamous letter to Schmitt, in which he acknowledges the importance of Schmitt's work on the seventeenth-century doctrine of sovereignty for his own analysis of the royal hero in the Baroque plays. He also acknowledges a methodological affinity with Schmitt (*GSI*:3, 887 and GB III, 558).[19] Benjamin's letter reveals little that is not apparent to a careful reader of *Trauerspiel* book, which, in its section on the sovereign, directly references Schmitt's *Political Theology* (although Benjamin specifically highlights the significance of *Dictatorship* in his letter). The subsequent discovery of this letter nevertheless provoked a scandal, no doubt due to its addressee.[20] Mainly because of his embrace of Nazism, Schmitt was considered to be an unsavory correspondent for Benjamin, a left-wing Jewish intellectual who ultimately took his life while fleeing Nazi-dominated Europe. The editors of the first volume of Benjamin's collected correspondence, Theodor Adorno and Gershom Scholem, excluded the letter from their 1966 edition of Benjamin's *Briefe*.[21] Adorno also erased the reference to Schmitt in Benjamin's endnotes to the *Trauerspiel* book, which was published in his 1955 edition (with Gretel Adorno) of Benjamin's *Schriften*.[22] When Benjamin's letter was finally published, in Rolf Tiedemann and Hermann Schweppenhäuser's 1974 edition of a volume in the *Gesammelte Schriften*, the reaction was explosive. In Jacob Taubes's words, Benjamin's letter was nothing less than "a ticking bomb," which "comprehensively shatters our preconceptions regarding the intellectual history of the Weimar period" (Taubes 2013: 16; cf. Bredekamp 2016: 680–2). More recent scholarship has moved past the cry of scandal, and has begun to examine the substance of Schmitt's influence on Benjamin. Without denying this influence, much of the recent literature has demonstrated that Benjamin subtly but significantly subverts Schmitt's ideas.[23] The chapters in Part I advance the view that Benjamin differs in significant ways from Schmitt—a claim that is supported by several of the other chapters in this volume.

These differences come to the forefront in Benjamin's portrayal of the sovereign hero of the Baroque trauerspiel. Despite citing Schmitt's theory of sovereignty, which famously regards the sovereign as the one who decides on the state of exception, Benjamin portrays the sovereign hero of the Baroque dramas as afflicted by melancholy, which renders him all but incapable of making a decision. Two of the chapters in this section, Paula Schwebel's "Melancholy Sovereignty and the Politics of Sin," and Miguel Vatter's "Sovereignty and Revolutionary Astropolitics: Benjamin, Baroque Trauerspiel and Calderón's *Life Is a Dream*," take up Benjamin's non-Schmittian approach to sovereignty. In divergent but complementary ways, moreover, both chapters consider Benjamin's analysis of melancholy to be of significance for understanding how he parts ways with Schmitt.

In Chapter 1, "Melancholy Sovereignty and the Politics of Sin," Schwebel focuses on Benjamin's analysis of what medieval theologians referred to as acedia. She argues that the sovereign's acedia is the most visible sign that an altogether different political theology is at work in the Baroque trauerspiel than in Schmitt's *Political Theology*. Schmitt regards the sovereign as a secularization of the voluntarist God. According to Schwebel, however, the Baroque sovereign's acedia marks a decisive alteration of the Schmittian analogy between the sovereign and God. Acedia was understood as a state of sin, and its significance for the Baroque imaginary of sovereignty, Schwebel argues, points to an Augustinian tradition of political theology, which Francis Oakley has called a "politics of sin." Augustinian ideas made a comeback in the Lutheran

Reformation and are visible in the Lutheran-steeped German Baroque plays. According to a politics of sin, the state is imposed on fallen humanity as both a punishment for original sin and a remedy against the disorder wrought by the Fall. The function of secular authority, accordingly, is to impose a penal order on guilty humanity and, through coercion, to restrain its vicious impulses. Schwebel's chapter considers the difference that it makes when sovereignty is derived, not from a secularization of the concept of divine supremacy, but from humanity's fallen condition, and the supposed need to hinder transgressions. While Benjamin's analysis of the Baroque plays suggests that a politics of sin is at work in his literary sources, Schwebel argues that Benjamin himself advances a subtle critique of a politics of sin. In contrast to Augustine's reading of Genesis 1 and 2, which focuses on the concept of original sin and God's justice in punishing guilty creation, Benjamin turns to Genesis to argue that creation as such is good, and that the imposition of judgments on an otherwise innocent creation is itself guilty of an injustice.

In Chapter 2, "Sovereignty and Revolutionary Astropolitics: Benjamin, Baroque Trauerspiel and Calderón's *Life Is a Dream*," Vatter develops a complementary but divergent analysis of the significance of melancholy in Benjamin's interpretation of the Baroque trauerspiel, He draws out the connections between Benjamin's argument and Aby Warburg's theory of Renaissance "heroic melancholy." Vatter turns to Benjamin's analysis of Calderón, specifically, Calderón's *Life is a Dream* (*La Vida es Sueño*). It may be said that Benjamin invokes Calderón as a foil to bring out the national peculiarities of the German trauerspiels of the Nuremberg and Silesian schools. Both the German and Spanish plays contend with the theological necessities of what Benjamin describes as the secularization of history. Benjamin clarifies that this does not mean that religious concerns have withdrawn or become insignificant. But he argues that the world of the Baroque plays is confined to immanence or denied direct access to transcendence. Benjamin finds in the Spanish dramas an attempt to compensate for the loss of the kingdom of grace by means of a playful reflection. By contrast, he claims that the German plays plunge headlong into the despair of a state of creation devoid of grace (*OT*, 68/*GSI*:1, 260). As Vatter acknowledges, it is often presumed that Benjamin identified more with the despairing attitude of the German plays. This is at least in part because Benjamin remarks that the Spanish plays, while aesthetically superior to the German works, are ethically less responsible (*OT*, 72/*GSI*:1, 263). Conceivably, Benjamin means by this that the Spanish works present creation as aesthetically fulfilled, but this fulfilment conceals and compensates for the withdrawal of the kingdom of grace, substituting semblance and artifice for a genuinely moral or religious resolution. Vatter, however, proposes an original and compelling rereading of Benjamin's argument, which brings to the fore the cosmological and astrological conceptions of revolutions introduced in the late Renaissance, which he demonstrates to be decisive for understanding Calderón's *Life is a Dream*. Building on Warburg's discovery of an "astropolitics" in the Reformation and Counter-Reformation, Vatter argues that this Renaissance conception of revolutions anticipates themes in Benjamin's own emerging thinking about revolutionary praxis. The focus on revolutionary praxis registers a further difference between Schmitt and Benjamin. Whereas Schmitt regards the sovereign's decision to suspend normal laws in the state of exception as a means for the state to preserve itself in situations that threaten the given order, Benjamin articulates the teachings of a "tradition of the oppressed," the task of which is to bring about a "real state of emergency," aligned with a revolutionary overthrow of state power, specifically in its authoritarian or fascist form ("On the Concept of History," Thesis VIII, SW4, 392/ WuN19, 74).

In Chapter 3, "Contra Schmitt: Leo Strauss, Walter Benjamin, and Jewish Political Theology," Batnitzky and Liska put Benjamin's entire *œuvre* under the microscope in order to disentangle his thought from Schmitt's. They approach this task of disentanglement by comparing Benjamin's relationship to Schmitt with that of another prominent German-Jewish thinker, Leo Strauss, who is also often associated with Schmitt. In both cases, they argue that Schmitt's towering role in the realm of political theology, and the tendency to interpret Strauss and Benjamin within a Schmittian framework, has led to a misunderstanding of their respective ideas. Batnitzky and Liska contend that disentangling Benjamin and Strauss from Schmitt is an invitation to question Schmitt's dominance in the field of political theology, and to highlight these German-Jewish thinkers' contributions to a possible Jewish political theology. A central point of divergence from Schmitt, common to both Benjamin and Strauss, is a rejection of the view that the redemption has already come. Batnitzky argues that the idea that the redemption has already occurred, and that Jesus is the Christ, is a central tenet of Schmittian political theology; she refers to this as Schmitt's "Christian triumphalism," and demonstrates that Strauss rejects it. In opposition to this view, she argues that Strauss develops an exilic political theology, which is committed to the idea that the redemption has not yet occurred. The absence of redemption, according to Batnitzky's reading of Strauss, is demonstrated in the Jewish history of suffering, or Jewish martyrdom. Unlike Christian martyrdom, which glorifies suffering, and regards Jesus's death as redemptive, Strauss considers Jewish suffering to bear witness to "the one thing needful," namely, *Tzedakah*, often translated as "righteousness and charity," or more simply, as justice. Batnitzky contends that Schmitt discounts both the importance of suffering, and its moral meaning as the absence of redemption. Liska argues that the absence of redemption is as central for Benjamin as it is for Strauss. But she highlights that Benjamin sees the world as unredeemed because of the ongoing condition of injustice and oppression—an idea that is not linked to Jewish suffering in particular, but to a more universal understanding of the lack of justice in the socio-political world. As Liska argues, the specificity of the Jewish people for Benjamin is not their suffering, but their sensibility for justice, which is linked, for Benjamin, to their messianic tradition.

Each of the chapters in Part II is devoted to examining the non-theocratic politics that explicitly or implicitly is developed in Benjamin's writings. It would help clarify this topic if we had, in its entirety, the corpus of texts that Benjamin wrote in the early 1920s under the working title "*Politik*." Much of the relevant material is considered lost, although his essay published in 1921, "Toward the Critique of Violence," is clearly part of this material. In the past two decades or more, there has been considerable research done on the genesis of Benjamin's project on politics. This research explores Benjamin's correspondence, his writings, and writings by those who influenced or might have influenced him.[24] Among the features of Benjamin's thought that emerge are abhorrence of theocracy and loathing of those aspects of ostensibly non-theocratic governance that nonetheless bear theocratic traces, such as the preoccupation with having a leader (Fenves 2021: 12). Part II elaborates this non-theocratic politics in Benjamin's work. Each of the chapters in this section examine an interaction of theology and politics that undermines theocracy and its authoritarian legacy. This interaction is brought to bear against living conditions that are oppressive in the pseudo-legitimacy that awards them the appearance of inviolable necessity. Whether or not it is explicitly theocratic in *content*, such an appearance of necessity is at least tacitly theocratic in *structure*. This is arguably the case, for instance, with law's purported transcendence of specific historical conditions. The chapters in Part II focus on Benjamin's endeavor to render manifest and to "profane" such residues of theocracy and their authoritarian implications. This endeavor will be elaborated as a form of justice.

In Benjamin's terms, the remnants of theocracy are "myth." Benjamin uses the term "myth" to designate the hypostatization of circumstances that—contrary to their self-acclamation as necessary, natural, or fated—are contingent, temporal, and historical.[25] This topic opens the way to discussions of Benjamin's theological conception of justice. In Chapter 4, "Nihilism as World Politics: Benjamin's Theology of Entropy," Agata Bielik-Robson discusses the justice with which matter defeats delusions of spirit. In Chapter 5, "My Kingdom for a Shirt: Untrammeled Atheism and Anarchism in Benjamin and Kafka," James Martel discusses Benjaminian justice as an-archic—that is, devoid of the hierarchies often dubiously associated with notions of God. In Chapter 6, "Study, Sovereignty, and Justice: Benjamin, Scholem, and Agamben," Brendan Moran discusses Benjaminian study as the justice that profanes the purportedly divine to arrive at a Kafkan politics in which study cannot desist before notions of the holy.

In Benjamin's anti-theocratic politics, there is opposition to myth as the demand for sacrifice. Any sacrifice exercised in Benjaminian politics is not demanded; a demanded sacrifice is mythic. In "On the Concept of History," Benjamin commends hate-filled sacrifice-preparedness fueled by remembrance of the injustice of previous and current generations' suffering (*SW*4, 394/ *WuN*19, 77; see too *WuN*19, 21–22, 38, 66, 101). It would be a sleight of hand to implicate Benjamin in the sort of authoritarian terrorist movements into which some of his readers ventured (Wohlfarth 2006). Yet Benjamin's writings, including the 1921 essay "Towards the Critique of Violence" connected with the aforementioned project on politics, address feelings that accept sacrifice that is *not* demanded by anyone (*TC*, 58/ *GS*II:1, 199–200). This sacrifice opposes the supposedly necessary sacrifice that myth propagates on its behalf.

It is time that makes non-mythic insubordination possible. In time, no rulership, oppressive or otherwise, has permanent validity. In contrast to mythic fatedness, which awards the appearance of necessity to contingent circumstances, time is an ally for liberatory politics. In a text of 1938 on Bertolt Brecht, Benjamin thus affirms someone who has undergone enormous duress under domination and yet has not completely acquiesced (*SW*3, 333/ *GS*II:2, 518). Time intrudes even in the most stifling conditions, and thereby does not abandon politics to myth. Time upsets denial or disregard of it. Time can concretely oppose myth in a myriad of contexts. There has accordingly been work that relates Benjamin's writings, including his expressly theological writings, not only to the critique of capitalism, to variants of anarchism, and to class conflict, but also to perspectives of the conquered in Latin America and to ecological concerns (Löwy 2019). In contrast to liberatory politics, myth is defeatist. Mythic is the punitive sense of necessity that demands suffering, respect, or simple submission to specific conditions. Myth treats living conditions as though they are deserved and as something for which one is fundamentally responsible. "The basic conception in myth is the world as punishment" (*SW4*, 403/ *WuN*19, 139), as Benjamin remarks in the paralipomena to "On the Concept of History." To such mythic living conditions (whether past or current), an oppositional hate and revenge, and a correlative destruction, can always take exception. Benjamin's nihilism and anarchism, discussed respectively by Agata Bielik-Robson in Chapter 4 and by James Martel in Chapter 5 of this volume, recognize that transience is a form of justice in that it prevails over myths of hypostasis, myths against time. Transience brings change; change can bring misery and can bring happiness, but the preponderance of transience assures that no specific misery has to be regarded as fate—namely, as something that had to happen or must happen.

With this approach to time, Benjaminian politics are always somehow theological. In his now famous notes of 1916 on "the category of justice," Benjamin explains: "[j]ustice . . . can only be as a condition of the world or as a condition of God" (2011). The relevant condition of the world could be called a condition of God, for it is undeniable. That which is undeniable is resistant to aggressions against it; it is resistant to this injustice. Yet the resistance, the justice, requires effort on the part of those who wish to be attentive to it. To do justice to this undeniable condition requires struggle against the aggressions that implicitly or explicitly deny the condition of the world/the condition of God. Justice is a struggle to assure that the undeniable is not ignored—to assure, in this sense, that the world is not denied. "Justice is the struggle to make the world into the highest good." Justice "constitutes a condition [*Zustand*] of the world" but also indicates "the ethical category of what exists [*des Existentent*]" (*TC*, 65/ Benjamin 1995: 401 translation modified).

If the inexhaustible condition of the world orients justice, it is quite conceivable that violation of this condition could occasion hatred, even revenge, against forces perpetrating the violation. The principal proviso is, however, a challenging one: assure that the hate, revenge, nihilism, or anarchism do not themselves metamorphize into myth—that is, into their own forced closures and denials. For this reason, as Brendan Moran notes in Chapter 6 of this volume, Benjamin's politics may be conceived as a politics of study—the study that never rests with such closures and denials. Among such closures and denials, Moran argues, are law and theocracy. The restlessness of study consists in being unhindered and unhampered. To that extent, study is anarchic and nihilistic as it enacts opposition to law and theocracy. With regard to the latter, Benjamin says in the "Theological-Political Fragment" that "the cardinal merit of Bloch's *Spirit of Utopia*" is "[t]o have repudiated with utmost vehemence the political significance of theocracy" (*SW3*, 305/ *GSII*:1, 203). Benjamin's opposition to theocracy is so thoroughgoing that it has been suggested Benjamin is actually warning against some of Bloch's own tendencies (Steiner 2016: 47–8). Benjamin's wariness of theocratizing law—even *implicitly* theocratic law—is correlatively vigilant.

Opposing all that is simply projected upon the world, the attentiveness of study involves justice. This justice would be nihilistic in its destructive approach to identification with such projections. In his essay of 1931 on Karl Kraus, Benjamin refers to an inheritance from Judaism whereby for Kraus, "justice and language remain founded in each other"; "[t]o worship the image of divine justice in language—even in the German language—this is the genuinely Jewish *salto mortale* by which Kraus tries to break the spell of the demon" (*SW2*, 443–444/ *GSII*:1, 349). The spell of the demon is the ban on exploring beyond norm and law. Roberto Esposito suggests that an increased privileging of norm and law, even for highly questionable practices such as forced euthanasia, paved the way in the Weimar Republic for a Nazism that itself was continuously seeking normative and legal means to justify its measures at the cost of justice to those most affected by those measures (Esposito 2008). This exclusionary *dispositif* is the progeniture of earlier political-theological justifications for disregard and aggression (Esposito 2015) and might be the context in which Benjamin marvels that *even in the German language* the Austrian Kraus demonstrates a preoccupation with the possible alliance of language with justice rather than with law and norm. Developing Hamlet's protest against "the Wittenbergian philosophy," passages of Benjamin's *Trauerspiel* book could be read as an anticipatory critique of the meshing of Lutheran hyper-normativity with authoritarianism (see *OT*, 140–41/ *GSI*:1, 317–18). For Benjamin, Kraus destroys such linguistic maneuverings that refuse justice. The justice involves "a humanity that proves itself by destruction" (*SW2*, 456/ *GSII*:1, 367). There emerges the justice with which the "new angel" frees humans by taking from them—rather than providing—any happiness that resides in a denial of time (456/367), any happiness that assumes it itself is fated and thereby has license to dominate others.

In Chapter 4, "Nihilism as World Politics: Benjamin's Theology of Entropy," Agata Bielik-Robson argues that throughout Benjamin's *œuvre* there is political theology based on "nihilism as world politics"—the formulation given in Benjamin's so-called "Theological-Political Fragment." Bielik-Robson shows how this fragment responds both favorably and critically to the 1918 edition of Bloch's *Spirit of Utopia*: favorably by showing the impossibility of a utopian theocracy, critically by implicitly questioning Bloch's investment in the hope of raising the world to an utterly spiritual level. Bielik-Robson contends that the "Theological-Political Fragment" contains notions of relevance to much that Benjamin wrote. This relevance includes divergence from Bloch's visions of an ultimate reconciliation of spirit and matter. Bielik-Robson elaborates Benjamin's notion of "transience" as allowing for a kind of hope in reverse, which does not entail a humanization of matter but rather a productive regression: a productive nihilism, in which messianic nature resists and counters messianisms of spirit. Benjamin's nihilism, Bielik-Robson clarifies, is not the same as loss of ability to create and affirm values; nor is it Weberian resignation in the face of modern disenchantment. Benjamin's nihilism involves, rather, an embrace of nature's "eternal and total passing away" (*SW3*, 305–6/ *GSII*:1, 203–4). This nihilism of matter in its transience undercuts human hubris. With this emphasis on material nature, something like a biopolitics and its concern with physicality emerge. The focus on nature's eternal passing away goes against the grain of the more spiritual theopolitics evident in Bloch, Gustav Landauer, Martin Buber, and Jacob Taubes. This nihilistic political theology is nonetheless hopeful. The hope in transience ("hope in reverse") opposes hope that is invested in the mythic and theocratic ideal of ultimately overcoming transience.

Benjamin's nihilism goes hand in hand with the anarchism discussed by James Martel in Chapter 5 of this volume: "My Kingdom for a Shirt: Untrammeled Atheism and Anarchism in Benjamin and Kafka." Benjaminian nihilism and anarchism both take critical aim at the myths that support power. These myths often depend on the hypostatization of that which is time-bound. Martel explores the centrality of anarchism to Benjamin's political thought. He argues that Benjamin's anarchism is a form of atheism. This might seem an incredible claim to make about Benjamin, someone whose thought is considered by many—including many in this volume—to be theological, albeit in an idiosyncratic way. Martel's point, however, is that Benjamin's particular form of political theology effectively removes much that is associated with God—especially false hierarchies that rely, tacitly or expressly, on metaphysical or theological claims. With the at least conceptual, critical destruction of these hierarchies, Benjamin leaves human beings relatively unhindered—a condition that Martel elaborates as anarchistic. Benjamin is shown to be an-archic and, relatedly, a-theological. This condition is not purely negative—that is, *against* archism and *against* theism. Martel argues that Benjamin's move is something like a negation of a negation. Examining Benjamin's readings of Kafka's stories and parables, Martel suggests that Kafka and Benjamin converge in engaging with the concept of divinity without succumbing to the kinds of lies and temptations that create hierarchies and other forms of rule. In doing so, Kafka and Benjamin avoid false ascriptions to the divine or to secularized versions of the divine. They are working with the divine to offset the kinds of occult theology that continue to structure modern forms of power and authority, regardless of whether or not the power and the authority expressly refer to this theological provenance. Benjamin decenters theology to make it a fount of inspiration and aid in anarchic human life.

In Chapter 6, "Study, Sovereignty, and Justice: Benjamin, Scholem, and Agamben," Brendan Moran explores ways in which the priority of studying sets Benjamin apart from any Schmittian notion of mythically secured sovereignty. Along with Gershom Scholem and Giorgio Agamben, Benjamin tries to offset voluntary or involuntary stultification under mythic rulership. Especially Benjamin and Agamben associate the inexhaustible potential for study with the pressure of time that undermines reluctance to study. Messianism is the pressure of time to go beyond, to study beyond, what is settled. The justice of *time* is that it recognizes the domination of no settled space over time. The justice of *study* is that it frees what is ostensibly settled from conclusions hitherto drawn about it. Whatever exceeds law, or exceeds other human constructions, appears distorted in relation to those constructions. Distortion complements study by accentuating the incompleteness of study, an incompleteness that includes the independence of distortion from law. Agamben claims that Scholem, in contrast, unwittingly becomes Schmittian in invoking a fundamental law, albeit a very unclear law, as sacredly valid. If Benjamin and Agamben are unSchmittian, it is in their regard for whatever is excluded by sovereignty that is itself associated with law and its representatives. As Moran attempts to indicate nonetheless, there might be passages or moments when Benjamin himself, however unwittingly, risks lapsing into affirmation of a quasi-Schmittian sovereignty.

Part III turns to the relationship of Benjamin's political philosophy with messianic time. Benjamin's political theology (if it is one), is centrally concerned with time. In other words, he characteristically takes up the question of time in connection to its political and theological import. The chapters in this section take diverse approaches to ideas of time, history, and the motif of the messianic in Benjamin's thought. Each poses the question, in some cases indirectly, of how Benjamin—drawing on Judaic messianism(s)—inter-articulates theology and politics in ways that are quite distinct from Schmittian political theology.

Benjamin's concern with the motif of messianic time may be traced from his early writings to his latest work. In his 1914–15 essay, "The Life of Students," Benjamin favorably relates "the idea of the French Revolution" to "the messianic realm" (*SW*1, 37/ *EW*, 197/ *GS*II:1, 75). Both the idea of the French Revolution and the messianic, as Benjamin conceives it, involve a confrontation of the historical situation with an idea of the redeemed world (i.e., the idea of a world in which justice and reason will have been realized). Benjamin returns to the idea of the messianic in his later work, most prominently in the 1940 theses "On the Concept of History," to characterize the revolutionary action of the historical materialist. Reference to the messianic arguably serves a critical function with respect to the historical situation, in that it reveals the discrepancy between the historical situation and the messianic ideal. Benjamin distinguishes messianic time from the representation of time as "empty and homogeneous" (*SW*4, 395/ *WuN*19, 78 translation modified; *WuN*19, 23–24, 39–40, 90, 102)—the time of some mathematics and of some physical processes. By the nineteenth century, a processual, linear conception of time had infiltrated dominant representations of history, imparting an uncritical idea of time as a linear, unidirectional movement. Benjamin notes that Marx—but especially his epigones, representatives of the Social Democratic left—embraced an idea of historical time as progressing inexorably toward a telos or end. Such a conception of time, as Massimiliano Tomba has suggested, also "processualizes" political ideas: demands for equality, or justice, for example, become dissipated in notions of gradual equalization and reform (Tomba 2013, "Preface"). This provides the comforting illusion that the passage of time alone will bring about the political transformation that is urgently required. For Benjamin, this conception of time had a narcotic effect (*AP* K1a, 6; N3, 4; O°, 71/*GSV*, 493; 578; 1033). He insists that to change the world, one must change time. Revolutionary politics would thus require a rethinking of historical time as such.

As a figure of time, conceived otherwise than as an "empty, homogenous" process, the messianic furnishes Benjamin with a conception of the historical world as incomplete; or to put this point slightly differently, it furnishes an image of the world as *unredeemed* (a theme that is registered in Batnitzky and Liska's chapter in Part I). The messianic idea involves a constant confrontation of the historical situation with an image of the redeemed world—a world in which justice reigns and relations of domination have been overcome. In Benjamin's theses "On the Concept of History," the messianic ideal is secularized, in a Marxist lexicon, as "class-free society." The messianic idea, for Benjamin, is not a passively-awaited world to come, beyond history; it is rather a task to be fulfilled *now*. This distinguishes Benjamin's idea of messianism from a (Christian) eschatological conception, as chapters in this section will discuss.

Arguably, Benjamin turns to the theological motif of Jewish messianism for its critical potential in disrupting what imposes itself as a fateful necessity.[26] This suggestion builds on arguments made in Part II (especially by Bielik-Robson and Moran), which analyze the political-theological significance of the Benjaminian concept of transience. The transience of material nature, for Benjamin, exhibits the indirectly redemptive quality of time, in that the continuous passing away of all things does not allow any contingent form of life to impose itself as necessary and eternal. Benjamin utilizes the term "myth," and the correlative term, "fate," to characterize that which arrogates to itself the stultifying semblance of necessity. The critical opposition of the messianic to myth and fate justifies our inclusion of Howard Eiland's chapter, "Benjamin's Concept of Fate," as Chapter 7 in this section. Eiland's chapter is unique in this section in focusing primarily on Benjamin's early work, up to and including his *Origin of the German Trauerspiel*. Accordingly, there are fruitful resonances between Eiland's chapter and the chapters on the *Trauerspiel* book in Part I (notably, Schwebel's and Vatter's). Eiland's chapter is, however, a helpful fit for Part III, because of its primary focus on Benjamin's conception of the *temporality* of fate.

Benjamin's notion of fate, and his turn to the theological concept of the messianic for its critical and liberatory potential in interrupting fate, reflects the influence of Hermann Cohen. A founding member of the Marburg School of Neo-Kantianism, Cohen was also a profoundly significant voice in twentieth-century Jewish Thought.[27] Cohen's influence is briefly discussed in Chapter 7, "Benjamin's Concept of Fate," by Eiland, and more extensively of course in Chapter 8, Tamara Tagliacozzo's "Fulfilled Time: Benjamin's Reception of Hermann Cohen's Idea of Messianism." As Yannik Thiem has argued, Cohen was critical of the Christian concept of original sin, which he saw as imposing a kind of fatalism detrimental to moral agency (Thiem 2009). Like Cohen, Benjamin uses the term "myth" to designate a sense of fatedness. As Cohen puts it, "[f]or [mythical faith], there is only surrendering to fate" (Cohen 1995: 190). Benjamin is likewise opposed to the mythical, as that which supposedly cannot be resisted, but can only be surrendered to. Like Cohen, moreover, Benjamin detects *Schuld* (guilt/debt) at the core of *Schicksal* (fate). The influence of Cohen's critique is evident in Benjamin's own speculations on the "guilt-context" that fatalism imposes on humanity, and its suffocation of possibilities for moral agency and freedom. As Cohen argued, in Athenian tragedy, demonic fate, with its spell of inherited guilt, is first broken through when the tragic hero recognizes his moral superiority to the gods. A new moral sublimity ruptures the hitherto inexorable cycle of guilt and atonement. Unlike Cohen, who had the utmost regard for law,[28] Benjamin proposes in his "Critique of Violence" that the ambiguous, archaic order of fate survives in the subjection of creaturely life to positive law.[29]

Eiland argues that in essays and fragments from the period 1914–23, and subsequently in *Origin of the German Trauerspiel*, Benjamin develops a concept of fate in antithesis to the principle of homogeneous continuum, a principle fundamental not only to chronological time but also to the narrative form of conventional historiography. With its roots in biblical and classical antiquity as well as early modernity, "fate" appears in Benjamin's political-theological aesthetic as the natural-historical "guilt-context of the living," involving an ambiguous conjuncture and inter-articulating of chronologically distinct moments. As a dialectical thinker, Benjamin does not simply oppose this idea of fate, but affirms and adapts at least one aspect of it: namely, the way in which the virtual correspondence of different moments in time breaks with a linear, or "empty and homogenous," conception of the temporal. While Benjamin is certainly critical of the way that fate has been deployed to mask despotism and every sort of machination, there is in Benjamin's early conceptualization of fate what Eiland characterizes as a field-theoretical principle of virtual synchronicity between different times, which leaves its stamp on Benjamin's later historical-materialist conception of historical time as the ever-new citation of what has been. The interplay of fore- and after-histories, constituting the forward- and backward-looking "dialectical image," critically recalls the intimately relayed manifestation of fate across stations of an individual life-form or historical object. Ultimately, Benjamin is critical of fate, but as Eiland argues, fate is overcome not by means of the self's "sovereign" decision (as in Schmitt), but by way of an act of "educational awakening," which stems from critical reflection. Eiland argues that for Benjamin, the nucleus of a political-theological project resides in this "[c]ritical reflection ... with a historical understanding animated by the promise of both freedom and justice," which "can transform an oppressive inheritance, deconstructing its terms in order to awaken dormant possibilities of practice." Such an awakening confronts fate, with its concomitant sense of inherited guilt, with an aim to "disclose alternative prospects of 'natural innocence,' originary openness," and freedom.

Benjamin's Judaic idea of the messianic was, of course, influenced by his friend, Gershom Scholem—in particular, by Scholem's characterization of the Lurianic Kabbalah, with its concepts of *shevirat ha-kelim* (the shattering of the vessels), and *tikkun* (their messianic recuperation and re-composition).[30] Cohen's influence, however, is also palpable in Benjamin's formulation of the messianic, as Tamara Tagliacozzo argues in Chapter 8, "Fulfilled Time: Walter Benjamin's Reception of Hermann Cohen's Idea of Messianism." What Scholem and Cohen have in common is that both regard the messianic as something that happens on the sociopolitical stage, as a redemption of the world, rather than an inner-redemption of the individual soul. Moreover, both Scholem and Cohen see a role for human agency in bringing about the messianic, whether through *tikkun* (Scholem), or through *mitzvot*—that is, good deeds, or ethical action (Cohen). Tagliacozzo supplies the Cohenian background for understanding the motif of the messianic across Benjamin's corpus. In elaborating the two philosophers' respective concepts of messianic time, she clarifies their convergences and divergences. According to Tagliacozzo, Cohen emphasizes the political significance of the prophetic ideals, which offer an idea of historical time that is not empty and homogenous, but that confronts historical circumstances with an ideal of justice to be fulfilled. Like Cohen, Benjamin takes up a secularized idea of the messianic as an ethico-political task to be fulfilled in this world. Benjamin diverges from Cohen, however, where Cohen conceives of the messianic as a regulative ideal, or infinite task, that is projected onto the future, and regarded as something to be approached gradually. Unlike Cohen, Benjamin does not recognize progressive advancement of history toward the fulfillment of prophetic ideals. Benjamin is concerned, rather, with redeeming the past so that it can interrupt pretenses of universal human progress (pretenses to which Cohen subscribes). Tagliacozzo concludes with a reaffirmation of how Benjamin could be taken to draw upon certain tendencies in Cohen's writing: a Judaic-messianic conception of history, an anti-ontology (i.e., a focus not on being as given, but on the incompleteness of what is, as a task to be fulfilled), and an anti-eschatology (i.e., that the Messiah is not the redeemer of a world to come, but of this world, now).

Chapter 9, Sami Khatib's "Beyond Mysticism and Apocalypse: Benjamin's Dislocation of the Messianic," is unique in this volume in arguing that Benjamin does not have a political theology. Most contributions to the volume imply, if not openly suggest, that Benjamin's writings demonstrate something like a non-Schmittian political theology, even if Benjamin does not identify it as such. Khatib contends that Benjamin's figure of the messianic does not constitute a contribution to the discourse of political theology and does not even designate a specific theological strand of messianic thought. Instead, politics and theology enter a (non-)relation whereby neither element collapses into the other. Throughout Benjamin's *œuvre*, two strands of messianic thought enter various combinations and transvaluations: (1) the mystical idea of a minimal messianic transformation or adjustment (*Zurechtstellung*) and (2) the apocalyptic rupture and intrusion of a radically heterogeneous dimension of transcendence—the Messiah—in human events. These two strands constitute traditions of messianic thought that inform well-known figurative images in Benjamin's later work—especially the figurative images in "On the Concept of History" (1940). The scenes and images evoked by these messianic figures—angel, puppet, dwarf, and little hunchback—have what some call an "epistemological function" whereby Benjamin's "image thinking" is not a straightforward conceptual elaboration but rather a presentation unfolding in the medium of those images and figures themselves. Khatib argues that these "thought images" (*Denkbilder*) cannot be disentangled by straightforward distinctions between initial expression and its signification, or between objective content and metaphor. Correlatively, politics cannot be the subject of messianic (or theological) predication. There can be no forced fusion of theology and politics, no credible identitarian conception of the messianic. For Benjamin, there is instead a messianic manifestation that is not itself identical with the messianic.

Chapter 10, Carlo Salzani's "A Hunchbacked Political Theology: Creaturely Biopolitics as The Self-Sublation of Distorted Life," does recognize something in Benjamin's work that might be a political theology, however unique. The theology famously enlisted to political ends in the first thesis of "On the Concept of History" is a theology of the missed or the distorted—hunchbacked—possibilities, and thus itself a "hunchbacked" theology.[31] Although the term "hunchbacked" is often considered offensive, Salzani notes that some claim a hunched back is the sign under which the whole of Benjamin's life should be put. Salzani extrapolates that the hunched back can also be said to mark Benjamin's peculiar style of political theology. The hunchbacked theology should help to enact the "real state of emergency" as a counter-articulation of the sovereign exception. Accordingly, this counter-articulation involves an essential distortion (*Entstellung*) that no *tikkun*—no healing—will ever rectify. Whereas there is a notion of "rectification" that informs the logic of the sovereign inclusive exclusion (also in the Foucauldian form of "normalization"), the messianic *tikkun*—though often translated precisely as "rectification"—must be different. In the 1934 Kafka essay, Benjamin writes that the distortion—the little hunchback—will disappear with the coming of the Messiah, and uses the verb *zurechtstellen* (to set right) to denote the "little adjustment" the Messiah will bring about, abiding thereby the metaphor of verticality that informs the sovereign logic of rectification. A preparatory note suggests, however, that the *tikkun* is not intended as a straightening of what is crooked, but rather as play that displaces. Salzani endeavors to elucidate the peculiar "hunchbacked" form political theology takes in Benjamin's messianism.

## Notes

1. The editors thank the volume's contributors for their input into this introduction. Only the editors are, of course, responsible for the final formulations.
2. Oliver O'Donovan 1996 traces the term "political theology," or "civil theology," back to Marcus Varro, a Roman writer in the first century BCE (cf. Rashkover and Kavka 2014: 2).
3. Putting his theory of the "state of exception" into practice, Schmitt acted as a legal representative of the Reich government in the case (*Preußen contra Reich*) which litigated the constitutionality of Hindenburg's declaration of a state of emergency. In *Political Theology*, Schmitt discusses Article 48 of the Weimar Constitution as granting the sovereign "unlimited power" (Schmitt 2005: 11–12). For Schmitt's detailed analysis of Article 48, see the appendix to his *Dictatorship* (Schmitt 2014: 180–226). For discussion of Schmitt's approach to Article 48, see: Meierhenrich and Simons 2016: 31–2; and Duncan Kelly 2016: 232–6.
4. For a discussion of Schmitt's "multifaceted participation" in the Nazi legal system, as well as his anti-Semitic attitudes, see, for example, Raphael Gross 2016: 96–116. For a concise summary of Schmitt's involvement with Nazism between 1933 and 1945, see Meirhenrich and Simons 2016: 8–10.
5. As chapters in this volume (notably Miguel Vatter's) suggest, Benjamin represents a distinctive voice in a larger debate over secularism and the "post-secular." See, for example, Benjamin's discussion of the haunting afterlife of Christian theological concepts of eschatology and original sin in the "guilt-context" that he identifies in the Baroque trauerspiel. For a discussion of the latter as distinct from Schmitt's conception of the secularization of theological concepts, see Annika (Yannik) Thiem 2013.
6. See Metz 2007 (1977). See also Hille Haker 2016, for a discussion of Metz's "new political theology" as a commentary on Benjamin's thought.
7. See, for example, Löwy, 1995; cf. 2005: 21.
8. For important studies that develop aspects of Benjamin's "Capitalism as Religion," see Elettra Stimilli 2017, 2018, as well as Baecker 2019.
9. See Fritsch 2005 for a study of the rapport between Derrida and Benjamin.
10. One of Butler's relevant essays appears in a volume edited by Colby Dickinson and Stéphane Symons on *Walter Benjamin and Theology*, which contains a number of essays pertinent to the topic of political theology—including a response by Astrid Deuber-Mankowsky (2016) to Butler's work on Benjamin's essay of 1921, "Toward a Critique of Violence."

11  See, for example, Saitya Brata Das 2018; Kirill Chepurin and Alex Dubilet 2021; Seán Molloy 2017; and Eric Nelson 2019.
12  See, for example, Miguel Vatter 2020; Saul Newman 2019 and Peter Langford and Saul Newman 2023.
13  See, for example, Jeffrey Robbins 2011.
14  See, for example, Pui-Lan Kwok 2021, Joshua Ralston 2018, and the special issue of *Political Theology*, edited by Robert Yelle (2022) on "Deprovincializing Political Theology."
15  To name only a few: Peter Fenves (2011); Daniel Bensaïd (2010); Daniel Weidner (2010); Gérard Raulet (2004); and Brian Britt (1996, 2016). Noteworthy in this context is also the recent book edited by Willem Styphals and Stéphane Symons (2019), in which the contributions provide an Anglophone audience with important discussions of the lineages and the debates within what is sometimes called political theology: Schmitt, Benjamin, Hannah Arendt, Hans Blumenberg, Jacob Taubes, and Jan Assmann. Another pertinent volume is that edited by Christine Blättler and Christian Voller (2016), which contains several essays quite specifically devoted to Benjamin's political philosophy. There is also an earlier volume edited by Bernd Witte and Mauro Ponzi with Claas Morgenroth and Karl Ivan Solibakke (2005) in which the essays often discuss Benjamin, Agamben, and others in terms of the confluence of theology and politics that might be detectible in globalization, capitalism, violence, and other spheres of human activity. Noteworthy too, moreover, are several books and many articles written by contributors to our volume; each contributor has written considerably on topics centrally related to the relationship of Benjamin with political theology, as footnotes and lists of references for the chapters indicate.
16  See Meierhenrich and Simons 2016: 16 for the felicitous expression, "other of order," and a discussion of Schmitt's fear of disorder.
17  See Matthias Lievens 2016, however, for an articulation of the significance of the meaning of history in Schmitt's work.
18  For analysis of this enigmatic notion, which appeared in Schmitt's thought beginning in 1930s, see: Lievens 2016: 414–9; and Felix Grossheutschi 1996. For discussion in this volume of Schmitt's interpretation of the *Katechon*, and how this registers a difference from Benjamin's approach to time and transience, see the chapters by Agata Bielik-Robson and Leora Batnitzky and Vivian Liska in this volume.
19  Benjamin's 1930 letter indicates that he derived from Schmitt's work, especially *Die Diktatur*, confirmation of his own mode of research in the philosophy of art, which he deemed similar to Schmitt's mode of research in the philosophy of state. In a 1928 version of his curriculum vitae, Benjamin elaborates on this claim, stating that just as Schmitt's analysis of the political integrates phenomena whose apparent territorial distinctness is an illusion, he himself approaches the work of art as "an integral expression of the religious, metaphysical, political, and economic tendencies of its age, unconstrained in any way by territorial concepts" (*SW*2.1, 78/ *GS*VI, 219).
20  In Agamben's words, Benjamin's letter has been considered scandalous (Agamben 2005a: 53.
21  Taubes recounts how Adorno denied the existence of Benjamin's letter to Schmitt (Taubes 2004: 98). For a discussion of Taubes's exchange with Adorno, see de Wilde 2011: 364.
22  See Benjamin, *Schriften*, eds. Theodor W. Adorno and Gretel Adorno, vol. 1, 183–4. Cf. *OT*, 65–6/ *GS* I:1, 245–6. For a discussion of the removal of the endnotes in the 1955 edition, see Moran and Salzani 2015: 4.

23  Marc de Wilde chronicles the different stages in the secondary literature since Benjamin's letter to Schmitt was first published in 1974. The earliest responses, he argues, were split between those who saw the letter as indicating a disturbing proximity between far left and far right-wing positions during the Weimar period (cf. Kennedy 1987; and Taubes 2013), and those who regarded the affinity expressed by Benjamin in his letter to Schmitt to be superficial and misleading (cf. Jay 1987; and Preuss 1987). De Wilde observes a subtler approach in more recent interpretations of the Benjamin-Schmitt relationship, citing Weber 1992 and Agamben 2005a, among others. These latter positions have emphasized that, while drawing on Schmitt's concepts and methods, Benjamin injected new meaning into these by transposing them into a different context (de Wilde: 2011: 365).
24  See Uwe Steiner 2001 and 2016 and Fenves 2021: 6, 12, 14–21, 36. A brief summary is available in Moran and Salzani 2015: 2–3.
25  Thijs Lijster (2011) compares Benjamin's conception of "myth" with usage made of this term in Horkheimer and Adorno's *Dialectic of Enlightenment* (2002) and with Lukács's (1971) conception of "second nature."
26  See Annika (Yannik) Thiem (2009) for one such argument.
27  For important studies which discuss Cohen's influence on Benjamin, see Astrid Deuber-Mankowsky (2000), Annika [Yannik] Thiem (2009), and Tamara Tagliacozzo (2017).
28  For a recent book on Cohen, which regards his ethics as arising out of law, see Hollander (2021).
29  See Thiem 2009, 15; cf. Hanssen 2000: 19–20.
30  See Scholem 1974, ch. 7. For discussions of *tikkun* in this volume, see chapters by Tamara Tagliacozzo and Carlo Salzani.
31  Here Salzani develops a formulation in Hamacher 2005.

# References

Agamben, Giorgio. (2005a), *State of Exception*, trans. Kevin Attell, Chicago: University of Chicago Press.

Agamben, Giorgio. (2005b), *The Time that Remains: A Commentary on the Letter to the Romans*, trans. Patricia Dailey, Stanford: Stanford University Press.

Baecker, Dirk, ed. ([2019] 2003; 1st edn), *Kapitalismus als Religion*, 4th edn, Berlin: Kulturverlag Kadmos.

Benjamin, Andrew. (2013), *Working with Walter Benjamin: Recovering a Political Philosophy*, Edinburgh: Edinburgh University Press.

Benjamin, Walter. (1955), *Schriften*, two volumes, eds. Theodor W. Adorno and Gretel Adorno, Frankfurt/M.: Suhrkamp.

Benjamin, Walter. (1995), "Aus dem mir geliehenen Notizbuche Walter Benjamins. 'Notizen zu einer Arbeit über die Kategorie der Gerechtigkeit,'" in Gershom Scholem (ed.), *Tagebücher nebst Aufsätzen und Entwürfen bis 1923. 1. Halbband 1913-1917*, Karlfried Gründer and Friedrich Niewöhner with Herbert Kopp-Oberstebrink, 401–2, Frankfurt/M.: Jüdischer Verlag.

Benjamin, Walter. (2011), "From a Notebook Walter Benjamin Lent to Me [Gershom Scholem]: 'Notes Toward a Work on the Category of Justice,'" in Peter Fenves (ed.), *The Messianic Reduction: Walter Benjamin and the Shape of Time*, 257–8, Stanford: Stanford University Press.

Bensaïd, Daniel. (2010), *Walter Benjamin: Sentinelle messianique à gauche du possible*, Paris: Les Prairies ordinaires.
Blättler, Christine and Christian Voller, eds. (2016), *Walter Benjamin: Politisches Denken*, Baden-Baden: Nomos Verlag.
Bredekamp, Horst. (2016), "Walter Benjamin's Esteem for Carl Schmitt," in Jens Meierhenrich and Oliver Simons (eds.), *The Oxford Handbook of Carl Schmitt*, 679–704, New York: Oxford University Press.
Britt, Brian. (1996), *Walter Benjamin and the Bible*, New York: Continuum.
Britt, Brian. (2016), *Postsecular Benjamin: Agency and Tradition*, Evanston: Northwestern University Press.
Butler, Judith. (2012), *Parting Ways: Jewishness and the Critique of Zionism*, New York: Columbia University Press.
Butler, Judith. (2016), "One Time Traverses Another: Benjamin's 'Theological-Political Fragment,'" in Colby Dickinson and Stéphane Symons (eds.), *Walter Benjamin and Theology*, 272–85, New York: Fordham University Press.
Butler, Judith. (2020), *The Force of Nonviolence: An Ethico-Political Bind*, London: Verso.
Chepurin, Kirill and Alex Dubilet. (2021), *Nothing Absolute: German Idealism and the Question of Political Theology*, New York: Fordham University Press.
Cohen, Hermann. (1995), *Religion of Reason Out of the Sources of Judaism*, trans. Simon Kaplan, Atlanta: American Academy of Religion Texts and Translation Series, Scholars Press.
Das, Saitya Brata. (2018), *The Political Theology of Schelling*, Edinburgh: University of Edinburgh Press.
de Wilde, Marc. (2011), "Meeting Opposites: The Political Theologies of Walter Benjamin and Carl Schmitt," *Philosophy & Rhetoric*, 44 (4): 363–81.
Derrida, Jacques. (1990), "Force of Law: The 'Mystical Foundation of Authority,'" trans. Mary Quaintance, *Cardoza Law Review*, 11:5–6 (July–August): 919–1045.
Derrida, Jacques. (1994) *Spectres of Marx*, trans. Peggy Kamuf, London: Routledge.
Deuber-Mankowsky, Astrid. (2000), *Der frühe Walter Benjamin und Hermann Cohen: Jüdische Werte, kritische Philosophie, vergängliche Erfahrung*, Berlin: Vorwerk 8.
Deuber-Mankowsky, Astrid. (2016), "Rhythms of the Living. Conditions of Critique: On Judith Butler's Reading of Walter Benjamin's 'Critique of Violence,'" in Colby Dickinson and Stéphane Symons (eds.), *Walter Benjamin and Theology*, 273–1, New York: Fordham University Press.
Esposito, Roberto. (2008), *Bíos: Biopolitics and Philosophy*, trans. Timothy Campbell, Minneapolis: University of Minnesota Press.
Esposito, Roberto. (2015), *Two. The Machine of Political Theology and the Place of Political Thought*, trans. Zakiya Hanafi, New York: Fordham University Press.
Fenves, Peter. (2011), *The Messianic Reduction: Walter Benjamin and the Shape of Time*, Stanford: Stanford UP.
Fenves, Peter. (2021), "Introduction," in Walter Benjamin, Peter Fenves, and Julia Ng (eds.), *Toward the Critique of Violence: A Critical Edition*, Stanford: Stanford University Press.
Fritsch, Matthias. (2005), *The Promise of Memory: History and Politics in Marx, Benjamin, and Derrida*, Albany: State University of New York Press.
Gross, Raphael. (2016), "The 'True Enemy: Antisemitism in Carl Schmitt's Life and Work," in Jens Meierhenrich and Oliver Simons (eds.), *The Oxford Handbook of Carl Schmitt*, 96–116, New York: Oxford University Press.
Grossheutschi, Felix. (1996), *Carl Schmitt und die Lehre vom Katechon*, Berlin: Duncker & Humblot.

Haker, Hille. (2016), "Walter Benjamin and Christian Critical Ethics—A Comment," in Colby Dickinson and Stéphane Symons (eds.), *Walter Benjamin and Theology*, 286–316, New York: Fordham University Press.

Hamacher, Werner. (2005), "'Now': Walter Benjamin on Historical Time," trans. N. Rosenthal, in Andrew Benjamin (ed.), *Walter Benjamin and History*, 38–68, London: Continuum.

Hanssen, Beatrice. (2000), *Critique of Violence: Between Poststructuralism and Critical Theory*, London and New York: Routledge.

Herrero, Montserrat. (2015), *The Political Discourse of Carl Schmitt: A Mystic of Order*, London and New York: Rowman and Littlefield International.

Hollander, Dana. (2021), *Ethics out of Law: Hermann Cohen and the "Neighbor,"* Toronto: University of Toronto Press.

Horkheimer, Max and Theodor W. Adorno. (2002), *Dialectic of Enlightenment*, trans. Edmond Jephcott, Stanford: Stanford University Press.

Jay, Martin. (1987), "Reconciling the Irreconcilable? Rejoinder to Kennedy," *Telos*, 71: 67–80.

Jennings, Michael. (2012), "Towards Eschatology. The Development of Walter Benjamin's Theological Politics in the Early 1920s," in Carolin Duttlinger, Ben Morgan, and Anthony Phelan (eds.), *Walter Benjamins anthropologisches Denken*, 41–57, Freiburg: Rombach.

Kelly, Duncan. (2016), "Carl Schmitt's Political Theory of Dictatorship," in Jens Meierhenrich and Oliver Simons (eds.), *The Oxford Handbook of Carl Schmitt*, 217–44, New York: Oxford University Press.

Kennedy, Ellen. (1987), "Carl Schmitt and the Frankfurt School," *Telos*, 71: 37–66.

Kwok, Pui-Lan. (2021), *Postcolonial Politics and Theology: Unraveling Empire for a Global World*, Louisville: Westminster John Knox Press.

Langford, Peter and Saul Newman. (2023), *Order, Crisis, and Redemption: Political Theology after Schmitt*, Albany: SUNY Press.

Lievens, Matthias. (2016), "Carl Schmitt's Concept of History," in Jens Meierhenrich and Oliver Simons (eds.), *The Oxford Handbook of Carl Schmitt*, 401–25, New York: Oxford University Press.

Lijster, Thijs. (2011), "The Interruption of Myth: Walter Benjamin's Concept of Critique," in Karin de Boer and Ruth Sonderegger (eds.), *Conceptions of Critique in Modern and Contemporary Philosophy*, 156–74, London: Palgrave Macmillan.

Löwy, Michael. (1995), "Walter Benjamin and Marxism," *Monthly Review*, 46 (9): 11–19.

Löwy, Michael. (2005), *Fire Alarm: Reading Walter Benjamin's 'On the Concept of History,'* trans. Chris Turner, London and New York: Verso.

Löwy, Michael. (2019), *La revolution est le frein d'urgence. Essais sur Walter Benjamin*, Paris: Éditions de l'éclat.

Lukács, Georg. (1971), *History and Class Consciousness. Studies in Marxist Dialectics*, trans. Rodney Livingstone, Cambridge: The MIT Press.

Meirhenrich, Jens and Oliver Simons. (2016), "'A Fanatic of Order in an Epoch of Confusing Turmoil': The Political, Legal, and Cultural Thought of Carl Schmitt," in Jens Meierhenrich and Oliver Simons (eds.), *The Oxford Handbook of Carl Schmitt*, 3–70, New York: Oxford University Press.

Metz, Johann Baptist. ([2007] 1977), *Faith in History and Society: Toward a Practical Fundamental Theology*, trans. J. Matthew Ashley, New York: The Crossroad Publishing Company.

Molloy, Seán. (2017), *Kant's International Relations: The Political Theology of Perpetual Peace*, Ann Arbor: University of Michigan Press.

Moran, Brendan and Carlo Salzani. (2015), "Introduction," in Brendan Moran and Carlo Salzani (eds.), *Towards the Critique of Violence: Walter Benjamin and Giorgio Agamben*, 1–15, London: Bloomsbury.
Newman, Saul. (2019), *Political Theology: A Critical Introduction*, Cambridge: Polity Press.
Nelson, Eric. (2019), *The Theology of Liberalism: Political Philosophy and the Justice of God*, Cambridge: The Belknap Press of Harvard University Press.
O'Donovan, Oliver. (1996), *The Desire of the Nations: Rediscovering the Roots of Political Theology*, Cambridge: Cambridge University Press.
Pasquino, Pasquale. (1986), "Bemerkungen zum 'Kriterium des Politischen' bei Carl Schmitt," *Der Staat*, 25: 385–98.
Preuss, Ulrich. (1987), "The Critique of German Liberalism: Reply to Kennedy," *Telos*, 71: 97–109.
Ralston, Joshua. (2018), "Political Theology in Arabic," *Special Issue of Political Theology*, 19 (7): 549–52.
Rashkover, Randi and Martin Kavka. (2014). *Judaism, Liberalism and Political Theology*, Bloomington: Indiana University Press.
Raulet, Gérard. (2004), *Positive Barbarei. Kulturphilosophie und Politik bei Walter Benjamin*, Münster: Verlag Westfälisches Dampfboot.
Robbins, Jeffrey. (2011), *Radical Democracy and Political Theology*, New York: Columbia University Press.
Salzani, Carlo. (2015), "From Benjamin's *bloßes Leben* to Agamben's *nuda vita*: A Genealogy," in Brendan Moran and Carlo Salzani (eds.), *Towards the Critique of Violence: Walter Benjamin and Giorgio Agamben*, 109–23, London: Bloomsbury.
Schmitt, Carl. ([2005] 1922; 1934), *Political Theology: Four Chapters on the Concept of Sovereignty*, trans. George Schwab, Chicago and London: University of Chicago Press.
Schmitt, Carl. ([2014] 1921), *Dictatorship*, trans. Michael Hoelzl and Graham Ward, Cambridge: Polity.
Schneider, Peter. (1957), *Ausnahmezustand und Norm: Eine Studie zur Rechtslehre von Carl Schmitt*, Stuttgart: Deutsche Verlags-Anhalt.
Scholem, Gershom. (1974), *Major Trends in Jewish Mysticism*, New York: Schocken Books.
Steiner, Uwe. (2001), "The True Politician: Walter Benjamin's Concept of the Political," trans. Colin Sample, *New German Critique*, 83 (Spring–Summer): 43–88.
Steiner, Uwe. (2016), "Walter Benjamins 'Wendung zum politischen Denken,'" in Christine Blättler and Christian Voller (eds.), *Walter Benjamin: Politisches Denken*, 33–71, Baden-Baden: Nomos Verlagsgesellschaft.
Stimilli, Elettra. (2017), *The Debt of the Living: Ascesis and Capitalism*, trans. Arianna Bove, Albany: State University of New York Press.
Stimilli, Elettra. (2018), *Debt and Guilt*, trans. Stefania Porcelli, London: Bloomsbury.
Styphals, Willem and Stéphane Symons, eds. (2019), *Genealogies of the Secular: The Making of Modern German Thought*, Albany: SUNY Press.
Tagliacozzo, Tamara. (2017), *Experience and Infinite Task: Knowledge, Language and Messianism in the Philosophy of Walter Benjamin*. London and New York: Rowman and Littlefield International.
Taubes, Jacob. (2004), *The Political Theology of Paul*, trans. Dana Hollander, Stanford: Stanford University Press.
Taubes, Jacob. (2013), *To Carl Schmitt: Letters and Reflections*, trans. Keith Tribe, New York: Columbia University Press.

Thiem, Annika [Yannik]. (2009), "Fate, Guilt, and Messianic Interruptions: Ethics of Theological Critique in Hermann Cohen and Walter Benjamin," PhD diss., University of California, Berkeley.

Thiem, Annika [Yannik]. (2013), "Theological-Political Ruins: Walter Benjamin, Sovereignty, and the Politics of Skeletal Eschatology," *Law Critique*, 24: 295–315.

Tomba, Massimiliano. (2013), *Marx's Temporalities*, Leiden and Boston: Brill.

Vatter, Miguel. (2020), *Divine Democracy: Political Theology after Carl Schmitt*, New York: Oxford University Press.

Weber, Samuel. (1992), "Taking Exception to Decision: Walter Benjamin and Carl Schmitt," *Diacritics*, 22 (3–4): 5–18.

Weidner, Daniel, ed. (2010), *Profanes Leben: Walter Benjamins Dialektik der Säkularisierung*, Berlin: Suhrkamp.

Witte, Bernd and Mauro Ponzi with Claas Morgenroth and Karl Ivan Solibakke, eds. (2005), *Theologie und Politik. Walter Benjamin und ein Paradigma der Moderne*, Berlin: Erich Schmidt Verlag.

Wohlfarth, Irving. (2006), "Entsetzen. Walter Benjamin und die RAF," in Wolfgang Kraushaar (ed.), *Die RAF und der linke Terrorismus*, Vol. 1, 280–314, Hamburg: Hamburger Edition.

Yelle, Robert, ed. (2022), "Deprovincializing Political Theology," special issue, *Political Theology*, 23 (1–2): 8–12.

Part I

# Contra Schmitt

## On Sovereignty and Political Theology

1

# Melancholy Sovereignty and the Politics of Sin[1]

Paula Schwebel

Walter Benjamin's discussion of the sovereign hero in the *Origin of the German Trauerspiel* reflects his serious engagement with Carl Schmitt's ideas.[2] However, there are significant differences between the imaginary of sovereignty in the German Baroque plays, as Benjamin portrays it, and the imaginary of sovereignty addressed by Schmitt in *Political Theology* and *Dictatorship*. Careful analysis of these differences helps to elucidate both Benjamin's treatment of sovereignty and his controversial relationship with Schmitt.[3]

The most obvious difference is that Schmitt makes it the sovereign's function to decide on the state of exception, whereas Benjamin demonstrates that the figure of the sovereign in the Baroque plays is all but incapable of making a decision (*OT*, 56/*GSI*:1, 250). Benjamin regards the sovereign's indecisiveness as a manifestation of melancholy—specifically, of the despair that medieval theologians called acedia: "The prince is the paradigm of the melancholic" (*OT*, 145/*GSI*:1, 321); "[t]he irresolution of the prince, in particular, is nothing other than saturnine acedia" (*OT*, 161/*GSI*:1, 333). The prince's melancholy accounts for his incapacity to carry out what, for Schmitt, is sovereignty's most important function: to act decisively to preserve the state in an emergency.

Scholars disagree about the import of Benjamin's juxtaposition of the melancholy, indecisive sovereign of the Baroque plays and Schmitt's sovereign decisionism. Max Pensky recognizes indecisiveness as a key feature of the sovereign's melancholy, yet he argues that Benjamin, like Schmitt, was a proponent of political decisiveness.[4] Lutz Koepnick and Dimitris Vardoulakis both suggest, to the contrary, that Benjamin's melancholic sovereign undermines Schmitt's decisionism. They argue that absolute power occasions melancholy, which inexorably impedes the exercise of power. For Koepnick, what makes power absolute is its rule over an "empty world" (cf. *OT*, 141/*GSI*:1, 317); yet this emptiness elicits depression, which erodes the sovereign's will to decisiveness (Koepnick 1996: 289).[5] Vardoulakis suggests instead that the melancholy of absolute power arises from the absolute freedom to decide, which deprives decision-making of an end or purpose (Vardoulakis 2013: 97).

I agree with Koepnick and Vardoulakis that Benjamin discerns an intrinsic connection between sovereign absolutism and the fall into melancholy acedia. I disagree, however, that this connection between melancholy and indecision is the gravamen of Benjamin's critique of Schmitt. I argue instead that the sovereign's acedia is only the most visible sign that an altogether different political theology of sovereignty than Schmitt's is at work in the *Trauerspiel* book. For Schmitt, the modern concept of sovereignty is a secularization of the omnipotent God of theological voluntarism.[6] Schmitt's argument revives the representation of sovereignty in one branch of early modern political thought.[7] But the representation of sovereignty that Benjamin discerns in the German Baroque plays points to an Augustinian tradition of political theology, which Francis Oakley has aptly characterized as a "politics of sin" (2015: 91–127). In this tradition, political subordination is a result of the Fall; it is not natural to humanity. The state is both a worldly remedy for the disorder brought into existence by fallen humanity and a divinely ordained punishment for sin. The state restores order and stability in the temporal world through penal and coercive means. But this order is marked as fallen by these very means, which have no place in the original order of creation. Oakley traces the development of this Augustinian idea through late medieval thought to its resurgence in Lutheranism. In the Lutheran-steeped literature that Benjamin treats, the sovereign is implicated—by virtue of his dominating rule—in the guilt and despair of fallen creation.

What is secularized in the politics of sin is not the concept of God's omnipotence, but the concept of original sin—Adam's Fall and the resulting guilt of creation. The concept of guilty humanity is taken up within secular political thought as a justification for authoritarian rule. Schmitt affirms this link in both *Political Theology* and *Dictatorship*.[8] But a politics of sin definitively alters the meaning of the Schmittian analogy between God and the sovereign. For Augustine, the source of original sin is Adam's pride in seeking "to be like God" (Augustine [426] 1998: XIV.13, 610; cf. Gen. 3.5). The dialectical image of sovereignty in the German Baroque plays simultaneously exhibits the sovereign's striving to be like God and its theological meaning as the fall into sin. Thus, Benjamin's literary sources furnish material for a critique of Schmitt's analogy between the sovereign and God.

Yet just as surely as the politics of sin differentiates the representation of sovereignty in the trauerspiel from Schmitt's theory of sovereignty, Benjamin's own position must also be distinguished from a politics of sin, although distilling Benjamin's critical voice from his philological one requires attention to subtle details. I argue that Benjamin rejects the spurious link between the presumptive guilt of fallen creation and the legitimation of domination. It is this link that the politics of sin and Schmitt's political theology have in common, despite their other differences.[9] Benjamin inverts the claim that human guilt legitimates political domination, arguing that domination itself is the source of melancholy and guilt in an otherwise innocent creation.

## The Politics of Sin from Augustine to Luther

What Oakley refers to as a politics of sin has roots in the Augustinian view that subordination is not natural to human beings but is a consequence of the Fall. It is a theologically grounded political philosophy, which treats secular authority as "a divinely ordained punishment and remedy for sin" (Oakley 2015: 91). Oakley traces the "penumbral presence" of this Augustinian philosophy into the late Middle Ages, and finds its reflorescence—along with Augustinian ideas in general—in the Protestant Reformation (ibid.: 92). Herein we find a historical connection to the Baroque trauerspiels; for, as Benjamin observes: "The great German dramatists of the Baroque were Lutherans" (*OT*, 140 /*GSI*:1, 317).

Augustine distinguishes between a natural order, immanent in original creation, and the order of the political state. Domination and servitude do not exist by nature among human beings; but Adam freely turns away from the natural order of creation, disordering the world by placing his own will at the center of existence, rather than obeying God's command (Augustine [426] 1998: XIX.15, 943). Original sin is henceforth the inheritance of Adam's descendants.[10] As a consequence of the Fall, human nature becomes vitiated, "changed for the worse" (Augustine [426] 1998: XIV.1, 581). The flesh triumphs over the spirit, producing incontinence of the will, enslavement to sin, and the necessity of suffering and death (Augustine [426] 1998: XIV.15, 612; XIV.1, 581).

After the Fall, human society is divided into two orders, which are intermingled in the temporal world, only to be separated at the Last Judgment. Citizens of the "earthly city" (Satan's kingdom) are condemned to eternal damnation in hell—a just penalty for original sin, according to Augustine. Citizens of the "city of God" (Christ's kingdom) are redeemed of their sins and saved—not by virtue of their own efforts, but by the "unmerited grace of God" (Augustine [426] 1998: XIV.1, 581). These two "cities" do not correspond to the institutions of the visible church and the state; rather, they are images for two different forms of human relatedness and community. The earthly city is inhabited by those who, like Adam, place self-love at the center of existence. Such people are avaricious, rebellious, and hungry for power and domination over others. The city of God, conversely, is inhabited by those who, like Christ, place love of God at the center of existence. They are humble, obedient, and realize their love of God in the world through love of the neighbor. Since the mass of humanity belongs to the earthly city, Augustine argues for the necessity of secular power, the function of which is to secure an external kind of peace and justice through coercive and penal means.[11] While the state establishes a certain order, as opposed to chaos, it is an "external, coercive, repressive, remedial order" (Deane 2013: 117). This is far removed from both the natural order of creation in Paradise, and the spiritual order of Christ's Messianic Kingdom, which, for Augustine, is the exclusive domain of true peace and justice. In pointed contrast to the eudaimonistic conception of politics in Plato and Aristotle, Augustine conceives of the state as a penal order, reserving true happiness for inhabitants of the city of God (Deane 2013: 11–12).[12]

A threefold distinction is thus established in Augustine's political thought, between (1) the original dominion of Adam in Paradise—a state in which all human beings are created equal and no one has dominion over another human being; (2) the secular power of the state, which wields the sword to restrain fallen humanity's vicious inclinations; and (3) the community of the elect, in which the faithful do good, not because of fear of punishment, but out of love for God. Oakley traces this threefold distinction into the late Middle Ages in works by Richard Fitzralph and John Wycliffe, who articulate the difference between Adam's "natural dominion," the "civil dominion" of the secular state, and the "evangelical dominion" of the true church (i.e., the community of the elect), which is a spiritual authority, rather than a coercive power.[13]

The Lutheran version of a politics of sin, while steeped in Augustinian thought, largely abandons the idea of Adam's natural dominion, which Luther associates with a superseded "Old" Testament.[14] Instead of a threefold distinction, Luther makes the twofold distinction between the coercive power of the state and the spiritual authority of the true church. Echoing Augustine's distinction between the city of God and the earthly city, Luther regards the world as divided into two kingdoms: the "kingdom of God," to which the community of the elect belong, and the "worldly kingdom," wherein the rest of humanity is condemned to damnation. In the kingdom of God, there is no need for coercive power. The true church—that trans-temporal, trans-spatial community of the elect—is subject only to the spiritual governance of God's Word over the inner heart. But Luther agrees with Augustine that, in the temporal world, governance through the sword is necessary—indeed, divinely ordained—for the restraint of sinners and the protection of the righteous.

Luther argues that through faith and faith alone, Christians stand before God as wholly righteous, redeemed of their sins. In their relationship to God, they belong to a wholly spiritual realm. Yet, inasmuch as they also exist in the temporal realm, all remain entangled in sin; for one is saved not by being free of sin, but despite being a sinner (Luther [1523] 1962: 90; cf. Oakley 2015: 112). Hence the necessity of secular power, the function of which is to mete out an external form of justice through law and punishment. It is understood that secular power will exercise this role in a tyrannical way; for princes, according to Luther, "are generally the biggest fools or the worst scoundrels on earth . . . They are God's executioners and hangmen; His divine wrath uses them to punish the wicked and to maintain outward peace" ([1523] 1962: 113). No matter how depraved the prince's behavior, Luther sees secular authority as the instrument through which God exercises his justice in the temporal world. Thus, he regards rebellion, even against a tyrant, as sacrilege.

Anticipating Benjamin, we can see that in a politics of sin the sovereign's rule is twined with despair. Reflecting Augustine's view that subjugation enters the world as a consequence of the Fall and a punishment for original sin, sovereignty is derived from the sunken condition of fallen humanity rather than the elevation of a Godlike ruler. Subjugation is a state of despair, both for the subjugator and the subjugated. For the subjugator, alienation abounds. Entangled in the temporal world, the essence of which is mutability and transience, the sovereign's power is fundamentally insecure, leading to perpetual fear and anxiety. Moreover, as God's executioner, the prince is alienated from God by his use of tyrannical, even sinful means, placing his own salvation in jeopardy.[15] The sovereign's anxiety, fear and alienation from God—in a word, his acedia—remove him from the unspoiled happiness of life in Paradise and from inner tranquility, which is the liberty of faith.

Of course, subjugation also produces suffering on the part of those who are subjected. To be subjected to a coercive, penal order is to be blocked from the spontaneous expression of one's natural inclinations.[16] According to Benjamin, this is a source of woe. The suffering of subjugated creation seems not to have troubled the architects of a politics of sin, who saw suffering as deserved punishment for original sin. But

Benjamin regards the suffering of subjugated creation as evidence of the guilt—that is, the injustice—not of creation, but of the penal order.

## The Politics of Sin in Benjamin's *Origin of the German Trauerspiel*

As Benjamin observes, the setting of the trauerspiel is the state of creation (*OT*, 72/GSI:1, 263-64). This is an unmistakably fallen creation, determined by the "creaturely guilt" of original sin (*OT*, 128-29/GSI:1, 308). In this state, suffering and death are unleashed as a matter of fatal necessity.[17] Nor is the sovereign exempt from this chain of calamities: "The plane of the creaturely state . . . quite unmistakably determines the sovereign as well" (*OT*, 72/GSI:1, 263-64). While a politics of sin is implicit in these lines, Benjamin never states explicitly that a different political theology than Schmitt's underlies the imaginary of sovereignty in the Baroque plays. Indeed, by prominently citing Schmitt as his source for illuminating the "new concept of sovereignty" that emerged in the seventeenth century, Benjamin leads us away from the insight that more than one justification of absolute sovereignty coexisted in this period of intense religious and political conflict (*OT*, 49-50/GSI:1, 245-46). What differences are entailed when sovereignty derives its legitimacy, not from a secularization of the God-concept, but from the putative need to impose a penal order on guilty creation?

First, reference to a politics of sin sheds light on the ambivalent characteristics of the sovereign's divine investiture, which Benjamin observes in the Baroque plays. While the sovereign is indeed divinely ordained, this does not mean what Schmitt takes it to mean; namely, that the sovereign bears the attributes of God (including the attribute of an omnipotent or unlimited will). Although he is "the lord of creatures," Benjamin makes it clear that the sovereign "remains a creature" (*OT*, 72/GSI:1, 264). What it means to be divinely invested within a politics of sin is to be an instrument of divine justice in the temporal world. The secular lord is an agent of divine justice, not because he is Godlike in any way, but because his cruelty and excesses are used by God to punish the sinful, test the righteous, and keep vice in check.[18]

Second, it follows that the view of sovereignty as instrumental in an economy of divine justice invalidates the analogy between the sovereign and God. For it is ultimately God's sovereignty that acts in history. Like an invisible hand, God intervenes in the course of history to turn even the most disordered acts of tyranny to providentially well-ordered ends. This supports the "specifically Baroque" idea—which we now recognize as characteristic of a politics of sin—that even if the sovereign is a depraved lunatic, the perception of his role as sacrosanct remains unscathed (*OT*, 54-55; 57/GSI:1, 249; 251). God's action in history is especially revealed in those moments when the sovereign *loses agency*, overcome by the excess of power expressed *through* him, rather than *by* him. What "continues to fascinate" is the incontinence of the sovereign's actions (*OT*, 57/GSI:1, 251). Descriptions abound of "the Caesar who loses himself in the intoxication of power" (*OT*, 56/GSI:1, 250), or the tyrant who erupts "like a volcano into frenzied rage" (*OT*, 55/GSI:1, 250). It is what is *unwilled* in the sovereign's conduct that points beyond the human will to divine providence: "precisely at the point where [the tyrant] unfolds power most deliriously . . . there is recognized the revelation of history, and at the same time, the authority that calls a halt to its vicissitudes" (ibid.). This stands in direct contrast to Schmitt's political theology, in which the sovereign, as an analogue of the omnipotent God, is conceived as the author of the political order—an order that emanates from his exercise of will, just as the order of creation emanates from God's will.

The main point of convergence between Schmitt's political theology and a political theology of sin is that both ground a concept of absolute sovereignty. But this similarity is misleading. The derivation of sovereignty from the guilt of fallen humanity is antithetical to its derivation from the secularized concept of an omnipotent God. For Schmitt, the specific manifestation of the sovereign's absolute power is a secularization of the theological concept of miracles (Schmitt [1922, 1934] 2005: 36). Miracles are a revelation of God's supremacy in the suspension of nature's normal laws. Suspension is categorically distinct from transgression: the latter contravenes the law while remaining *under* its power, while the former reveals a sovereign freedom that is *higher* than the law, in that the author of the law is not bound by law's necessity. This has its secular analogue, Schmitt argues, in the sovereignty that is revealed in the authority to suspend customary laws in the state of exception (Schmitt [1922, 1934] 2005: 5, 36). By contrast, the legitimation of unlimited dictatorship in a politics of sin is derived from God's justice in punishing transgression. The transgression that calls forth this punishment and thus grounds dictatorship is the guilt of creation as such, which unfolds from Adam's first transgression (*OT*, 129/*GSI.1*, 308).[19] The dogma of original sin provides theological justification for a fundamentally penal conception of the political order. The ideal of this order is the suppression of fallen humanity's (corrupted) nature—its immediacy or spontaneity—and the production of a *second* nature, which has been rigorously disciplined by penal law. This is antithetical to Schmitt's depiction of the unbound freedom of sovereign subjectivity from law's necessity. The imposition of a penal law over nature is intended to arrest the inclination to transgress *before* it has the chance to become an exception. Thus, Benjamin subtly alters Schmitt's meaning when he writes that "it is the most important function of the prince to avert" or exclude the exception (*OT*, 49/*GSI:1*, 245; cf. Weber 1992: 12).

According to Benjamin, the *raison d'être* of the sovereign's unlimited dictatorship is "the restoration of order" in the temporal world (*OT*, 59/*GSI:1*, 253). Ironically characterized as "the restoration of paradisiacal timelessness," this is decidedly not a restoration of Paradise itself (*OT*, 81/*GSI:1*, 271). Rather, *stability* (i.e., timelessness) is the single-minded goal, and it is pursued in the temporal world through unlimited dictatorship. In a passage that is precious for my argument, Benjamin indicates that the tyrant's dictatorship over the body politic—which has its counterpart in reason's dictatorial rule over the passions in the chaste heroine of the Baroque plays—results in the emergence of "an antihistorical new creation," which is "removed from the innocent first state of creation" (*OT*, 59/*GSI:1*, 253). With its implicit reference to the Fall, this remark both alludes to a politics of sin and directs a subtle protest against it. Whereas, in a politics of sin, authoritarian rule is justified by appeal to the guilt of fallen creation, Benjamin inverts the terms of this argument, suggesting that the imposition of dictatorial rule itself is responsible for creation's removal from natural innocence.[20]

Whereas natural life expresses itself spontaneously, subjugation under law blocks this expression, eliciting a mood of mourning, not least in the one who exercises rule: "spirit is the capacity to exercise dictatorship. This capacity requires strict internal discipline no less than the most unscrupulous external action," a comportment which "awakes, in the creature stripped of all naïve impulses, the mood of mourning" (*OT*, 89/*GSI*:1, 276). A duality is thus opened up within sovereignty, between the office of the sovereign and the personal characteristics of the prince.[21] According to the demands of his office, the sovereign must serve as an instrument of domination—an office that he is able to carry out effectively only insofar as he is capable of mastering his own impulses. As a person, however, the sovereign's will is "broken by emotion," revealing his indomitable despair (*OT*, 90/*GSI*:1, 277).

As involuntary, uncaused sorrow, melancholy is a mirror-image of faith; both reveal the limits of the human will.[22] For the Lutheran authors of the German trauerspiels, the despair of fallen creation—represented by the acedia of even the most highly enthroned of creatures—points beyond politics to faith. For faith alone—not human laws (or "works")—can save from the insuperable despair and guilt of the creaturely estate. As we will see, Benjamin repudiates the reversal from the depths of despair to faith, which is posited allegorically in the Baroque plays. For him, the melancholy of subjugated creation bears witness to the injustice of the penal order. This injustice is not resolved—but rather propped up—by Augustinian and Lutheran theology, which spuriously appeals to the realization of divine justice in the penal order of the state.

## The Fall of Adam and the Sovereign's Acedia

As long as we consider sovereignty in an exclusively political, or even political-theological register, we will overlook its primarily allegorical significance in the Baroque plays (*OT*, 205/*GSI*:1, 367). The plays are allegorical because they communicate a theological meaning through the vehicle of their secular plots.[23] The plots, which revolve around political intrigue and court life, have their allegorical meaning in salvation history. As I argue, the sovereign's fall into acedia has its allegorical significance in Adam's fall into sin. The connection to Adam is posited in Benjamin's discussion of the trauerspiel; as he notes, in the legal theory of the time, the sovereign's authority was thought to be derived from "the dominion over the world which Adam received as the crown of Creation as a whole" (*OT*, 73/*GSI*:1, 264). But the line of succession has passed through Adam's sin. If the sovereign is an allegory for Adam, it is for the *fallen* Adam. For although the creation that serves as the setting for the trauerspiel "still reflects the sun of grace," it is "[m]irrored . . . in the slough of adamic guilt" (*OT*, 128/*GSI*:1, 308).

The allegorical representation of sovereignty in the trauerspiel is illuminated by the theology of the Fall and the doctrine of original sin. According to Augustine, Adam and Eve deny their creaturely dependence on the Creator when they are persuaded by the serpent to "be like God" by eating of the tree of knowledge of good and evil ([426] 1998: XIV.13, 610; cf. Gen. 3.5).[24] Adam's prideful refusal to accept his status as a creature—superior to all other creatures, but subordinate to God—is the root of original sin. His aspiration to be like God leads to humanity's fall away from God: "By striving after more, man is diminished; when he takes delight in his own self-sufficiency, he falls away from the One who truly suffices him" (ibid.: XIV.13, 610). The trauerspiels condense this idea into an image of the sovereign, who, striving for absolute power, falls into acedia—that state of sin in which the soul is alienated from God.[25] As a critical counterpart to Schmitt's analogy between the sovereign and God, Benjamin poses the trauerspiel's image of the sovereign's fall into acedia—a dialectical image, because it simultaneously expresses the sovereign's superbia (his prideful aspiration to achieve Godlike supremacy) and its theological meaning as the fall into sin.

Acedia reflects the psychology of a soul that has fallen in turning away from God. According to Augustine (a Platonist in this regard), the soul moves toward and becomes like that which it loves (Deane 2013: 40). The soul that loves God moves toward him and becomes more like him, without, however, collapsing the ontological distinction between Creator and creature. The soul that turns away from God—by seeking to *be like God*, rather than *being-in-relation* to God—falls ever further from God. This takes the form of an emanative descent, which reverses the Platonic ascent to the highest form of the good (*OT*, 162/*GSI*:1, 334). The soul that loves God—the one, eternal, incorporeal, unchangeable Being—is sustained in being, wisdom, and goodness. But the soul that turns away from God, through its disordered desires, becomes entangled in what is most insubstantial, mutable, and ultimately unreal (Augustine [426] 1998: IX.17, 382; cf. Deane 2013: 40). Whereas the love of God [*caritas*] is eternally fulfilling, the lust for earthly things [*libido*] is insatiable. As soon as one desire has been satisfied, another arises to take its place (Deane 2013: 45). The compulsive infinity of earthly desires leads the fallen soul into an abyss. In Benjamin's recapitulation of this idea, "it belongs to all virtue to have before it an end—namely, its model in God, just as all depravity opens an infinite progress into the depths" (*OT*, 251-52/*GSI*:1, 404); "immersion [in earthly things] led only too easily into the bottomless" (*OT*, 144/*GSI*:1, 320).[26]

Guilty creation's emanative descent is captured, first of all, in a play on light symbolism. Like the sun, God's light sustains created life in being (Augustine [426] 1998: X.2, 393–4). But the soul that turns away from God is plunged into darkness and icy cold, impenetrable by the rays of God's grace.[27] Darkness and cold are associated with hell and the dominion of the devil.[28] According to Augustine's allegorical interpretation of Genesis, the Creator's initial division between light and darkness refers to the fall from grace of the rebellious angels, who turned from God's light toward the darkness (Augustine [426] 1998: XI.19, 473; XI.33, 494).[29] Evil, in the Augustinian tradition, has no substantive being of its own; it is privative. This is symbolized by the absence of God's light, which plunges the fallen angels—henceforth demons in hell—into impenetrable darkness, signifying a lack of truth and being.[30] In the medieval discourse of acedia, which makes its return in Baroque allegoresis, this darkness is conceived as a state of spiritual sleep, in which the soul becomes vulnerable to demonic dreams (*OT*, 157/*GSI*:1, 330).[31]

In Augustine's account, the story of the angelic fall frames the story of Adam's fall, since Adam "resembles the devil" in his prideful disobedience to God ([426] 1998: XIV.4, 586). But Adam's fall into sin is differentiated from the angelic fall by the introduction of the element of flesh. It is not simply a rebellious will that prompts Adam to disobey the command of God; his love for Eve—the flesh of his flesh—leads him to turn away from God, the breath of his breath.[32] Whereas God is eternal, incorporeal, and immutable, flesh is a medium of continual transformation and transience, which reaches its limit only in death. Adam's disobedience—a misuse of his freedom and a disordered love for what is lower—is punished by the triumph of flesh over spirit. Henceforth, the fallen creature becomes disobedient to himself: "his very mind, and even his lower part, his flesh, do not obey his will" (ibid.: XIV.15, 612; cf. Deane 2013: 42). Contra Schmitt, for whom the sovereign has the Godlike attribute of an unlimited will, the trauerspiel's tyrant exposes his fallenness through incontinence or loss of sovereignty over his own self.

The representation of acedia evolves two images to express the fallen soul's alienation from God. On the one hand, an image of restlessness evokes the agitation of a soul that does not rest in God.[33] On the other hand, an image of heaviness evokes the gravitational force exerted on the soul by earthly things, pulling it downward (*OT*, 157-58/*GSI*:1, 330-31).[34] The former is evident in the sovereign's incapacity to decide: "[t]he tempo of [his] affective life quickens to such an extent that calm actions, slowly ripened decisions, are seen less and less often" (*OT*, 90/*GSI*:1, 277). This is no mere indecisiveness; it is that state of sin—namely, acedia—in which the soul, having lapsed from its true rest in God, spins out in dizzying, disoriented activity (*OT*, 160-61/*GSI*:1, 332-33).

The latter image of weightiness—the gravitational pull exerted by temporal things on fallen creation—is implicit in the peculiar manner in which fate unfolds in the trauerspiel. Consistent with the Augustinian view of love as a motive force, which draws the soul toward what it loves, Benjamin describes how "once human life has sunk into the bonds of the merely creaturely, the life of seemingly dead or inanimate things gains power over it as well" (*OT*, 132/*GSI*:1, 311). According to Augustine, the righteous pass lightly through the world, making use of things as needed, but not becoming attached to them as they transit through this world on their way to God's world ([c. 407] 2009: XL.10, 604; cf. Deane 2013: 43–4). But the life of guilty creation becomes *entangled* in the temporal world, trapped and weighed down by earthly things.[35] This takes the form of a fatal compulsion, since "man is necessarily a slave to the things by means of which he seeks to be happy. He follows them whithersoever they lead." And "those who think to escape servitude by not worshipping anything are in fact slaves of all kinds of worldly things" (Augustine [390] 2005: XXXVIII.69, 70; cf. Deane 2013: 41). The fateful entanglement of guilty life in the world of things yields another facet of the trauerspiel's dialectical image of sovereignty: the master, propped up by his property, is enslaved to things by his compulsive lusts. Since neither property nor slavery existed in the original state of creation, their entry into life marks its condition as fallen. Idolatry, the worship of things, is also implicit in this description. Benjamin's discussion of the entry of property (i.e., stage props) into the drama of fate conceivably has its background here (*OT*, 132-33/*GSI*:1, 311-12).

The representation of the sovereign as bestial rounds out the trauerspiel's allegorical representation of the sovereign as fallen Adam. In the original order of creation in Paradise, according to Augustine, human life is situated midway between the life of angels and the life of beasts ([426] 1998: XII.22, 533; cf. Deane 2013: 42). But fallen humanity sinks into bestiality, and has the capacity to surpass even the beasts in cruelty (Augustine [426] 1998: V.19, 224; cf. Deane 2013: 42). This is expressed in the dialectical image of the lowly animal rising up in the loftiest of worldly creatures. In Benjamin's words, "in the ruler, the most exalted of creatures, the animal can rise up with unsuspected powers" (*OT*, 74/*GSI*:1, 265). In demonstration of this point, Benjamin cites the following lines from the chorus of Andreas Gryphius's first trauerspiel, *Leo Armenius, Oder Fürsten-Mord* [Leo Armenius, or Murder of a Prince]: "You, who have lost the image of the Highest, / Behold the image born unto you. / Ask not, 'Why does it enter in a stable?' It seeks us, who are more bestial than a beast" (*OT*, 74/*GSI*:1, 265; cf. Gryphius [1646] 1882: act IV, 387 ff.). As these lines suggest, the element of flesh, through which human life is bound to transience, suffering, and death, is also what enables sinful humanity's redemption in Christ. For God humbled himself by taking on the form of flesh in Christ in order to save the elect from eternal punishment. In Christ's sacrificial death, the flesh is sundered from spirit, preparing the soul for its entry into eternal life. This is the allegorical significance of the sovereign's death, which coincides with salvation in the trauerspiel's redemptive ending. For, as Benjamin notes, death occurs in the trauerspiel not merely as punishment for sin, but as expiation of guilty life (*OT*, 130/*GSI*:1, 310).

## The Allegorical Significance of Sovereignty in *Leo Armenius*

Confirmation of the allegorical significance of Adam's fall into sin and its expiation in death is found in Gryphius's *Leo Armenius*. While its plot is taken from secular history rather than liturgy or scripture, the play refers allegorically to salvation history. At the outset of the play, we encounter Michael Balbus, who is scheming to assassinate the emperor, Leo. As the plot unfolds, Balbus is found out and sentenced by Leo to be executed on Christmas day. But Leo's wife, Theodossia, persuades Leo to defer the execution so as not to sully the day of celebration for Christ's birth. In the interim, Leo falls into a terrifying dream, which prophecies his death. He is subsequently murdered in the church while touching the cross. As Judith Aikin observes, the play is an allegory for "the onset of the Age of Grace (the New Testament)" from out of "the end of the historical period ruled by the Law of Moses (the Old Testament)" (1982: 58). The death scene, which takes place during the Christmas service, represents "the end of the old Leo, whose sense of justice is that of revenge, and the birth of the new Leo, who can show mercy, confess sin, imitate Christ" (ibid., 55-6). This construction reflects the contrast between the temporal justice of the secular sovereign—exercised tyrannically through vengeance and punishment—and the spiritual justice of Christian mercy and love. It also reflects the contrast between the "first Adam"—king and lord of all creation in the Old Testament, whose sin led to the forfeiture of his original dominion and the imposition of a penal order on fallen humanity—and the "second Adam" (i.e., Christ)—the messianic King of the New Testament, whose redemptive work heralds a new, spiritual life of humanity (cf. Paul, Romans 5: 12-21 and 1 Corinthians 15: 20-28).

Rather than a temporal unfolding of salvation history, the trauerspiel presents its concealed drama of salvation spatially, in the constellation of its allegorical personae (*OT*, 67; 82/*GSI*:1, 260; 271). This spatial configuration explains why the Baroque typology of sovereignty is Janus-faced; for instead of presenting, as a temporal succession, the conversion from tyranny to martyrdom, the sovereign represents tyrant and martyr simultaneously. These "antitheses play into each other, in unparalleled ... fashion" in *Leo Armenius* (*OT*, 54; 58/*GSI*:1, 249; 252).[36] Fallen creation evolves its own constellation, expressed through the penal coupling of guilt and coercive power. Thus, Leo, the vengeful tyrant, has his complement in the figure of the intriguer, the scheming Balbus, whose unexplained rebelliousness is an allegory for Satan's rebellion against God, or for Cain, the first inhabitant of the devil's kingdom (*OT*, 87/*GSI*:1, 275). The dyad of guilt and punishment—image of fallen creation—is juxtaposed to the figure of the martyr, allegorized in Leo's death. But Benjamin notes that the representation of martyrdom does not escape immanence.[37] As an image for the pious mortification of the flesh, martyrdom is suggested in the plays in representations of bodily suffering, frequently involving the violent dismemberment of the corpse (*OT*, 58; 235-36/*GSI*:1, 252; 391).

Prior to his death—indeed, drawing him toward death by a demonic fatality—Leo plunges into acedia. Benjamin quotes at length from *Leo Armenius*:

> Leo Armenius speaks of the prince in this manner: "His heart sinks at the thought of his sword. When he sits at his table, the mixed wine in its crystal turns to gall and poison. With the fading of day there comes creeping the sabled throng, the armies of anxiety, to watch and wake in his bed. In his ivory, in his purple and scarlet, he never finds rest. . . . And should he be granted a short sleep, then Morpheus assails him and paints in darkest colors in the night what he thought by day, and terrifies him now with blood, now with crashing throne and flames, with anguish and death and stolen crown." (*OT*, 146/*GSI*:1, 322; cf. Gryphius [1646] 1882, act 1, scene 4, 385 ff.)

Leo's acedia results from his disordered love, which is misdirected toward worldly things (his sword and crown, his ivory, purple and scarlet) rather than God. Contemplation of these things causes his heart to sink—to be weighed down. Since worldly things are transient, Leo is beset by fear and anxiety over their loss. His anxiety peaks with "the fading of day"—allegory for the turn away from God's light and truth toward darkness and delusion. His mind, having wandered from true rest in God, is restless. When he is finally able to sleep—the spiritual sleep of the soul—he is assailed by demonic dreams. Under the fatal compulsion of his dreams, he is moved to visit the prison where Balbus is housed, precipitating the events that culminate in his murder. Both the mind's vertiginous plunge into a phantasmagorical dreamworld and the body's restless motion are symptomatic of acedia.[38]

Leo's free-fall into the phantasmagoria of acedia meets its limit only in death, which coincides with his martyrdom. For just as the death of Christ redeems human sin,

Leo's death is an allegory for divine grace and God's mercy toward sinners: "Death provides the freedom for the soul to enter the bliss of eternal life" (Aikin 1982: 50). The sovereign's death is an allegory for both the transience and vanity of human life and for the soul's liberation from its earthly bonds.

The trauerspiel's redemptive ending stages the conversion from a worldly perspective to the perspective of faith, in which the soul "awakens" from the nightmare of acedia in God's world (*OT*, 254/*GSI*:1, 406). This awakening is a transformation of perspective, rather than of the world—from fallen subjectivity to the redeemed subjectivity of faith. The self that was entangled in the worldly—its bonds to the temporal world represented by its appearance in constellation with other allegorical figures—is transformed into a spiritual self, which finds itself alone before God. From the vantage point of faith, the self that awakens in God's world recognizes the alien world which had impinged upon it in acedia as phantasmagorical. The entire world of *vanitas*, which had unfolded from the perspective of acedia, is absorbed back into the perspective of faith, supposedly without remainder (*OT*, 257/*GSI*:1, 407). The allegorical figures devised to represent life enmeshed in vice—the tyrants and intriguers—signify "precisely the nonbeing" of what they represent; the merely privative nature of evil (*OT*, 255/*GSI*:1, 406).

Benjamin advances two criticisms of the perspectival inversion in the trauerspiel's redemptive ending. First, he contends that both the subject's descent into an underworld of demonic phantasmagoria and its ascent to the heaven of God's world are posited only within allegories. Both remain aesthetic constructs—mere sallies of the imagination, which fail to escape the immanence of the temporal world. While there is some truth or "fidelity" (*Treue*) in acedia's presentation of the worldly as an anguished hellscape, Benjamin condemns as "faithless" (*treulos*) the leap toward an illusory heaven (*OT*, 161-62; 255/*GSI*:1, 333-34; 406). By aesthetic sleight of hand, the play's ending substitutes an image of the redeemed world for the unredeemed, broken, despairing condition of creaturely life.

Second, Benjamin objects to the idea that evil is absorbed back into the nothingness of a merely privative idea in God's world. While he agrees with Augustine that evil lacks an objective correlate in the original state of creation, it meanwhile becomes "anchored deep in reality" in the fallen world—not by the guilt of creation—but "by means of punishments" (*OT*, 256/*GSI*:1, 407).[39] And punishment does not disappear with the reversal into faith; it is merely transformed. For while the penal order imposed by the earthly sovereign emanates from a *vacillating* subjectivity—an instrument rendered ineffective by the infirmities of flesh—it is construed, in the theology of original sin, as having its ultimate anchor in God's omnipotent sovereignty, which unleashes on fallen creation the eternal punishments of hell.

> And while, with the earthly tribunal, the vacillating subjectivity of judgment is anchored deep in reality by means of punishments, in the heavenly tribunal the semblance of evil comes wholly into its own. There the avowed subjectivity comes to triumph over every deceptive objectivity of law and assimilates itself, as the work of "highest wisdom and primordial love," as hell, to divine omnipotence. (*OT*, 256/*GSI*:1, 407; cf. Dante Allighieri 1892: 13)

It is certainly an inversion to present this vision of totally efficacious, eternal punishment as "the work of 'highest wisdom and primordial love.'" That allegorical signification can diverge so fantastically from reality is an indictment of "fallen" language, an idea that I touch on in the final section.

## By Way of a Conclusion: Adam's Naming of Creation

Benjamin's analysis of the imaginary of sovereignty in the Baroque trauerspiels demonstrates that the plays themselves unfold a politics of sin. Read alongside Schmitt's theory of sovereignty, Benjamin's literary sources do critical work. Specifically, the plays evolve a dialectical image of sovereignty, which simultaneously expresses the human being's striving to *be like God* and its theological meaning as a sinful falling away from God, made manifest in the sovereign's acedia. But Benjamin is in no way sympathetic to a politics of sin. As I have suggested, he inverts its terms: whereas the architects of the politics of sin regard human nature as vitiated by original sin, and as needful of a penal order to restrain its inclinations, Benjamin regards the penal order itself as a source of woe for subjugated nature. As he suggests, it is not nature that is guilty; rather, guilt (or injustice) accrues to the penal order, which seeks to hinder creation's self-expression.

Benjamin's critique of a politics of sin is subtle in the *Trauerspiel* book. Much of the text is a commentary on the trauerspiels themselves, which makes it difficult to distill Benjamin's critical voice from his attempt to give expression to the ideas at stake in his literary sources. But Benjamin provides insight into an order more appropriate to innocent creation in his work on an Adamic theory of language.[40] Benjamin's linguistic Adamicism is typically not read as a contribution to political theology. However, its precise bearing on the questions discussed in this chapter may be brought into relief by juxtaposing Benjamin's interpretation of Genesis to Augustine's. Augustine's reading of Genesis revolves around three moments: (1) the cardinal good of creaturely obedience to the Creator, symbolized in Paradise by God's command not to eat of the tree of knowledge; (2) original sin, as Adam and Eve's willful transgression of God's command; and (3) the divine justice of eternal punishment, which passes into all of Adam's descendants through the corruption of human nature and its subjection to death—corruption that cannot be removed by human means, but only by God's grace. Augustine subsumes secular politics under divine justice, viewing it as the instrument by which God punishes guilty creation in the temporal world. He thus legitimates an authoritarian and penal political order. Benjamin resists the penal implications of the Augustinian interpretation of Genesis at every step. The main points of his Genesis interpretation are: (1) an idea of the creation as God's self-expression, which gives rise to a created order in which each singular being immediately expresses God in expressing itself; (2) the "fall" of language, which coincides with the introduction of an order of judgment, which is extrinsically and coercively imposed over creation; and (3) the suffering, or lament of nature, which arises from the hindrance of its self-expression through its subjection to judgment and the penal order to which judgment gives rise.

What makes a comparative reading of Augustine and Benjamin fruitful and illuminating is that both distinguish between an immanent order in creation, and a "fallen" order, which is extrinsically imposed on creation. The contrast between an immanent order and an imposed order explains a structural similarity between "fallen" politics and "fallen" language. Whereas the former involves the imposition of conventional laws on citizens of the state, the latter involves the imposition of conventional significations on nature. Both reveal their coercive quality, Benjamin argues, insofar as they hinder nature's self-expression. Benjamin's idea that creation expresses itself rejects a foundational premise of the politics of sin: namely, that after the Fall, nature becomes disorderly, requiring the imposition of an extrinsic, coercive order as a remedy against chaos. Against this view, he argues that, even after the "fall" of human languages, creation continues to express itself; however, it now finds its expression hindered—blocked by extrinsic means—which gives rise to nature's mournfulness.

It is admittedly controversial to suggest that Benjamin, like Augustine, upholds an idea of an immanent order in creation. This is thorny, since the notion of an immanent order in creation has been harnessed to abusive claims about forms of life that are supposedly unnatural, or "disordered." Arguably, we find a problematic version of this idea in Augustine, whose vision of the order immanent in creation is unabashedly hierarchical and moralistic. God is above the rest of creation, and human beings, although subordinate to God, have dominion over all "irrational" creatures (Augustine [426] 1998: XIX.15, 942; cf. Genesis 1:26). According to Augustine, the original and supposedly proper order of creation is retained only as long as the first human beings are duly obedient to God's command. From this we learn that, for Augustine, human beings were created for obedience. The potential for an authoritarian politics is already implicit here, and in the attendant suggestion that creation is not self-sufficient. Once Adam and Eve transgress God's command, they deprive themselves—and all of their descendants—of God's light, which is authoritative without being coercive. Henceforth (with the exception of those elect, who are redeemed of their sins by God's grace), fallen humanity requires subjugation under extrinsically imposed and coercive laws. Thus, Augustine maintains that fallen humanity is justly placed in a condition of bondage (ibid., XIX.15, 943).

In contrast to Augustine's vision of an immanent order in creation, which centers around a structure of command and obedience, Benjamin's notion of immanent order is anchored in an idea of the self-expression of singularities. As such, it may be read as resistance against the view that some forms of expression are improper, or "against nature." Rather than an abstract determination, or judgment that certain forms of expression are good or evil, Benjamin's argument yields a criterion of adequacy: an expression is adequate when it is able to unfold itself completely.[41] Each created being expresses itself to the full extent of its power. Nonhuman creation is limited in the degree to which it can express itself, since it is non-verbal (*SW* I, 67/*GS*II.1, 147). The uniqueness of Adam's language of names is that it raises the self-expression of the rest of creation to a higher power, rendering it "more perfect" by transposing the mute, material language of things into the medium of sound (*SW* I, 70/*GS*II.1, 151). In Adam's naming of creation, Benjamin finds an alternative to the Augustinian idea of original dominion in Paradise. Whereas Augustine gravitates toward the statement of Adam's rule over the rest of creation in Gen. 1:26, Benjamin takes up the idea, in Gen. 2:18-20, where God brings the creatures to Adam to name. Accordingly, Adam is not "the lord of nature" by *ruling over* nonhuman creation; rather, Adam's names give voice to creation's own self-expression (*SWI*, 65/*GSII*.1, 144). Benjamin acknowledges that there is an intimation of hierarchy in the difference between the rest of creation's mute, material language, and the Adamic language, which unfolds in the spiritual medium of sound. Unlike Augustine, however, Benjamin does not celebrate this hierarchy; he regards it as an intimation (already in Paradise) of the mournfulness of subjugated nature.[42]

A second point of divergence between Augustine's interpretation of Genesis and Benjamin's may be found in how each interprets the symbolism of the tree of knowledge of good and evil. For Augustine, the tree of knowledge symbolizes the good of obedience to commands and the evil of transgression. The fruit itself is not bad to eat, Augustine avers, since nothing God creates is bad. What is evil is the transgression of the command ([426] 1998: XIII.21, 568). For Benjamin, by contrast, the tree of knowledge is an emblem of the entry of *judgments* into human language (*SW* I, 72/*GSII*.1, 154). Benjamin agrees with Augustine that nothing that God creates is evil; therefore, the judgment of good and evil is "vain," in the sense that the term "evil" does not name or give voice to the expression of any being. Rather, it subjects beings to an abstract judgment, imposed from without (*SW* I, 71-72/*GSII*.1, 153-54). Although judgment is vain, it is not without effect: the establishment of judgment over creation introduces a particular kind of evil into the world. It coincides with the "fall" of human language—the imposition of a regime of arbitrary significations onto nature (*SW* I, 71/*GSII*.1, 153). Moreover, as Benjamin makes clear in the *Trauerspiel* book, the order of judgment is anchored in reality by punishments (*OT*, 256/*GSI*:1, 407). Benjamin thus directly broaches the nexus between the fall of language and fallen politics. Fallen language and fallen politics both establish an extrinsically imposed and conventional order over creation. Schmitt makes this extrinsically imposed and arbitrary order the essential characteristic of law—namely, its imposition by the dictate of the sovereign's will.

Whereas Augustine justifies the imposition of an extrinsic order on creation by appeal to the putative disorder of fallen nature, Benjamin maintains that creation itself does not fall. Creation continues to express an immanent order in expressing itself; but it now finds its expression hindered, subjected to an extrinsic order of judgments. Subjugated nature's self-expression becomes an expression of suffering: that is, an expression of its being limited by something extrinsic to itself. Benjamin frames this hindrance as the lament or suffering of subjugated nature (*SW* I, 72-73/*GSII*.1, 155). He articulates this idea, first in his essay "On Language as Such," then in a fragment on "The Role of Language in Trauerspiel and Tragedy" (both from 1916), then finally, in the *Trauerspiel* book (*OT*, 226/*GSI*.1, 383). I find his most pregnant expression in the fragment, since it articulates in overtly political terms the point of connection between the mournfulness of nature and its subjugation under a penal order:

> [T]he essence of the trauerspiel is already contained in the old adage that all of nature would begin to mourn if ever it were endowed with language...whereas

creation wished only to pour forth in purity, it was man who bore its crown. This
is the significance of the king in the trauerspiel. . . . These plays represent the
stemming of nature, a tremendous damming up of feeling. . . . [S]orrow fills the
sensuous world in which nature and language meet. (*OT*, 269/*GS*II.1, 138-39)

Encapsulated here is Benjamin's crucial objection against a politics of sin. Creation strives to express itself—to "pour forth in purity." But it finds its self-expression blocked by an order that is extrinsically imposed on it. This order encompasses what Benjamin calls "fallen" language (i.e., language as a system of arbitrary significations) and "fallen" politics (i.e., the repressive, penal order of the state). The fallen order is set athwart creation's self-expression, hindering it, damming it up, and filling the sensuous world with sorrow.

Benjamin's resistance against an extrinsically imposed order—whether of juridical law or arbitrary, subjective significations—centers around his fidelity to creation's self-expression. Although Benjamin does not believe it possible to resurrect an Adamic language of names, he retains an idea that things express themselves, and that the task of the philosopher is to translate the material language of things into a verbal language, without imposing an arbitrary, subjective schema on things, as it were, from above (*OT*, 14/*GS*I.1, 217). Benjamin's appeal to creation's self-expression provides a critical vantage point from which to recognize the domination and subjective arbitrariness involved in any extrinsically imposed order—a critique that extends to both the politics of sin and Schmittian sovereignty.

## Notes

1 I am grateful to Brendan Moran for his editorial interventions and to Miguel Vatter and Dimitris Vardoulakis for comments on an earlier draft. I discussed ideas with Vivian Liska, Carl Schwebel, and Shoshana Schwebel, each of whom helped me clarify my argument. I dedicate this chapter to Shoshana, with gratitude for our lifelong exchange of ideas.
2 In a letter to Schmitt, Benjamin acknowledges the importance of Schmitt's work on the seventeenth-century doctrine of sovereignty in *Dictatorship* and in *Political Theology* for his own discussion of the royal hero in the Baroque plays (*GS*I:3, 887 and *GB*III, 558). He makes direct reference to *Political Theology* in the *Trauerspiel* book. See *OT*, 49-50/*GS*I:1, 245-46, and *OT*, 87/*GS*I:1, 275, where Benjamin cites the identical passage from Frédéric Atger's doctoral dissertation (Atger 1906: 136) as does Schmitt in *Political Theology* (Schmitt [1922, 1934] 2005: 46-7). Moreover, his "Curriculum Vitae (III)" of 1928 attests to Schmitt's methodological influence on his study of works of art (*SW*2:1, 78/*GS*VI, 219).
3 Benjamin's engagement with Schmitt is controversial due to Schmitt's radical conservatism and his subsequent embrace of Nazism. For an overview of the secondary scholarship on this issue, see de Wilde: 2011.
4 On Benjamin's demand for decisiveness, see Pensky 1993: 12. On Benjamin's treatment of Schmitt and the theory of sovereign decisionism in particular, see ibid: 77-78.
5 See also Ferber, who concurs with Koepnick (2013: 93–6).

6   Voluntarist theology emphasizes that God's omnipotence implies a capacity to do anything that is logically possible, including suspending his own prior decrees. What is transferred into secular politics is not simply the attribute of omnipotence, but the conceptual link between omnipotence and its revelation in the miraculous suspension of the normal laws of nature. Schmitt finds the secular analogue of this idea in the sovereign's decision to suspend customary laws in the state of exception (Schmitt [1922, 1934] 2005: 36).

7   Schmitt finds a precedent for his account of sovereignty in Jean Bodin's *Six Books of the Commonwealth* (Schmitt [1922, 1934] 2005: 8–10). For a discussion of theological voluntarism in Bodin's theory of sovereignty see: Engster 2001, 47–81. On theological voluntarism as formative of the modern concept of absolute sovereignty, see Oakley 1984 and Elshtain 2008.

8   In *Political Theology*, Schmitt contends that a fundamental determinant of political thought is whether humanity is conceived of as "by nature good" or "by nature evil" ([1922, 1934] 2005: 56). Advocates for authoritarian rule find justification in the dogma of original sin and the natural evil of humanity (ibid.: 55-60). In *Dictatorship*, Schmitt references Luther among the thinkers of a politics of sin: "In every discussion that seeks to justify political or statal absolutism, the natural human inclination towards evil is postulated as an axiom, in order to justify the authority of the state. And, however different the theoretical interests of Luther, Hobbes, Bossuet, de Maistre and Stahl may have been, this argument appears significantly in all of them" ([1921] 2014: 6).

9   According to Brian J. Fox, original sin is "one of the most important theological concepts Schmitt finds transposed into political theory" (2017: 10). As mentioned in note 7, Schmitt argues that all theories of state may be distinguished by whether they presuppose humanity to be by nature good or evil. Positioning himself on this spectrum, Schmitt argues in 1932 that because the concept of the political comes down to the friend-enemy distinction, "all genuine political theories presuppose man to be evil, i.e., by no means an unproblematic but a dangerous and dynamic being" ([1932] 2007: 61).

10  There is precedent for Augustine's idea of original sin in Paul's Letter to Romans 5:12. However, see Agamben for a discussion of the interpretive liberties taken by Augustine in establishing that it was sin, rather than death, which passed into all men through Adam (Agamben 2020: 16–27).

11  Agamben traces the origination of the political concept of the masses to Augustine's notion of the *massa peccati* (the mass of sin), the *massa damnata* (the damned masses) (2020: 41–44).

12  This is decisively opposed by Benjamin, who argues in his "Theological-Political Fragment" that "the secular order should be erected on the idea of happiness" (*SW* 3, 305-6/*GSII*.1, 203-4).

13  The principal primary sources are *De pauperie Salvatoris* (On the Poverty of the Savior [1351-7]) by Richard Fitzralph (c. 1300-1360), and a pair of treatises, *De dominio divino* (On Divine Dominion [1373-4]) and *De civili dominio* (On Civil Dominion [1375-6]) by John Wycliffe (1328-84).

14  Luther's disregard for Adam's original dominion has polemical stakes, which are apparent in his rebuke of the Peasants' Revolt of 1524-25: "It does not help the peasants when they pretend that according to Genesis 1 and 2 all things were created free and common. . . . For under the New Testament, Moses does not count; for there stands our Master, Christ, and subjects us, along with our bodies and our property, to

the emperor and the law of this world, when he says, 'Render to Caesar the things that are Caesar's' [Luke 20:25]" (Luther [1525] 1997: 188-93, 189-90).

15  As Luther writes, "Who is not aware that a prince is a rare prize in heaven?" ([1523] 1962: 120).

16  Luther's idea of the subjection of humanity to secular power is conceived as a hindrance to the natural expression of creaturely inclinations: "In the same way a savage wild beast is bound with chains and ropes so that it cannot bite and tear as it would normally do, even though it would like to," human beings are subjected "to the sword so that, even though they would like to, they are unable to practice their wickedness" ([1523] 1962: 90).

17  Fatalism is implicit in the notion of original sin. According to Augustine, once human nature becomes vitiated by Adam's sin, it is "bound by the chain of death and justly condemned," unleashing "the whole series of calamities by which the human race is led by a succession of miseries from its depraved origin, as from a corrupt root, even to the ruin of the second death [damnation], which has no end, and from which only those who are redeemed by the grace of God are exempt" ([426] 1998: XIII. 14, 556). See Annika [Yannik] Thiem: 2009 for an important study of Benjamin's critique of original sin and the fatalism that it implies.

18  According to Augustine, God makes "good use even of wicked wills" ([426] 1998: XI.18, 471). As a consequence of this view, Augustine maintained that subjects owe complete obedience to their rulers (Deane 2013: 69). Luther concurs, upholding the Pauline view that even a tyrant should be regarded as "the servant of God to execute wrath on the wrongdoer" (Romans 13:4).

19  The concept of guilt in the trauerspiel, as Benjamin recognizes, is natural or creaturely guilt. This raises a theological paradox, since the nature that God created is good. However, as Agamben points out, Augustine resolves this paradox by introducing *a history within nature*—namely, the history of the Fall (Agamben 2020: 30-1). As Benjamin puts it, "nature . . . which bears the imprint of the course of history, is fallen nature" (*OT*, 191/*GSI*.1, 356). While Adam fell into sin as a result of his free choice to transgress God's command, the corruption of human nature after the Fall is propagated through natural means. Agamben notes that Augustine uses vegetal language to characterize the transmission of natural guilt to fallen humanity, using the word *propagare*, the original meaning of which is "to plant a seedling" (ibid: 39). Perhaps alluding to this background, Benjamin suggests that in the trauerspiel, both death and meaning are likened to seeds, which come to fruition in the creature's unredeemed state of sin (*OT*, 174/*GSI*.1, 343).

20  Benjamin also discusses the natural innocence of creation in "Goethe's Elective Affinities" (*SW*1, 297-360/*GSI*.1, 123-201) and "Fate and Character" (*SW*1, 201-206 /*GSII*.1, 171-179). For an analysis of innocent nature in these other texts by Benjamin, see Moran 2015: 80-4.

21  As Franz Neumann argues, Lutheran political thought introduces a split within sovereignty—a distinction between the *office* of the sovereign, deemed sacrosanct, and the *personal characteristics* of the prince (compare with Benjamin, *OT*, 56/*GSI*:1, 250). For Neumann, the divorce between office and officeholder foreshadows the abstract character of human relations in bourgeois politics ([1942, 1944] 2009: 85-92; 88). For Benjamin, the split within sovereignty is fundamentally melancholy. This is where Benjamin comes closest to Freud's conception of melancholy—especially where the splitting of the ego, characteristic of melancholia, evolves into a distinction within

the subject between a repressive superego and a repressed, guilt-laden ego (see Freud [1917] 2005 and [1923] 1960).
22 On the religious significance of melancholy as uncaused sorrow, see Ferguson 1995: 163–8.
23 Allegory, which derives from the Greek *allos* [other] and *agoreuein* [to speak openly, to speak in the assembly], indicates a mode of veiled or indirect communication, where what is said has a concealed significance in addition to its literal meaning (Fletcher 2012: 2).
24 Augustine wrote five commentaries on Genesis: *On Genesis: A Refutation of the Manichees* (De Genesis contra Manichaeos [388–89]), *Unfinished Literal Commentary on Genesis* (De Genesis ad litteram liber unus imperfectus [393–5]), the final three books of his *Confessions* [400], *The Literal Meaning of Genesis* (De Genesi ad litteram [401–16]), and books XI-XIV of *The City of God against the Pagans* (De civitate Dei contra paganos [426]). Unless I have specific reasons to discuss his other interpretations, I will focus on *The City of God*.
25 Augustine does not use the language of acedia, which originated in fourth-century monasticism in works attributed to Evagrius Ponticus and John Cassian. Their ideas were introduced to Western Europe, more than a century and a half later, by Gregory the Great, of whom Siegfried Wenzel writes, "It is generally assumed that his thought depended largely on St. Augustine, but a careful analysis of details ... reveals much originality" (Wenzel 1960: 26).
26 Augustine's conception of love as a motorial force, which draws the soul toward what it loves, sheds light on the significance of Benjamin's claim that mourning is determined by an "astounding tenacity of the intention, a tenacity appertaining, among other feelings, perhaps only to love" (*OT*, 142/ *GSI*:1, 318). Augustine considers the misdirected love of earthly things to be demonic, as demonstrated by the phantasmagorical unreality of its objects and its bottomless infinity. This demonic characterization is emphasized in the medieval and Baroque discourse of acedia. Benjamin counters this demonic association by juxtaposing it to the Renaissance and antique conception of melancholy as divine madness. In this vein, mourning's "tenacity of intention," which is borne out in its immersion in the depths of profane creation, is not demonic but reflects "a distant light"—an expression of the divine in creation (*OT*, 162-163/GSI.1, 334). For further discussion of the distinction between medieval acedia and Renaissance melancholy, see notes 30, 32, and 33 in this chapter. See also the section on melancholy in Rrenban 2005: 170–4.
27 According to Augustine, the sinful will is "darkened and chilled" ([426] 1998: XIV.13, 608).
28 Benjamin cites Aegidius Albertinus: "It is generally cold and always winter in the royal courts, for the sun of justice is remote from them.... Hence courtiers shiver from sheer cold, fright, and woe" (*OT*, 147/*GSI*:1, 322; cf. Albertinus 1617: 411). Thus, court life is an allegory of hell (ibid).
29 Genesis does not address the creation of angels, their battle, or the fall from grace of the rebellious angels. But Augustine interprets the separation of light from darkness in Genesis 1:4 as an allegory for the angelic fall. The allegory of the angelic fall is pivotal to Benjamin's section on allegory in the *Trauerspiel* book (*OT*, 247-252/*GSI*:1, 400-404). This section is bolstered by three references to Augustine's *City of God*, all of which concern the allegorical transformation of an inherited imaginary of the pagan gods into demons in Christian hell (*OT*, 241, 245, and 252/*GSI*:1, 395, 399, 404).

30 For Augustine, the mind that turns away from God's light "lives according to a lie" ([426] 1998: XIV.4; cf. Paul, Romans 1:25; cf. Deane 2013: 40).
31 The disturbance of sleep by demonic dreams is discussed by Augustine, but not in connection to the concept of acedia ([426] 1998: XXII.23, 1156). This connection is first made in a commentary on Psalms attributed to Origen, but possibly by Evagrius Ponticus (cf. Wentzel 1960: 7–8). While dreams come to have a "purely demonic" character in the medieval and Baroque representation of acedia, they were conceived of as prophetic conduits of divine insight in the Renaissance, building on the antique conception of melancholy as divine madness (*OT*, 150; 154/*GSI*:1, 235, 328). For an exploration of the significance of dreams in the Renaissance discourse on melancholy, and the implications of this idea for Benjamin's thought, see Miguel Vatter's chapter in this volume.
32 Following St. Paul's interpretation of Adam's sin (1 Timothy 2:13-15), Augustine argues that Adam was not deceived by the serpent; only Eve was ([426] 1998: XIV.11, 606). Her transgression separates her from God and from Adam, which Adam feels as a loss, prompting him to disobey God's command in order to be with her again (cf. Wetzel 2012: 167–85).
33 Augustine begins his *Confessions* with the statement that "our heart is restless until it rests in you" ([400] 2008: I.1, 3). Translator Henry Chadwick connects this idea to Plotinus's view that the soul rests only in the One. This image is also found in the monastic discourse on acedia, described by Evagrius as "vagrant thoughts," which detach the mind from God (cf. Wentzel 1960: 13). As Benjamin notes, in the Renaissance conception of melancholy, restlessness gains a more positive association with the influence of Saturn, which, as the most distant planet, makes the soul "rise ever higher, and finally grants it the utmost knowledge and prophetic gifts" (*OT*, 152/*GSI*:1, 326-27; cf. Giehlow 1904: 14).
34 For Augustine, "We are pressed down by the corruptible body" ([426] 1998: XIV.3, 583-84; cf. Wisdom 9:15). But sin is not caused by the body; it is rather caused by the soul that turns away from God and is "weighed down with the desires that be of the earth" ([c. 407] 2009: XVIII.7, 327-28). In keeping with the more positive discourse on melancholy in the Renaissance, Benjamin shows that Ficino connects the idea of gravity to depth of concentration, which "leads to an understanding of the very deepest truths" (*OT*, 158/*GSI*:1, 330-31; cf. Ficino [1482] 1998, I.4, 115; cf. Klibansky, Panofsky, and Saxl [1964, 1990] 2019: 259). But the medieval and Baroque conception of acedia conceives of the earthbound soul as drawn down into a bottomless abyss, as discussed earlier (see note 26).
35 Benjamin repeatedly invokes the "entanglements" [*Verwicklungen*] of fallen creation. (Although *Verwicklungen* is typically translated as entanglements [for example, at *OT* 115, 129, 133, 210/*GSI*.1, 297, 308, 311, 371], it is sometimes rendered as "intrigues" [at *OT*, 74/*GSI*:1, 265], "plot strands" [at *OT*, 85/*GSI*:1, 274], and even "intricacy" [at *OT* 210/*GSI*:1, 371]). The concept of entanglement appears frequently in Augustine ([*irrētio*], which means to ensnare, trap, or entangle). For the latter, becoming ensnared in earthly things detains people from seeking God's world. See, for example: Augustine [426] 1998: I.9, 14; IX.2, 360; and X.10, 406.
36 Benjamin connects this simultaneity to the tendency of secularized history to grasp temporal data in a spatial image: "For where it is a matter of making time present in space—and what else is the secularization of time but its transformation into the strictly present?—then the most radical procedure is to make events simultaneous" (*OT*, 209/*GSI*.1: 370).

37  As I have argued elsewhere, Benjamin holds that a predominant representation of the martyr in the Baroque trauerspiel evolves from seventeenth-century Neostoicism (Schwebel 2021: 109–35). The image of the martyr as a "radical stoic" takes the form of reason's rule over the passions (*OT*, 59-60/*GSI*:1, 253). Stoicism conflicts with Augustinian and Lutheran theology by bringing perfection within reach of the human will, rather than regarding salvation as wholly dependent on God's grace. By implication, Benjamin suggests that all of the trauerspiel's allegorical types, including the martyr, represent possibilities for playing out subjectivity within the restricted domain of secular existence. Accordingly, each represents an aspect of *misplaced* human sovereignty: namely, the vain striving on the part of finite humanity to reach transcendence, whether through efforts of reason or of the will. This challenges Aikin's interpretation of the martyr as an allegory for Christ (Aikin 1982: 53–8).

38  Elsewhere, Gryphius characterizes the fallen soul's enthrallment to the worldly as a delusive dream from which one must endeavor to awaken: "*Auff meine Seel/ auff! auff! entwach aus diesem Traum!/ Verwirff was irrdisch ist / und trotze Noth und Tod!*" (Alms 2007: 212; cf. Gryphius 1968: 97). In his sonnet, "*An die Welt*," Gryphius suggests that, in this dream-state, the soul is especially vulnerable to the "black of night," which "overwhelms us at midday"—an allusion to the "noonday demon" of acedia (Alms 2007: 212; cf. Gryphius 1968: 10).

39  Benjamin's account of evil as privative is given both in his essay "On Language" (*SW*I, 71/*GS*II.1, 152-53), and reiterated in *OT*, 255-56/*GSI*:1, 407.

40  Benjamin's discussion of Adam's language of names and the subsequent "fall" of language unfolds across different works. These are, primarily, his essay "On Language as such and on the Language of the Human" (*SW*I, 62-74/*GS*II.1, 140–57), his fragment "On the Role of Language in Trauerspiel and Tragedy" (*OT*, 267-270/*GS*II.1, 137–40), the "Epistemo-Critical Foreword" to the *Trauerspiel* book (especially at *OT*, 14/*GS*I.1, 217), and the section on allegory, which revisits ideas from Benjamin's essay "On Language," especially regarding language's "fall" (see, in particular, *OT*, 226 and 255-256/*GS*I.1, 383 and 406-407).

41  I argue that this criterion of adequacy has its grounding in Benjamin's appropriation of a Leibnizian philosophy of expression. See Schwebel 2018, Schwebel 2015, and Schwebel 2012. For a discussion of the concept of adequacy in Leibniz and Benjamin, see in particular Schwebel 2012: 70–5.

42  According to Benjamin, the elevation of the Adamic name-giver above the thing that is named "perhaps always remains an intimation of mourning," even in Paradise (*SW* I, 73/*GS*II.1, 155). He suggests, moreover, that the hierarchy of expressive power in Paradise anticipates the multiplicity of human languages, even before this is explicitly addressed in the biblical story of Babel: "Since the unspoken word in the existence of things falls infinitely short of the naming word in the knowledge of man, and since the latter in turn must fall short of the creative word of God, there is a reason for the multiplicity of human languages. . . . (According to the Bible this consequence of the expulsion from Paradise admittedly came about only later)" (*SW* I, 70-71/*GS*II.1, 152; cf. Gen. 11: 1-9).

# References

Agamben, Giorgio. (2020), *The Kingdom and the Garden*, trans. Adam Kotsko, Kolkata: Seagull Books.

Aikin, Judith Popovich. (1982), *German Baroque Drama*, Boston: Twayne Publishers.
Albertinus, Aegidius. (1617), *Lucifers Königreich und Seelengejaidt, oder Narrenhatz*, Augspurg: N. Hainrich/Aperger.
Allighieri, Dante. (1892), *La Divina Commedia*, ed. Carlo Witte, Berlin: R. v. Decker.
Alms, Anthony. (2007), "Theology, Trauerspiel, and the Conceptual Foundations of Early German Opera," PhD diss., The City University of New York, New York.
Atger, Frédéric. (1906), *Essai sur l'histoire des doctrines du contrat social*, Nimes: Imprimerie Coopérative 'La Laborieuese'.
Augustine. ([390] 2005), "True Religion," trans. Edmund Hill, in Boniface Ramsey (ed.), *Augustine: On Christian Belief*, 15–100, Hyde Park and New York: New City Books.
Augustine. ([400] 2008), *Confessions*, trans. Henry Chadwick, Oxford and New York: Oxford University Press.
Augustine. ([426] 1998), *The City of God against the Pagans*, trans. R. W. Dyson, Cambridge and New York: Cambridge University Press.
Augustine. ([c. 407] 2009), *Homilies on the Gospel of John 1–40*, trans. Edmund Hill, Hyde Park and New York: New City Books.
De Wilde, Marc. (2011), "Meeting Opposites: The Political Theologies of Walter Benjamin and Carl Schmitt," *Philosophy and Rhetoric*, 44 (4): 363–81.
Deane, Herbert A. (2013), *The Political and Social Ideas of St. Augustine*, Tacoma: Angelico Press.
Elshtain, Jean Bethke. (2008), *Sovereignty: God, State, and Self*, New York: Basic Books.
Engster, Daniel. (2001), *Divine Sovereignty: The Origins of Modern State Power*, Dekalb: Northern Illinois Press.
Ferber, Ilit. (2013), *Philosophy and Melancholy: Benjamin's Early Reflections on Theater and Langauge*, Stanford: Stanford University Press.
Ferguson, Harvie. (1995), *Melancholy and the Critique of Modernity: Soren Kierkegaard's Religious Psychology*, London and New York: Routledge.
Ficino, Marsilio. ([1482] 1998), *Three Books on Life*, trans. and eds. Carol V. Kaske and John R. Clark, Tempe: Arizona Center for Medieval and Renaissance Studies.
Fletcher, Angus. (2012), *Allegory: The Theory of a Symbolic Mode*, Princeton and Oxford: Princeton University Press.
Fox, Brian J. (2017), "Carl Schmitt and the Nineteenth-Century Catholic Reaction on Original Sin," *Telos*, 178: 9–32.
Freud, Sigmund. ([1917] 2005), "Mourning and Melancholia," trans. Shaun Whiteside in *Sigmund Freud: On Murder, Mourning and Melancholia*, 203–18, London: Penguin Books.
Freud, Sigmund. ([1923] 1960), *The Ego and the Id*, trans. Joan Riviere and revised by James Strachey, New York and London: W.W. Norton and Co.
Giehlow, Karl. (1904), "Dürers Stich 'Melencolia I' und der maximilianische Humanistenkreis," *Mitteilungen der Gesellschaft für vervielfältigende Kunst*, 27 (3): 6–18.
Gryphius, Andreas. ([1646] 1882), "Leo Armenius oder Fürsten-Mord," in Andreas Gryphius, Hermann Palm, and Nicolas Caussin (eds.), *Andreas Gryphius Trauerspiele*, 6–135, Tübingen: Litterarischen Verein in Stuttgart.
Gryphius, Andreas. (1968), *Gedichte: Eine Auswahl*, ed. Adalbert Elschenbroich, Stuttgart: Reclam.
Klibansky, Raymond, Panofsky Erwin, and Saxl Fritz. ([1964, 1990] 2019), *Saturn and Melancholy: Studies in the History of Natural Philosophy, Religion, and Art*, Montreal and Kingston: McGill-Queen's University Press.
Koepnik, Lutz P. (1996), "The Spectacle, the 'Trauerspiel,' and the Politics of Resolution: Benjamin Reading the Baroque Reading Weimar," *Critical Inquiry*, 22 (2): 268–91.

Luther, Martin. ([1523] 1962): "Temporal Authority: To What Extent It Should be Obeyed," trans. J. J. Schindel, *Luther's Works*, Vol. 45, Philadelphia: Muhlenberg Press.

Luther, Martin. ([1525] 1997), "Against the Robbing and Murdering Hordes of Peasants," trans. Charles M. Jacobs, in *Works of Martin Luther*, Vol. 4, 188-93, Albany: The Ages Digital Library Collections.

Moran, Brendan. (2015), "Nature, Decision and Muteness," in Brendan Moran and Carlo Salzani (eds.), *Towards the Critique of Violence: Walter Benjamin and Giorgio Agamben*, 73-90, London: Bloomsbury Academic.

Neumann, Franz. ([1942, 1944] 2009), *Behemoth: The Structure and Practice of National Socialism, 1933-1944*, Chicago: Ivan R. Dee.

Oakley, Francis. (1984), *Omnipotence, Covenant and Order: An Excursion in the History of Ideas from Abelard to Leibniz*, Ithaca: Cornell University Press.

Oakley, Francis. (2015), *The Watershed of Modern Politics: Law, Virtue, Kingship, and Consent (1300-1650)*, New Haven: Yale University Press.

Pensky, Max. (1993), *Melancholy Dialectics: Walter Benjamin and the Play of Mourning*, Amherst: University of Massachusetts Press.

Rrenban, Monad. (2005), *Wild, Unforgettable Philosophy in Early Works of Walter Benjamin*, Lanham: Lexington Books.

Schmitt, Carl. ([1921] 2014), *Dictatorship: From the Origin of the Modern Concept of Sovereignty to Proletarian Class Struggle*, trans. Michael Hoelzl and Graham Ward, Cambridge: Polity Press.

Schmitt, Carl. ([1922, 1934] 2005), *Political Theology: Four Chapters on the Concept of Sovereignty*, trans. George Schwab, Chicago: The University of Chicago Press.

Schmitt, Carl. ([1932] 2007), *The Concept of the Political*, trans. George Schwab, Chicago: The University of Chicago Press.

Schwebel, Paula. (2012), "Walter Benjamin's Monadology," PhD diss., University of Toronto, Toronto.

Schwebel, Paula. (2015), "Monad and Time: Reading Leibniz with Heidegger and Benjamin," in Andrew Benjamin and Dimitris Vardoulakis (eds.), *Sparks will Fly: Benjamin and Heidegger*, 123-44, Albany: State University of New York Press.

Schwebel, Paula. (2018), "Constellation and Expression in Benjamin and Leibniz," in Caroline Sauter and Nassima Sahraoui (eds.), *Thinking in Constellations: Walter Benjamin in the Humanities*, 51-82, Cambridge: Cambridge Scholars Publishing.

Schwebel, Paula. (2021), "Sovereign/Creature: Neostoicism in Benjamin's *Origin of the German Trauerspiel* and His Response to Carl Schmitt's *Political Theology*," in Kurt Lampe and Andrew Benjamin (eds.), *German Stoicisms: From Hegel to Sloterdijk*, 109-35, London: Bloomsbury Academic.

Thiem, Annika [Yannik]. (2009), "Fate, Guilt and Metaphysical Interruptions," PhD. Diss., University of California, Berkeley.

Vardoulakis, Dimitris. (2013), *Sovereignty and its Other: Toward the Dejustification of Violence*, New York: Fordham University Press.

Weber, Samuel. (1992), "Taking Exception to Decision: Walter Benjamin and Carl Schmitt," *Diacritics*, 22 (3/4): 5-18.

Wenzel, Siegfried. (1960), *The Sin of Sloth: Acedia in Medieval Thought and Literature*, Chapel Hill: The University of North Carolina Press.

Wetzel, James. (2012), "Augustine on the Origin of Evil: Myth and Metaphysics," in James Wetzel (ed.), *Augustine's City of God: A Critical Guide*, 167-85, Cambridge: Cambridge University Press.

# 2

# Sovereignty and Revolutionary Astropolitics

## Benjamin, Baroque Trauerspiel, and Calderón's *Life Is a Dream*[1]

Miguel Vatter

For Agnes Heller *in memoriam*

## Introduction: Baroque Drama and Marxist Critique

The *Origin of the German Trauerspiel* is certainly one of the key texts from which to establish Walter Benjamin's relation to the discourse of political theology. For Benjamin, the Baroque drama is centrally concerned with the dynamic of secularization thematized by Max Weber and Carl Schmitt at the beginning of the twentieth century. In *Political Theology: Four Chapters on the Concept of Sovereignty*, Schmitt argued that the Baroque sovereign brought civil peace through a decision on the state of exception, which, like a divine miracle, interrupts the ruinous course of events and re-establishes legal order. For Benjamin, however, Baroque drama thematizes another meaning of secularization, namely, the radical bifurcation between profane historical becoming and the sacred path to salvation. Especially in the German trauerspiel, which Benjamin reads as heavily influenced by the Lutheran rejection of "good works" and the doctrine that only faith saves, history is represented as a "drama of fate" wherein politics becomes a stage for evil; the world is entirely predetermined and without intrinsic purpose; and life itself is guilty and must consequently perish.

When "time is out of joint" and salvation is no longer up to the individual's freedom but depends entirely on God's unfathomable grace, drama (*Spiel*) becomes a reflection on mourning and sorrow (*Trauer*). In Baroque drama, this activity of reflection is often thematized by the device of a "play within the play." As Benjamin shows, the manner and purpose of reflection varies across national dramaturgical traditions. Thus, in Shakespeare's *Hamlet* reflection leads the hero into a melancholic state of indecision, resolved in the end by the inner certainty of being a puppet in God's hands.[2] Reflection in the German trauerspiel is intended to reveal the forsaken nature of creaturely life: "with tears it begins and with weeping it ends. Yes, time likes to play with us even after death, when putrefaction, maggot, and worm burrow in our dead bodies" (citing Daniel Caspar von Lohenstein) (*OT*, 70). In Calderón's drama, instead, the hero's reflection on fate seems to playfully extract him or her from destruction, as if "the only means of salvation is through never-ending dialectical reflection" (*SW*1, 380).

With which of these configurations of reflection and fate does Benjamin's thought have more affinity? It has often been remarked that Benjamin identified with the melancholic's mortifying gaze on history as a long-running catastrophe, sharing Franz Kafka's bitter saying that there is "an infinite amount of hope . . . —but not for us"[3] At the same time, Benjamin's political thought is indelibly associated with the attempt to introduce a messianic conception of time into historical materialism, one that would bring about a "real state of exception," analogous to a general strike rather than to a *coup d'État*.[4] While finishing the *Trauerspiel* book, Benjamin also seems to have undergone something of a conversion toward communism on the island of Capri, in part through conversations with Ernst Bloch and Asja Lacis, in part by reading György Lukács's *History and Class Consciousness*.[5] Can one discern in the *Trauerspiel* book an esoteric teaching on the relation between history as fate, dialectical reflection, and revolutionary praxis?

In "What is Orthodox Marxism?", the introductory essay to *History and Class Consciousness*, Lukács argues that the "method" of dialectical materialism is less a matter of applying abstract theoretical categories to historical reality than of apprehending how historical reality develops its own criticism of itself. To illustrate this idea, he refers to a famous letter by Karl Marx to Arnold Ruge of September 1843. In this letter, critique is defined in terms of "making the world aware of its own consciousness, in arousing it from its dream of itself, in explaining its own actions to it. . . . [I]t will then become plain that the world has long since dreamed of something of which it needs only to become conscious for it to possess it in reality" (Marx 1844).[6] In the *Arcades* project Benjamin explicitly returns to this citation and to the motif of the *Zeit-Traum* (dream-time) to understand the meanings of critique and revolution.[7] As will become clear from the analysis of Calderón's *Life Is a Dream*, Marx's dictum coincides with the dramatic "stuff" of Calderón's play in which political reality and action are entirely encapsulated within a complex dialectic of dreaming and awakening. It is conceivable that Benjamin, while composing his *Trauerspiel* book, could have been struck by the dialectical reflection on dreaming found in both Calderón and Marx thanks to the mediation of Lukács's text.

For sure, Benjamin avers that only in Calderón "could the consummate art form of the Baroque trauerspiel be studied. What makes for its validity—validity of the word as of the object—is not least the precision with which 'mourning' [*Trauer*] and 'play' [*Spiel*] can harmonize with each other" (*OT*, 68).[8] Unlike its German counterpart, where the play shows how mourning succumbs to melancholia, Benjamin identifies in *Life Is a Dream* the conception of a new prince who acts as a "secularized power of redemption" by reflecting upon the mysterious relation between dream and reality, according to which "the dream arches over waking life like the vault of heaven" (*OT*, 68). In the fourth section of this chapter, I show that Benjamin's understanding of the crisis of eschatology in Baroque drama depends on his adoption of Aby Warburg's pioneering study of astrology, cosmology, and Lutheranism. Warburg uncovers an astral theology and an "astropolitics" that serves as a guiding thread from the Renaissance of Machiavelli and Bruno through the Reformation and into the Baroque. This astral theology understands *natura* as *Deus in rebus* (God in things), to cite Bruno's formulation in *The Expulsion of the Triumphant Beast*.[9] Warburg's hypotheses on the ambivalent function of astral determinism in early modernity helps Benjamin conceive of how Baroque drama, having excluded eschatology, is thrown back onto the state of nature and, through allegory, articulates a form of redemption that is immanent to the drama of fate. I argue that Calderón's *Life Is a Dream* offers such an astropolitical response to the antinomies of Lutheranism in its *ponderación misteriosa*. By following the astral and oneiric motifs in Benjamin's own text, it is possible to offer a redemptive reading of the "playful" and "reflexive" components of Calderón's trauerspiel in the direction that Benjamin himself may have found most conducive to his own approximation of communist praxis.

## Secularization and the Question of Baroque Eschatology

The theological situation of the Baroque is characterized by "the collapse [*Ausfall*, loss, failure] of all eschatology." "Nothing was more alien. . . than expectation of an end time" (*OT*, 66). In this sense, the Baroque inaugurates what Charles Taylor calls a secular age, "in which the eclipse of all goals beyond human flourishing becomes conceivable" (Taylor 2007: 19). In contrast to the Baroque, the medieval world was still characterized by "hierarchical complementarity": the priestly/monastic order of society gives up the pursuit of worldly goals in order to keep open the passageway to transcendence for the rest of society through "good works" (Taylor 2007: 19). This medieval world was shaken by Luther's rejection of indulgences and his theology of *sola fides*. Although the Counter-Reformation may have re-established "the hierarchical tendency of the Middle Ages"—after the interlude constituted by the Renaissance, which to Benjamin appears "not as an irreligious, pagan age but as a span of nonclerical freedom in the life of faith" —this restoration occurs "in a world that was denied immediate access to the beyond" (*OT*, 66). Luther's "Two Kingdoms" doctrine divided "Christendom or Europe . . . into a series of European Christendoms whose historical actions no longer claim to be integrated in a process of salvation" leading to "boundless despair" (*OT*, 65).

When the Christian Church is no longer seen as placeholder for the coming of God's Kingdom on Earth, the world is represented as an "immanent frame" that appears to modern individuals to be as deterministic as cosmic fate had appeared to the ancients (Taylor 2007). It is in this sense that for Benjamin the Baroque drama is a "drama of fate." The loss of a graduated path, a stairway to Heaven, coupled with the Lutheran and then Calvinist radical undecidability of salvation, plunges the Baroque age, on Benjamin's telling, into melancholia. As Freud hypothesizes, in the melancholic, the ambivalence felt toward the object of love by the loving ego is turned against itself, leading to feelings of unworthiness, baseness, and guilt occasioned not by any immoral acts but simply by the fact of living.[10] Lutheranism and Calvinism responded by universalizing and secularizing the renunciation of the world that characterizes the priestly order, thereby internalizing this renunciation into everyday life through inner-worldly asceticism: "a disciplined personal life," "a well-ordered society," and a "correct inner stance" became the expression of a secular world (Taylor 2007: 82).

For Giorgio Agamben, the Baroque's desire to immanentize order covers an underlying "gigantomachy over a void." Benjamin and Schmitt are said to have staged an indirect discussion about this void, before, during, and after the composition of the *Trauerspiel* book. Whereas Schmitt understood this void in terms of the sovereign's capacity to create order *ex nihilo* through the state of exception, for Benjamin, "the paradigm of the state of exception is no longer the miracle... but the catastrophe" (Agamben 2005: 55). According to Agamben's controversial hypothesis, Benjamin's manuscript originally contained the phrase "there is *a* Baroque eschatology" which the editors of the critical German edition changed into "there is *no* Baroque eschatology [Es gibt (*k*)*eine* barocke Eschatologie]" (Agamben 2005: 56).[11] At issue is the correct interpretation of Benjamin's central hypothesis that in the Baroque "there is a mechanism that multiplies and exalts everything earth-born before it is delivered over to its end. The beyond is emptied of everything in which even the slightest breath of world can be felt, and from it the Baroque extracts a profusion of things that tended to elude every formation [*Gestaltung*] and at its high point brings them to light in drastic form so as to clear a last heaven and so place it, as vacuum, in a condition to swallow up the earth one day with catastrophic violence" (*OT*, 51). Agamben sees in this passage evidence of a "'white eschatology'—which does not lead the earth to a redeemed thereafter, but consigns it to an absolutely empty sky—that configures the baroque state of exception as catastrophe. And it is again this white eschatology that shatters the correspondence between sovereignty and transcendence, between the monarch and God, that defined the Schmittian theologico-political" (Agamben 2005: 56).[12] Yet, Agamben's reading downplays the cosmological subtext of the "contemplative necessities" of the Baroque. Since history no longer has a transcendent "End" as *Ziel* or goal, it extends "*into the immeasurable [ins Ungemessene]*" (*OT*, 65, emphasis mine). This idea of an indefinite extension makes sense within a Newtonian universe where the "absolute" nature of time is linked with the "infinity" of space. This cosmological context turns out to be crucial for what Benjamin characterizes as the spatialization of history in the Baroque.

The absence of eschatology in the Baroque is internally related to the transition from a finite "cosmos" to an infinite "universe."[13] Within a finite, closed understanding of the cosmos, the belief in the "vault" of heaven over our heads makes it also possible to imagine that there exists a Heaven "above" the vault. But once the vault is broken through, and all one perceives is infinite *empty space and empty time*, the "vacuum," then this leads to a loss of faith in Heaven. In this sense, the trauerspiel is "bound up in a strict immanence and without the prospect onto the beyond of the mystery plays" (*OT*, 67). Evidence that the meaning of Benjamin's passage cited earlier should be understood cosmologically is given by the precise use of the term "mechanism." What is alluded to here is Newtonian mechanics, made possible by Galilean dynamics and by the Copernican rediscovery of heliocentrism. It is infinite space that "clear[s] a last heaven [*einen letzten Himmel zu räumen*]" and sucks up the new "profusion of things that tended to elude every formation," by which Benjamin seems to allude to modern atomism and its "vacuum" that destroyed belief in the Aristotelian "forms."

The image of the "cataract" that the Baroque individual fears will tear him or her away from the world and drag them into nothingness, with "catastrophic violence" (*OT*, 50–51) corresponds best to what Giorgio de Santillana has called the modern idea of "fate," wherein the "Necessity of things, the logic of History and the logic of technology are combined into one power" called progress. Santillana draws a striking analogy between such modern fate and the phenomenon of black-body radiation in thermal equilibrium with its environment, for instance, in a perfectly insulated oven in which black bodies are placed and heated at a very high temperature. If one were to peek into the oven once thermal equilibrium is reached, one would see only light; all form and distinction having vanished, the oven would appear perfectly empty.[14]

## The Function of *Spiel* in the Representation of History

The cosmological and astral dimensions are essential to both hypotheses formulated by Benjamin about the representation of history in the trauerspiel.[15] The first hypothesis is that history is represented spatially and as such it is naturalized.[16] This is a representation of history without any interventions by God, without miracles. If the Baroque closes the door on eschatology thanks to its new cosmology, it becomes clearer why it would simultaneously seek "consolation in the renunciation of a state of grace by returning to the bare state of creation," that is, to the state of nature (*OT*, 67/*GSI*.1, 260, translation modified). The second hypothesis is that the trauerspiel represents history as a "play" not only of fate but, above all, *with* fate.[17] Play, *Spiel*, stands for both the staging of historical events as a fateful concatenation, and for a self-reflection of the play that ushers in a moment of transcendence.[18] These two meanings are captured by the idea of the world as a stage (*theatrum mundi*), which means that theater is part of life, but also that all life is theater. In *Hamlet or Hecuba: The Interruption of Time into Play*, Schmitt criticized posthumously Benjamin's reading of the trauerspiel for not appreciating the "tragic" dimension of the first meaning of play. I argue that Benjamin valorized Calderón's *Life Is a Dream* precisely because of the political implications of the second meaning of play.

In formulating his thesis that the Baroque drama reverses the meaning of history from being the path of salvation into being a permanent catastrophe characterized by fate and guilt, Benjamin claims: "Here, as in other spheres of life in the Baroque, what is decisive is the transposition of originally temporal data [*ursprünglich zeitlichen Daten*] into a spatial unreality and simultaneity [*räumliche Uneigentlichkeit und Simultaneität*]. It leads deep into the structure of this dramatic form" (*OT*, 67). Although Benjamin is explaining how the German trauerspiel no longer sees the events of the historical *saeculum* "as stations on the path to salvation" but rather as "natural history" (*OT*, 67), the spatiotemporal language employed here is post-Einsteinian and is likely to have derived directly from his encounter with Lukács's *History and Class Consciousness*. Benjamin's expression refers to Lukács's engagement with Bergson's conception of *durée* in his analysis of reification and is resonant with the Bergson-Einstein polemic on the relativity of time.[19]

The reference to the Einsteinian frame, and to Bergson's contestation of it, reappears when Benjamin explains the Baroque fascination with clock time:

> the image of the moving hand is, as Bergson has shown, indispensable for the representation of nonqualitative, repeatable time of mathematical natural science. In such time is enacted not only the organic life of the human being but also the doings of the courtier and the acts of the sovereign, he who, according to the occasionalist image of the divine potentate, immediately intervenes in the affairs of state at every moment in order to arrange the data of the historical process in a, so to speak, spatially measurable, regular and harmonious succession. (*OT*, 87)

This, then, is one sense in which the sovereign is the "representative" of history: if history is naturalized, and nature operates on "clock-time," then the sovereign is a stand-in for the Deist idea of God as watchmaker.

Benjamin thus re-inscribes Schmitt's foundational analogy between sovereign and God of *Political Theology* within the more fundamental cosmological context. There is some irony in Benjamin's not citing Schmitt, but rather citing Schmitt's citation of Frédéric Atger: "the prince develops all the virtualities of the state by a sort of continuous creation. The prince is the Cartesian God transposed into the political world" (*OT* 87/GSI.1, 275, translation modified). This citation is intended to show that the theory of the mechanistic universe that Descartes (but also Hobbes) advanced, and that underpinned the construction of the sovereign, undermines at the same time the theological ground of this sovereignty on Schmitt's reading of them, namely, the possibility of miraculous intervention within the machine of the state in the form of the state of exception.[20]

Schmitt criticized Benjamin's interpretation of the Baroque trauerspiel because, even if "the theatre piece ... is in itself but a game [*Spiel*/play]," still "we must draw a distinction between tragic play [*Trauerspiel*] and tragedy." The "seriousness of the authentically tragic should not disappear" (Schmitt 2006: 33). This seriousness is given by reference to the underlying historical reality and political conflict that is represented in the modern tragedy. Schmitt's point is that if it is true that the world is a stage, and this is nowhere more the case than in the kingly courts, where everybody is playing a role, still for Shakespeare the theater was not separated from "the play of real life" (Schmitt 2006: 35). In the case of *Hamlet*, the play is a representation of history because it draws its subject matter from the key circumstances in the lives of James I and his Catholic mother, Mary Queen of Scots: the former's inability to decide for Protestantism and against Catholicism; the latter accused of conspiring to kill her own Stuart husband and father of the future king James I.[21] For Shakespeare, theater was more like life—which is tragic—whereas in Continental Baroque drama, life was more like theater—which just makes us feel sad. "The tragic ends where play-acting begins, even if the play is meant to make us cry, a sorrowing play for a wretched audience, a deeply moving sad play" (Schmitt 2006: 34).[22]

For Schmitt, a trauerspiel is a dramatic form in which "fate" is a theatrical effect (a game) generated by the play's representation in order to elicit sorrow in the audience because it brings to evidence that there is no salvation to be found in history or through the state. However, for Schmitt, Shakespeare's tragedy is something different than a trauerspiel because "all the players are aware of an irrevocable reality which no human brain has devised, but on the contrary, is there, thrust in like the dumb rock against which the play breaks, and the surge of the truly tragic moves forward in a cloud of foam" (Schmitt 2006: 38). For Schmitt, the "play within a play" staged by Hamlet before his mother and uncle is not the place where "transcendence was allowed to have the last word only in the worldly disguise of a play within the play" (*OT*, 69), but to the contrary reveals the brutality and "barbarism" of a politics when it is deprived of the sense for the state.[23] The playful dimension of the trauerspiel will always break against the rock of *Realpolitik*. It is as if Schmitt were commenting that Benjamin's image of the cataract, which rushes away all lives in the progress of history through empty time, is itself an illusion: the cataract will eventually crash against the real of historical actuality, thus revealing the limits of reflection.

Does Benjamin's *Trauerspiel* book contain, as it were, an *ante litteram* response to Schmitt's posthumous critique? I believe such a response can be reconstructed by pursuing the sense in which Spanish drama elevated play/*Spiel* to a degree unseen in the German trauerspiel. Unlike its German counterpart, the Spanish drama does not begin and end in tears. The reason is that the Spanish trauerspiel "resolves the conflicts of a state of creation without grace playfully reduced [*spielerisch verkleinert*], so to speak, within the compass of the court and of a kingship that proves to be a secularized power of redemption [*säkularisierte Heilsgewalt*]" (*OT*, 68/GSI.1, 260).[24] Benjamin claims that Calderón "rather than Shakespeare" was for the Romantics the dramatist *kat exochen* because of "the incomparable virtuosity of reflection that his heroes call upon at every moment in order to turn the order of fate around in their hands like a ball, exposing to view now one aspect, now another" (*OT*, 71). The "order of fate" is an astronomical and astrological turn of phrase, and what Benjamin means is that the reflection at issue in the trauerspiel turns on "playing" with the orbs, not only of the Earth, but of planets and stars, that have been set "out of joint."[25] The Spanish *teatro del mundo* brings cosmology into everyday life, not only in the sense of astrology (the horoscope as prediction of our destiny, as ruling over our daily events), but also in the sense of the new astronomy and cosmology in which humanity becomes aware of its own decentred place within an "open" universe.[26] The real "gigantomachy over a void" is determined by the fact that our planetary ball is orbiting around in an "empty" and "infinite" universe. It is the universe itself that relativizes *Heilsgeschichte* to insignificance. But, at the same time, the Copernican view on planetary "revolutions" is inextricably connected to a revolutionary origin of modern legitimacy, and planetary orbits call for a return to nature, to creation, to new beginnings, in order to find therein a possible source of salvation.

Benjamin posits the specific difference of German trauerspiel in contrast with this astronomical reflection in Calderón. The moralism of Lutheranism "always striving—as its vocational ethic so emphatically proclaims—to bind the transcendence of the life of faith to the immanence of daily life" forbids the astral element in play. "The conclusion of the German Trauerspiel . . . is—morally, though certainly not artistically—more responsible than that of the Spanish drama" (*OT*, 72). In order to understand the strange new elliptical orbit of Benjamin's reflection, with Lutheran morality at one of its foci and astrology at the other, it is necessary to briefly examine Aby Warburg's discovery of the astropolitics of Lutheranism.

## Lutheranism and the Problem of Astral Fate

The Baroque trauerspiel is a "play of fate" in a distinctly Christian sense of the term:

> [a]t the core of the idea of fate, rather, is the conviction that guilt—which, in this context always means creaturely guilt (in Christian terms, original sin), not a moral failing of the one who acts—however fleeting its manifestation, gives rise to causality as instrument of ceaselessly unrolling fatalities. Fate is the entelechy of occurrence in the field of guilt. (*OT*, 129)[27]

The ancient notion of fate as astral determinism is replaced by the idea of guilt as original sin, and by the belief that the order of nature will bend and follow the "entelechy" of the revealed divine economy of sin and redemption. Yet Benjamin's at least partial adoption of Aby Warburg's research into the astrology of Lutheranism considerably complicates the aforementioned schema.

Lutheranism is characterized by the contradictory gesture of religiously dismissing good works as a path to salvation, to the benefit of pure faith, coupled with the political demand that the Lutheran subject develop a strong sense of civic virtue and rightful action. Luther himself abandons his initial "storming of the work" when the sense grows upon him that if only grace can save, then this must mean that the world is indeed dominated by irresistible fate.[28] "There was a share of Germanic paganism and dark belief in the omnipotence of fate expressed in the overburdened reaction that, in the end, drove from the field the good work as such, and not just its meritable and penitential character. Human actions were deprived of all value. Something new came into being: an empty world" (*OT*, 141).

Melanchthon, the great philosopher of Lutheranism, was particularly persuaded of the need to employ astrology and the new cosmology as indicators of divine providence.[29] The Catholic enemies of the Reformation tried to pin the birthday of Luther in 1484 as proof that he was born under the "malignant" influence of Saturn, and that his reform was the work of the devil. Melanchthon engaged in battle with these astrologers trying to fashion a counter "astropolitics": he "adopted *the astrology of the ancient world as an intellectual defense against a cosmically predetermined earthly fate*. So strong, indeed, was his *faith in the stars* that in this matter he constantly risked—as elsewhere he avoided—a confrontation with his more powerful friend" (Warburg 1999a: 603, emphasis mine). Here Warburg explicitly names the "faith in the stars" as the countervailing, even redemptive response to a belief in "predetermined earthly fate" that, according to Benjamin, emerged in Luther himself as a reaction to his "storming of the work."[30]

The Arabic medieval transmission of Hellenistic astrology in the West, chiefly through ninth-century CE Persian astronomer Abu Ma'shar (Albumasar), established that "a new prophet required the cosmic sanction of a conjunction of superior planets, and of Saturn and Jupiter in particular" (Warburg 1999a: 612, emphasis mine). After very long, but finite periods of time, celestial revolutions would bring down one religion and see the emergence of a new one.[31] In Ficino and Machiavelli, among other Renaissance thinkers, this motif played an important role in their critiques of Christianity and in the various attempts to recover an "ancient theology" shared by pagan cultures.[32] Obviously, it was not farfetched to see in Luther such a "new prophet" brought into existence by such a major "conjunction" of Saturn and Jupiter.[33]

The reception of Arabic astral determinism in the Italian Renaissance amplified the "fear of Saturn" as the most malignant planetary influence. If this malign influence could be seen in the medieval monastic *acedia*, in the Baroque, with the evacuation of eschatology and under the guise of Copernican astronomy, it appears as *melancholia*. However, Warburg famously interpreted Dürer's engraving *Melencolia I* as suggesting the possibility that "a malignant, child-devouring planetary god, whose cosmic contest with another planetary ruler seals the subject's fate," could be "humanized and metamorphosed" into "the image of the thinking, working human being" (Warburg 1999a: 644). For Warburg this early modern recovery of ancient paganism discloses the hope of attaining some sort of "middle" or "prudential" point, which is symbolized by the Lutheran, "revolutionary" conjunction of Saturn with Jupiter, that Melanchthon identifies with Dürer's "heroic melancholy" (Warburg 1999a: 644) (*OT*, 155).[34]

This interpretative horizon casts a different light on Benjamin's fundamental thesis that the trauerspiel "theatricalizes" all of history because it reverses the progression of history in empty time back on to an initial stage of creation. Against the backdrop of Renaissance astropolitics, this spatialization of historical time becomes the staging for revolutions, understood as the movement of "return to beginnings."[35] Politically speaking, this means that the Baroque "theater of the world" not only stages the Christian natural paradise, but also the pagan myth of the Golden Age. The stars may reflect, in their own way, that "light of grace" found in the "state of creation" prior to the Fall of Adam, of which Benjamin speaks.

## The Astropolitics of *Life Is a Dream*

Frederick De Armas has convincingly shown the presence of an "astropolitics" at the heart of *Life Is a Dream*.[36] Basilio, the tyrannical father of Segismundo, is an "astrologer-king": "For when in my charts I see manifest the news of coming centuries, I earn the thanks owed to time for revealing what I have told" (I,6 102).[37] Explaining why he had his own son and rightful heir entombed alive in a tower, Basilio recounts the details of Segismundo's birth and the bad omens of his horoscope: "Resorting to my studies, I saw in them and in everything else that Segismundo would be the most reckless of men, the cruelest of princes, and the most perverse of monarchs" (I,6 103). While the astrological charts place the son under the sign of Saturn, the "most impious planet," by imprisoning him in a tower the father acts like the titan Kronos/Saturn who attempts to devour his own son, Zeus/Jupiter, only to be outwitted: "Like Saturn, he must eventually face his rebellious son" (Armas 1987: 117). Segismundo's character is thus astrally overdetermined: he is a new Jupiter who also happens to fall under the influence of Saturn. This opens the fundamental puzzle of the play: how can Jupiter be the harbinger of a return to the Age of Saturn? How can a (legitimate but unrecognized) king (Segismundo in the tower) occasion a revolution against another (legitimate but tyrannical) king (Basilio the astrologer-king) in order to restore an original state of justice?

My hypothesis is that through the conflict between Basilio and Segismundo, Calderón is reflecting on the fundamental problem of modern revolutions and the legitimacy of tyrannicide found in Protestant political thought such as the French Monarchomachs and the German Calvinist Althusius. These authors posed the question: how can a revolution, which is an illegal act, possibly bring about a new state of justice, unless it is itself legal in some natural sense of right, and assuming the traditional distinction between natural and positive rights? During the seventeenth century this problem would lead to the formulation of the idea of "constituent power."[38] But the idea has older, Platonic and Machiavellian, antecedents that are referenced in Calderón's drama.[39]

Plato gives two versions of the myth of Saturn/Kronos in *Statesman* and *Laws*, namely, the doctrine of a periodic and eternal return of the world to an initial stage of justice and peace overseen by Saturn, where no human rules over other humans or animals.[40] Plato suggests that humans live under Saturn when they are ruled by a "living law" (or divine intellect) rather than by other human beings.[41] The latter corresponds to the political form of rule found in the age of Jupiter/Zeus. Plato's reading of the Age of Saturn is an allegory for the subversive idea that what makes someone a legitimate king is neither force nor consent but rather the possession of a quasi-mathematical "kingly science" that can anticipate what is the right thing to do in any given circumstance. After Plato, an astro-political interpretation of the myth of Saturn was developed according to which the intellect of the "wise man" is superior to the fate prescribed by the stars. Assuming that the "wise man" can know with precision the motion of the stars and planets, and given that these motions determine whatever happens on earth, it is possible to predict what is going to happen and take measures to prevent the event from happening. Basilio represents this belief of Ptolemaic extraction: "Thus lending credence to the fates whose soothsaying had foretold such disaster in their fatal prophecies, I determined to lock up the beast that had just been born, hoping that a wise man might rein in the influence of the stars" (I,6 103).

Machiavelli offers a different interpretation of the myth of Saturn. In *The Prince* and in the *Discourses on Livy*, he argued that no human mind could predict the changes of fortune, and this cast into question the claims of certain practitioners of astrology. For Machiavelli, instead, good or bad fortune was a function of the "match" between the nature of the times—which he often understands as determined by the stars—and the character or *virtù* of the actors. This "match" was never predetermined but had to be put to a test, in the sense of *agon* or "play."[42] Hence, Machiavelli recommended that it was always better to be "audacious" rather than "respectful" if one wanted to change one's status in the world.[43] *Life Is a Dream* stages the way in which Segismundo refutes the astrological formula in his own person, and to this extent it can be said that Calderón here follows a Machiavellian motif.

The play begins in earnest when Basilio decides to "test" the truth of his astrological beliefs by introducing an "experiment" that is intended to falsify the initial astrological hypothesis: "I realize how erroneous it was to place easy credence in predictions of the future, since, even if the prince's inclination places obstacles in his path, they might not overcome him; because even the most contemptuous fate, the most wayward inclination, or the most perverse planet can only influence the will, not force it" (I,6 103–4).[44] In this passage Basilio opposes the "malignant" astrological conception of Saturn against the Christian conception of "free will" that is beyond the influence of the stars. On both accounts one can see here at work Warburg's hypothesis: first, the presence of a modern, Keplerian scientific attitude toward hypotheses (namely, that they need to be tested), and, second, a Lutheran idea of conscience as ground of a "good will." By setting Segismundo free under experimental conditions, Basilio seeks to "test" the hypothesis of a "good will" immune to astral fate. As it turns out, Segismundo's *virtù* will beat the stars, but in an entirely different way from the one desired by his father, namely by giving proof of a heroic melancholy which is as much Saturnine as it is Lutheran.

## From the Interpretation of Stars to the Interpretation of Dreams

Textually, the transition from the astro-political to the oneiric-political motif first occurs when Basilio explains to Clotaldo, his advisor and sole guardian of Segismundo in the tower, the reason for the stratagem of the dream. If Segismundo turns out to be the tyrant predicted by the stars, then Basilio wants him to believe that his short-lived time as a prince in the court was only a dream: "and he will do good to understand this, Clotaldo, because in this world everyone who lives dreams [*hará bien cuando lo entienda/ porque en el mundo, Clotaldo/ todos los que viven sueñan*]" (II,1 111, translation modified). The wordplay in Spanish is the most important in the entire play. On the one hand, it "is good" for Segismundo to believe that "in the world, those who live are dreaming." Such a "lesson" will serve him well in the sense that his punishment will be proportional to the guilt, to the "original" sin. The conceit that in this world most humans live in a dream is an allusion to the Platonic cave: those who lack the wisdom of philosopher-kings (in this case, astrologer-kings) are destined to live in a world of shadows and illusions. On the other hand, the wordplay alludes to the fact that Segismundo, once he truly "wakes up" to life being a dream, will do "good works" (*hará bien*) in a very worldly, Machiavellian sense, cognizant of the limitations of Platonic or idealistic philosophy in a world where many are "not good."

The "play within the play" at the heart of *Life Is a Dream* consists in arranging things such that Segismundo would believe that his experience at court was only a dream, an illusion. This meta-theatrical artifice leads Segismundo into an "infinite" and "dialectical" self-reflection that, *pace* Schmitt, does not *oppose* historical reality to reflection but makes them *coincide* in the form of *the revolutionary act*. The reason for the coincidence of the real with reflection is that the motif of "life as a dream" is the carrier of the allegorical component of the trauerspiel. For Benjamin, the allegorical vision of the world pierces through the illusion that the world is a totality of objective facts. From an allegorical point of view, anything can mean anything else, and so, in the end, nothing means anything at all, just like a dream seems to mean nothing at all, unless one has certain keys to interpret it. The connection between allegory and dreamwork is given by the concept of a rebus.[45] To see life as a dream is to see reality as a rebus to decipher. The "melancholic science" that Segismundo attains in his dialectical reflection is designed not only to interpret (the rebus of) reality, but to change it.

Benjamin finds the connection between allegory and rebus in the Renaissance conception of the hieroglyph as "something like a natural theology of script" (OT, 178).[46] According to this theology of writing, the more human writing seeks to express the divine, the more it tends toward the hieroglyphical form because the latter captures the divinity of nature itself. Benjamin is adopting Bruno's dictum that *Natura est Deus in rebus* (Nature is God in things). Here is the key to the dialectical inversion enacted by the trauerspiel that Benjamin associates with the "antinomies of the allegorical" (OT, 184ff). If allegory allows anything to mean everything or nothing at all, it empties the world of significance. Yet, at the same time, in virtue of its hieroglyphical writing, these same meaningless things can signify the divine. They "acquire a potency that makes them appear incommensurable with profane things and elevates them to a higher plane. . . . In allegorical perception, then, the profane world is both elevated in rank and devalued" (OT, 184).

The idea of secularization as a reduction of history to nature is connected with the idea of allegory *only* on condition that the writing of nature is understood to contain a divine meaning or idea: "For, in the Baroque, nature is considered as functioning for the purpose of expressing its meaning . . . What prevails is the rigid countenance of signifying nature, and history is to remain once and for all shut up in the stage property" (OT, 179–80). This insight leads Benjamin to two postulates linked with his idea of "natural history." The first postulate is the well-known image of historical progress as an accumulation of ruins, later found in the theses "On the Concept of History" (Thesis IX): "When, with the trauerspiel, history becomes part of the setting, it does so as script. 'History' stands written on nature's countenance in the sign-script of transience. The allegorical physiognomy of natural history, which is brought onstage in the trauerspiel, is actually present as ruin" (OT, 188). The second postulate, which Benjamin explicitly associates with Calderón's trauerspiel, is that nature is conceived as "*eternal transience*: in that alone did the *saturnine gaze* of those generations recognize history. Dwelling in their monuments (the ruins) . . . are Saturn's animals" (OT, 190, emphasis mine). The concept of "eternal transience" is related to Benjamin's equally famous idea expressed in the *Theologico-Political Fragment* according to which the *messianic* conception of nature is characterized by the "eternity of downfall . . . [T]he rhythm of this eternally transient worldly existence . . . is happiness" (SW3, 306).[47] Benjamin connects both postulates through the idea of "Saturn's animals," which contains a Warburghian bipolarity: political rulers are saturnine beasts who turn history into a pile of ruins; but these ruins contain also an animal of Saturn like Segismundo whose actions, carried out under the emblem of "life is a dream," signify the possibility of redeeming nature from out of itself, rather than through a transcendent gift of grace or through a sovereign imposition of the state of exception.[48]

## Life as a Dream, the Pathos Formula of Revolution

When Segismundo awakens to find himself a prince in his father's court, he accepts the transition from prisoner to prince, from slave to master, without questioning the reality of the distinction. He then proceeds to abuse his new social status. When Clotaldo, who represents the Baroque figure of the intriguer, avers to Segismundo the reasons why his father imprisoned him at birth, and why his father has now restored him to the position that he was always expected to occupy, Segismundo flies into a rage, accuses Clotaldo of treason, and wants to kill him on the spot. This incident reveals Segismundo as one of "Saturn's animals," but his anger is equally motivated by a sense of what is right "by nature": "when the law isn't just, the king needn't be obeyed; and what's more, I was his prince" (II 1, 114). What is legitimate for the human king or Jupiter (in this case, Basilio) is not legitimate for the Saturnine prince (here Segismundo), and vice versa, just like political or positive right is the determinate negation of natural right.

Seeing the disruptive behavior that Segismundo's attachment to the idea of a natural equality and liberty causes in the court, his father decides to put an end to the experiment and lock him back in the tower, making it appear as if he had dreamt up the whole episode. Back in the tower and about to wake up, Segismundo speaks in his dream: "A pious prince is he who punishes tyrants. Clotaldo shall die by my hands! My father shall kiss my feet!" (II 2, 130, translation modified). It is significant that this utterance, unlike the others, is spoken in a dream, as if to signify Segismundo's "true" desire as a "new" type of prince whose legitimacy resides in punishing tyrants masquerading as kings.

When Segismundo wakes up again in the tower, he does not let go of the reality of his previous experience in the court, and believes he is still dreaming. He confesses to Clotaldo his true desire, and the intriguer tries to convince Segismundo that his period in the court was the real dream: "Because we had spoken about that eagle beforehand, once you fell asleep you dreamed of being a ruler. But in your dreams it would be fitting, Segismundo, to show more respect to he who raised you with such care; for even in dreams it pays to do what's right [*que aun en sueños/ no se pierde el hacer bien*]" (II 2, 131, translation modified). This will turn out to be the *pathos formula* that determines the rest of the development of the play.

Segismundo's second great soliloquy reflects upon the point just made by Clotaldo about dreams: "What is life? A frenzy. What is life? A vain hope, a shadow, a fiction. The greatest good is fleeting, for all life is a dream and even dreams are but dreams" (II 2, 132). Rejecting both the idea that he was awake in the court, dictated by his drives, as much as the idea that he is awake in the tower, dictated by Clotaldo's deception, Segismundo understands the formula that "all life is a dream" to mean that both tower and court were real parts of his life, and that in both he was dreaming: "he who lives dreams what he is until waking." Segismundo believes that there is no social reality that is independent from illusion or ideology.[49] But he also learns the necessity to "repress this proud condition [*fiera condición*], this fury, this ambition, in case we are dreaming." "Fiera condición" means both "proud condition" and "the condition of beasts of prey." The necessity of repression follows from the rejection of the phantasy of omnipotence or the "unbridled" pursuit of mastery. To live is to dream, and this means, politically speaking, that the pursuit of absolute mastery or sovereignty is vain. As one of Saturn's animals, Sigismundo breaks with the politico-theological analogy between the sovereign and God.

Thus, the first thesis of Segismundo's new "kingly science" based on the formula that "life is a dream" concerns the inherent contingency and fragility of all human "states of affairs." That any existing social order of things can be cancelled, as when one passes from dreaming to waking, is the first condition of revolutionary action. Segismundo voices the awareness of anyone who has lived through a revolution; namely, the nearly instantaneous crumbling of an entire social order and the emergence of a completely new world, such that for those who live through this transition it seems as if the past world had been "nothing but a dream" and had vanished completely. Thus, on one side, the change of order is so complete that the past seems like a "dream" with respect to the present; conversely, the past had to be lived "as a dream" from which one could awaken in the revolutionary change; otherwise, there would have been no such change in the first place.

After Segismundo is again imprisoned in the tower, the soldiers acting in the name of the people storm the tower and liberate him. They elevate Segismundo to the status of what Machiavelli calls the "civil prince": a prince who has in the armed people, rather than in the aristocracy, the foundation of his power. Calderón stages a plebeian revolt against the king led by a "new prince" ("new" in the sense that his claim to ruling no longer depends on dynastic succession) in which "popular power" bests astrological "fate" or "fortune." The soldier who frees him from the tower suggests the idea that Segismundo's previous experience of a change of condition was a dream *in the sense of an announcement of the future, a prophecy*, which is now finding its realization: "Great things are always announced in premonitions, which must be what you had if you dreamt this moment" (III 1, 136). This change of interpretation with respect to the problem of predicting the future is what allows Segismundo to adopt the formula of "life as a dream" in a revolutionary sense. But it is equally a signature of a Lutheran position, since, as Warburg argues, for Melanchthon and Luther astrological predictions about the future are warranted if they refer to events that can be traced back to biblical prophecy.

To the soldier's prophetic interpretation of the formula "life as a dream" Segismundo responds: "You're right; it was a premonition. And just in case it was correct, given that life is so short, let's dream, my soul, let's dream again. But this time we must be vigilant and aware that we shall awaken from this delight at the best moment" (III 1, 136). Here Segismundo gives the last dialectical turn to the formula "life as a dream." The dream stands for an idea of the future as something better than the present, as an *ideal* that allows us to move against the present order of things, hence the incitement to "dream once again." This is the sense of a revolutionary dream that one associates with the "I Have a Dream" speech of Martin Luther King (whose name expresses in itself a Baroque political program!).

When Clotaldo confronts Segismundo as head of the rebel army and asks what he thinks he is doing, Segismundo responds with Clotaldo's own words, which have now acquired a radically new and subversive meaning: "That I'm dreaming, and that I want to do what's right, for it pays to do what's right even in dreams [*Que estoy soñando y que quiero/ obrar bien, pues no se pierde/ el hacer bien aun en sueños*]" (III 4, 137). Here the sense of "good works" or "doing good" (*obrar bien*) refers to the realization of the very thoughts Segismundo had uttered while asleep, that is, that the true prince's duty is to overthrow a tyrant. Segismundo's unconscious wish can now be fulfilled because it turns out to be shared by the whole of society, or at least by the class of the oppressed, the plebeians.

## Conclusion: *Ponderación Misteriosa* and Constituent Power

Just as Benjamin says, *Life Is a Dream* ends in a quintessentially *spielhaft* (playful) way with a shocking "*côup de théatre*," a flabbergasting display of theatricality: Segismundo's punishment of the plebeian soldier who had freed him and occasioned the "successful" revolution (which in a way is also a restoration). Unlike in Schmitt's reading of *Hamlet*, at stake here is not the entrance of a real dynastic succession family drama into the *Spiel*, but the irruption of the "armed people," which is perhaps not without relation to the problem of divine violence in Benjamin. This political actor, the armed people, was first conjured up by Machiavelli in *The Prince*. This last scene of the play is at once the highest moment of the *Spiel* and contains the most enigmatic *ponderación misteriosa*, which requires Segismundo to punish the "loyal" rebel (the soldier) and to forgive the "legitimate" tyrant (Basilio).

Segismundo's last action has always puzzled commentators.[50] It is undoubtedly a Machiavellian gesture and sheds a problematic light on the previous act of Christian "forgiveness" and "mercy" lavished on Segismundo's father. I suggest that Segismundo's actions point to a conception of politics that unifies Christianity with Machiavellism *otherwise* than through the doctrine of "reason of state."[51] Segismundo is facing a problem inherent to every revolutionary process: how and when does the revolution "end" and the state "begin"? It is possible to give a reading of the punishment of the rebel soldier as an answer to this complicated political problem.[52]

On this reading, the rebel soldier represents the forces of the revolution that take themselves to be the "real" as opposed to understanding that they too are "living the dream." One attains here the apex of the dialectical reflection on revolution: after revealing the unreality or dream-like consistency of the old order of things, and the consequent victory of the revolution, the problem becomes that of becoming conscious of the equal but opposite unreality of the revolution itself, to prevent the bad infinity of an endless or permanent revolution. The concept of permanent revolution rests on the idea that the present state of things is illusory and *only* the revolutionary act is real and true. The punishment of the revolutionary soldier, in this sense, would disabuse the revolutionary forces of the belief in the "reality" of this new order of things, and thus maintain, for the rebel soldier, just as it is for the new prince, the critical principle of "life as a dream." Hence it is appropriate for Segismundo to return the rebel soldier to the tower, just as Segismundo was returned there after his initial becoming prince, when he abused his sovereign power in the belief that such power was real and absolute.

In this case, Segismundo's "Machiavellian" treatment of the soldier stands as a punishment to the latter's mindset that "the ends justify the means" (e.g., a better regime justifies the breaking of legality, the violence of civil war, etc.) which is a principle that does not permit the establishment of a rule of positive law. If understood this way, Segismundo as sovereign is closer to Benjamin's reconstruction of the Baroque conception of sovereignty, where the function of sovereignty is that of "excluding" the state of exception, rather than "deciding" on it. But does this mean, as Cacciari argues in his important interpretation of Benjamin and Hofmannsthal's two versions of *The Tower*, that "kingship, therefore, is being legitimized in two directions: as decision . . . and as foundation of an apparent peace preserved by means of norms and laws that can be applied"? (Cacciari 2009: 77–8). Has Segismundo simply transmuted the doctrine of constituent power into a decisionistic justification of the rule of law, and adopted the sophists' saying that "might makes right"?

Another reading is possible if one acknowledges that Segismundo is following to the last consequence the radicalization of the pathos formula that "life is a dream." To the general admiration of the court for his last action against the rebel, Segismundo replies:

> What's so amazing, what's so shocking, given that my teacher was a dream? And I still fear, deep down inside, that one day I shall awaken to find myself locked away in my cramped prison. And if that doesn't happen, it's enough to dream it's so, for that's how I came to realize that all human joy is, in the end, as ephemeral as a dream. So I'd like to take advantage of this happy moment while I can . . . and ask you to overlook our flaws, for forgiveness should come naturally to noble souls.
> (III 3, 153)

These concluding words place the punishment of the soldier in a different light: the place to which the ex-revolutionary is banished is also the place from which the current prince hails and to which he is afraid of returning, as befits the dialectical and unending transition from Saturn to Jupiter and Jupiter to Saturn. In this sense, Calderón seems to recognize the affinity between new prince and plebeian soldier. But, likewise, Segismundo argues that the formula "life as a dream" can account for both the need for subversive actions and for forgiveness, as if the "righting of wrongs" needs itself, always, to be "righted" by being forgiven—in short, the formula of "life as a dream" disallows any position that is "justified in itself." The search for justification never attains a "happy end" (least of all in Luther, of which Luther was aware). Finally, Segismundo acknowledges that "a dream was my teacher," and that he fears "waking up" from this dream. Segismundo's anxiety is no longer associated with falling into a dream-state or discovering oneself dreaming, but, to the contrary, it is the anxiety of falling outside of the dreaming. To understand this anxiety, it would be necessary to return to the peculiar crossing in the twentieth century of psychoanalysis and Marxist theory, a task of vast proportions and possibly interminable.

One of the last commentaries on this crossing was given by a well-known essay on "Left Melancholy" by Wendy Brown. Brown employs this term coined by Benjamin, and then draws from his *Trauerspiel* book in order to comment on the problem of a Left that is paralysed by its inability to avow the loss of an idealized form of communism. This is the form of communism that places theory always in advance of praxis, unlike Marx's conception of criticism in his letter to Ruge. For Brown, this melancholic form of Leftism is more in love with its "[l]eft passions and reasons[,] ... [l]eft analyses and convictions" than with "the existing world that [it] presumably seeks to alter" (Brown 1999: 21). As I understand it, Brown was not recommending turning toward some form of political "realism." On the contrary, she was suggesting that Left melancholy fixates itself on a reified reality that prevents it from dreaming again in the kind of way that is needed to change the world. In this essay I have argued that to recapture this political meaning of dreaming it is illuminating to engage in astral politics. It is no coincidence that Benjamin's first published book after his turn to communism, *One-Way Street*, concludes on an astropolitical motif. Benjamin indicates clearly the highest political function of the "ecstatic contact with the cosmos": "If one had to expound the teachings of antiquity with utmost brevity while standing on one leg, as did Hillel that of the Jews, it could only be in this sentence: 'They alone shall possess the earth who live from the powers of the cosmos'" (*SW*1: 486).

## Notes

1 I would like to give my thanks to the editors for their patience with an unwieldy first draft, and their careful reading and editorial suggestions. I would also like to thank Andreas Greiert for our continued exchanges on Walter Benjamin.

2 "His [Hamlet's] life, as the exemplary object of his mourning, points, before its extinction, to the Christian providence in whose bosom his mournful images turn into blessed existence. Only in a life of this princely sort is melancholy, on being confronted with itself, redeemed" (*OT*, 163).

3 See "Franz Kafka on the Tenth Anniversary of His Death" in *SW*2.2, 794–818. For a recent discussion, see Wortham 2020.

4 See the eighth thesis in "On the Concept of History" (*SW*4, 392) and "Toward the Critique of Violence" (*TC*, 39–61). For commentary, Derrida 2001, Agamben 2005, and Martel 2012.

5 See Wolin 1981 and Greiert 2011. In a letter to Scholem recounting his encounter with *History and Class Consciousness*, Benjamin writes: "what struck me was the fact that Lukács, proceeding from political considerations to a theory of knowledge ... arrives at principles which are very familiar to me and endorsed by me" (*GB*1, 351–5). On the events in Capri, see now Eiland and Jennings 2016.

6 Marx's letter is cited in Lukács 1968: 2. For a discussion of the citation in relation to Benjamin, see Rancière 1996.

7 The citation of Marx's letter to Ruge appears in *AP*, N5a, 1. Benjamin's neologism of "*Zeit-Traum*" (*AP*, K1, 1) is a playful variant of the German expression *Zeitraum* (a period or extension of time) which had just been revolutionized by Einstein's theory of special relativity and its concept of *Raumzeit* or space-time. For long-running commentaries on dream and historical consciousness in the later Benjamin, see

Buck-Morss 1991: ch. 8 passim and Friedlander 2012: ch. 5. See also Lindner 2008, Weidmann 2000, and Gelley 2019.
8 Of the few attempts to analyze Benjamin's Calderón-interpretation one of the earliest and best is found in Cacciari 2009. The Spanish trauerspiel is entirely absent in Haas and Weidner 2014. But see Lorenz 2013 who employs Francisco Suarez as a master text to decode Calderón's discourse on sovereignty, a thesis already anticipated in the monumental study by Regalado 1995. For a general overview of the state of the question of research in English and German on Benjamin and trauerspiel see Newman 2012.
9 On Bruno and Shakespeare, see Gatti 2011. For a very interesting discussion of Warburg's late interest in Bruno, see Johnson 2012: ch. 7 passim.
10 Fiorini, Bokanowski, and Lewkowicz 2007.
11 For this debate, see Prozorov 2010.
12 Here Agamben follows the reading of Weber 1992.
13 See Cassirer 1963, Koyré 1957, Blumenberg 1989, Westman 2011.
14 See the essay "Fato Antico, Fato Moderno" in Santillana 1968: 344–5. It is tempting to associate Benjamin's description of the cataract with a "planetary" view on the Anthropocene and climate change.
15 For two other approaches to the problem of historical representation in Benjamin, see Andrew Benjamin 2013 and Ross 2018.
16 See the claim that in the trauerspiel "temporal process is caught up and analysed in a spatial image" (*OT*, 82).
17 "When the drama of play [*Trauer-spiel*] is confronted with historical subjects it finds itself compelled to develop the logic of fate as 'game'" (*SW1*, 373).
18 In one of the famous formulations: "In the court the trauerspiel sees the eternal, natural décor of the course of history" (*OT*, 82).
19 For a discussion of this engagement with Bergson in Lukács, see Vatter 2014b. On the Bergson-Einstein polemic of those years, see Canales 2016.
20 For Schmitt's response to this objection, see the 1937 essay "The State as Mechanism in Hobbes and Descartes" in the appendix of Schmitt 2008.
21 On Schmitt's critique of Benjamin, see Galli 2012, Weber 1992, reprised in a new version in Weber 2008, and Kahn 2003. In his treatment of the "gigantomachy" between Schmitt and Benjamin, Agamben does not discuss this text nor the problem of *Spiel*. This discussion is also absent in Ferber 2013.
22 To prove this point, Schmitt discusses Act 2, scene 2, in which Hamlet comments on a theatrical representation of the death of Priam and Hecuba's tears. "But Hamlet does not cry for Hecuba. He discovers with some amazement that there are people who by virtue of their trade shed tears for things that in actual reality of their existence, in their real situation, are indifferent to them" (Schmitt 2006: 37).
23 Schmitt's well-known claim is that English Baroque drama represents a *national decision* for a "maritime way of life" that separates England from the Continental idea of "state police" with its victory over the 'barbaric middle ages'" and inaugurates the capitalist and imperialist "new global order of land and sea" (Schmitt 2006: 55).
24 Bettina Menke reduces the element of *Spiel* in the trauerspiel to that of "reine Spaß" (pure fun), which corresponds to her reading of the politics of the trauerspiel centered on the "inauthentic" means employed in political intrigue and in diplomacy. For these claims, see Menke 2009 and Menke 2006. For a critique of Benjamin's use of *ponderación misteriosa* to understand the German trauerspiel, see Weber 2004.
25 For a cosmological reading of the Hamlet myth, see Santillana and Dechend 1969.

26 This point has been now demonstrated conclusively by Regalado 1995: 455–94. Regalado, however, is unaware of Warburg's research on Lutheran astropolitics and thus arrives at conclusions quite distinct from those I shall put forward.
27 On this conception of fate, see Benjamin 1997a: ch.3 passim, and Benjamin 2013. See Paula Schwebel's chapter in the present volume for a discussion of fate in connection with original sin. For a discussion of fate in Benjamin's corpus more broadly, see Howard Eiland's chapter in this volume.
28 This point, that Luther's rejection of "good works" should not be totalized into a rejection of work as such, has been made brilliantly and, to my mind, definitively by Erik Erikson 1993. Erikson ends his book with a citation from Calderón.
29 On Melanchthon's relation to astrology and modern cosmology, see Westman 2011. On astrology in Maximilian I's court, see now Hayton 2015.
30 For alternative discussions of Warburg's and Benjamin's approaches to Lutheranism and astrology, see Newman 2011 and Johnson 2016.
31 See here "Italian Art and International Astrology in the Palazzo Schifanoia" in Warburg 1999b. For Abu Ma'shar's text on the conjunctions, see Abu Ma'shar 2000. For a general discussion of astrology and the cycles of religions in the Renaissance see Garin 1983.
32 On astral determinism, see Cumont 1960 and Santillana 1968. On these themes in Ficino, see Romandini 2006 and Vasoli 1999; for Machiavelli, see Vatter 2017, 2011.
33 On the possibility discussed in the late Renaissance that Luther might be a "fourth Plato" who would revive the "ancient theology" and bring down Christianity, see Monfasani 2008.
34 Benjamin speaks of "a dialectical tension in the representation of Saturn" (*OT*, 154), an idea he takes from Warburg's essay on Luther and astrology. He refers to the 1923 book by Saxl and Panofsky, *Dürer's 'Melencolia I'. Eine quellen- und typengeschichtliche Untersuchung*, which would later be expanded into Klibansky, Panofsky, and Saxl 2019.
35 On Machiavelli and the theory of "return to beginnings" as formula for political revolution, I refer to Vatter 2014a and now Marchesi 2023.
36 See Armas 1987, Armas 1986, Armas 2001, and Armas 2017.
37 In what follows I use the English translation found in Calderón de la Barca 2004 with occasional modifications. The notation refers to act, scene, and page number in translation.
38 On the origins of constituent power in the seventeenth century, see Schmitt 2014, Negri 1999 and Kalyvas 2005. For a reading of the problem of political succession in *Life Is a Dream* based on the "King's two bodies" see Balazs 2015.
39 For the Platonic influence in *Life Is a Dream*, see Kluge 2008.
40 On the myth of Saturn in Greek thought see Lovejoy and Boas 1997.
41 On this conception of the "living law" see now Vatter 2021.
42 On the conception of "play" in Machiavelli, see now Marasco 2021.
43 See my discussion in Vatter 2014a.
44 For a "Pascalian" reading of this experimental cosmology see Regalado 1995: 486–9.
45 Obviously, Benjamin was aware that for Freud, the dreamwork is the rebus: this is the language in which the unconscious "writes" itself in dreams. However, the Freudian use of rebus is never cited in his discussion of rebuses in the *Trauerspiel* book.
46 It would take me too far afield to engage the problem of the hieroglyph more fully in connection with the motif of dream interpretation. But see here the essential discussion in Derrida 2016 and Sloterdijk 2009.

47  For a discussion of this concept in light of cosmology, see Vatter 2014b.
48  On this line of interpretation, see now Greiert 2022.
49  I refer to the Freudian and Lacanian interpretations of Calderón discussed throughout in Regalado 1995.
50  See Hall 1968 and Heiple 1973: 3, 8.
51  For the classic statement on "reason of state," see Meinecke 1997.
52  The problem of the punishment of the rebel soldier is what motivates Hugo von Hofmannsthal's two versions of *The Tower* as Cacciari 2009 has shown. Benjamin's *Trauerspiel* book and Hofmannsthal's plays are mutually imbricated.

# References

Abu Ma'shar. (2000), *On Historical Astrology: The Book of Religions and Dynasties*, eds. Keiji Yamamoto and Charles Burnett, Leiden: Brill.
Agamben, Giorgio. (2005), *State of Exception*, Chicago: University of Chicago Press.
Armas, Frederick A. de. (1986), *The Return of Astrea. An Astral-Imperial Myth in Calderón*, Lexington: University Press of Kentucky.
Armas, Frederick A. de. (1987), "Icons of Saturn: Astrologer-Kings in Calderón's Comedias," *Forum for Modern Language Studies*, 23 (2): 117–30.
Armas, Frederick A. de. (2001), "Segismundo/Philip IV: The Politics of Astrology in *La vida es sueño*," *Bulletin of the Comediantes*, 53 (1): 83–100.
Armas, Frederick A. de. (2017), "Rubens, Calderón and the Gods of *La vida es sueño*: Uranus, Saturn and Jupiter," *Hipogrifo: revista de Literatura y Cultura del Siglo de Oro*, 5 (1): 103–14.
Balazs, Zoltan. (2015), "Artificial Eternity: The Problem of Political Succession in Pedro Calderón della Barca's *Life is a Dream* and Heinrich von Kleist's *The Prince of Homburg*," *Contemporary Political Theory*, 14 (1): 2–22.
Benjamin, Andrew. (1997), *Present Hope: Philosophy, Architecture, Judaism*, London: Routledge.
Benjamin, Andrew. (2013), *Working with Walter Benjamin: Recovering a Political Philosophy*, Edinburgh: Edinburgh University Press.
Benjamin, Walter. 2019. *Origin of the German Trauerspiel*, trans. Howard Eiland, Cambridge, MA: Harvard University Press.
Blumenberg, Hans. (1989), *Genesis of the Copernican World*, Cambridge: MIT Press.
Brown, Wendy. (1999), "Resisting Left Melancholy," *Boundary 2*, 26 (3): 19–27.
Buck-Morss, Susan. (1991), *The Dialectics of Seeing: Walter Benjamin and the Arcades Project*, Cambridge: MIT Press.
Cacciari, Massimo. (2009), "Impracticable Utopias: Hofmannsthal, Lukács, Benjamin," in Massimo Cacciari (ed.), *The Unpolitical: On the Radical Critique of Political Reason*, 45–91, New York: Fordham University Press.
Calderón de la Barca, Pedro. (2004), *Life's a Dream*, trans. Michael Kidd, Denver: University Press of Colorado.
Canales, Jimena. (2016), *The Physicist and the Philosopher: Einstein, Bergson and the Debate That Changed Our Understanding of Time*, Princeton: Princeton University Press.
Cassirer, Ernst. (1963), *The Idea of the Individual and the Cosmos in Renaissance Philosophy*, Chicago: University of Chicago Press.

Cumont, Franz. (1960), *Astrology and Religion among the Greeks and Romans*, New York: Dover.
Derrida, Jacques. (2001), "Force of Law. The 'Mystical Foundation of Authority,'" in Gil Anidjar (ed.), *Acts of Religion*, 230–98, New York: Routledge.
Derrida, Jacques. (2016), *Of Grammatology*, Baltimore: Johns Hopkins University Press.
Eiland, Howard and Michael W. Jennings. (2016), *Walter Benjamin: A Critical Life*, Cambridge: Harvard University Press.
Erikson, Erik H. (1993), *Young Man Luther: A Study in Psychoanalysis and History*, New York: W.W. Norton & Company.
Ferber, Ilit. (2013), *Philosophy and Melancholy: Walter Benjamin's Early Reflections on Theatre and Language*, Stanford: Stanford University Press.
Fiorini, Leticia Glocer, Thierry Bokanowski, and Sergio Lewkowicz, eds. (2007), *On Freud's "Mourning and Melancholia," Contemporary Freud*, London: Routledge.
Friedlander, Eli. (2012), *Walter Benjamin: A Philosophical Portrait*, Cambridge: Harvard University Press.
Galli, Carlo. (2012), "*Hamlet*: Representation and the Concrete," in Graham Hammill and Julia Reinhardt Lupton (eds.), *Political Theology and Early Modernity*, 60–83, Chicago: University of Chicago Press.
Garin, Eugenio. (1983), *Astrology in the Renaissance: The Zodiac of Life*, New York: Viking.
Gatti, Hilary. (2011), *Essays on Giordano Bruno*, Princeton: Princeton University Press.
Gelley, Alexander. (2019), *Benjamin's Passages*, New York: Fordham University Press.
Greiert, Andreas. (2011), *Erlösung der Geschichte vom Darstellenden. Grundlagen des Geschichtsdenkens bei Benjamin 1915-1925*, München: Wilhelm Fink.
Greiert, Andreas. (2022), "Kein politischer Sinn der Theokratie. Zur Walter-Benjamin-Deutung bei Jacob Taubes und Gershom Scholem," *Allgemeine Zeitschrift für Philosophie*, 47 (2): 175–99.
Haas, Claude, and Daniel Weidner, eds. (2014), *Benjamins Trauerspiel. Theorie-Lektüren-Nachleben*, Berlin: Kulturverlag Kadmos.
Hall, H. B. (1968), "Segismundo and the Rebel Soldier," *Bulletin of Hispanic Studies*, 45 (3): 189–200.
Hayton, Darin. (2015), *The Crown and the Cosmos: Astrology and the Politics of Maximilian I*, Pittsburgh: The University of Pittsburgh Press.
Heiple, Daniel L. (1973), "The Tradition behind the Punishment of the Rebel Soldier in *La vida es sueño*," *Bulletin of Hispanic Studies*, 50 (1): 1–17.
Johnson, Christopher. (2012), *Memory, Metaphor and Aby Warburg's Atlas of Images*, Ithaca: Cornell University Press.
Johnson, Christopher. (2016), "Configuring the Baroque: Warburg and Benjamin," *Culture, Theory and Critique*, 57 (2): 142–65.
Kahn, Victoria. (2003), "Hamlet or Hecuba: Carl Schmitt's Decision," *Representations*, 83 (1): 67–96.
Kalyvas, Andreas. (2005), "Popular Sovereignty, Democracy, Constituent Power," *Constellations*, 12 (2): 223–44.
Klibansky, Raymond, Erwin Panofsky, and Fritz Saxl. (2019), *Saturn and Melancholy*, Montreal: McGill's-Queens University Press.
Kluge, Sofie. (2008), "Calderón's Anti-Tragic Theater: The Resonance of Plato's Critique of Tragedy in *La vida es sueño*," *Hispanic Review*, 76 (1): 19–52.
Koyré, Alexandre. (1957), *From the Closed World to the Infinite Universe*, Baltimore: The Johns Hopkins Press.
Lindner, Burkhardt, ed. (2008), *Walter Benjamin. Träume*, Frankfurt: Suhrkamp.

Lorenz, Philip. (2013), *Tears of Sovereignty: Perspectives of Power in Renaissance Drama*, New York: Fordham University Press.
Lovejoy, Arthur O. and George Boas. (1997), *Primitivism and Related Ideas in Antiquity*, Baltimore: The Johns Hopkins University Press.
Lukács, Georg. (1968), *History and Class Consciousness*, Cambridge: MIT Press.
Marasco, Robyn. (2021), "Machiavelli and the Play-Element in Political Life," *Political Theory*: 1–21. http://doi.org/10.1177/00905917211046573.
Marchesi, Francesco. (2023), *Ritorno ai princìpi. Concezioni della storia da Machiavelli alla Rivoluzione francese*, Rome: Carocci editore.
Martel, James. (2012), *Divine Violence: Walter Benjamin and the Eschatology of Sovereignty*, London: Routledge.
Marx, Karl. (1844), "Letter from Marx to Arnold Ruge September 1843," in Karl Marx and Arnold Ruge (eds.), *Deutsch-Französische Jahrbücher, 1844*. https://www.marxists.org/archive/marx/works/1843/letters/43_09-alt.htm.
Meinecke, Friedrich. (1997), *Machiavellism: The Doctrine of Raison d'État and Its Place in Modern History*, London: Routledge.
Menke, Bettina. (2006), "Reflexion des Trauer-Spiels. Pedro Calderón de la Barcas *El mayor monstruo, los celos* nach Walter Benjamin," in Bettina Menke, Eva Horn, and Christoph Menke (eds.), *Literatur als Philosophie. Philosophie als Literatur*, 269–77, Munchen: Wilhelm Fink.
Menke, Bettina. (2009), "Zur Kritik der Gewalt. Techniken der Übereinkunft, Diplomatie, Lüge," in Hendrik Blumenrath et al. (eds.), *Techniken der Übereinkunft. Zur Medialität des Politischen*, 37–56, Berlin: Kulturverlag Kadmos.
Monfasani, John. (2008), "A tale of two books: Bessarion's *In Calumniatoris Platonis* and George of Trebizond's *Comparatio philosphorum Platonis et Aristotelis*," *Renaissance Studies*, 22 (1): 1–16.
Negri, Antonio. (1999), *Insurgencies: Constituent Power and the Modern State*, Minneapolis: University of Minnesota Press.
Newman, Jane O. (2011), *Benjamin's Library. Modernity, Nation and the Baroque*, Ithaca: Cornell University Press.
Newman, Jane O. (2012), "Tragedy and 'Trauerspiel' for the (Post-)Westphalian Age," *Renaissance Drama*, 40: 197–208.
Prozorov, Sergei. (2010), "The Katechon in the Age of Biopolitical Nihilism," *Philosophy and Social Criticism*, 36 (9): 1053–73.
Rancière, Jacques. (1996), "The Archeomodern Turn," in Michael Steinberg (ed.), *Walter Benjamin and the Demands of History*, 24–40, Ithaca: Cornell University Press.
Regalado, Antonio. (1995), *Calderón. Los orígenes de la modernidad en la España del Siglo de Oro*, 2 vols. Vol. 1, Barcelona: Ediciones Destino.
Romandini, Fabián Ludueña. (2006), *Homo oeconomicus. Marsilio Ficino, la teología, y los misterios paganos*, Buenos Aires: Miño y Dávila Editores.
Ross, Alison. (2018), *Revolution and History in Walter Benjamin: A Conceptual Analysis*, London: Routledge.
Santillana, Giorgio de. (1968), *Reflections on Men and Ideas*, Cambridge: MIT Press.
Santillana, Giorgio de and Hertha von Dechend. (1969), *Hamlet's Mill: An Essay on Myth and the Frame of Time*, Jaffrey: David R. Godine Publisher.
Schmitt, Carl. (2006), *Hamlet or Hecuba: The Irruption of Time Into Play*, trans. Simona Draghici, Corvallis: Plutarch Press.
Schmitt, Carl. (2008), *The Leviathan in the State Theory of Thomas Hobbes*, Chicago: University of Chicago Press.

Schmitt, Carl. (2014), *Dictatorship: From the Origin of Modern Concept of Sovereignty to Proletarian Class Struggle*, trans. Michael Hoelzl and Graham Ward, London: Polity.

Sloterdijk, Peter. (2009), *Derrida, an Egyptian: On the Problem of the Jewish Pyramid*, London: Polity.

Taylor, Charles. (2007), *A Secular Age*, Cambridge: Harvard University Press.

Vasoli, Cesare. (1999), *Quasi sit deus. Studi su Marsilio Ficino*, Lecce: Conte Editore.

Vatter, Miguel. (2011), "La política del gran azar: Providencia y legislación en Platón y el Renacimiento," in Miguel Vatter and Miguel Ruiz Stull (ed.), *Política y acontecimiento*, 23–58, Santiago: Fondo de Cultura Económica.

Vatter, Miguel. (2014a), *Between Form and Event. Machiavelli's Theory of Political Freedom*, Paperback ed., New York: Fordham University.

Vatter, Miguel. (2014b), *The Republic of the Living. Biopolitics and the Critique of Civil Society*, New York: Fordham.

Vatter, Miguel. (2017), "Machiavelli, 'Ancient Theology', and the Problem of Civil Religion," in Nadia Urbinati, David Johnston, and Camila Vergara (eds.), *Machiavelli on Liberty and Conflict*, 113–38, Chicago: University of Chicago Press.

Vatter, Miguel. (2021), *Living Law: Jewish Political Theology from Hermann Cohen to Hannah Arendt*, New York: Oxford University Press.

Warburg, Aby. (1999a), "Pagan-Antique Prophecy in Words and Images in the Age of Luther (1920)," in Aby Warburg (ed.), *The Renewal of Pagan Antiquity*, 760–75, Los Angeles: Getty Research Institute Publications.

Warburg, Aby. (1999b), *The Renewal of Pagan Antiquity*, Los Angeles: The Getty Research Institute Publications.

Weber, Samuel. (1992), "Taking Exception to Decision: Walter Benjamin and Carl Schmitt," *Diacritics*, 22 (3–4): 5–18.

Weber, Samuel. (2004), "Storming the Work: Allegory and Theatricality in Benjamin's Origin of the German Mourning Play," in Samuel Weber (ed.), *Theatricality as Medium*, 160–81, New York: Fordham University Press.

Weber, Samuel. (2008), *Benjamin's-Abilities*, Cambridge: Harvard University Press.

Weidmann, Heiner. (2000), "Erwachen/Traum," in Erdmut Wizisla Michael Opitz (ed.), *Benjamins Begriffe*, 341–62, Frankfurt: Suhrkamp.

Westman, Robert S. (2011), *The Copernican Question: Prognostication, Skepticism, and the Celestial Order*, Berkeley: University of California Press.

Wolin, Richard. (1981), "From Messianism to Materialism: The Later Aesthetics of Walter Benjamin," *New German Critique*, 22: 81–108.

Wortham, Simon. (2020), *Hope: The Politics of Optimism*, London: Bloomsbury.

3

# Contra Schmitt

## Leo Strauss, Walter Benjamin, and Jewish Political Theology

Leora Batnitzky and Vivian Liska

Leo Strauss and Walter Benjamin have rarely been put into conversation.[1] Little seems to bring together the conservative and dialogical Strauss and the radical and dialectical Benjamin. That such a conversation between the political philosopher regarded as a precursor of neo-conservativism and the idiosyncratic Marxist who continues to inspire the contemporary left can benefit from a comparison of their respective relationships to Carl Schmitt is far from self-evident. Yet, investigating the purported proximity of both Strauss and Benjamin to certain aspects of Schmitt's thought harbors the promise of illuminating not only their divergent approaches to political theology, but also the current interest in Schmitt's anti-liberal thought. It could help explain why today not only rightist political thinkers, but figures on the left such as Chantal Mouffe, Giorgio Agamben, Susan Buck-Morss, Slavoj Žižek[2] as well as some scholars associated with centrist or liberal ideas such as the legal scholar Paul Kahn would turn to Hitler's "crown jurist" to support their respective theoretical and political agendas. Obviously, these thinkers don't adopt Schmitt's thought as a whole, but his anti-democratic and anti-liberal thought, his approach to the state of exception and his decisionism remain a significant reference for all of them.

An exploration of what in Schmitt's thought both attracted and repelled Strauss and Benjamin, who were so patently on different sides of the political spectrum, can contribute to an understanding not only of divergent trends among German-Jewish thinkers of the twentieth century, but also shed light on disquieting intellectual developments and their potential antidotes in the present.

Some attribute Schmitt's current relevance to attributes of our historical moment and political circumstances. As when Schmitt wrote, democracies are again revealing their fragility and flaws. Adherents of Schmitt generally argue that political liberalism is overly optimistic in its view of human nature and is thus blind to the inherently antagonistic nature of politics so central to Schmitt's critique of liberalism. For Schmitt's rightist followers, there can be no functioning legal order without a sovereign authority. For them, the current weakness of parliamentary democracy proves this.

For his aficionados on the left, Schmitt can inspire an anti-statist rebellion against dysfunctional legal systems and parliamentary governments. Voices from both the right and the left oppose constraints of legality stemming from what they consider a meaningless, impersonal bureaucracy such as the European Union. On the right, Schmitt is invoked in reactions to 9/11, to Trump, to the populist governments in Poland and Hungary, or to the impossibility of implementing democracies in the Middle East. On the left, Schmitt is often called upon against Western liberal democracies' imperialism, police power, biopolitics, and more.[3]

Intellectually, the turn to Schmitt in our days can be explained in light of what preceded it: deconstruction's playful indeterminacies, its undermining of binary oppositions, its aporias and aesthetic acrobatics, may indeed have stretched its critique, beyond operative thresholds, of authority and decisiveness, its celebration of deferral and delayed action, as well as the blurring of boundaries through finding the "other" in every "same"—in short, everything Schmitt opposes. The backlash against deconstruction manifests itself—even in those who started out within its fold—in a desire for political *Eigentlichkeit*: authenticity, intensity, heroic force and immediate political action that can counteract the paralysis caused by the infinite aporias at the heart of the deconstructive paradigm, particularly Derrida's mode of deferral.[4] Finally, those who proclaim a so-called postsecular turn invoke Schmitt's belief in the impossibility of a full secularization and the continuing or renewed, though often hidden, relevance of religious ideas.

Schmitt's political theology is, for all these reasons, a highly topical and volatile issue and, given the existing attempts to associate both Strauss and Benjamin with him, a perfect medium to envisage their conversation.

## Disentangling Strauss from Schmitt (Leora Batnitzky)

### Absence of Redemption

In February 1962, Leo Strauss gave a lecture at the University of Chicago's Hillel, entitled "Why We Remain Jews: Can Jewish Faith and History Still Speak to Us?" Strauss remarked at the beginning of the lecture that the title was strange; he had agreed to "why we remain Jews," about which he claimed he would have something to say but was surprised by the subtitle, chosen by someone at Hillel—"Can Jewish Faith and History Still Speak to Us?"—about which he did not feel qualified to speak. Like Churchill's well-known quip that "democracy is the worst form of government—except for all the others that have been tried," Strauss's claim in "Why We Remain Jews" is that remaining Jews for those who can no longer believe in the faith of their ancestors is untenable. Except that the alternatives are all worse. Here we can appreciate why Strauss may have felt unable to speak to the subtitle of his lecture, for even if he could offer an answer to why we remain Jews, he would seem unable to offer any positive content to the question of whether "Jewish faith and history still speak to us."

Given this description of Strauss's lecture, it may seem surprising that I will argue in this chapter that a statement Strauss makes in this lecture does in fact give voice to what I will contend is a twentieth-century Jewish political theology that begins to offer an answer to the question of how Jewish faith and history still speak to us. Here is the statement:

> The Jewish people and their fate are the living witness for the absence of redemption. This, one could say, is the meaning of the chosen people; the Jews are chosen to prove the absence of redemption. (Strauss 1997a: 327)

Using the term "political theology" to characterize Strauss's thought is unexpected. But, as I will argue, this is only surprising because the reception of Strauss remains ensnared with that of Carl Schmitt. It is undeniable that Strauss and Schmitt had a relationship, but the significance of this relationship is at the very least overstated.

No one has shaped the receptions of Schmitt and Strauss more than Heinrich Meier who claims that we ought to understand Strauss through the lifelong "secret dialogue" he had with Schmitt (Meier 2006). Meier identifies "political theology" with Schmitt and "political philosophy" with Strauss. Admittedly, there is much truth to this distinction between Schmitt and Strauss or between political theology and political philosophy. To state the obvious, Schmitt was, after all, explicitly committed to what he called "political theology" and Strauss devoted his life to studying and reinvigorating "political philosophy." Yet Meier's sharp dichotomy between political theology and political philosophy (or between Schmitt and Strauss) is based on a particular reading of Strauss through the lens of Schmitt that assumes two things: first, that Strauss demands that we *decide* for either political theology or political philosophy and second that Strauss *decides* for political philosophy.

## Indecision and Ambivalence

I am of course using the term "decide" deliberately. Political theology for Schmitt is not only (in Meier's words) "political doctrine that claims to be founded on faith in divine revelation" but it is also coeval with the sovereign's decision. Indeed, it may not be an overstatement to suggest that the themes and content of Schmitt's political theology all follow from his claim about decision (Schmitt 1985: 5–35). But my argument here is that Strauss's thought is properly characterized not in terms of Schmittian decision but rather in terms of hesitation or ambivalence. Remarkably, as Eugene Sheppard has noted, in his eulogy for Strauss at the Van Leer Institute, Gershom Scholem portrayed Strauss as a man "*be-naftulav*," meaning a man of agitations or hesitations (Sheppard 2007).[5] My suggestion is that hesitation, agitation, and also ambivalence characterize not just Strauss as a person but also Strauss's conception of the *undecidable* contest between Athens (or political philosophy) and Jerusalem (or political theology).

Meier's characterization of Strauss as having decided for Athens rather than Jerusalem, or for political philosophy rather than political theology, is steeped in two basic Schmittian assumptions, first, about the definition of faith as fundamentally irrational, and second, about the absolute (as opposed to relative) necessity of decision as the defining feature of the choice between Athens and Jerusalem, as well as of political life more generally. Space does not permit an examination of these points in any detail but for the purposes of this chapter it is sufficient to note that Strauss rejects both of these assumptions as distinctively Christian assumptions and that his depiction of the vitality of the West is rooted in the West's *hesitation in deciding*, even in its refusal to decide, between Athens or Jerusalem.[6] Philosophy and revelation reflect two ways of thinking, but more basically they are two ways of life. Strauss does maintain that every individual must make a choice between the two. However, while each individual must live according to one or the other of these two frames of ultimate concern, this does not mean that either one of these positions is justified such that the possibility of the other one is rendered inadmissible. It is the very structure and character of the choice that forbids Strauss or anyone else from excluding the possibility of the other. Put somewhat differently, it is only because both are valid that one can speak of a choice.

Hesitation, agitation, and also ambivalence characterize Strauss's conception of premodern rationalism and of Maimonides in particular (Batnitzky 2021). Maimonides is Strauss's paradigm of true rationalism because, according to Strauss, Maimonides critically conceives the relation between Athens and Jerusalem not by synthesizing them but rather by acknowledging the challenges and limits that each one poses to the other. The hesitation that marks the relationship between Athens and Jerusalem finds a counterpart in Strauss's claim about the absence of redemption. Here too Strauss's engagement with Maimonides holds the key. Strauss's political theology is found *not* in Maimonidean prophetology (as Vatter 2021 argues) but rather in the rabbinic Judaism that Maimonides is both shaped by and shapes. This rabbinic Judaism is predicated on *the end of prophecy* and it is fundamentally an exilic Judaism (Bokser 1983). Following Maimonides, Strauss's fundamental premise is that the messianic era is *not* here—we remain in a world that is not yet redeemed. For Strauss (and for Maimonides), exile itself is not only a real political condition but also a theological one. Strauss explicitly links the absence of redemption to exile, or *galut*, which he defines as "the notion, that there is something—a deep defect—in our situation as Jews, and this deep defect in our situation as Jews is connected with the deep defect with the situation of man. That was an implication of the traditional Jewish faith" (Strauss 1997a: 339). Exile is a theological-political condition that happens in a space and time saturated with hesitation and ambiguity. Exile is the time and space in which we wait for a decision that has not yet been made.

The connection between Strauss's hesitation between Athens and Jerusalem and his account of *galut* helps us disentangle Strauss from Schmitt and helps us begin to fill out this political theology by way of Strauss's engagement with some of his German-Jewish contemporaries. In particular, Strauss, like Franz Rosenzweig and Yitzhak Fritz Baer (both discussed in this chapter), grounds his political-theological musings on a rejection of Christian triumphalism.

Christian triumphalism is at the heart of Schmitt's political theology. Here are a few examples. In *Roman Catholicism and Political Form*, Schmitt argues that the Catholic Church embodied the ideal of political theology because it "represents the Person of Christ Himself: God become man in historical reality" (Schmitt 1996: 19). In *Political Theology*, decision is not just analogous to miracle but to the miracle of all miracles: God's incarnation, which is reenacted in the eucharist. Like transubstantiation, in decision "a transformation takes place every time" (Schmitt 1985: 31). Schmitt also makes Christology essential to restoring legal personality after Kelsen's critique of it (ibid: 36–52). But nowhere is Schmitt's Christian triumphalism more evident than in his interpretation of Hobbes's contention, in the third book of *Leviathan*, that the "one article of faith" necessary for the sovereign is "Jesus is the Christ." For Schmitt, Hobbes's insistence that "Jesus is the Christ" is testament to a specifically Christian faith and the continuity between political theology and the liberal rule of law, both of which are grounded on exception and decision (Schmitt 2008: 243). "Jesus is the Christ" is the glue that makes, as Schmitt puts it in *Constitutional Theory*, "an invisible being visible and present through a publicly present one" (Schmitt 1985: 233). In all of these cases, Schmitt's twin theological and political premise is that Christ has already come. It is this premise that Strauss rejects.

According to Strauss, "the absence of redemption" means that Jesus is not the Christ and that redemption has not come. As we have seen, *galut* is the absence of redemption; this is a rejection of the Christian claim that redemption has come (Christian triumphalism). Strauss's statement that the Jews are "the living witness for the absence of redemption" clearly echoes Augustine in linking Jews and Judaism with witness, exile, and the unredeemed nature of the world.

> What was written of Cain was a figure of them [the Jews] . . . [T]hey should not be destroyed and . . . it adds at once: "Scatter them by thy power." For, if they had remained in one part of the earth, they would not have added their testimony to the preaching of the Gospel, which bears fruit all over the world. Therefore: "Scatter them by thy power," that . . . they do not forget, and which foretold Him whom they do not follow. (Augustine 1953: 246)

For Augustine, the degradation of Jewish exile provides an answer to a vexing question for the early Church. If the redeemer has come, then why is the world not yet redeemed? For Augustine, Jewish denial of Christ stands in the way of redemption but Jews also witness, almost despite themselves, the prefiguration of Christ's coming in God's covenant with them.

Strauss revalues Augustine's theological-political constellation by providing a *different answer* to the question of why we remain in an unredeemed world:

> The Christian assertion that the redeemer has come was always countered by our ancestors with the assertion that the redeemer has not come. One can perhaps say—and I say this without any animus—that the justification of Judaism in its fight with Christianity was supplied by the Crusades. One only has to read that history as a Jew to be satisfied with the fact that one is a Jew. (Strauss 1997a: 322)

Strauss's mild disclaimer "I say this without any animus" is an attempt to blunt what is in fact a very sharp Jewish response to Augustine's political theology: historical Christian violence against the Jews displays the lie at the heart of Christianity. Christian love is actually hatred. If the redeemer had come, such suffering born of hatred would no longer exist. It is in this sense that "[t]he Jewish people and their fate are the living witness for the absence of redemption" (ibid: 327).

Strauss's theo-political transvaluation of a key theme in Christian theology, and in Augustine's thought in particular, was not especially unique for a German Jew. Franz Rosenzweig, to whom Strauss dedicated his first book (Strauss 1997b), also plays on Augustine to upend Christian triumphalism. Note for instance Paul's words in 2 Corinthians 3:13, a central text for Augustine: "We are not like Moses, who would put a veil over his face to prevent the Israelites from seeing the end of what was passing away." Rosenzweig, whose influence on him Strauss repeatedly mentioned, transvalues the image of Jewish blindness that would later become the Christian anti-Jewish image of the blindfolded synagogue: "Is not part of the price that the Synagogue must pay for the blessing in the enjoyment of which she anticipates the whole world, namely, of being already in the Father's presence, that she must wear the bandages of unconsciousness over her eyes?" (Rosenzweig 1969: 114). While Rosenzweig emphasizes the anticipation of redemption whereas Strauss stresses the absence of redemption, both understand Jewish exile, or *galut*, as a condition that continues to upend not Jewish chosenness but Christian triumphalism.

## Martyrdom and the Seriousness of Life

Elaborating on his statement that "one only has to read that history [of the Crusades] as a Jew to be satisfied with the fact that one is a Jew," Strauss quotes Baer, whom he calls "the greatest living Jewish historian," and refers to his short book titled, appropriately, *Galut* (published first in Hebrew in 1936 and then in English translation in 1947). Let us highlight two sentences of Baer's, which are particularly important for the political theology I have been outlining in this chapter: "In this age [of the First Crusade], religious-national martyrdom reaches its highest expression. These martyrs are no seekers after death like the early Christians, no heroes challenging destiny" (Strauss 1997a: 323).

Following Baer, Strauss defines Jewish martyrdom against Christian triumphalism. And Strauss's answer to "why we remain Jews" is bound to the history of Jewish martyrdom:

> Our past, our heritage, our origin is then not misfortune, as Heine said, and still less, baseness. But suffering indeed, heroic suffering, suffering stemming from the heroic act of self-dedication of a whole nation to something which it regarded as infinitely higher than itself—in fact, which it regarded as the infinitely highest. No Jew can do anything better for himself today than to live in remembering this past. (Strauss 1997: 323)

It is important to emphasize that Strauss, following Baer, insists that he is not valorizing martyrdom. Instead, his claim is that Jewish martyrdom is witness to "the one thing needful," "righteousness and charity" (ibid: 327), discussed further in this chapter. Here we may understand that for Strauss Jewish martyrdom is witness to the absence of redemption, once again in sharp distinction to the Christian interpretation of Jesus's martyrdom as redemption itself.

Baer's account of Jewish martyrdom provides a useful lens through which to understand Strauss's critique of Schmitt in his 1932 review of *The Concept of the Political*. Strauss's critics continue not only to entangle Strauss with Schmitt but also to be especially outraged by his criticism that Schmitt's concept of the political still remains on the "horizon of liberalism" (Meier 2006: 119). But not only is this statement taken entirely out of context, it also misses what is in fact Strauss's *moral* criticism of *The Concept of the Political*. Strauss helps Schmitt understand that his critique of liberalism is predicated on "what the opponents of the political want," which is "tantamount to the establishment of a world of entertainment . . . [,] a world without *seriousness*." For this reason, Strauss maintains, affirming the political "is ultimately nothing other than the affirmation of the moral" (ibid: 117). And nothing is more serious than the morality of self-sacrifice. Schmitt remains within the horizon of liberalism for Strauss because he does *not* provide a *moral justification* for self-sacrifice, otherwise known as martyrdom. Schmitt's "political," like his "political theology" more broadly, discounts not only the importance of suffering but also its moral meaning: the absence of redemption.

The political theology of the absence of redemption, unlike political theologies tied to Christian martyrdom, does not glorify or seek suffering or death. Instead, what is important about martyrdom is its possibility. A life that cannot account for the possibility of self-sacrifice is a life that does not take life seriously. Unlike Schmitt, who cannot affirm the moral underpinnings of the political, Strauss's reference to martyrdom does precisely that. Jewish martyrdom is witness to the one thing needful in a world that remains unredeemed: righteousness and charity. Notably, with the pairing of "righteousness and charity," Strauss alludes to the Hebrew term *Tzedakah*, which means both simultaneously, though it is often translated simply as "justice." Strauss's implicit reference to *Tzedakah* further differentiates Judaism from Christianity, since the latter often posits a dichotomy between justice, understood legalistically, and charity or mercy, which are not legalistic. *Tzedakah* as righteousness and charity encompasses inter-personal as well as communal obligations.[7]

I have argued in this chapter that Strauss's statement that "[t]he Jewish people and their fate are the living witness for the absence of redemption" is a twentieth-century Jewish political theology. This political theology begins to offer an answer to the question of how Jewish faith and history still speak to us. I have done so by connecting what I have called Strauss's hesitation about decision with the absence of redemption and the state of exile. I turn now to consider three ways that the analysis offered in this part of this chapter helps us begin to do so.

First, sovereignty, along with decision, remains a hallmark of Schmitt's political theology, but sovereignty and political theology need not be inextricably tied to each other. As we have seen, the absence of redemption is a political theology of exile, not of sovereignty. Appreciating Strauss's hesitation about decision allows us to break free of Schmitt's framework, which inextricably links political theology with sovereignty. But one obvious question this argument raises is how this political theology of exile relates to Zionism. Ambivalence is the point. Strauss raises strong concerns about what he argues are deeply impoverished conceptions of Judaism and Jewishness offered by a variety of forms of Zionism (Strauss, 1997b, 5–6). Strauss in fact contends that Zionism has the capacity to annihilate what is most profound in the Jewish tradition. Still, Strauss supports some form of politically sovereign Jewish existence. For Strauss, Zionism does not negate exile but stands alongside it because Zionism and exile *both* attest to the unredeemed nature of the world. Rather than reflecting political or conceptual inconsistency or weakness, a political theology of the absence of redemption shows not just that sovereignty and political theology need not always be bound together but also that sovereignty and exile need not negate one another. In the twenty-first century, hesitation about the absolute decision for sovereignty or exile may well be the most honest and compelling response to many of today's theological-political difficulties.

Second, as briefly discussed, Schmitt's Christian triumphalism is found in his view that decision decides something inevitable, or something that has already happened. Drawing out the implications of the inevitability of decision, Agamben writes:

> Schmitt's adoption of the figure, or myth, of the Christian Epimetheus neglects an important theological legacy and resembles the status of irresponsible guilt (or innocent responsibility) that seems to define the ethical tenor of our times, and which Nazi officials, beginning with Adolf Eichmann (who declared himself guilty before God, but not before the law), consistently invoked to justify their acts. A decision that decides something always already decided, a historical act that has lost its meaning in history, can only either take responsibility for an error whose price it is not obliged to pay or discount the importance of the suffering for which it is responsible. (Agamben 2017: 462)

As Agamben shows, Schmitt's Christian triumphalism goes hand in hand with his contention that a decision has already been decided. This triumphalism eliminates human responsibility for decision because a decision that has already been decided could not have been otherwise. Schmitt's Christian triumphalism, to be sure, reflects at best a distorted Christian theology. Nevertheless, a rethinking of Christian triumphalism at the very least makes room for more robust non-Christian political theologies while also challenging anyone interested in a Christian political theology to reassess a Christian conception of time, *for the very sake of the possibility of morality*. As we have seen, at stake for Strauss in rejecting Christian triumphalism is nothing less than human freedom and moral responsibility because nothing has been decided in advance. If human beings act differently, with righteousness and charity, there may indeed be less suffering in the world. And recognizing human freedom and responsibility also means bearing witness to the significance, though not the inevitable necessity, and certainly not the desirability, of human suffering.

Third, hesitation about decision and deferral more generally do not imply standing still and doing nothing. Rather, hesitation and deferral suggest that until the messianic era, all decisions or actions are at best impermanent or provisional. Put somewhat differently, hesitation and deferral mean that we remain in the position of always beginning again. While I would not include her thought in the twentieth-century Jewish political theology of the absence of redemption described in this chapter, Hannah Arendt's musings on beginnings seem particularly apropos here. Whereas

Schmitt's sovereign makes the same already decided decision each time he decides for the friend and against the enemy, Arendt's conception of natality suggests that each provisional decision by a plurality of individuals provides a new beginning. As she puts it, "The miracle that saves the world, the realm of human affairs, from its normal, 'natural' ruin is ultimately the fact of natality, in which the faculty of action is ontologically rooted. It is, in other words, the birth of new men and the new beginning, the action they are capable of by virtue of being born" (Arendt 1958: 247). Living in the absence of redemption is living by virtue of the miracle of natality, which is "the exclusive prerogative of man; neither a beast nor a god is capable of it" (ibid: 22–23). Arendt believes that the world of beasts or the world of a god are ones below or beyond morality. An unredeemed world is a human world because it is a moral one in demanding, by virtue of its unredeemed nature, the one thing needful: Tzedakah. The future is not foreclosed in this unredeemed world; rather, the future remains open as we human creatures continue to begin again and again, in recognition that the end is not yet here.

## Disentangling Benjamin from Schmitt (Vivian Liska)

In 1930, Benjamin summed up a discussion he had with Bertolt Brecht about his relationship to Carl Schmitt: "Agreement. Hatred. Suspicion" (*GSII*:3, 1372).[8] Two insights—one affective, the other methodological—can be derived from this short, paradigmatically dialectical comment. Benjamin's approach to the German jurist is not only ambivalent in the sense of hesitant and inconclusive: it is radical and extreme, both in its polarity and its dialectic mode. This mode echoes an idea expressed most succinctly in Hegel's *Wissenschaft der Logik* (*Science of Logic*, 512): "Die wahrhafte Widerlegung muß in die Kraft des Gegners eingehen und sich in den Umkreis seiner Stärke stellen; ihn außerhalb seiner selbst anzugreifen und da Recht zu behalten, wo er nicht ist, fördert die Sache nicht." (Effective refutation must infiltrate the opponent's stronghold and meet him on his own ground; there is no point in attacking him outside his territory and claiming jurisdiction where he is not.) It is in the spirit of this idea that Benjamin entered the realm of Schmitt, came close to his thought and "stole" some of his weapons to defeat him and what he stands for.

Disentangling Strauss from Schmitt, as Leora Batnitzky has done so convincingly, yields a Jewish political theology based primarily on the notions of the "absence of redemption," "indecision," and the "seriousness of life." She focuses on Strauss's rejection of Schmitt's "Christian triumphalism" with his insistence on the Jews' ongoing suffering as evidence of the "absence of redemption," on Strauss's denunciation of Schmitt's decisionism with a demonstration of Strauss's indecision, ambivalence, and oscillation between different positions that contrast with Schmitt's resolve, and on Schmitt's critique of modernity's frivolousness and superficiality with Strauss's affirmation of the readiness for martyrdom signifying the "seriousness of life." Both Benjamin and Strauss were undoubtedly attracted to Schmitt's thought where it provides a critique of the "lightness of being" they perceived as the basic mood of the Weimar Republic. Both rejected modernity's complacency, its lack of depth, gravitas, and a sense of meaning and orientation, which they found, to some extent, in the Jewish tradition. The "absence of redemption" and its implications are also central for Benjamin, but they ultimately point in a different direction.

Benjamin's relationship with Schmitt's thought was both more intense and more antagonistic than Strauss's. Implicitly, the subliminal "dialogue" between them has been described by Agamben as "a sort of obscure chess match" (Attell 2009: 821); explicitly, Benjamin's relationship to Schmitt consisted mainly of several cross-references between the two and a very controversial, almost subservient letter from Benjamin to Schmitt.[9] I will be concerned here with the three notions at the heart of Schmitt's political theology that Benjamin has dealt with directly: sovereignty, decisionism, and the state of exception. I will, in this context, invoke Benjamin's dialectical messianism, which I will contrast with Strauss's concern about Christian triumphalism, Benjamin's call for rupture, interruption, and a "spontaneous grip" (*hurtigen Handgriff*), where it differs from Strauss's indecision and ambivalence, and Benjamin's notion of the "moment of danger" where it offsets Strauss's idea of morality and the readiness for martyrdom invoked by Batnitzky in her characterization of Strauss's relationship with Schmitt.

## Christian Triumphalism, the Absence of Redemption and the Dialectics of Messianism

The "absence of redemption" is equally essential for Benjamin as it is for Strauss. For Benjamin, however, this idea is not so much directed against "Christian triumphalism" as it is against a liberal, bourgeois contentment and illusion of harmony that is blind to injustice and political oppression. Benjamin's messianism simultaneously negates the Enlightenment belief in the autonomy of the subject. The Messiah is, for him, a force that is unpredictable and awaited, but redemption can be touched upon by humans precisely by pointing out its lack in the here and now. In this respect, Benjamin's antidote to Schmitt is revolutionary messianism.

For Schmitt, in accordance with his Catholicism, history is merely "the time that remains" (see Agamben 2005b). The end of times is kept away by the *katechon*, the "restrainer" who wards off the antichrist (embodied, among other instances, by liberal modernity) and thus also the apocalypse that would bring about the kingdom of heaven on earth. By contrast, Benjamin invokes the "fall into history" from the Book of Genesis and the Kabbalistic "breaking of the vessels," whereupon a state of perfection will only return with the coming of the Messiah. The main way of doing justice to the absence of redemption is to point to the unredeemed state of the world manifest in the reigning injustice and the "tradition of the oppressed" (*SW*4, 392/ *GS*I:2, 697). This is, for Benjamin, a socio-political fact: "As long as there still is one beggar," Benjamin writes, "there will still be myth" (*SW*2, *688/GS*VI, *208)*. Fighting the myth of mere immanence, as articulated in Benjamin's conception of "Capitalism as Religion"—thus in an already secularized version of this myth—is the task underlying Benjamin's political theology (*SW*1, 288–291/*GS*VI, 100–103).

At the heart of Batnitzky's case for Strauss's political theology is the idea that the Jewish people and their fate are the living witness for the absence of redemption. For

Benjamin, by contrast, the absence of redemption is not manifest in Jewish suffering (which is particular), but in a lack of justice (which is universal). The specificity of the Jewish people lies not in their suffering, but in their special sensibility for justice, which he derives from their messianic tradition rather than from their history of oppression. For Benjamin, "the Jewish man of letters" bears "the new social consciousness" (*GBI*, 83), which, freed of well-worn patterns of thought and ways of behaving, and in the simultaneity of close observation and critical distance, reveals an alternative to "*das Gegebene*," to the status quo of the world.

Benjamin's dialectical political theology is most explicit in his "Theologico-Political Fragment," his most overtly messianic text: "Nothing that is historical," Benjamin famously writes,

> can intend to refer to the messianic from itself out of itself. For this reason, the kingdom of God is not the telos of the historical dynamic; it cannot be established as a goal. From the standpoint of history, it is not the goal but the end. Thus the order of the profane cannot be built on the idea of the kingdom of God. (*SWIII*, 305)[10]

In his explication of Benjamin's dense text, Eric Jacobson states that "what is not under question is the firm separation between theology as a form of critical understanding and politics in its materialist realization" (Jacobson 2003: 32). Benjamin indeed depicts "messianic intensity" (*messianische Intensität*) and the "dynamics of the profane" (*Dynamis des Profanen*) in the form of two parallel arrows, the one pointing to this-worldly human happiness, the other to the kingdom of God. The arrows point in opposite directions but propel one another forward. The divine kingdom thus cannot be established through progress in history; for Benjamin its anticipation is not in a straight line with its telos. It is, instead, conceived dialectically, through the mighty detour of achieving happiness—understood primarily as justice—on earth.

For Benjamin, the Messiah cannot be brought about by human action directly. However, Benjamin, unlike Strauss, regards redemption not only as a lack but as a direction for the "right life" which consists of an attentiveness for messianic "spark[s]" (*SW4*, 391/*GSI*:2, 695) and "splinters" (*SW4*, 397/*GSI*:2, 704) that save not only the future, but also the past and above all the present—Benjamin's "now-time" (*Jetztzeit*) (*SW4*, 395/*GSI*:2, 701). These messianic fragments are embodied in worldly, everyday experiences, modes of being in the world, in various unexpected figures and dispositions ranging from Proust's *mémoire involontaire* to the ability to capture fleeting moments of insight, from the *flâneur* to the collector, from the translator to the materialist historian, from the storyteller to the last reminiscences of the dying person.

In his theses "On the Concept of History," Benjamin describes theology and its way of acting in the world in terms that clearly distinguish it from the grand scheme of a Schmittian political theology centred around divine sovereignty. In his famous first thesis, Benjamin depicts theology as a secret force hidden in a chess automaton "constructed in such a way that it could respond to every move by a chess player with a countermove that would ensure winning the game" (*SW4*, 389/*GSI*:2, 693). What ensures the player's victory is that "a little hunchbacked dwarf," who was an expert chess player, "guided the puppet's hand by means of strings." Benjamin provides his seminal *Denkbild* with a key to its riddle: "We can," he writes, "imagine a philosophic counterpart to this apparatus. The puppet, called 'historical materialism,' is to win all the time. It can easily be a match for anyone if it enlists the services of theology, which today, as we know, has become small and ugly and has to keep out of sight" (*SW*4, 389/*GS*I:2, 693).

This view of theology is, in many ways, an antidote to Schmitt's idea of sovereignty. Theology, while essential to defeating the opponent—in Benjamin's case, undoubtedly fascism and Nazism—doesn't provide authority from above, but instead is enlisted as an extraneous force that limits human empowerment, though without divesting the worldly from the possibility of intervening. The exact function of theology in this game is open to discussion, but it is a *weak* force; it does not operate out of authority but rather keeps in check the power of the autonomous subject as conceived by the Enlightenment. We can now confront Benjamin's explicit references to Schmitt's idea of sovereignty with what Benjamin himself calls this "*weak* messianic power" (*SW*4, 390/*GS*I:2, 694).

In his letter to Schmitt as well as in his book on the German *Trauerspiel*, Benjamin quotes Schmitt and expresses a debt to his notion of sovereignty. However, as others have pointed out, Benjamin is also clearly distancing himself from Schmitt (cf. Agamben 2005a: 53; and Bredekamp 1999: 261–3). For the latter, the sovereign is derived from, analogous to, or modeled on an omnipotent divinity, by endowing a human ruler with transposed (secularized) divine authority, and by granting that ruler the right and power to suspend the law at will. In contrast to Schmitt, Benjamin regards the sovereign as a thoroughly profane creature, a point he highlights in the Baroque plays, but that is also fundamentally in accordance with the Jewish tradition. Benjamin also rejects Schmitt's association of the sovereign's divine authority to suspend the law with God's arbitrary suspension of the laws of nature in miracles. In Judaism, however, biblical miracles are never arbitrary but always part of the covenantal relationship. Divine justice as presented in Benjamin's "Critique of Violence"—in its biblical example of Korach—is rooted in the Israelites' trust and thus in a mutual covenantal bond. Where for Schmitt, the sovereign is a kind of incarnation of God, Benjamin's sovereign remains creaturely and ultimately fails in the clash between his worldly power and his fallibility as a human.

Furthermore, in "Critique of Violence," Benjamin's indictment of law-instating and law-sustaining state violence is offset by a legitimate "divine violence," but he emphasizes that it is not for humans, thus not for a sovereign, to decide when and where it is applicable:

> But if, with respect to violence, its standing resource [*Bestand*] as pure, immediate violence is also secured beyond law, this proves that, and how, there is a possibility of revolutionary violence, which is the name reserved for the highest manifestation of pure violence through human beings. Not equally possible, and also less urgent for human beings is, however, the decision concerning when pure violence was realized in a particular case. For only mythic violence, not divine violence, can be recognized as such with certainty, unless it be through incomparable effects, for the de-expiating force [*Kraft*] of violence is not disclosed to human beings. (*TC*, 60/*GS*II:1, 202)

While this notion and Benjamin's use of it have often been criticized, among others by Jacques Derrida (Derrida 1992: 3–67), Benjamin insists that humans cannot use violence to decide when a concrete situation requires or justifies "divine violence": it is thus impossible in the name of God.[11]

Schmitt's political theology has attracted those who, like Benjamin and Strauss, rejected the progressive linear process of rationalization of modernity described by Max Weber. For Strauss, this idea of progress is an illusion that empties life of all meaning. For Benjamin it perpetuates the dismal status quo. Benjamin named this void "homogenous, empty time" (*SW*4, 396/*GSI*:2, 704) and called for its urgent interruption. Schmitt's sovereign decision enables such a rupture, but Benjamin, though tempted by this thought, also warns against its dangers.

There is a direct link between Benjamin's warning against deciding on "divine violence" and his relation to Schmitt's decisionism. Benjamin was attracted to Schmitt's temporality of decision that is not derived from reasoning, particularly its suddenness, which is opposed to the liberal idea of a slow, gradual reform, or to Kant's "infinite task."[12] For Benjamin, however, decision ought to come not from above but, in a revolutionary movement, from below. Benjamin's writings abound with images of abruptness—he speaks of the revolution as "pulling the emergency brakes of history" (*SW*4, 402/*GSI*, 1232), the interruption of "empty, homogenous time" in the moment of standstill, of a shock of awakening and an "abrupt departure from time of normality" (*SW*4, 395–6/*GSI*, 700–1). That Benjamin was undoubtedly tempted by the Schmittian decisive gesture linked to a political theology is nowhere more explicit than in a letter to Gershom Scholem, where Benjamin speaks of his desire "to take leave of the purely theoretical sphere . . . through religious or political conduct" (*C*, 300/*GB*III, 158–9). Hewing close to Schmitt's decisionism, Benjamin (paradoxically) explains his hesitations about joining the Communist party: He speaks of an "indispensable prerequisite that every observation of action proceed ruthlessly and with radical intent. Precisely for this reason, the task is not to decide once and for all, but to decide at every moment. But to decide! . . . My own conviction would be to proceed radically, never consistently, in the most important matters" (*C*, 300/*GB*III, 158–9). Yet even where Benjamin comes close to Schmitt's decision, he divests it of its finality and decisiveness, evoking the possibility—even the necessity—of what could be seen as the idea of a new beginning appropriate for each new circumstance.

Schmitt describes his idea of decision in terms of a radical sovereign power: "A pure, non-argued and not discussing, not self-justifying decision, thus an absolute one created out of nothing" (Schmitt 1985: 66, with my modifications).[13] Schmitt justifies his idea of sovereign decision in juridical terms: there is an inevitable inherent decision in legal matters; impartiality and the idea that a just ruling can be derived from reasoning and justification is an illusion. Schmitt makes an important point that there are indeed, in the end, arbitrary decisions even in the most legalized context. But this doesn't mean that we must affirm sovereign decisionism as a positive value in and for itself (rather than minimizing the arbitrariness).

For Benjamin, by contrast, the sovereign finds himself in a situation in which a decision is as imperative as it is impossible: The antithesis between the power of the ruler and his capacity to rule led to a feature peculiar to the trauerspiel, which can be illuminated only against the background of the theory of sovereignty. Because he is not Godlike, "the prince, who is responsible for making the decision to proclaim the state of emergency, reveals, at the first opportunity, that he is almost *incapable* of making a decision" (*OGT*, 71/*GS*I:1, 250; see also Weber 1992: 14).

## Decisionism, Ambivalence, and Attentiveness

In contrast to Strauss, Benjamin's antidote to Schmittian decisionism does not lie in indecision and ambivalence or oscillation between "Athens" and "Jerusalem," but in a dialectical "interplay" of antitheses, which Benjamin describes in relation to Kafka's writing as an "ellipsis" between Jewish tradition and "modern city dweller" (*C*, 563/*GB*VI, 110). Benjamin certainly does not embrace a Schmittian absolute decisionism. In invoking the Messiah, he admits to a force that must come from the *outside*, as well as from an interiorized, non-rational instinct that can be practiced. Ultimately, Benjamin transforms the voluntarist decision into a bodily presence of mind (*leibhaftige Geistesgegenwart*) (*OGT*, 99/*GS*IV.1, 142), which is precisely not fully willed, but instead calls for a lucidity and vigilance, an attentiveness to the danger of the concrete situation.

Another instance concerning the question of decisionism can yield significant insights into the role that Jewish tradition plays in it. Barely discussed in the abundant literature on Benjamin and Schmitt is an instance where Benjamin reads Kafka in light of the Jewish tradition, more particularly the Talmudic tradition. In his magisterial essay on the occasion of the tenth anniversary of Kafka's death, Benjamin states that Kafka's prose resembles the Haggadah in what may "appear to the reader like obsessiveness" (*kann beim Leser den Eindruck der Verstocktheit hervorrufen*). Benjamin explains the comparison in this way:

> We may remind ourselves here of the form of the Haggadah, the name Jews have given to the rabbinical stories and anecdotes that serve to explicate and confirm the teachings—the Halakhah. Like the Haggadic, the narrative parts of the Talmud, [Kafka's] books too, are stories; they are a Haggadah that constantly pauses, luxuriating in the most detailed descriptions, in the simultaneous *hope and fear* that it might encounter the Halkhik order, the doctrine itself en route. (*SW* 2, 496/*GS*II:2, 679; emphasis mine)

Benjamin calls this ambivalence between hope and fear of encountering the law "*Verzögerung*" (deferral, or postponement), and he finds in Kafka's resistance against fulfillment and completion not just "the true workings of grace"—but also, arguably, a counterforce to Schmitt's decisionism.

## The State of Exception, the Seriousness of Life, and the Moment of Danger

In *Gefährliche Beziehungen* (Dangerous Liasons), Susanne Heil writes about the commonalities between Benjamin and Schmitt: "The two thinkers shared the critique of a liberalism lacking in seriousness, extremity and depth" (Heil 1996: 10). In this respect there is thus an obvious proximity between Strauss and Benjamin. Earlier Batnitzky explains Strauss's attraction to Schmitt in terms of a shared insistence on the "seriousness of life." Disentangling Strauss from Schmitt, she associates Strauss's invective against modernity's lack of seriousness with meaningful Jewish readiness for martyrdom and morality expressed in righteousness and charity. In contrast to Strauss, Benjamin rejects martyrdom as belonging to the mythical world, hails the revolution instead of a normative morality as an expression of the "seriousness of life," and conceives of the latter as the "moment of danger" in the face of an exceptional situation, which Schmitt calls *Ernstfall* (serious case).

For Schmitt, the "seriousness of life" manifests itself in the state of exception, in which the sovereign is the one who has the power to suspend the law in a concrete situation of emergency—supposedly to maintain the law in a "moment of danger." Benjamin's text reverses the role of the sovereign in a barely noticeable turn in the argument: "Whereas the modern concept of sovereignty amounts to a supreme executive power on the part of the prince, the Baroque concept emerges from a discussion of the state of emergency, and makes it the most important function of the prince to *avert* this" (*OGT*, 65/*GSI*:1, 245; emphasis mine. See also Weber 1992). But this function could be understood as a sign that, as Benjamin writes, the *Baroque* has no eschatology, thus—contrary to his own political theology, *no possibility of redemption*. In this case the function of the *prince* and his potentially oppressive power would be what for Schmitt is embodied in *liberalism, Judaism and modernity*: for Benjamin, the figure of the *katechon*, who, as restrainer, keeps the antichrist and the apocalyptic—and ultimately salvational—end of history *away*. Benjamin's reversal of Schmittian categories is more direct in relation to what constitutes the "moment of danger." This expression, which becomes crucial for Benjamin in his "On Concept of History," written shortly before his death in 1940, in the midst of the experience of Nazi terror, is often attributed to him as first author. Schmitt, six years earlier, uses it in the most problematic context. In an article titled "Der Führer schützt das Recht," (The Führer protects the Law) published on August 1, 1934 in the *Deutsche Juristen-Zeitung*, Schmitt writes: "The Führer protects the law from the worst abuse when, *in the moment of danger*, he immediately establishes justice by virtue of his leadership as supreme judge" (Schmitt 1934: 946, emphasis mine).[14] Benjamin radically inverts this expression in his sixth thesis of "On the Concept of History": "To articulate the past historically does not mean to recognize it 'the way it really was' (Ranke). It means to seize hold of a memory as it flashes up *at a moment of danger*. Historical materialism wishes to retain that image of the past which unexpectedly appears to man singled out by history *at a moment of danger*" (*SW* 4, 391; with my modifications and emphasis).[15] Where Schmitt hails the dictatorial gesture of Hitler as the sovereign *Führer* who empowers himself by placing himself above the law, Benjamin calls on the "subject of history" to grasp an "image of the past" that "flashes by" in a desperate attempt to save it from the "heap of rubble"— the *Trümmerhaufen* (*SW*4, 392 / *GSI*:2, 698)—to which human history has been reduced, not least, one could say, by the likes of Schmitt and those who, then and now, succumb to his seductions.

## Conclusion

In the 1980s, when the ban on Schmitt was lifted by a disappointed and disoriented left in search for new anti-liberal inspiration, those who revived his reputation did so apologetically. Two decades later, both the uneasiness and the provocation had disappeared. Schmitt was no longer considered a controversial thinker of the past but an inspiration to understand the present. This "taming" of Schmitt, which turned him into a respectable source of insights occurred partly through an insistence on his proximity to widely acknowledged figures such as Benjamin and Strauss, but at the price of entangling these with all that is problematic about Schmitt. We have attempted in this chapter to distinguish between them and him. Saving Benjamin and Strauss from their purported proximity to Schmitt allows us to think of their legacies anew. Most importantly in the context of this chapter, disentangling Benjamin and Strauss from Schmitt invites us to question the legitimacy of Schmitt's towering role in the realm of political theology and to highlight these German-Jewish thinkers' contribution to a twentieth-century Jewish political theology.

## Notes

1. An important exception is the excellent article by Philipp von Wussow (Wussow 2021: 323–42).
2. For a fine overview of the Schmitt reception on the left see Amine Benabdallah (Benabdallah 2007).
3. See a discussion about Schmitt invoking these political contexts titled "Dancing with the Enemy" (Liska et al., 2021).
4. See for example Agamben's critique of Jacques Derrida's reading of Kafka's "Before the Law" where Agamben calls Derrida's attitude a "petrified and paralyzed messianism" and calls for its interruption (Agamben 1999: 171).
5. My argument builds on Sheppard's but it goes further in insisting not only, as Sheppard does, that the politics of exile shaped Strauss's intellectual development but also, and in my opinion more importantly, that Strauss puts forward a political theology of the absence of redemption the idea of which is expressed by *galut*.
6. For a brief overview of this topic see Batnitzky 2021.
7. For more on this topic, see the former Chief Rabbi of Great Britain, Jonathan Sacks 2016.
8. "Schmitt / Einverständnis, Hass, Verdächtigung." Diary entry, April 21, 1930.
9. Benjamin's letter to Schmitt has first been published in: *GSI*, 887. For the English translation, see Weber 1992: 5.
10. "Nichts Historisches [kann] von sich aus sich auf Messianisches beziehen wollen. Darum ist das Reich Gottes nicht das Telos der historischen Dynamis; es kann nicht zum Ziel gesetzt werden. Historisch gesehen ist es nicht das Ziel, sondern Ende. Darum kann die Ordnung des profanen nicht am Gedanken des Gottesreichs aufgebaut werden" (*GSII:1, 203*).
11. Brendan Moran has pointed out that, contrary to this claim, Benjamin does designate certain forms of killing, war, and punishment as "divine violence" (Moran 2018: 253).

12  See Benjamin's fragment "Zweideutigkeit des Begriffs der 'unendlichen Aufgabe' in der kantischen Schule" (*GS*VI, fr 32, 53).
13  "Eine reine, *nicht* räsonnierende und *nicht diskutierende*, sich *nicht* rechtfertigende, also aus dem *Nichts* geschaffene absolute *Entscheidung*" (Schmitt 2004: 205).
14  "Der Führer schützt das Recht vor dem schlimmsten Missbrauch, wenn er *im Augenblick der Gefahr* kraft seines Führertums als oberster Gerichtsherr unmittelbar Recht schafft."
15  "Vergangenes historisch artikulieren heißt nicht, es erkennen, 'wie es denn eigentlich gewesen ist'. Es heißt, sich einer Erinnerung bemächtigen, wie sie *im Augenblick einer Gefahr aufblitzt*. Dem historischen Materialismus geht es darum, ein Bild der Vergangenheit festzuhalten, wie es sich *im Augenblick der Gefahr* dem historischen Subjekt unversehens einstellt" (*GS*I:2, 695; with my emphasis).

# References

Agamben, G. (1999), *Potentialities: Collected Essays in Philosophy*, trans. Daniel Heller-Roazen, Stanford: Stanford University Press.

Agamben, G. (2005a), *State of Exception*, trans. Kevin Attell, Chicago: University of Chicago Press.

Agamben, G. (2005b), *The Time That Remains: A Commentary on the Letter to the Romans*, trans. Patricia Dailey, Stanford: Stanford University Press.

Agamben, G. (2017), "A Jurist Confronting Himself: Carl Schmitt's Jurisprudential Thought," in Jens Meierhenrich and Oliver Simons (eds.), *Oxford Handbook of Carl Schmitt*, 457–70, New York and Oxford: Oxford University Press.

Arendt, H. (1958), *The Human Condition*, Chicago: University of Chicago Press.

Attell, Kevin. (2009), "An Esoteric Dossier: Agamben and Derrida Read Saussure," *ELH*, 76 (4): 821–46.

Augustine (1953), *The Fathers of the Church 20*, Washington, DC: Catholic University of America Press.

Batnitzky, Leora. (2021), "Leo Strauss," in Edward N. Zalta (ed.), *The Stanford Encyclopedia of Philosophy* (Summer 2021 Edition). Available online: https://plato.stanford.edu/archives/sum2021/entries/strauss-leo/ (accessed May 22, 2023).

Benabdallah, Amine. (2007), *Une Réception de Carl Schmitt dans l'extrême gauche: La théologie politique de Giorgio Agamben*, MA diss., Institut d'Etudes Politiques de Paris, Ecole Doctorale de Sciences Po.

Bokser, B. (1983), "The Wall Separating God and Israel," *The Jewish Quarterly Review*, 73 (4): 349–74.

Bredekamp, H (1999), "From Walter Benjamin to Carl Schmitt, via Thomas Hobbes," trans. M. Thorson Hause and J. Bond, *Critical Inquiry*, 25 (2), (Winter: 1999): 261–3.

Derrida, J. (1992), "Force of Law: The Mystical Foundations of Authority," in D. Cornell, M. Rosenfeld, and D. G. Carlson (eds.), *Deconstruction and the Possibility of Justice*, trans. M. Quaintance, 3–67, London: Routledge.

Hegel, G. W. F. (2010), *Science of Logic*, trans. George Di Giovanni, Cambridge: Cambridge University Press.

Heil, S. (1996), *'Gefährliche Beziehungen': Walter Benjamin und Carl Schmitt*. Stuttgart: J. B. Metzler.

Hobbes, T. *Leviathan*, ed. Jonathan Bennett. https://www.earlymoderntexts.com/assets/pdfs/hobbes1651part1.pdf.

Jacobson, E. (2003), *Metaphysics of the Profane: The Political Theology of Walter Benjamin and Gershom Scholem*, New York: Columbia University Press.

Liska, V. et al. (2021), "Dancing with the Enemy," *Theoria Ubikoreth* [*Theory and Criticism*], 55: 227–56 (in Hebrew).

Meier, H. (2006), *Leo Strauss and the Theologico-Political Problem*, trans. Maurcus Brainard, Cambridge: Cambridge University Press.

Moran, B. (2018), *Politics of Benjamin's Kafka: Philosophy as Renegade*, London: Palgrave Macmillan.

Rosenzweig, F. (1969), *Judaism Despite Christianity: The Letters on Christianity and Judaism Between Eugen Rosenstock-Huessy and Franz Rosenzweig*, ed. Eugen Rosenstock-Huessy, Alabama: University of Alabama Press.

Sacks, J. (2016), "Tzedakah: The Untranslatable Virtue." Available online: https://rabbisacks.org/covenant-conversation/reeh/tzedakah-the-untranslatable-virtue/ (accessed May 22, 2023).

Schmitt, C. (1.8.1934), "Der Führer schützt das Recht," *Deutsche Juristen-Zeitung*.

Schmitt, C. (1985), *Political Theology: Four Chapters on the Concept of Sovereignty*, trans. George Schwab, Cambridge: The MIT Press.

Schmitt, C. (1996), *Roman Catholicism and Political Form*, trans. G. L. Ulmen, Westport: Greenwood Press.

Schmitt, C. (2004), *Politische Theologie. Vier Kapitel zur Lehre von der Souveränität*, Berlin: Duncker & Humblot.

Schmitt, C. (2008), *Constitutional Theory*, trans. and ed. J. Seitzer, Durham: Duke University Press.

Sheppard, E. (2007), *Leo Strauss and the Politics of Exile: The Making of a Political Philosopher*, Waltham: Brandeis University Press.

Strauss, L. (1997a), "Why We Remain Jews," in Kenneth Hart Green (ed.), *Jewish Philosophy and the Crisis of Modernity*, 311–56, Albany: State Unviersity of New York Press.

Strauss, L. (1997b), *Spinoza's Critique of Religion*, trans. E. M. Sinclair, Chicago: University of Chicago Press.

Vatter, M. (2021), *Living Law: Jewish Political Theology from Hermann Cohen to Hannah Arendt*, Oxford and New York: Oxford University Press.

Weber, S. (1992), "Taking Exception to Decision: Walter Benjamin and Carl Schmitt," *Diacritics*, 22 (3/4)["Commemorating Walter Benjamin"]: 5–18.

Wussow, Ph. von (2021), "Leo Strauss and Walter Benjamin: Thinking in a Moment of Danger," in Jeffrey A. Bernstein and Jade Larissa Schiff (eds.), *Leo Strauss and Contemporary Thought: Reading Strauss Outside the Lines*, 323–42, Albany, NY: State University of New York Press.

Part II

# Critique of Law and Theocracy
# Nihilism, Anarchism, and the Justice of Study

# 4

# Nihilism as World Politics

## Benjamin's Theology of Entropy

Agata Bielik-Robson

> Gibt es wirklich die Zeit, die zerstörende?
> Wann, auf dem ruhenden Berg, zerbricht sie die Burg?
> Dieses Herz, das unendlich den Göttern gehörende,
> wann vergewaltigt's der Demiurg?
> Ach, das Gespenst des Vergänglichen,
> durch den arglos Empfänglichen
> geht es, als wär es ein Rauch.
>
> Rainer Maria Rilke[1]

In my chapter, I will try to demonstrate that there is a consistent project of a political theology in Benjamin's whole *œuvre* and that it takes the form of "nihilism as world politics."

This idea originates in Benjamin's "Theological-Political Fragment," written in response to Ernst Bloch's 1918 edition of *Geist der Utopie*. It is comprised partly of praise and partly of a disguised polemic against Bloch, who gets explicitly credited for having proved the impossibility of a utopian theocracy (a compliment not at all obvious with regard to Bloch) and then tacitly trashed for his investment in the messianic "principle of hope," staked on the gradual raising of the world to the spiritual level. In my analysis of the "Fragment"—which, as I will argue, had a lasting influence on Benjamin's political thinking—I want to point to the theological elaboration of the concept of transience (*Vergängnis*), which may be read as Benjamin's own version of a "metaphysics of entropy" and the corresponding notion of a *hope in reverse*. Bloch approaches his "principle of hope"—eventually to become the title of his *opus magnum*—in a traditional manner of Jewish messianism, filtered through his appropriation of Hegel and Marx, according to which the world has an objective tendency to press toward the redemptive *telos* when spirit and matter will have found perfect reconciliation. Contrary to this, Benjamin sees the "messianic intensity" of thinkers like Bloch as a source of misfortune and unhappiness. Thus, paraphrasing Kafka, if there is hope, it is not for "us," if we imagine ourselves as the messianic agents pressing for the redemptive goal of history. It is rather a *hope in reverse*, realizing itself not in the Blochian progress of the world toward the "humanization of matter" (Bloch 2009: 232) but in the regressive downward movement of the eternal Fall, in which matter resists and counteracts the messianic agency of the spirit.[2]

## The Crimson Thread of Negation

Let's assume, for the sake of this chapter, that Scholem was right in his dating of the "Fragment." The direct crucial reference to Bloch's first edition of *The Spirit of Utopia* is a strong argument in favor of the earlier date, around 1920–2. Scholem attached great importance to the "Fragment"—perhaps because it contained in a nutshell the doctrine of antinomianism which he later attributed to the tradition of "Jewish Gnosis": what I call here a *hope in reverse* borrows retroactively from Scholem's analysis of the Sabbatian *good deed in reverse* (*mitzvah ha-ba'ah ba-averah*), which violated the law in order to satisfy the body. Also, Scholem's suggestion that the Sabbatian antinomian theology balanced on the "fine line between religion and nihilism" seems to fit perfectly well with Benjamin's vision of nihilism as a new world politics that should locate its hopes in the happiness of matter, peacefully falling to the rhythm of transience (Scholem 1991: 109). However, Adorno's testimony, dating the "Fragment" as one of the latest of Benjamin's creations, should not be easily dismissed either: many elements of this text could be read as mirroring themes which Benjamin developed only in the 1930s—most of all, in his interpretations of Kafka, Brecht, and Bachofen. In what follows, I will thus read the "Fragment" as simultaneously an early fulcrum and a late summary—that is, as a document which presents the antinomian doctrine of the liberation of matter in the most essential and condensed form.

The main argument of the "Fragment" consists in the negation of *any* link between redemption and the profane order of history:

> Only the Messiah himself completes all history, in the sense that he alone redeems, completes, creates its relation to the messianic. For this reason nothing historical can relate itself on its own account to anything Messianic. Therefore, the Kingdom of God is not the *telos* of the historical dynamic; it cannot be established as a goal. From the standpoint of history, it is not the goal but the terminus [*Ende*]. Therefore, the secular order cannot be built on the idea of the Divine Kingdom, and theocracy has no political but only a religious meaning. To have repudiated with utmost vehemence the political significance of theocracy is the cardinal merit of Bloch's *Spirit of Utopia*. (SW3, 305)[3]

According to the "Fragment," world politics, equated by Benjamin with the nihilistic pursuit of happiness, is always in blatant contradiction to the divine order. While the former's goal is "worldly restitution," that is, the full realization of the metaphysical essence of the world—the latter's goal is *restitutio in integrum*, aiming at making whole the pleroma of immortal life:

> Messianic intensity of the heart, of the inner man in isolation, passes through misfortune, as suffering. To the spiritual *restitutio in integrum*, which introduces immortality, corresponds a worldly restitution that leads to the eternity of downfall, and the rhythm of this eternally transient worldly existence, transient in its totality, in its spatial but also in its temporal totality, the rhythm of Messianic nature, is happiness. For nature is Messianic by reason of its eternal and total passing away. To strive after such passing, even for those stages of man that are nature, is the task of world politics, whose method must be called nihilism. (SW3, 305-6)

While these two metaphysical orders of restitution—of the natural world, on the one hand, and of the divine immortal pleroma, on the other—never collide, there is nonetheless a third element that insinuates itself in between the two: history. History arises as an attempt to mediate between God and Nature, but always in vain: after all, "nothing historical can relate itself on its own account to anything Messianic" (*SW3*, 305). History can do nothing to either hasten or slow down the coming of the Messiah whose advent will crown the process of the "spiritual *restitutio in integrum*." The "Fragment" may thus be seen as a variation on the Scholemian *Leben in Aufschub*, "life in deferral," in which the whole of historical time reduces to the passive awaiting of the Last Judgment, which in its "stuckness" contributes nothing to the final verdict (Scholem 1963: 73f). In Benjamin's reading, however, the condition of passive *Aufschub* is not to be overcome by a messianic politics, which would activate the so far dormant spark of the human soul. Rather, this requires the politics of global nihilism, which would undo the errancy of history and turn it back to the rhythm of transience, as the natural form of time that is not destined to accumulate, build, and reform, but simply to "decompose."[4] Nature as the "total passing away" is not to be sublated into accumulative history and subordinated to its human *telos* set on the ideal of permanence (*Dauer*). On the contrary, history must recognize itself as an error of impossible mediation and peacefully dissolve into nature, so it can now serve the metaphysical purpose of "worldly restitution."

What kind of theology could stand behind such a "nihilistic" rejection of history as nothing but a futile delay or error? The Blochian reference immediately points to Marcion, extolled by Ernst Bloch as a "great man" who truly understood the biblical archetype of Exodus, envisioning it as a historical exit from natural bondage in the hope of achieving the promised land of universal redemption.[5] Benjamin applies the Marcionite theme differently, using it, *pace* Bloch, for an anti-historical argument. While for Bloch, Marcion's merit lies in "conceptualising God as history," for Benjamin the reverse is true: *God is non-history*. He is a radically *alien God* who can never reconcile himself with the world; there is no possible bridge or mediation that could heal this absolute antithesis "in time." While Bloch takes from Marcion a dramatic Gnostic scenario of two warring principles—Creation versus Redemption—which plays itself out in historical dialectics, Benjamin takes from Marcion his rigid dualism, where God the Creator and God the Redeemer remain strictly opposed to one another, beyond any possibility of dialectical negotiation. The creaturely realm can thus be maintained only at the cost of the radical promise of immortal pleromatic life—while the realization of the latter, the proper *restitutio in integrum*, can only mean the destruction of the world as necessarily marked by mortality. The Other of the world can never return to the immortal One to form with it once again an integral whole of the Hegelian-Blochian "All-in-All." The rift is essential: the nature of the world lies in "its eternal and total passing away," while the nature of the Divine-Messianic lies in "immortality." The God of redemption—the Messiah—must thus remain radically *alien*, for no thing in this world is capable of anticipating his advent. No positive traces and no indications, however weak, can lead us toward the messianic fulfilment.

No thing can do this, but, perhaps, *nothing* can? Since the historical and the eschatological time always run in parallel, the notorious question—what to do?—cannot be answered in directly messianic terms. However, it can be answered in purely immanent and mundane terms, which are dictated by world politics conceived as political theology: not so much a global politics that should encompass the whole planet (that too), but rather the politics of the world as *ens creatum*, occupying one pole in this curious non-relation which Benjamin constructs between the Messianic and the profane. The essence of this politics, the goal of which is "worldly restitution," is nihilism, understood by Benjamin in a precise and specific way as an *affirmation of nothing*. Not nihilism as the Nietzschean loss of the ability to create and affirm values, not nihilism as the Weberian resignation in face of modern disenchantment, and not nihilism as repressive desublimation, the way it will later be understood by the members of the Frankfurt School. Benjamin's nihilism is theological and metaphysical at once: by embracing nothingness as constituting the essence of the world in "its eternal and total passing away," it allows the world to restitute itself as such, that is to realize its metaphysical essence. Thus, if Benjamin affirms the pursuit of happiness of the creaturely realm, he does so without liberal progressive hope or any historical investment in the melioration of social reality. Happiness is not an elusive *telos* of history striving to realize the ideal of justice, but an affirmation of the constitutive nothing that manifests itself in the creaturely rhythm of transience, not to be condemned but embraced in the natural attunement to the world of *flux* and finitude.

About fifteen years later (if we stick to the early dating of the "Fragment"), in his 1935 piece on "Johann Jakob Bachofen," Benjamin will ascribe this "nihilistic" approach to communism.[6] The Bachofen essay reveals Benjamin's communist sympathies at this point as deriving less from his studies of Marx than from his fascination with the archaic world of the *Mutterrecht*, where the primordial communist society lived in a blissful attunement with the flow of living and dying, which, according to the Swiss anthropologist, perfectly matched the Ovidian description of the Golden Age as *sponte sua, sine lege*, "spontaneous and lawless." For Benjamin, communism opposes progressive liberalism precisely in abandoning all illusions of "spiritual progress" and in the realization of nihilism as the politics perfectly attuned to the created, finite, radically non-divine world. Clearly preferring Bachofen's vision of libidinal communism to the Marxist (after all, progressive) version, Benjamin praises the "prophetic side of Bachofen" (*SW*3, 12), which manifested itself in his growing influence on both right-wing (Ludwig Klages) and left-wing (Friedrich Engels) radical theories of social utopia.[7] He feels attracted by the Bachofenian primal world of hetaerical fluidity or "general promiscuity," where all things enter into "ephemeral constellations," based on the idea of free love and loosely choreographed by the rhythm of transience, which constitutes the only rule of "that entire creation" (best depicted by Hieronymus Bosch in his *Garden of Earthly Delights*). In this happy world, deprived of rigid dualisms, life and death do not form an opposition either; they commingle in a fluid relationship:

> Hence the formulation *die unbeweinte Schöpfung*, which defies all translation— *creation whose vanishing calls forth no lament*. It arises from matter itself—but the word *Stoff* [matter, stuff] suggests tufted, dense, gathered material. It is the agent of the general promiscuity which characterized the most ancient human community, with its hetaerical constitution. And from this promiscuity not even life and death were exempt; *they commingled in ephemeral constellations according to the rhythm which governed that entire creation*. Thus, in that immemorial order, death in no way suggests a violent destruction. (*SW3*, 13-14; emphasis added)⁸

In Bachofen's rendering of the Golden Age, death is not a misfortune to be lamented. As the negation of a separate life, it is a welcome event that fulfils the more primordial wish to return to the womb/tomb, which undoes the error of fragmentation and restitutes "the entire creation" to its wholeness. While "messianic intensity" characterizes the subject with its separate dimension of inwardness—"the inner man in isolation"—the rhythm of transience encompasses the whole as one creation destined to "pass away." Yet this "downfall" should not be conceived in the tragic mode of *Untergehen*, "going-under," which would "call forth a lament": this is how it is perceived by the "inner man," who suffers because of his painful desire for immortality. The "passing away" can also be blissful, as long as it isn't disturbed by impossible longings, originating in a futile rebellion against the preestablished conditions of creaturely finitude: "For in happiness all that is earthly seeks its downfall and only in good fortune is its downfall destined to find it" (*SW3*, 306).

Transience is the main theme of the "Fragment," as it is the *thema regium* of the Weimar "theology of crisis" (*Krisetheologie*), which re-awakened the Marcionite dualistic gnosis after centuries of repression and its "Hegelian" slumber. According to Karl Barth, the true *kerygma* or revelatory message of Christianity is a non-negotiable Not thrown against the worldly condition of flesh, fall, and sin, which can manifest itself in the world only as a "crimson thread" of its inner negation/ nihilization, or creaturely transience (*Vergängnis*):

> The most radical ending of history, the negation under which all flesh stands, the absolute judgment, which is the meaning of God for the world of men and time and things, is *also* the crimson thread which runs through the whole course of the world in its inevitability . . . No road to the eternal meaning of the created world has ever existed, save the road of negation. This is the lesson of history. (Barth 1968: 77; 87; emphasis added)

Thus, while "the old world [is] a completely closed circle from which we have no means of escape" (Barth 1968: 187), and no messianic striving can ever make possible an Exodus out of the "iron cage," the only possible means to help the world conform to the justice of the absolute judgment is to hasten its end: to facilitate the negation which is already operative in the domain of flesh as its inherent *Vergängnis*. The lesson of history, therefore, is not a Hegelian-Blochian *telos* in which matter will rise to the sublime heights of the Spirit—after all, "the smell of death reaches to the highest and most sublime realms of human activity" (Taubes 1954: 236–37)—but a message contained in the very negativity of finite material existence. Not only is it not to be counteracted by the messianic intensity of striving toward an improved—ultimately immortal—way of being, but must be assisted and enhanced as the only element of the profane order that is capable of maintaining a relation with the transcendent one: transience as the immanent likeness and image of the Grand No.[9]

Just like Marcion in the second century and Karl Barth in the twentieth in their respective commentaries on Paul's *Epistle to Romans*, Benjamin also refers to Paul's famous saying on the fleeting figure of the world ("For this world in its present form is passing away," 1 Cor. 7:31), which he interprets as the spontaneous movement of being left to its own devices. It is in the nature of the world to pass, to fade away, to dissolve into nothing.[10] In Paul, as well as in his commentators throughout the ages, this is not necessarily a damning sentence on the world's worthlessness: it is rather a matter-of-fact diagnosis which perceives profane existence as inescapably finite. Even in Barth, who comes the closest to the Gnostic condemnation of matter as evil, it is precisely transience which links immanence to transcendence by the "crimson thread": if there is a divine signature here on earth, it is not in its beauty and glory, but in the negation paving its way through created nature. Benjamin takes on the Barthian motif and gives it an unexpected Bachofenian twist. The self-nihilating tendency, due to which the created world is not made to last, should not be disturbed by pseudo-messianic efforts to raise it (*steigern*) to a higher and more durable mode of existence, but rather "assisted" as the only possible relation between the worldly and the Messianic: "the order of the profane assists, *through being profane*, the coming of the Messianic Kingdom" (*SW*3, 305; emphasis added). When Benjamin writes that "*nothing* historical can relate itself on its own account to anything Messianic," we should thus read it literally: if there is a relation, it lies precisely in *nothing*, in the self-neantizing rhythm of transience that governs the entire creation. Hence, the only conceivable function of world politics is to *let the world go*—let it dissolve into transience, which is its metaphysical destiny. "The order of the profane should be erected on the idea of happiness" (*SW*3, 305), writes Benjamin in reference to Aristotle's definition of politics as realizing the desire of all men to be happy,[11] but it is only from the perspective of "messianic intensity" that "the quest of free humanity for happiness runs counter to the messianic direction." In fact, when seen not from the "heart" of the "inner man," but from the body dancing to the rhythm of transience, these two orders assist one another in fulfilling their respective "restitutions": "But just as a force, by virtue of the path it is moving along, can augment another force on the opposite path, so the secular order—because of its nature as secular—promotes the coming of the Messianic Kingdom" (*SW*, 305). Happiness is a state of a true wholeness, a reintegration in which the world realizes its essence of the "eternal downfall" and thus, through its immanent self-negation, "increases" and enhances the force of the Grand No of the messianic order with which it has *nothing* in common.

The true task of world politics, therefore, would be *not* to oppose transience by introducing a mirage of immortality or the Hegelian "objectivity and permanence" (Hegel 1977: 118) as the goal of historical striving, but to go with the flow, expose and embrace the "nothing" which underlies all creaturely *hevel* [vanity]. The only conceivable permanence here is the eternal passing away as the never-ending night of *sacred entropy* which political theology must endorse by adjusting to its rhythm.[12] Now, the crucial point is to conceive correctly the seemingly oxymoronic phrase: "eternity of downfall." Does it refer to the Greek notion of eternity of *physis* as immutable in its perennial mutability, stabilizing becoming in the endless cycle of *genesis kai phthora*? Or does it rather indicate the metaphysical truth of all material nature as essentially born ready to die, with an emphasis on the "downfall"? If we follow the latter conjecture, nature itself would not have to be eternal as in the Greek cosmology; it could just as well end at one point in natural history, the way it was envisaged by Karl Barth. So, perhaps, there is hope in the idea of nature's easeful passing away, bringing about an end to the eternal cycle of "becoming and perishing"? A hope that it may find "good fortune" precisely in its downfall, disturb the balance of growth and decay, by augmenting the latter and, in this manner, finally *end*? By rejecting the Hegelian dialectical scheme of gradually mending the world by ascending to spiritual heights (history of progress as one way of escaping the cycle), and instead investing in the radical nihilization of the profane order, Benjamin offers a new notion of the Fall, as well as a new notion of hope. The lucky downfall, mimicking (and simultaneously mocking) the Christian-Augustinian concept of *felix lapsus* or "fortunate fall," does not indicate a chance to rise again and regain a spiritual perfection that would be higher than in the prelapsarian state. It indicates, rather, a transience taken to the second power, quickened and enabled, which would complete the Fall and quietly dissolve the world into nothing. In Barth, there is still a vengeful apocalyptic expectation that this world will end with a bang: the botched enterprise of being will go down in fire and suffering, when confronted with the "holy terror" of the intervening Parousia. None of this is detectable in Benjamin. More consistent with Barth's own conviction that "the old world [is] a completely closed circle from which we have no means of escape" (Barth 1968: 187), Benjamin can only imagine the passing away of the whole world as its internal affair of immanent negation in which the entropic tendency of all being is gently "assisted" in order to finally realize the Fall: the "worldly restitution" is the ultimate completion of *felix lapsus*. The only hope, therefore, which the worldly beings can harbor, lies in the active "seeking [of their] downfall."[13]

## "The Quest of Free Matter for Happiness": *Plumpes Denken*

The focus on happiness as perfectly attuned to the "rhythm of transience"—the happy cadence of the material creation as always already falling—brings to mind not only Bachofen and his "nihilistic" vision of archaic communism but also another distant voice from the Marcionite era: Basilides. It is a cardinal merit of Giorgio Agamben to have spotted in Benjamin's "Fragment" an echo of the Basilidian teachings, which went against the mainstream of Alexandrian Gnosticism by taking the side of "tormented matter" (Agamben 2004: 90).[14] While the majority of the Gnostics, Marcion included, supported the interests of the Spirit (*pneuma*) against the material world (*hyle*), in which they saw the main source of evil and oppression, Basilides inverted this tendency and challenged Spirit as the cruel "persecutor of matter" that needs to be brought to metaphysical justice. In Basilides, as if inverting the Marcionite narrative, Spirit invades Matter from the outside, as an alien and parasitic *life-form* which creates havoc in the hitherto peaceful material nature. It disturbs its profane order, by pushing all natural beings out of joint and forcing them to want things which they do not possess and which do not lie in their natures. Basilides calls this artificial and perverse force a *desire*. In his commentary on Paul's *Epistle to Romans* (yet another among those already mentioned), he claims that it is precisely due to the desire imbued by Spirit that "fish strive to graze on the hills with the sheep" (Agamben 2004: 90), while human being, *a fortiori*, begins to long for immortality and "becoming like gods." Spirit, therefore, not only does not help the material world to achieve its redemption; even if it wished to perfect Matter, *pneuma*, being so tragically incompatible with *hyle*, can merely colonize it, disturb its natural rhythm, and make it deeply and irredeemably unhappy. The only solution, therefore, is to separate the two alien principles: to make Spirit go back to where it came from—the restored pleroma of the immortal Great Life—and to leave Matter alone to its own intrinsic and self-nihilating rhythm of happiness, which is perpetual downfall and transience. The "unlucky" complicity of spirit and matter must be broken, so they both can realize their own paths toward *restitutio*. Matter, therefore, must be abandoned to *ex-piration* as the very opposite of *in-spiration*: it must give out the Spirit, as one gives out the last breath, and quietly return to its own way of being, which, because of its perfect attunement to the rhythm of passing away, is indistinguishable from the entropic element of always already *dying*. The state in which Matter is abandoned to itself is called by Basilides "Great Mercy," as well as "Great Ignorance": since Matter is irreparable, it can only be mercifully left in peace, unbothered by the knowledge of alien spiritual affairs and their unhelpful "messianic intensities."[15] The Basilidian motif of *messianic separation*, the goal of which is to disable Spirit's parasitic preying upon Matter, underlies the whole of Benjamin's "Fragment": the principle of Matter is represented by the "order of the profane," while the principle of Spirit is called "messianic intensity." The former is "erected on the idea of happiness," while the latter "passes through misfortune, as suffering." Nature cannot be redeemed, but it can nonetheless "assist, through being profane, the coming of the Messianic Kingdom." Benjamin calls it "the quietest approach," *ein leisestes Nahen* (*SW*3, 306) of the messianic realm: though we can do nothing to provoke the advent of the Kingdom directly, we can help nature in its spontaneous tendency toward self-neantization, as the fulfilment of its true metaphysical essence, no longer bothered by the alien desire of Spirit. Just like Basilides, who believed that nature's eternity of the cycle is only relative and, when no longer bothered by Spirit, Matter will eventually succumb to its entropic destiny, Benjamin also stakes his hopes on the world peacefully dissolving into nothingness. The Messianic Kingdom is not its goal, but we can still make it possible, by simply *letting the world end*: when it all expires without trace—and all matter evaporates, fallen into the absolute coldness of the finally realized maximum of entropy—then the Messiah can set in, precisely as no longer needed or expected.[16]

Thus, if nature is here called messianic, it is only due to its indirect and oblique relation to the Kingdom; the more easily it passes away, according to its inherent *principle of entropia*, the sooner the Messiah's *utopia* is to be fulfilled, but—*pace* Bloch—there is no *spirit of utopia* or *principle of hope* operative in the immanent world. The deeper the Fall of the profane order, the higher the chance of the Messianic coming, which not only will not crown the "historical dynamic," but close it once and for all as a fully separate and finished chapter—*not* to be continued. The "storm blowing from Paradise" (*SW*4, 392), falsely called progress, can only be stilled by *ein leisestes Nahen*, the least obtrusive approach.[17]

Benjamin's theology of entropy fits well with the antinomian rule—*the worse, the better* (or, in Hölderlinian terms: "where there is danger, there grows the chance of salvation").[18] This rule is as old as the Jewish-messianic tradition, which, since the Talmud, acknowledges the strict connection between the depth of the fall and the approaching "birth pangs of the Messiah."[19] Yet, the difference between the violent advent of the Kingdom, dreaded by the rabbis, and Benjamin's "quietest approach" lies in the disparate way in which they perceive the apocalyptic finale. The Talmudic tradition, continued by Scholem, sees it as an inescapably vehement event, full of "messianic intensity," "misfortune and suffering"—while Benjamin conceives of it as a quiet end of history, in which material nature, finally left to its own mortal devices, will happily accept its truth in time, decay and death, and will terminate silently, without cries of protest; even more, blissfully. The night of nature will thus be saved as precisely the unsavable, that is, saved from the messianic Spirit and its misguided efforts to redeem Matter; saved from any desire for salvation.

The "Fragment" could thus be the first (or the last, depending on the dating) exercise in Benjamin's project of *plumpes Denken*, formulated by him in his review of Brecht's *Dreigroschenroman*: a rough kind of thinking, attuned to material needs as separate from false desires, and guided by the Basilidian rule according to which nothing may long after anything contrary to nature and thus suffer pain.[20] To Bertolt Brecht's deliberate crudeness of *erst Fressen!* Benjamin cannot help but add a theological dimension. It is the voice of liberated matter, free at last from the violations of Spirit, for the first time speaking out and for itself, plump and not at all subtle: "the word *Stoff* suggests tufted, dense, gathered material" (*SW*3, 13). In the "Fragment," therefore, Benjamin prophesizes the Basilidian take on the end of history as it will soon be envisaged by Alexandre Kojève: not as the proud Hegelian *telos* of *Heilsgeschichte*, in which Spirit finally paves the way toward the ultimate idealization of matter, but just the *end* in which humankind, led by nihilistic world politics—renamed by Michel Foucault and Giorgio Agamben as biopolitics—abandons history as a failed project and sinks back into animal rhythm of transience, spun between birth and death and devoid of any aura of immortality. Instead of the misguided spiritual striving for a more sublime—permanent, immortal—form of life, the messianic nihilism actively "strive[s] for such a passing away—even the passing away of those stages of man that are nature" (*SW*3, 306). It is not just a question of tolerating those stages as impediments that pose resistance to the project of spiritual reform of the world and human life. When Benjamin announces in "World and Time" that his "definition of politics [is] the fulfillment of an unimproved humanity" (*SW*1, 226), he does not mean a practice of condescending to the imperfect or the deficient: *die Erfüllung der ungesteigerten Menschhaftigkeit* indicates an autarchy of those *Stufen* of being-human which do not participate in any ascension (*Steigerung*) toward self-improvement. The idea is indeed quite revolutionary: those stages in which matter reveals its essential irreparability (*Ungesteigertheit*) are to be actively sought out and enhanced. What formerly, from the spiritual point of view, appeared as death, loss, and ruin—the destructive effects of time defying our desire for permanence—now should appear as a *rhythm*: an undisturbed flow of time, structured precisely as the *flux* and shaking off of all stable forms.

In Benjamin's "Fragment," the idea of happiness is strongly linked to the concept of the happy fall, *felix lapsus*: the downfall is like falling in love—a free-fall in free love. The orgiastic element is signaled here by "the quietest approach": an implicit praise of physical love and its orgasmic happiness which is the most fleeting of all experiences and totally resists any attempt to make it permanent. Orgasm, *le petit mort*, cannot last: it is the very opposite of the Hegelian "objectivity and permanence," which can be gained only through "fleetingness staved off."[21] It is the epitome of the "ephemeral constellation" (*SW3*, 14) in which happiness is indistinguishable from as-if-dying, passing away in the Pauline *hos me* manner, absolute expenditure, exhaustion, abandon. To accept and enhance this "stage"—the orgasmic passing moment of sexual climax without lasting commitments, focused solely on the *transe of transience*—means to be able to love time: to love the way it brings joy in order to momentarily take it away. Martin Hägglund calls such attitude a *chronophilia*: a happy recognition that we are capable of loving only what is destined to pass. Time, the Rilkean Demiurge of this world, gives and takes away, all in one instant—and love can cherish only what exists in transience. In our aching hearts, filled with messianic intensity, we inevitably grow a strain of *chronophobia*, striving to make our object of love eternal, but this "habit of the heart" goes against the very nature of love and its central experience of "little death." In wishing to make love permanent, we kill love itself.[22]

In Saint Augustine, the paradigmatic *chronophobe*, the heart is the center of a "noble desire" which longs for what is most denied to man on earth—immortality—and, as such, constitutes the paradigmatic Basilidian longing to be something totally other than we are here and now, that is, finite: the Augustinian heart will not rest in its "messianic intensity" until it rests with God, *inquietum est cor nostrum donec requiescat in te*.[23] Benjamin contests Augustine's restless desire for immortality as the opposite of natural "good fortune": he wants the heart, in which spirit and matter come into a confused clash, to dissolve, so they can become once again separate. Contrary to those theologians, from Augustine to Hegel, who claimed that, in this way or another, *finitum capax infiniti*—the finite being can carry the infinite—Benjamin sides with thinkers of the opposite conviction, Karl Barth included: *finitum non capax infiniti*. *Erlösung*, therefore, is most of all a *Lösung*—a dissolution of the heart-knot and separation of the two incompatible elements which, when colliding, only create pain of the "living contradiction" (Hegel 1969: 770).

The loss of aura, therefore, which used to surround mortal things with the halo of eternity and, as Benjamin states quoting Hegel, "strips away the 'semblance and deception of this false, transient world' from the 'true content of phenomena'" (*SW3*, 127) is *not* be deplored. All that matters is joining the stream of finitude in "the time that remains," in which human life can still undo the error of the intense desire for immortality, planted in the heart of the "inner man," untie the knot of misery, in which the alien Spirit entered into an unhappy relation with the body, and pull the brake on the errancy of history, led by a false promise of the spiritualization of matter.[24] If such simplified *plumpes Leben* is eventually to achieve its inherent form of life, it will no longer be opposed to the transient nature of time: it won't be a Platonic form imposed as a lasting paradigm on the passing matter, but a plastic shape made out of the rhythm itself, the rhythmic-choreographic figure incipient to the material element of *Khora* which, for Plato, constituted merely an amorphic chaos, capable only of passive reception of the forms impressed on it from the above. *Pace* the whole history of Western philosophy, which based its understanding of *morphe* on the Platonic notion of eternal and purely spiritual paradigms, Benjamin perceives the fluid hetaeric element of matter as imbued with its own morphic capacity, engendering a *khoragraphic* transic dance to the rhythm of transience. Paraphrasing Paul's saying from 1 Cor. 7:31 on the figure of the world passing away, we could thus say that Benjamin's *morphe* of the natural world of matter resides precisely *in* its passing away: not in the opposition to the transient finitude, but in its full unequivocal embracement. It is thus only when we give up the Platonic dualism of form and matter—where the former is exposed to the destructive influence of the latter as plunging eternity into the decay of temporal existence—that we will be able to see that the transience is not an enemy of *morphe*, but possesses its own spontaneous rhythmic form of self-organization which, as Benjamin notes in his essay on Bachofen, "arises from matter itself" (*SW3*, 13).[25]

The main stake of this "Basilidian" political-theological project—and simultaneously the only criterion of its success—is to make pain go away. *No aura, no cry*—the truly *unbeweinte Schöpfung* as the theological matrix of *die ungesteigerte Menschhaftigkeit* can now do totally without the Hegelian pain as "the living contradiction," in which the infinite clashes with the finite, as well as without the Lévinasian arrows of radical alterity, painfully stuck in the flesh and goading it against its natural inertia.[26] The Hegelian "pain" is precisely what Kafka, in his parable on Hunter Gracchus, calls *das Unglück*: the misfortune which befalls an essentially happy human animal—"gladly living and gladly dying," that is perfectly attuned to the natural rhythm of transience[27]— who suddenly gets derailed and sent on the waters of endless drifting or "the errancy of history." The only way to undo the "mishap" is to restitute the *felix lapsus* as the happy orgiastic free-falling of all flesh as playing to the rhythm of the hetaeric fluidity and general promiscuity of all things. Benjamin finds the glimpses of this happier solution both in Bachofen's description of the matriarchal arche-communism and in Kafka's depiction of *die Vorwelt* as the "swamp world" (*SW2*, 808), preceding the history which began with the act of creation, when the Spirit hovering over the waters descended upon the *tohu va-vohu* in order to turn it into a solid hard ground. While the heart of the "inner man" knows nothing but permanent suffering, because he cannot forget that he is going to die (*memento mori*), the *vorweltlich, pre-creational* realm of matter is the source of infinite pleasure—Gracchus's "gladness"—because it is immersed in the dark watery element of oblivion (*Vergessenheit*). *Vergängnis*, therefore, must be coupled with *Vergessenheit*; it is precisely the merciful oblivion or the Basilidian Great

Ignorance that allows each and every material creature to *enjoy* the way of all flesh, experienced not as a destructive transience but as a rhythmic flow.

## Sacred Entropy: "The Great Process of Decomposition"

In one of his 1923 letters to Florens Christian Rang, Benjamin introduces yet another concept belonging to the orbit of his "Basilidian" political theology: *die gerettete Nacht*, the "night preserved."[28] While referring to the Hölderlinian figure of *die Nacht der Erde*, the night of the world deserted by gods, Benjamin's phrase gives it an ambivalent spin: what the romantic *topos* presents as abandonment and a hopeless plunge into *Weltdämmerung*, becomes, in Benjamin's elaboration, a fortuitous escape from too much of the light—the blinding light of revelation—which would make the life of nocturnal beings on earth impossible. Their ontological weakness demands that they are left alone in the benign darkness as the natural element of their "nihilistic" constitution: *die gerettete Nacht*, therefore, denotes the world of nature as a closed system of immanence, which should be preserved precisely as such—*verschlossen*, hermetic and isolated, made immune to the intrusions of the spirit. Agamben's reading of Benjamin's "night preserved" brings forward the implicit Basilidian touch: *die gerettete Nacht* is the Night of Matter liberated from the torments and terrors of the Spirit and veiled by the Great Ignorance:

> Here nature, as the world of closedness [*Verschlossenheit*] and of the night, is opposed to history as the sphere of revelation [*Offenbarung*] ... The "saved night" is the name of this nature that has been given back to itself, whose character, according to another of Benjamin's fragments, is transience and whose rhythm is beatitude ... The saved night is a *relationship with something unsavable*. (Agamben 2004: 81–2; emphasis added)

For Agamben, who reads Benjamin as the "modern Basilidian" (as if in a polemic with Taubes's description of him as a "modern Marcionite" [Taubes 2006]), the choice between the closed immanence of nature and the open futurity of history should be decided for the sake of the former: human beings must give up on the "interminable errancy—history" (Agamben 2016: 272) as the false adventure of "messianic intensity" and instead choose the immanence of nature, that is come to terms with something essentially and fundamentally irreparable, which can exist only as falling and failing. For the inhabitants of the Night, to be is also always to not be; the Pauline derealizing *hos me* (as if not) is inscribed into their mode of (non)being.

Given the astonishing career of Gnostic literature in the Weimar era, it should not surprise us that all those motifs—Marcionite versus Basilidian—reappear in Benjamin in a modernized form. It is even less surprising if we consider that the old Basilidian motif of the self-expiration of the world of Matter lends itself as a perfect canvas for metaphysical speculations on the newly discovered law of entropy as the energetic deterioration of a closed physical system that would eventually lead to the thermal death of the universe. The key to this new sense of doom is precisely the "closedness,"

*Verschlossenheit*, which reverberates in Barth's description of the world as "the completely closed circle from which we have no means of escape" (Barth 1968: 187), as well as in Benjamin's letter to Rang on the closed night of creation and, subsequently, in Taubes's Weberian portrayal of the modern disenchanted universe as an "iron cage."[29] From the second half of the nineteenth century onward, Western thought stands under this new terrifying principle, which only intensifies the already long shadow thrown on it by Arthur Schopenhauer: from the seed planted by Carnot, Kelvin, Clausius, and Helmholtz, there grows a dark vision prophesying a final doom of the whole material universe. If the cosmos is not infinite, but finite, then, perhaps, the same rule of the degenerating isolated system applies to the totality of being which, someday in the remote future, will also grow cold and dissipate, thus extinguishing all more complex energetic systems—most of all, life.

There is practically no thinker who would not comment, openly or implicitly, on what became immediately dubbed as *Naturdämmerung*: "the twilight of nature" revealing the benighted condition of all material being. Ernst Bloch's *Spirit of Utopia* is a paradigmatic response to the anti-spirit of *entropia* in its passionate defence of "messianic intensity": for Bloch (as for Rilke), who interprets entropy in purely Gnostic terms, it is the very signature of the evil Demiurge ruling over the creaturely realm. When narrating about the Janus-faced modernity, torn between the horrors of the entropic real and the messianic hope for an Exodus out of the iron cage of the closed physical system destined to die, Bloch insists on keeping "a different order of wisdom than the one that describes a cycle of universal cooling, a new flare-up, and another phase of cooling—a carousel of entropy and anti-entropy from which mechanical philosophy draws its final conclusion" (Bloch 1998: 313).[30] If Benjamin has his own response to the "carousel of entropy and anti-entropy"—which may indeed underly his notion of myth as based on the closed system of becoming and perishing, coming into force for the first time in "Toward the Critique of Violence"[31]—it is very different than Bloch's new wisdom.

In *The Messianic Reduction*, Peter Fenves claims that Benjamin was very attentive to the scientific discoveries of his time and reacted to them vividly in his writings (Fenves 2011: 12–13).[32] Fenves does not mention the discovery of the second law of thermodynamics, but would it be farfetched to read the "Fragment" as a theological elaboration of the concept of the transience (*Vergängnis*)—that is, as Benjamin's own version of the "metaphysics of entropy"? The term—*die Metaphysik der Entropie*—has been applied recently to a thinker who could have influenced, directly or indirectly, Benjamin's intuitions, namely Philip Mainländer: an avid reader of Schopenhauer, he was probably the first philosophical theologian to reflect on—and eagerly embrace—the hypothesis of the thermal death of the universe.[33] According to Mainländer, transience, which runs through the whole of nature, should not be resisted, but hastened, since it is an expression of the passage of God himself moving from being to nothingness. Once this passage is complete and the sacred entropy runs its course, the world and God alike will have found their redemption (*Erlösung*) in being liberated from the error of becoming. What Barth will later call "the lesson of history" is already here, in Mainländer's *Philosophie der Erlösung* (1876), a negative knowledge (*gnosis*) about the error of creation, which should never be repeated. It is not enough to replace it with a

New Creation—as the Book of Revelation promises, making the Lamb say: "Behold, I make all things new!" (Revelation 21:5). Creation *as such* is an irreparable mistake/mishap which must be undone once and for good (*Ungeschehenmachen*), so God can "restitute" his wholeness in the pleroma of non-existence.

But why this torturous detour, which can confirm the superiority of nothingness only through the Fall into being? God, conceived by Mainländer as *Überwesen*, originally willed Nothing, but in the "simple simplicity" of his primordial state could *not* not become: his nature contained a necessity to be. The world, which had resulted from this compulsion to be, is an unfortunate realization of the original obstacle (*Hindernis*), but also a means to the end of nonbeing (*Nichtsein*) and, in fact, the only possible means to this end: it simply must run its course, expire, and thus finally extinguish the divine *Seinszwang*. In Mainländer's system, it is a role of the human being to acquire this higher knowledge and achieve "the culminating point in one's development, when our striving after destruction [*Strebung nach Vernichtung*] will be fulfilled" (Mainländer 1989: 49). But, unlike Schopenhauer, who advocated a Buddhist *ascesis*, Mainländer sees this *gnosis* as liberating and joyful. In a passage closely resembling Benjamin's musings on Bachofen, he reveals himself as a partisan of a happy communist state which will have abolished all laws and allow for a free exercise of *Lebenskräfte*, including free love, so the vital force can be spent as quickly as possible:

> My philosophy looks at the ideal state, at communism and free love, and teaches to a free, no longer suffering people the message of the death of humanity [*der Tod der Menschheit*] . . . This death will be followed by the death of the whole organic life on our planet . . . And then God will have finally crossed the path from his Over-being, through his Becoming, to his Not-being; he will have found through the process of the world [*Weltprozess*] what he, hindered by his original essence, could not have achieved immediately: the non-existence [*Nichtsein*] . . . the absolute *nihil negativum*. (Mainländer 1989: 93–6)

Benjamin's messianic calculation of the *Pfeilrichtungen* (arrow directions) of forces, which ultimately cooperate despite their seemingly disparate directions, is also confirmed by Mainländer: "the more strongly one wills life, the more quickly will the vital power be exhausted and the non-being be achieved" (Mainländer 1989: 121). *Wille zum Leben* is thus only a thin mask of *Wille zum Tode*, but Mainländer does not want to unmask it: when a philosopher learns about the futility of his will to live, his heart becomes heavy and unhappy. Then, instead of spending the living force, he becomes an ascetic, who unwillingly slows down the entropic process of the world's self-destruction. But when relieved of this burden, he throws himself into the rhythm of transience and thus contributes to the universal *Schwächung der Kraftsumme* (weakening of the sum of energy) that restitutes the world to its proper function, which is to facilitate the process of the divine *restitutio in integrum*. The coming communist state—"the city of eternal peace, Nirvana, the new Jerusalem" (Mainländer 1989: 153)—is envisaged by Mainländer as an avant-garde of the creation, a fulcrum of the happy Fall which, as if in the inverted Augustinian narrative, is to be followed by all nature.[34]

With this idea applied to Benjamin's "Fragment," his insistence on the indirectly messianic role of "nihilism as world politics" becomes strikingly clear. While the material world can never raise itself (*steigern*) to a messianic perfection, it can nonetheless play a crucial role in fostering the process of the divine sinking (*Untergehen*), the goal of which is the ultimate *Ruhe* or the Shabbat of the nirvanic *Nichtsein*, never again to be bothered by the flawed desire to create. The sacred entropy becomes thus an indirect means to a redemptive end: it is a "rhythm" that must be obeyed and by no means disturbed by "messianic intensity," wanting perfection from the essentially flawed being. Although the empty time of the natural realm, with its monotonous clockwork beat, cannot ever coincide with the fullness of the messianic time, it can nonetheless help the latter to arrive; it is precisely in the ultimate realization of its emptiness—the fact that it constitutes *nothing*—that it reveals the worldly time as the Rilkean *Zeit, die zerstörende* or the time of decay. For this deeply negative Gnostic line—from Basilides, through Schopenhauer and Mainländer, to Benjamin and Agamben—the fullness of *restitutio in integrum* remains a strictly *meontological* concept: it can be attributed solely to the pleroma of non-existence, never to the worldly realm of being.

With Benjamin, therefore, biopolitics—the new science of those dark "transformations taking place in that great flowing stream of human physicality" (*SW1*, 230)—acquires its own political theology. Very different from the original Schmittian theological justification of political sovereignty, and its later avatar in the concept of the *katechon* as the "restrainer of the apocalypse,"[35] it also goes against the grain of the messianic theopolitics of such thinkers as Landauer, Buber, Bloch, and Taubes. Neither an apocalypse from above, nor an apocalypse from below, Benjamin's "quietest approach" brings a vision of an end as always already inscribed in the world's "eternal downfall" and tying it by a "crimson thread of negation" (Barth 1968: 77) or "a great process of decomposition" (*SW1*, 226) to the otherwise non-approachable transcendence. The goal of the new "nihilistic world politics" is thus nothing but happiness, or rather, *nothing as happiness*: a blissful *trance of transience*, which gives up any hope for the messianic improvement of being, but does not end up hopeless. The "Fragment" may be a *Verfallsgeschichte*, but with a spin. Contrary to the widespread metaphysical pessimism of the Weimar era, Benjamin finds hope in reverse in the very narrative of the Fall: the messianic good deed resides in the sacred entropy that is always already ending the enterprise of being, quietly and mercifully.

## Notes

1 Rainer Maria Rilke, *Die Sonette an Orpheus. Zweiter Teil*, Nr. 27, in (Rilke 1955: 769). In Robert Temple's translation: "Does time really exist, time the destroyer?/ When will it break down the castle into mere fragments?/ When will this heart which has always been in the service of the gods/ Be governed by the Creator, the Demiurge?/ Oh, the spectre of perishability,/ How it infiltrates and passes through the innocently receptive,/ As if it were smoke!"
2 Benjamin quotes Kafka's *dictum*—"Oh, plenty of hope, an infinite amount of hope—but not for us" in his essay on Kafka (*SW2*, 798). If, for Benjamin, Kafka's work reveals

a "sickening of tradition" (*SW*3, 326), then, as Brendan Moran rightly suggests, "we can be recognized as hopeless insofar as we embrace [sickened] traditions" (Moran 2018: 39)—and the messianic tradition of hope in historical progress, as represented by Bloch, is certainly one of them. According to Moran, such a realization requires "an epic honesty—the honesty that impels, and seeks in all of us, a restlessness in relation to established forms" (Moran 2018: 40). Here I will attempt to show that, while disillusioned with the sickened forms of historical messianism, Benjamin will nonetheless seek hope elsewhere—in the new language of materialist theology, subversive toward the deadened, established forms of spiritual traditions and honest to the point of crudeness (*Plumpheit*).

3  A similar intuition on the impossibility of theocracy appears in Benjamin's little piece called "World and Time" (composed around 1919-20), which supports Scholem's hypothesis of early dating: "authentic divine power can manifest itself *other than destructively* only in the world to come (the world of fulfillment). But where divine power enters into the secular world, it breathes destruction. That is why in this world nothing constant and no organization can be based on divine power, let alone domination as its supreme principle" (*SW*1, 226; emphasis original).

4  Compare again "World and Time": "In the revelation of the divine, the world—the theater of history—is subjected to a *great process of decomposition*, while time—the life of him who represents it—is subjected to a great process of fulfillment . . . But perhaps in this sense the profoundest antithesis to the 'world' is not 'time' but 'the world to come'" (*SW*1, 226; emphasis added).

5  Even before Adolf von Harnack and Karl Barth, the two protestant theologians responsible for the Marcionite renaissance in Weimar period, marked by total disillusion with the Hegelian paradigm of progress, it was Ernst Bloch who, already in 1918, insisted on the relevance of Marcion, consisting "precisely in the fact that Marcion, a great man, conceptualized this God as history" (Bloch 1918: 330). In his study on Marcion, published in 1924, Harnack describes this second-century Gnostic as "the only thinker in Christianity who took fully seriously the conviction that the Deity who redeems one from the world has absolutely nothing to do with cosmology and cosmic teleology" (Harnack 1990: ix).

6  However, Benjamin's interest in Bachofen dates back much earlier: see his 1926 "Review of Bernoulli's *Bachofen*" (*SW*1, 426-27).

7  According to Michael Löwy, however, there is no need to distinguish firmly between the Bachofenian and the Marxist variants of communism: "In the theological writings of [Benjamin's] youth, there are frequent references to a lost paradise, but in the 1930s primitive communism comes to play this role—as, indeed, it does for Marx and Engels, who were attentive readers of the Romantic anthropology of Maurer and Bachofen, as well as the works of Morgan . . . Rejecting conservative (Klages) and fascist (Bäumler) interpretations, Benjamin stresses that Bachofen 'had explored to previously unplumbed depths the sources which, through the ages, had fed the libertarian ideal' . . . As for Engels and Paul Lafargue, their interest was also attracted by Bachofen's work on matriarchal societies, in which there was apparently a high degree of democracy and civic equality, together with forms of primitive communism that thoroughly 'overturned the concept of authority'" (Löwy 2005: 12-13). On Benjamin's appropriation of Marxism see footnote number 17.

8  Bachofen's vision of the prehistoric cosmochaos of fluidity and dedifferentiation will also resonate in Benjamin's description of Kafka's *Vorwelt* as the night preceding the formation of social hierarchies and structures, based on the solar myths and their

strict law of the day: "Kafka did not consider the age in which he lived as an advance over the beginnings of time. His novels are set in a swamp world. In his works, the creature appears at the stage which Bachofen has termed the hetaeric stage. The fact that this stage is now forgotten does not mean that it does not extend into the present. On the contrary: it is present by virtue of this very oblivion ... Everything forgotten mingles with what has been forgotten of the prehistoric world, forms countless uncertain and changing compounds, yielding a constant flow of new, strange products" (SW2, 808–10).

9  It is, therefore, hard to believe that Benjamin never read Karl Barth, as he claims in one of his letters from 1939, to Karl Thieme: "Reading your book, I regretted not knowing Barth so that I could do justice to how your way of thinking is related to dialectical theology" (C, 1994, 605). Perhaps, he never studied him thoroughly, but the "Fragment" is imbued with the peculiar aura of Barthian Paulinism, which had deeply infected other Jewish thinkers of the Weimar era: Ernst Bloch, Gershom Scholem, Franz Rosenzweig, Hans Jonas, Karl Löwith, and Hannah Arendt. The affinity between Benjamin and Barth never escaped Jacob Taubes, who in *The Political Theology of Paul* praises the former for having a kind of a theocratic "hardness similar to that of Karl Barth," as opposed to a "wishy-washy" type of hopeful messianism of striving (or what Benjamin calls *Steigern*, SW1, 226), characteristic of Bloch and Adorno:

> We can strive until the day after tomorrow; if there's no drawbridge, what's the point? That's Karl Barth, isn't it, this total disillusionment, and I don't see how you can get past that ... You can do it however you want, but there it ends: If God is God, then he can't be coaxed out of our soul. There is a prius there, and a priori. Something has to happen from the other side; then we see, when our eyes are pierced open. Otherwise we see nothing. Otherwise we ascend, we strive until the day after tomorrow (Taubes 2003: 75–6).

10  It was again Jacob Taubes, who spotted the presence of Paul in Benjamin's "Fragment": "I contend that this concept of nihilism, as developed here by Benjamin, is the guiding thread also of the *hos me* in Corinthians and Romans. The world decays, the *morphe* of this world has passed. Here, the relationship to the world is, as the young Benjamin understands it, world politics as nihilism ... Benjamin differs from Paul, however, in the thought of the autonomy of that which he calls here the profane" (Taubes 2003: 72–4). Compare also Agamben's commentary in *The Time That Remains*: "To my knowledge, Taubes was the only scholar to note the possible influence of Paul on Benjamin, but his hypothesis referred to a text from 1920s, the *Theological-Political Fragment* which he connected to Romans 8:19–23. Taubes's intuition is certainly on the mark ... but there are also substantial differences between the two texts. While, for Paul creation is unwillingly subjected to transience and destruction and for this reason groans and suffers while awaiting redemption, for Benjamin, who reverses this in an ingenious way, nature is messianic precisely because of its eternal and complete transience, and the rhythm of this messianic transience is happiness itself" (Agamben 2005: 140–1; translation slightly altered).

11  "Let us say what we claim to be the aim of political science—that is, of all the good things to be done, what is the highest. Most people, I should think, agree about what it is called, since both the masses and sophisticated people call it happiness, understanding being happy as equivalent to living well and acting well" (Aristotle 2004: 5).

12  The biblical word *hevel*, so central to Kohelet, connotes not just the vanity-signifying futile efforts of finite life. In fact, the name "Abel" is closely related to *hevel* and refers

to the brother more beloved by God than Cain who infamously rebelled against the condition of transience and, as such, may be regarded as the first bearer of "messianic intensity": "And the Lord had regard for Abel and his offering, but for Cain and his offering he had no regard" (Gen. 4:4–5). Could it be that Benjamin intuits an affirmative view of contingency as part and parcel of Jewish revelation? In his essay on Kohelet, Ethan Dor-Shav argues that the name "Abel" is the Greek translation of *hevel*, which should be read as legitimizing the transience of all created being rather than warning against its futility. The life of Abel is short and fleeting, but it is precisely his life ordered according to the "rhythm of transience," which pleases God, not his brother's (Dor-Shav 2008: 217).

13  In yet another commentary on Paul's *Epistle to Romans*, Agamben, referring both to Paul and Benjamin, writes: "In pushing each thing towards itself through the *as not*, the messianic does not simply cancel out this figure, but it makes it pass, it prepares its end. This is not another figure or another world: *it is the passing of the figure of the world*" (Agamben 2005: 24–25; emphasis added). Also, in a little piece from 1921, "The Meaning of Time in the Moral Universe," Benjamin defines temporality as a force helping or assisting the world's self-obliteration in the merciful manner which can avoid apocalyptic punishment: "time . . . helps, in ways that are wholly mysterious, to complete the process of forgiveness, though never of reconciliation" (*SW*1, 287). The divine No, therefore, would thus appear in two distinct yet related forms: *in* the world as the time (Rilke's *die Zeit, die zerstörende*) which delays the final blow, by accommodating it as the "crimson thread" of inherent negation, on the one hand— and *out* of the world as the apocalyptic annihilation striking in a timeless now, on the other: "Retribution [*Vergeltung*] is fundamentally indifferent to the passage of time, since it remains in force for centuries without dilution, and even today . . . a heathen conception still pictures the Last Judgment along these lines" (*SW*1, 286). Although falling and failing, the creation can nonetheless be forgiven; if it attunes itself to the passage of time, it will pass away spontaneously, thus evading the Grand No of the violent apocalyptic finale.

14  Benjamin never refers to Basilides himself, but that does not invalidate Agamben's interpretation. The Weimar renaissance of Gnosticism in all its possible variants and shades was such an intense cultural phenomenon that Benjamin was steeped in it from the beginning of his intellectual career. On the ubiquity of the Gnostic motives in pre-war German philosophy and theology and subsequent efforts to "overcome Gnosticism," see: Lazier 2012, especially the chapters "The Gnostic Return" and "Romans in Weimar," 27–48.

15  In the words of Basilides himself: "When, then, the whole Sonship shall have ascended, and passed beyond the Great Limit, the Spirit, then shall the whole creation become the object of the Great Mercy; for it groaneth until now and suffereth pain and awaiteth the manifestation of the Sons of God, namely that all the men of the Sonship may ascend beyond it [the creation]. And when this shall be effected, God will bring upon the whole universe the Great Ignorance [*Mahā-pralaya*], in order that all things may remain in their natural condition, and nothing long for anything which is contrary to its nature. Thus all the souls of this state of existence, whose nature is to remain immortal in this state of existence alone, remain without knowledge of anything different from or better than this state; nor shall there be any rumour or knowledge of things superior in higher states, *in order that the lower souls may not suffer pain by striving after impossible objects*, just as though it were fish longing to feed on the mountains with sheep, for such a desire would end in their destruction.

*All things are indestructible if they remain in their proper condition, but subject to destruction if they desire to overleap and transgress their natural limits*" (Mead 2012: 270–1; emphasis added).

16 Comp. Franz Kafka: "The messiah will come only when he is no longer necessary; he will come only on the day after his arrival; he will come, not on the last day, but on the very last" (Kafka 1961: 81).

17 Against the claim that Benjamin's vision of politics underwent "the profound upheaval occasioned in the mid-1920s by his discovery of Marxism" (Löwy 2005: 5), I believe the reverse is true: Benjamin thoroughly changed the Marxist doctrine, by turning it into a puppet of his own theological game. In the "Paralipomena to 'On The Concept of History,'" Benjamin openly calls Marx's theory erroneous, even if he immediately attempts to delegate this error to Marx's social-democratic epigones: "The structure of Marx's basic idea is as follows: Through a series of class struggles, humanity attains to a classless society in the course of historical development. = *But classless society is not to be conceived as the endpoint of historical development.* = From this erroneous conception Marx's epigones have derived (among other things) the notion of the 'revolutionary situation,' which, as we know, has always refused to arrive. = A genuinely messianic face must be restored to the concept of classless society and, to be sure, in the interest of furthering the revolutionary politics of the proletariat itself" (*SW*4, 402–3; emphasis added). But, dissociated from the "errancy of history," the revolutionary politics turns out to be as "nihilistic" as the "world politics" in the "Fragment" or in Benjamin's praise of the Italian Strike in "Critique of Violence." Here, as in the earlier writings, doing *nothing* or making *nothing* happen does not indicate a lack of activity but precisely an active "striv[ing] for such a passing away" (*SW*3, 306), the goal of which is to introduce a true "state of emergency," as opposed to the one in which we live and which became a rule (*SW*4, 392): an exceptional miraculous suspension of all the laws governing the structures of being. Hence the idea of "pure means" as the "omission of an action" (*SW*1, 239), aiming precisely at *nothing*: not a positive transformation of the world into a new classless form which would crown the historical striving/ *Steigerung* of mankind (as in Marx's "erroneous" revision of the Hegelian historiosophy), but rather a revolutionary *de-formation* in which all the structures and hierarchies of the great chain of being would be deactivated and dissolved back into the hetaeric *flux* of dedifferentiation. Once again commenting on Marx's "error," Benjamin writes: "Marx says that revolutions are the locomotive of world history. But perhaps it is quite otherwise. Perhaps revolutions are an attempt by the passengers on this train—namely, the human race—to activate the emergency brake . . . In this moment, time must be brought to a standstill" (*SW*4, 402–3). Revolution, therefore, is not a progressive move, investing in historical "improvement," but rather a fundamentally regressive one, based on the Gnostic model of *regressio* as undoing or interrupting the entanglement of form and matter and thus *restituting* the integral order of the profane as the material realm shedding all stable forms and structures—the class hierarchy included: "Classless society is not the final goal of historical progress but its frequently miscarried, ultimately *achieved interruption*" (*SW*4, 402; emphasis added). Even the *Thesen*, therefore, reveal Benjamin's attachment not so much to the Marxist political programme as to what Brendan Moran quite rightly calls "Kafkan politics": the dedifferentiating interruptions which assault the world of structure from the prehistoric realm of *Vorwelt*, where it is impossible "to speak of any order or hierarchy" (*SW*2, 799). The "Kafkan" revolution would thus be a lesson of radical *communitas* that comes from the

pre-creational night to disturb the societal order of the law of the day, which Benjamin calls a myth: "Exceptions to discernible myth may be regarded as outgrowths of the *Vorwelt*, the world that no myth incorporates or controls" (Moran 2018: 273).

18  In his essay on "Two Poems of Hölderlin," Benjamin indeed suggests that the "spiritual principle" of "becoming-one (*Einswerdung*)" with the world requires a "total submission" (*Hingabe*) to the "danger" of death (*SW*1, 34) as the final seal of finitude and transience. For Benjamin, it would be precisely this danger which coincides with *die Rettung* as realized in the idea of *die gerettete Nacht* [the night preserved]: see footnote nr 28.

19  See *Midrash Tehilim*: "Israel speaks to God: When will You redeem us? He answers: When you have sunk to the lowest level, at that time I will redeem you" (Scholem 1991: 11–12), or in *Sanhedrin 98a*: "May he come, but I do not want to see him" (ibid., 13), about which Scholem succinctly comments: "the redemption, then, cannot be realized without dread and ruin" (ibid., 13). "There can be no preparation for the Messiah. He comes suddenly, unannounced, and precisely when he is least expected or when hope has long been abandoned" (ibid., 11).

20  In "Brecht's *Threepenny Novel*," written in 1936, Benjamin defines *plumpes Denken* as the type of thinking whose "sole function is to direct theory toward practice": "a thought must be crude to find its way into action . . . The forms of crude thinking change slowly, for they are created by the masses" (*SW*3, 7), here understood as the fundamental matter-*Stoff* of every society.

21  "Desire has reserved to itself the pure negating of the object and thereby its unalloyed feeling of self. But that is the reason why this satisfaction is itself only a fleeting one, for it lacks the side of objectivity and permanence. Work, on the other hand, is desire held in check, fleetingness staved off; in other words, work forms and shapes the thing" (Hegel 1977: 118). For Hegel, desire is a wish to destroy the object which it consumes and, as such, is one of the primary manifestations of *die Furie der Zerstörung*—an energy which must be restrained and tamed, so it can serve the purpose of the work understood as a "delayed destruction," transforming the contingent object into something more lasting. For Benjamin, who opposes Hegel on all fronts, desire is to be released in its originary pure negativity, so it can aid *die Zeit, die zerstörende* in the entropic work of bringing the world to its end.

22  In what could be the best commentary on Benjamin's "Fragment," Hägglund writes: "There is thus an internal contradiction in the so-called desire for immortality. If one were not attached to mortal life, there would be no fear of death and no desire to live on" (Hägglund 2008: 2). In *Dying for Time*, Hägglund calls this contradiction a double bind characteristic of the human "chronolibido": "Desire is chronophobic since whatever we are bound to or aspire for can be lost: it can be taken away from or be rejected by us. Yet, by the same token, desire is chronophilic, since it is because we are bound to or aspire for something that can be lost that we care about it, that we care about what happens" (Hägglund 2012: 14). For Hägglund, the best expression of the ambivalent nature of human desire is music: the succession of notes that relentlessly pass away, which can be given a form only thanks to the retention of their traces, as if in the constant work of mourning (Hägglund 2012: 36). Benjamin, however, is more radical in the "Fragment": his insistence on rhythm only does away with the retentive musical structure and relieves the body from the burden of memory, which is the last-ditch effort of resistance to transience. The rhythm, therefore, is truly oblivious and unmourned, *unbeweint*: there is no trace of mourning in adjusting to it. Benjamin, always attuned to the developments of mass culture, could thus be said to

affirm a tendency which his friend, Adorno, vehemently opposed, that is, the gradual disappearance of musical structure for the sake of the purely rhythmic form based on simple repetition. While describing the average consumer of pop-music, Adorno targets obedience to the rhythm as the apocalyptic sign of the ultimate victory of the meek: "This obedient type is the rhythmical type . . . Any musical experience of this type is based upon the underlying, unabating time unit of the music—its 'beat' . . . To be musical means to [these people] to be capable of following given rhythmical patterns without being disturbed by 'individualizing' aberrations . . . This is the way in which their response to music immediately expresses their desire to obey . . . Thus do the obedient inherit the earth" (Adorno 1998: 207).

23  "Thou awakest us to delight in Thy praise; for Thou madest us for Thyself, and our heart is restless, until it repose in Thee" (St. Augustine 2014: 3).

24  It is perhaps in this context that we should read the conclusion to another little piece from 1920, "On Love and Related Matters," devoted to sexual revolution: "As we peer into the darkness of the transformations taking place in that great flowing stream of human physicality, our sight fails as we contemplate a future . . . Here flows the dark stream that for the most noble may prove to be their predestined grave. The only bridge that spans that stream is the spirit. Life will pass over it in a triumphal chariot, but perhaps only slaves will remain to be harnessed to it" (SW1, 230). While this piece is still written from the perspective of the waning spirit and its "noble desires," which peer into the dark flow of materiality and, terrified by the Shelleyan "triumph of life," see *nothing*—the "Fragment," having adjusted its sight to the night of the profane order, endorses these "transformations" and locates in them a fulcrum of a new world politics.

25  This immediately brings to mind another closely related politico-theological project that also sprang from Benjamin's unique appreciation of *materia prima*: Derrida's foray into the "Khora of the political" as a new element of the "democracy to come," whose inhabitants—*les voyous* or "the rogues"—will no longer follow the preestablished and external social laws, but will be allowed to "deviate" according to their incalculable singularities and achieve their own internal forms of being (Derrida 2005: 44).

26  Compare Lévinas writing openly against the principle of inertia and entropic dissipation: "Inertia is certainly the great law of being; but the human looms up in it and can disturb it. For a long time? For a moment? The human is a scandal in being, a 'sickness' of being for the realists, but not evil" (Lévinas 2000: 115).

27  "I had been glad to live and I was glad to die . . . Then came the mishap" (Kafka 1952: 185). On which Benjamin comments: "From the 'nethermost regions of death' blows the wind that is favorable to him—the same wind which so often blows from the prehistoric world in Kafka's works, and which also propels the boat of the hunter Gracchus" (SW2, 815). It is thus quite justified to see this *vorweltlich* wind, which reminds us of our radical finitude, as an antidote to the seemingly progressive "storm blowing from the paradise," which imbues humankind with false hopes in immortality.

28  Walter Benjamin to Florens Christian Rang, December 9, 1923 (C, 224).

29  See Jacob Taubes, "The Iron Cage and the Exodus from It, or the Dispute over Marcion, Then and Now": "In the *cosmos atheos* of the modern age, there is no point of escape 'beyond' the world. Therefore, neither can there be any Gnostic exodus from the world in the modern age" (Taubes 2009: 138). The connection between the Marcionite Gnostic doctrine of the Alien God and the scientific climate of late

modernity, marked by Rudolf Clausius's discovery of the law of entropy in 1865, was made by Harnack himself in the 1920 "Foreword to the First Edition" of his book on Marcion: "The new life of faith and freedom was for him something so 'alien' as over against the world that he based its emergence upon the same doubtful/daring hypothesis by which Helmholtz proposed to explain the emergence of organisms on the earth" (Harnack 1990: ix). In 1884, Hermann von Helmholtz proposed a cosmozoic theory according to which life did not arise spontaneously on earth, but came from outer space in the form of micro-organisms traveling with meteorites and comets. Since matter throughout the universe is generally hostile to the anti-entropic process of life, life constitutes an absolute exception: it was born accidentally and only once on an alien distant planet and propagates itself against the cosmic odds.

30  On the Jewish-messianic reactions to the discovery of entropy, see Wołkowicz 2007: 212–13.
31  The theme of an idle alternation of growth and decay as characteristic of myth emerges in the last paragraph of "Toward the Critique of Violence," where Benjamin looks at human history as a cyclical "oscillation" of "a dialectical rising and falling in the lawmaking and law-preserving forms of violence": "The law governing this oscillation rests on the circumstance that all law-preserving violence, in its duration, indirectly weakens the lawmaking violence it represents, by suppressing hostile counterviolence ... This lasts until either new forces or those earlier suppressed triumph over the hitherto lawmaking violence and thus found a new law, destined in its turn to decay. On the breaking of this cycle maintained by mythic forms of law ... a new historical epoch is founded. If the rule of myth is broken occasionally in the present age, the coming age is not unimaginably remote" (SW1, 251–52). But, as already suggested, the breaking of this cycle can come only from the deliberate enhancement of the "crimson thread of negation," which official history does not want to see: "Benjamin's proposed critique of violence is at least partly a critique of the attempted closure of history from the force of 'decay' [*Verfall*]" (Moran 2015: 73).
32  At the same time, Fenves points to the special place of the category of *Vergängnis* as one of the "defining attributes" of Benjamin's œuvre (2011: 156).
33  Horstmann 1989: 20.
34  Even if Benjamin never read *Philosophie der Erlösung*, its radical teaching could have reached him via Gustav Landauer, whom he definitely had read, and not only as the translator of Meister Eckhart. In Landauer's 1893 novel, *Der Todesprediger*, the main character voices opinions very close to Mainländer's thanatic anarchy, which are crystallized in the slogan *Es lebe der Tod!* also quoted approbatively in Mainländer's book: "Hoch lebe unser Tod!" (Mainländer 1989: 94).
35  The concept of the *katechon* (in Luther's translation *der Aufhalter*, "the restrainer") derives from Paul's Second Letter to Thessalonians (2:3–2:8). See also Schmitt 2002, most of all the chapter "The Christian Empire as a Restrainer of the Antichrist (*Katechon*)," 59–61.

# References

Adorno, Theodor W. (1998), "On Popular Music," in John Storey (ed.), *Cultural Theory and Popular Culture: A Reader*, 197–209, Athens: The University of Georgia Press.

Agamben, Giorgio. (2004), *The Open: Man and Animal*, trans. Kevin Attell, Stanford: Stanford University Press.
Agamben, Giorgio. (2005), *The Time That Remains: A Commentary on the Letter to the Romans*, trans. Patricia Dailey, Stanford: Stanford University Press.
Agamben, Giorgio. (2016), *The Use of Bodies. Homo Sacer IV, 2*, trans. Adam Kotsko, Stanford: Stanford University Press.
Aristotle (2004), *The Nicomachean Ethics*, trans. Roger Crisp, Cambridge: Cambridge University Press.
St. Augustine of Hippo (2014), *Confessions*, trans. E. B. Pusey, Cambridge: Harvard University Press.
Barth, Karl. (1968), *The Epistle to the Romans*, trans. Edwyn C. Hoskyns, Oxford: Oxford University Press.
Bloch, Ernst. (1918), *Der Geist der Utopie*, Leipzig and Munich: Verlag von Duncker und Humblot.
Bloch, Ernst. (1998), *Literary Essays*, trans. Andrew Joron, Stanford: Stanford University Press.
Bloch, Ernst. (2009), *Atheism in Christianity*, trans. J. T. Swann, London: Verso.
Derrida, Jacques. (2005), *Rogues. Two Essays on Reason*, trans. Michael Naas, Stanford: Stanford University Press.
Dor-Shav, Ethan. (2008), "Ecclesiastes, Fleeting and Timeless: Part I," *The Jewish Bible Quarterly*, 36 (4): 211–22.
Fenves, Peter. (2011), *The Messianic Reduction: Walter Benjamin and the Shape of Time*, Stanford: Stanford University Press.
Harnack, Adolf von. (1990), *Marcion: The Gospel of the Alien God*, trans. John E. Steely and Lyle D. Bierma, Jamestown: Labyrinth Press.
Hägglund, Martin. (2008), *Radical Atheism: Derrida and the Time of Life*, Stanford: Stanford University Press.
Hägglund, Martin. (2012), *Dying for Time: Proust, Wolf, Nabokov*, Cambridge: Harvard University Press.
Hegel, G. W. F. (1969), *Science of Logic*, trans. A. V. Miller, London: Allen and Unwin.
Hegel, G. W. F. (1977), *Phenomenology of Spirit*, trans. A. V. Miller, Oxford: Oxford University Press.
Horstmann, Ulrich. (1989), "Philipp Mainländer's Metaphysik der Entropie. Vorwort zur *Philosophie der Erlösung*," in Ulrich Horstmann (ed.), *Philipp Mainländer, Philosophie der Erlösung*, 9–30, Frankfurt am Main: Insel Verlag.
Kafka, Franz. (1952), *The Selected Short Stories*, trans. Willa and Edwin Muir, New York: Schocken.
Kafka, Franz. (1961), *Parables and Paradoxes*, ed. Nahum Glatzer, New York: Schocken.
Lazier, Benjamin. (2012), *God Interrupted: Heresy and the European Imagination between the World Wars*, Princeton: Princeton University Press.
Lévinas, Emmanuel. (2000), *Entre Nous: Thinking of The Other*, trans. Michael B. Smith and Barbara Harshav, New York: Columbia University Press.
Löwy, Michael. (2005), *Fire Alarm: Reading Walter Benjamin's "On the Concept of History,"* London: Verso.
Mainländer, Philipp. (1989), *Philosophie der Erlösung*, ed. Ulrich Horstmann, Frankfurt am Main: Insel Verlag.
Mead, G. R. S. (2012), *Fragments of a Faith Forgotten*, London: Forgotten Books.
Moran, Brendan. (2015), "Nature, Decision and Muteness," in Brendan Moran and Carlo Salzani (eds.), *Towards the Critique of Violence: Walter Benjamin and Giorgio Agamben*, 73–90, London: Bloomsbury.

Moran, Brendan. (2018), *Politics of Benjamin's Kafka: Philosophy as Renegade*, London: Palgrave Macmillan.
Rilke, Rainer Maria. (1955), *Sämtliche Werke. Band 1*, Frankfurt am Main: Insel Verlag.
Schmitt, Carl. (2002), *The Nomos of the Earth in the International Law of the Jus Publicum Europaeum*, trans. G. L. Ulmen, New York: Telos Press Publishing.
Scholem, Gershom. (1963), *Judaica 1*, Frankfurt am Main: Suhrkamp.
Scholem, Gershom. (1991), *The Messianic Idea in Judaism: And Other Essays on Jewish Spirituality*, New York: Schocken.
Taubes, Jacob. (1954), "Theodicy and Theology: A Philosophical Analysis of Karl Barth's Dialectical Theology," *The Journal of Religion*, 34 (4): 231–43.
Taubes, Jacob. (2003), *The Political Theology of Paul*, trans. Dana Hollander, Stanford: Stanford University Press.
Taubes, Jacob. (2006), "Walter Benjamin – Ein moderner Marcionit? Scholems Benjamin-Interpretationreligionsgeschichtlich überprüft," in Elettra Stimilli (ed.), *Der Preis des Messianismus. Briefe von Jacob Taubes und Gershom Scholem und andere Materialien*, 53–66, Würzburg: Königshausen & Neuman.
Taubes, Jacob. (2009), *From Cult to Culture: Fragments Towards a Critique of Historical Reason*, ed. Aleida Assmann, Stanford: Stanford University Press.
Wołkowicz, Anna. (2007), *Mystiker der Revolution. Der utopische Diskurs um die Jahrhundertwende*, Warsaw: Warsaw University Press.

# 5

# My Kingdom for a Shirt

## Untrammeled Atheism and Anarchism in Benjamin and Kafka

James Martel

## Introduction

Anarchism, it is often assumed, is an inherently atheistic form of politics. The anarchists of the Spanish Revolution in 1936 destroyed every church they could get their hands on. The Paris Communards didn't destroy churches in their brief time in power but they desanctified and reoccupied them, using them as sites for their local clubs and workers councils. And yet, for all of this, there is a way in which true atheism is very hard to achieve. One can burn down a church and still subscribe to theistic principles insofar as those get smuggled into a basic concept like modernity or temporality, the building blocks of our contemporary world. More precisely, atheism per se does not necessarily rescue the would-be anarchist from the effects of the theism that it sets out to oppose. As Andrew Benjamin argues:

> [T]he attempt to counter religion with the assertion of atheism is . . . premised on a failure to grasp the way in which religion is deployed within the political . . . Religion structures every aspect of life and thus every subject position, even that subject position that defines itself as "irreligious." Hence the response to religion has to be a political one and not the evocation of the critical paucity of atheism. (Benjamin 2013: 2)

It would appear then that we need a new form of atheism, one that both recognizes and breaks from all forms of theism, including those that help to structure the concept of atheism itself. This is not just a matter of ceasing to believe in God; as I'll argue further, the actual existence of God is almost beside the point. It is not God per se but rather the political-theological structure of Western forms of religion which have been transformed into a secular structure that I would call archism. Archism is the opposite of anarchism and is ubiquitous even as it avoids being either recognized or (usually) named. This is a form of power based on hierarchy and domination. As I will argue further, such hierarchies represent a metaphysics of power, wherein externalities such as God or nature are used to bolster what I will claim to be entirely arbitrary and human power structures so that they cannot be questioned or challenged. Archism takes on various political forms ranging from fascism to liberal democracy. In all these systems, an allegiance to hierarchy (albeit more or less overt depending on the form) and a belief in the representative powers of the state or other falsely mimetic forms (which supplant and replace the political life of virtually all of its subjects) accords with an overriding commitment to capitalism at all costs.

Archism, as I will argue further, is at its base a theistic phenomenon even as its modern form appears to be entirely secular. Archism is served by a metaphysics of both time and space wherein some particular aspect is held above other aspects as a basis for rule. This space (the White House, the Kremlin) is better than that space. This person (the President, the movie star) is better than that person. This time (the future, the past) is better than that time. The world is taxonomized, organized, and ranked according to the transcendent categories that archism engages in, that is to say, the externalities that are evoked (some overtly religious, some secular, but in all cases metaphysical and hence theistic) to justify its hierarchies of authority and power. Given the power and ubiquity of archism and given that atheism itself—at least in terms of how we usually think about these things—offers no respite from the power structures that it serves, how can we start to think about an atheism which sheds its occult metaphysical and theological premises and, by extension, an anarchism that does so as well?

Atheism and anarchism have a long history of being associated together but in this chapter I will argue that their connection is as much conceptual as it is historical. Anarchism, precisely because it seeks an end to any kind of hierarchy, is explicitly opposed to the theological bases for those hierarchies. And atheism, because it seeks to break once and for all from these very same externalities, seeks a political expression that supports and promotes that vision.

In order to think more about this question, in what follows I will turn to an analysis by Walter Benjamin of the writings of Franz Kafka and, in particular, a pattern in many of the latter's tales wherein atheism—and hence anarchism—are only achieved by directly engaging with and then explicitly rejecting the theistic. As I will show further, the path to atheistic anarchism is not simply to will theism out of existence but instead entails an engagement with the most fantastic aspects of archist authority— including the archist authority of God—in order to face down and reject, rather than evade, the power of archist theism. The nature of theism, as already noted, is so easily disguised that anything short of a direct recognition and acknowledgment of its insidious character will lead to just more of the same. Accordingly, I will look at two passages in particular that lay out how Benjamin thinks about Kafka's work and how they in turn help us to understand how an atheistic anarchism can best be enacted.

## Archism and Mythic Violence

Before turning to Benjamin's analysis of Kafka, I want to first briefly discuss the connection between what I have been calling archism and what Benjamin calls mythic violence, one of his most important political (and theological!) concepts. This background will be useful in coming to terms with what Benjamin is referring to when he makes his claims about Kafka's writing and what it offers us.

Benjamin sets out the concepts of mythic and divine violence in his "Toward the Critique of Violence," written in 1921. Speaking of mythic violence, Benjamin tells us that "[f]ar from opening up a purer sphere, the mythic manifestation of immediate violence reveals itself to be at the deepest level identical with all legal violence and transforms a vague intimation of its problematical character into a certainty concerning the perniciousness of its historical function, the annihilation of which thus becomes a task" (*TC*, 57; see too *SW1*, 249).

For Benjamin then, all forms of law (at least the dominant, Western version that claims to have a monopoly on that term), as well as the state itself, are actually illicit. Mythic violence for Benjamin is a form of projection whereby terrestrial (hence human) powers which have no absolute or ontological right to rule base their power on transcendent categories of either a theological or secular nature. In both cases, some metaphysical object (God, nature, reason, or what have you) is claimed as the basis for the right to rule. Such rule is therefore received as an unimpeachable mandate wherein the subjects of that power must completely submit. Such power is therefore mythic because it is based on false theological foundations. Like myths that are based on gods who do not exist, mythic violence ascribes its origins to non-existent but highly influential sources. It is violent (in the original German the word *Gewalt* also means something like force) because it remains insecure about its source of authority. It must kill, Benjamin tells us, not just once but over and over again to continually reestablish its "right" to dominate the rest of us.

Benjamin's concept of mythic violence corresponds very well with what I have been calling archism. One could say that mythic violence is the name of the system that produces hierarchies and self-authorizing forms of power and that archism is the name of the result of that system. In my view, it is better to speak of archism rather than simply of the state or the law because archism is a broader concept. Perhaps even more importantly, the term covers capitalism as well. Capitalism is inherently archist because it necessarily presupposes and reproduces a metaphysics of hierarchy. In the fascist mode of capitalist archism that hierarchy is fairly open. In the liberal mode it is disguised by phantasms of equality. Either way, capitalism cannot exist without a prior and archist structure. To speak of archism allows us to understand how a substantially hierarchical system can survive the death of one of its key elements, like the state (the death of which is arguably happening in the present moment). Archism is the broader category for which the concept of the state is just one example.

For Benjamin there is a way for those externalities that archism relies upon to take revenge on the mythic forms of violence that have been incurred in their name. In his "Critique of Violence," Benjamin contrasts mythic violence with divine violence. Divine violence is for Benjamin a way for that very same externality, used as a source for mythic violence, to counteract the lies established in its name. Divine violence creates no new truths on earth but merely removes the falsities that have been attributed to the divine itself.

Benjamin describes the dichotomy between mythic and divine violence by telling us: "Mythic violence is blood-violence over mere life for sake of violence itself; divine violence is pure violence over all of life for the sake of the living" (*TC*, 57–8; See too *SW*1, 250). Whereas the former is anxious and self-oriented, requiring the sign of blood and reducing its subject populations to "mere life," the latter is oriented toward all of the living and is confident both in its existence and in its power.

As previously noted, I don't think that it matters in the end whether God really exists or not. The mere idea of God (or some secular corollary) is enough to create a basis for mythic violence. Yet, by the same token, the idea that the blank screens upon which archons project their desires could talk back, could resist the archons' own projections, already goes a long way in undermining the otherwise uninterrupted power structures based on mythic violence. Here, we see the true vulnerability of mythic violence and hence archism as well. Insofar as it is always anxious about its right to rule—even about whether it actually exists at all—such power forms are always vulnerable to the possibility of exposure. Archism always risks being shown to be the self-positing system that it actually is, even if that exposure is only theoretical or remains in the realm of pure potentiality.

## At the Foot of Castle Hill

At this point, let me look at the first of two passages that I want to focus on from Kafka, to give a better sense of how Benjamin learns from Kafka, not only how mythic violence can be resisted, but also how a different political model—an anarchist atheism—may be pursued. Both passages can be found in his text "Franz Kafka: On the Tenth Anniversary of his Death." Paradoxically, neither of the passages I want to focus on are actually by Kafka himself. They are both rather from Jewish folklore and writings; but for Benjamin, they nonetheless epitomize what he is talking about in terms of Kafka himself.

The first passage comes when Benjamin tells us a parable about why Jews prepare a Sabbath feast, something that he then links up with Kafka's novel, *the Castle*. He writes:

> The legend is about a princess languishing in exile, in a village whose language she does not understand, far from her compatriots. One day this princess receives a letter saying that her fiancé has not forgotten her and is on his way to her.—The fiancé, so says the rabbi, is the Messiah; the princess is the soul; the village in which she lives in exile is the body. She prepares a meal for him because this is the only way in which she can express her joy in a village whose language she does not know.—This village of the Talmud is right in Kafka's world. For just as K. lives in the village on Castle Hill, modern man lives in his own body: the body slips away from him, is hostile towards him . . . The air of this village blows about Kafka, and this is why he was not tempted to found a religion. The pigsty which houses the country doctor's horses; the stuffy back room in which Klamm, a cigar in his mouth, sits over a glass of beer; the manor gate which brings ruin to anyone who knocks on it—all these are part of this village. The air in the village is permeated

with all the abortive and overripe elements that form such a putrid mixture. This is the air that Kafka had to breathe throughout his life. He was neither mantic nor the founder of a religion. How was he able to survive in this air? (*SW2*, 805-806)

In this passage, Benjamin lays out a mode of connecting to the divine that does not entail mythic violence. The princess does not project onto the Messiah what he or she would like to eat. She does not confabulate some amazing dish of which only a Messiah is worthy. Instead, she just cooks what she does best. It's almost like a joke. Question: what do you make when the Messiah is coming over for dinner? Answer: Meatloaf! The point is that the act of reverence does not attempt to transcend the human sphere; it remains very much within the ordinary ways of life with which human beings engage. What the princess deems most delicious in her repertoire of cooking will have to do, is in fact enough. In other words, rather than reach for the divine in our relationship with it, we use it as an opportunity to determine for ourselves what we deem best. The divine, in this way, serves only as a means for a human community to make and form its own judgments. Rather than producing hierarchy based on some transcendent value that only a few have access to and can thus do the judging and ranking on behalf of the rest of us, this reinforces the ordinary life that we live together. As Benjamin tells us in his "Critique of Violence," divine violence is for the "living," that is to say for all of us who are currently alive in our ordinary existence (arguably it is for the dead as well but that is a different discussion).

Connecting this story to Kafka's novel *The Castle* is telling insofar as the denizens of Castle Hill on the whole do *not* follow this advice. The people in the village that K. encounters when he arrives in the village are in a fully fetishistic mode. They want and even need the castle and its inhabitants to be higher, better, truer than any of them. Their lives are completely occupied by imagining and possibly even having connections with the castle (the actual material existence both of the castle and of its occupants is never a fully settled thing in the book). All the "communications" (if that's what they are) with the castle are distorted and unclear. There is a telephone in the village from which calls sometimes arrive but all you hear is a static that might sound like angels singing but it could be something else too. K. gets a letter upon arriving in the village but the signature is blurry and he can't make it out. None of that, however, matters. The subjects of the village have given their entire life over to the castle and in fact the obscurity of signs from the castle offer plenty of opportunity for the villagers to engage in mythic violence, projections, and determinations that are attributed to the castle itself.

It is hard to overstate how much the castle anchors and delineates the lives of the villagers. Many of the women in the village fall in love with men from the castle. K. himself falls in love with the women who fall in love with the men from the castle. All in all, there is hardly any word, action, or thought that is not in some way motivated by or in reaction to the castle and those who are imagined to live in it.

There is something collective about the response to the castle even as personal relationships are individuated (and ranked) according to one's status vis-à-vis the castle's residents. Even "seeing" the castle is not something that comes automatically to a new observer but rather must be learned from the collectivity. When K. first arrives, he can't really determine what he is looking at when he looks in the direction of the castle.

> On the whole the Castle, as it appeared from this distance, corresponded to K.'s expectations. It was neither an old knight's fortress nor a magnificent new edifice, but a large complex made up of a few two-story buildings and many lower, tightly packed ones; had one not known that this was a castle, one could have taken it for a small town. K. saw only one tower, whether it belonged to a dwelling or a church was impossible to tell. (Kafka 1998: 8)

Left to his own devices, K. cannot quite make out the edifice which organizes the entire village. It takes the help of the local schoolteacher (an enforcer of village orthodoxy) to really see it, or at least believe that he was seeing it:

> "You're taking a look at the Castle?" [the teacher] asked, more gently than K. had expected, but as though he did not approve of what K. was doing. "Yes," said K., "I'm a stranger here, I only arrived yesterday evening." "You don't like the Castle?" the teacher said quickly. "What?" countered K., somewhat baffled, but then, rephrasing the question more delicately, he said: "Do I like the Castle? What makes you think I don't like it?" "Strangers never do," said the teacher. (Kafka 1998: 9)

This then is the opposite of what the princess does in the story that Benjamin relates. Rather than using some externality as a way to come to terms with what she herself deems important, the people in the village, and K. along with them, use the castle to project all kinds of phantasms about power and authority. Even if the castle turns out to be empty or personified (a very strong possibility according to Olga, who is one of the few truth-tellers in town) the villagers are so invested in these acts of mythic violence that they cannot and would not want to do otherwise (Kafka 1998: 180-6).

There is one exception in the village, Olga's sister Amalia, who spurned the advances of one of the "gentlemen of the castle" (Kafka 1998: 192-6). Amalia is the one rebel in her village, refusing to submit herself to the whims of the castle (or perhaps the imagined whims for that matter). She leads an honest but lonely life as no one else in the village will have anything to do with her. Her family sticks with her but suffers accordingly. Collectively they pay a very high price for not going along with the phantasms that otherwise structure and motivate Castle Hill.

Yet, for all of this, Benjamin does not see Kafka as abandoning the world in favor of the phantasms of mythic violence. Recall that Benjamin writes:

> The air of this village blows about Kafka, and this is why he was not tempted to found a religion. The pigsty which houses the country doctor's horses; the stuffy back room in which Klamm, a cigar in his mouth, sits over a glass of beer; the manor gate which brings ruin to anyone who knocks on it—all these are part of this village.

Rather than advocating for a full surrender to mythic violence, Benjamin tells us that Kafka was "not tempted to found a religion." He remains, like the princess in the story earlier, very much influenced by and engaged with ordinary human life ("the living"), even if the characters of his book are all too ready to subsume ordinary life to that of the castle.

Recall too that Benjamin goes on to write: "The air in the village is permeated with all the abortive and overripe elements that form such a putrid mixture. This is the air that Kafka had to breathe throughout his life." The villagers' obsession with the castle gets to the point that their own life and the material world around them becomes de-realized, in effect transferring their own solidity to the castle which in some sense then becomes more real than reality itself, certainly more interesting, more important, and so on. Kafka himself however does not forget, cannot in fact forget, the material world as such. Its stenches, its materiality, and its effects are all in evidence throughout this work. Even as we watch the villagers choose fantasy over reality time and time again, they cannot choose to eliminate material reality itself. Indeed, insofar as the power of the castle is an entirely parasitical one, it requires material reality as well as human subjects as a basis to rule from and over.

This once again demonstrates what might be an unexpected vulnerability of the castle and of mythic violence (and hence, archism) more generally: the relationship between the castle and the village is not reciprocal. The castle requires the villagers to rule over, it requires them in fact to exist at all. The villagers in turn do not need the castle, as Amalia discovers in her own lonely way. Their ordinary life, once again what Benjamin is referring to when he speaks of "the living," serves as a permanent resource for resistance, a way that divine violence, even if it is not something that humans can directly engage in themselves (a big question for Benjamin), remains available.

But note that this idea does not quite constitute a full atheistic expression. Recall that the princess chose to make dinner for the coming Messiah, thereby recognizing the latter's existence and exceptionality (even if her dinner isn't exceptional, her guest certainly is!). By the same token, other acts that human beings engage in can acknowledge—even if they do nothing more than that—the divine, even as those human subjects are determining for themselves what it is that they value and why.

What this first passage suggests is a kind of moderate atheism ("[Kafka] was neither mantic nor the founder of a religion") wherein one remains engaged with God or theism in order to allow the blankness of this relationship to return human attention to the living themselves (constituting what Aryeh Botwinick, among others, would call a "negative theology," a concept with a long history) (Botwinick 1997: 11). Here, God or externality is not the prime focus even as it remains an object of veneration. But it is still critical, still central to the functioning of this form of engagement. To get to a more robust form of atheism—one that doesn't replace but rather reinforces the incipient atheism of the first passage—let me now turn to the second passage.

## My Kingdom for a Shirt

The second passage that I would like to focus on comes a bit later in the essay on Kafka. Here, Benjamin tells what initially appears to be merely a funny story from Jewish folklore. He writes:

In a Hasidic village, so the story goes, Jews were sitting together in a shabby inn one Sabbath evening. They were all local people, with the exception of one person no one knew, a very poor, ragged man who was squatting in a dark corner at the back of the room. All sorts of things were discussed, and then it was suggested that everyone should tell what wish he would make if one were granted him. One man wanted money; another wished for a son-in-law; a third dreamed of a new carpenter's bench; and so each spoke in turn. After they had finished, only the beggar in his dark corner was left. Reluctantly and hesitantly he answered the question. "I wish I were a powerful king reigning over a big country. Then, some night while I was asleep in my palace, an enemy would invade my country, and by dawn his horsemen would penetrate to my castle and meet with no resistance. Roused from my sleep, I wouldn't have time even to dress and I would have to flee in my shirt. Rushing over hill and dale and through forests day and night, I would finally arrive safely right here at the bench in this corner. This is my wish." The others exchanged uncomprehending glances. "And what good would this wish have done you?" someone asked. "I'd have a shirt," was the answer. (SW2, 812)

Benjamin further tells us: "This story takes us deep into the household that is Kafka's world. No one says that the distortions which it will be the Messiah's mission to set right someday affect only our space; surely they are distortions of our time as well" (SW2, 812).

While the story of the beggar appears purely comical, Benjamin alerts us to the fact that there is something serious afoot here. In speaking of the "distortions which it will be the Messiah's mission to set right," the distortions themselves are instances of mythic violence. The Messiah's "set[ting it] right" is the response of divine violence. So far so good, but what about the political upshot of this story in terms of how it might be connected to anarchism (or atheism for that matter!)? By bringing up the Messiah doesn't Benjamin himself threaten a kind of archist metaphysics after all because clearly the Messiah is better and higher than anyone else? If, as Benjamin says earlier, these distortions of time and space must be unmade, and if that unmaking is done—can only be done—by a Messiah, what role does that leave for ordinary people and what, if anything, does this have to do with the story of the beggar? I will try to answer these questions in reverse order, for once we understand the story of the beggar a bit more, it helps us to understand how a system that relies on a Messiah can at the same time allow for a kind of untrammeled anarchism (with "untrammeled" being the operative word as I will explain further). Such an arrangement allows the power and collective action of the living, of people in all of their ordinariness and profanity, to be both expressed and acted upon.

To explain this better, let me return to the story itself. The beggar tells us that he wishes to be a king but that includes a wish that the king be deposed and only be able to keep his shirt (which is nevertheless an improvement over his current situation as he is dressed in rags). His audience is confused. Why does he need to go through the whole drama of being a king in order to get a shirt? Why not just ask for the shirt directly? But it is here that the connection to Kafka becomes clearer because as Benjamin points out, throughout Kafka's writing, we see a similar pattern of reaching for the highest only to end up with something much humbler (something I will expand upon shortly).

Whereas the other people in the story go directly to what they want: money, a son-in-law, and so on, the beggar goes into the acme of archist phantasm in order to come back to what he wants. In doing so, he engages in a version of what Žižek, citing Lacan, calls "traversing the fantasy" (Žižek 2000: 61)—that is, going to the extreme of a given myth (in this case) in order to come out at the other end. If you merely ask for something, even if it is as humble or lowly as a shirt, you end up trapped within the fantasy or, as Benjamin puts it, the "distortion," the mythic violence that the Messiah has to set right. Archism as an entire system, particularly in its capitalist mode, is based on lies that promise a bright future of material goods, personal satisfaction, safety and, in a sense some kind of release from the human condition (from disease, and above all, from death). Therefore, the subject of archism is expected, even required, to wish for things. Because archism ranks us, part of the way it demonstrates that rank is in terms of whose wishes get rewarded and whose do not. But even for the most privileged subject of archism, it is impossible to be granted their ultimate wish to escape fleshly mortality (as Nietzsche tells us, the Enlightenment teaches one to hate one's body and to wish to be a higher, noumenal subject, thereby cancelling out the person that one actually is).

The beggar gets around this by going to the acme of archist phantasm, to wish himself to be at the very peak position (the king!) and then, allowing the phantasm to fall apart, he returns to the level of ordinary human life in order to end up with a suitably humble wish: a shirt. This arc describes both a theological conviction (hence [a]theistic) and a political one ([an]archistic) in that the messianic possibility inherent in the idea of salvation is effectively bypassed even as the desire for political power over others is annulled, once again, by traversing the fantasy. Another way to say this is that given that for Benjamin we all have a built-in tendency toward fetishism and a desire for transcendent rescue, whether by a Messiah or by the state or other archist contrivance, rather than pretend that such desires don't exist, we must engage in them directly in order to render them harmless.

Benjamin himself gives a version of this same treatment in the "Critique of Violence" when he discusses the commandment "Thou Shalt Not Kill." He tells us that "no judgment of the deed [of killing] follows from the commandment" (*TC*, 58; See too *SW*1, 250). He furthermore says that the commandment "exists not as a standard of judgment, but as a guideline of action for the agent or community who have to confront it in solitude and, in terrible cases, take on the responsibility of disregarding it" (*TC*, 58; see too *SW*1, 250). Here, we see a bit more clearly what Benjamin also sees in Kafka. The subject of the commandment seems to have a clear order from God, but even in such a case, Benjamin says we cannot assume that we understand what the commandment actually tells us. Here, Benjamin is showing the way that divine violence can subvert or "right" mythic violence. Against the assumption that we unproblematically know what this commandment means (the mythic approach wherein we project our own assurances onto the screen of divine externality), he complicates this by saying that even in this situation, we must wrestle with the meaning, both alone and in our communities and at times we must even "disregard" (the German term *abzusehen* also implies turning our back on) the commandment entirely (*GSII*:1, 201).

This last move is perhaps the ultimate example of atheism in Benjamin's own writing. We look right at God, or at least a representation of God, and we turn the other way. This is not the usual style of atheism wherein we simply declare that we no longer believe in God. This is in the face of a deity who may or may not exist (as in *The Castle,* we never know for sure, but the powerful effect of that possibility cannot be denied) and we turn our backs nonetheless. That is what atheism looks like for Benjamin.

In light of this, the story of the beggar makes a bit more sense. Unlike his fellow companions, the beggar does not work within the existing system of mythic violence. Instead, he sketches out the entire arc of such fetishism and ultimately turns his back on it. He feels the allure of being king and having endless riches (we all do) but he abandons that fantasy and in doing so is "rewarded" (if that is the right word to use) with an experience of a tangible material object, something that he *can* have, as opposed to what he wants to have, what he is expected to want.

The radical nature of this venture is not in any way recognized by his companions. They are completely flummoxed by his decision to forego so readily the possibility of being and remaining a king. This shows the mindset from within the confines of mythic violence because they are dealing on a purely phantasmic level. If you were already going to wish that you could be a king (wherein they may admire but also understand his audacity) why on earth would you then wish to lose that position? This seems to suggest that there are rules and internal logics to such fantasies so that if you actually do wish for X, you must stick to that desire throughout. In a way, then, the radically atheist (and anarchist) modality that is being set forth by the beggar hides in plain sight. The others do not recognize this for what it is, so dazzled are they (like the dwellers of Castle Hill) by the phantasms which they seek to serve. Nor do they (or the archist forces themselves for that matter) recognize the dire, indeed existential, threat that such a move poses to archism as such.

## A Never Finished Wall

I have dwelt mainly on two important passages in Benjamin's essay on Kafka but there are many other places in the text where a similar argument may be seen. For example, there are Benjamin's comments on Kafka's portrayal of students. Of one of these portrayals, Benjamin says "Perhaps these studies had amounted to nothing. But they are very close to that nothing which alone makes it possible for something to be useful" (*SW*2, 813). The idea of a "nothing" that "alone makes it possible for something to be useful" is akin, I would argue, to the radical use of the divine as evinced by the princess in the first passage I looked at. It is "nothing," not known, not understood and definitely not spoken for, but it has the power nonetheless for actualizing "something," that is the world in all of its material ordinariness.

Benjamin goes on to say about the students that,

[t]he gate to justice is study. Yet Kafka doesn't dare to attach to this study the promises which tradition has attached to the study of the Torah. His assistants are sextons who have lost their house of prayer; his students are pupils who have lost the Holy Writ [*Schrift*]. Now there is nothing to support them on their "untrammeled, happy journey." (*SW*2, 815/ *GS*II:1, 437)

Here, the loss of the "truth" of scripture and religion, far from being a catastrophe is, for Kafka, a kind of blessing. It means that these signs and portents cease to demand that they be read in one way only (the "true" and mythological meaning of the text) and are radically available for the students to decide for themselves what these texts mean. This is not the usual secularist version of doing away with scripture. Scripture is still crucial. It is still studied, but it has been liberated from its connection to mythic authority and violence. Knowing that they have "lost the Holy Writ," the sacred truth at the basis of study, students can now safely ponder the texts; hence "the gate to justice is study."

In German, Benjamin refers to "*leere fröhliche Fahrt*" (*GS*II.2, 436, 437). The notion of an "untrammelled, happy journey" comes from an aphorism by Kafka (Kafka 2006: 52. See Moran 2018: 169). The concept of being "untrammeled" is one that Benjamin explicitly or implicitly repeats in his essay on Kafka at several points. It suggests a sense of being freed, of having the reins of power detached, and hence leads us closer to the anarchist upshot of his reading of Kafka. For Benjamin, the idea of being untrammeled can be seen even in some of Kafka's most oppressive novels such as *The Trial*, wherein the failure of archist power to be absolute is endlessly exposed and experienced.

One text which may be especially apt in showing the way that such power can never be totalizing is Kafka's short story "Building the Great Wall of China." Here, despite literally trying to wall themselves into an absolute monarchy—seemingly a model for total sovereignty if there ever was one—we see surprising and vital forms of freedom and resistance. In that story, the narrator, a subject from Southeast China, tells us that the project to build the great wall was never intended to be completed. It is built in sections that are very far away from each other and some sections are pulled down by nomads even as other sections are being built up. The narrator speculates that this incompletion reflects the fact that, as with the Tower of Babel (the connection between the two tasks is made explicit), the task of actually finishing the wall is impossible. Indeed, if it were somehow to be finished, the wall would have a negative effect on the workers and the empire alike: "The hopelessness of such work, which, however industriously performed, would not achieve its goal at the end of a long life, would have driven them to despair and, most important, diminished their usefulness to the work. It was for this reason that the system of piecemeal building was decided upon" (Kafka 2007: 115).

More to the point (and the narrator is fairly explicit about this), there is a fear that the Wall would be seen as challenging God's role as creator of wonders and miracles. The author tells us that: "you must admit that deeds were accomplished at that time that fall just short of the building of the Tower of Babel, although they are the very opposite when it comes to being pleasing to God—at least according to human reckoning" (Kafka 2007: 115–16). Here, we see that whereas the Tower may have been an affront to God, the Great Wall, precisely since it is never intended to be finished, pleases God, perhaps because it shows a certain humility on the part of even the most august human leader, the emperor of China.

This humility is reinforced when the narrator begins to tell us how, whereas formally the worship of the emperor is a religious priority for his subjects, in practice the emperor plays very little role in anyone's life. He tells us for example that China is so vast that Peking, the capital, is as if infinitely far away from any other place in the realm. He tells us that even in Peking "especially in the court, there is some clarity on this matter [about the empire]" (Kafka 2007: 119). He also tells us that:

> Our country is so vast that no fairy tale can do justice to its size, the heavens barely span it. And Peking is only a dot, and the emperor's palace only a smaller dot. The emperor as such, to be sure, is for his part great through all the hierarchies of the world. But the living emperor, a man like us, rests as we do on a couch that, while generously proportioned, is still comparatively narrow and short. Like us he sometimes stretches his limbs, and when he is very tired, he yawns with his finely chiseled mouth. (Kafka 2007: 119)

He tells us that even if the emperor were to send a message directly to one of his subjects, the messenger would never make his way out of Peking, much less arrive in whatever small village in which the intended recipient of the village lived. Peking itself, even the court room, would infinitely expand to ensure that such a message never made it through. For this reason, he tells us further that "[a]nyone intent on concluding from such phenomena that we basically have no emperor at all would not be far from the truth. Again and again I need to assert: there is perhaps no people more loyal to the emperor than our people in the south, but this loyalty does not benefit the emperor" (Kafka 2007: 122). Here we see that at the heart of the ultimate phantasm of political authority, there is in effect no actual ontological origin, no place that is inherently and unavoidably superior. The empire is too vast, too awe inspiring, to functionally exist. This reminds me of Benjamin's own discussion, made in opposition to Carl Schmitt's notion that "sovereign is he who decides upon the exception" (Schmitt 1976: 19) in his *Origin of the German Trauerspiel*, wherein he depicts the portrayals of monarchs as hopelessly and impossibly indecisive (*OT*, 56). For Kafka and Benjamin alike, the actual human beings who hold such positions are not any different from the rest of us and hence cannot carry such a burden, and cannot represent such power.

In this way, we see once again how divine violence rises up to defeat the mythic. The divine is too huge and too majestic to contain and reinforce the lies that are attributed to it by human beings. The very universe itself stands as a kind of challenge to the phantasms of would-be earthly archons.

Even for students (the same subjects that Benjamin refers to in his essay) in "The Great Wall of China" we see that they too are in a similar position vis-à-vis the doctrines that underlie the empire and its political and theological bases. How would it be possible to learn and understand a system that was so vast, so beyond the ken of human imagination? The answer is that it is not possible and so the students in effect don't have to worry about actually discovering the truth. The narrator tells us:

The farther down one goes to the lower schools, the more, understandably enough, people's doubts about their own knowledge vanish and a wave of half-education surges up high as mountains around a few theorems that have been rammed into the students' minds for centuries; and although these have lost none of their eternal truth, they also remain eternally unknown, amid this vapor and fog. (Kafka 2007: 119)

Here too, there is no call for students to simply stop studying but what we see instead is that the act of studying becomes a fully human one. Bereft of any hope, they are nonetheless inspired:

Just so, as hopelessly and hopefully, our people view the emperor. They do not know which emperor is reigning, and there is even doubt about the name of the dynasty. A lot of this sort of thing is learned by rote at school, but the general uncertainty in this respect is so great that even the best students are drawn into it. (Kafka 2007: 120)

What these students (and by extension, the rest of us) can learn is their own knowledge, their own best guesses about the universe and what it entails. So untrammeled, they are free to think and ponder both together and alone. They too have, in effect, turned their back on the deity insofar as the deity has nothing directly to tell them. But if they were to give up on scripture altogether, this would be a grave error because, for Kafka, as for Benjamin too, we all live on Castle Hill. That is to say, we all live animated by the expectation of the divine and some kind of divine or Messianic rescue. If we tried to really walk away from this altogether, we would have no inspiration at all. The divine stands as something unknowable and that unknowledge is precisely what can inspire us to seek some values and decisions of our own (it is of course also the eternal temptation toward mythic violence; it is both at once).

## What Kind of Messiah?

This discussion offers us another version of the passage about the princess who makes dinner for the Messiah. Just as she chooses to make a human dish for an inhuman entity (meatloaf!), so too do the students find their own values in the face of the obscurity and the immensity of the divine. This tells us that we are not fated to mythic violence, that we can use the very metaphysical objects that tempt us toward archism to discover instead our own all-too-human collective desires and wishes. Rather than a vertical, archist visitation from above, this can be a horizontal and anarchist project of collective meaning-making.

But this still leaves unanswered one big question, which I raised earlier. If we need a Messiah then aren't we still in effect subject to the whims of mythic violence after all? Are we not still dependent on some externality by which we gain, in effect, our freedom, even from Messiahs?

By way of an answer, I would begin by noting the discrepancy between the two main passages that I quoted from earlier. In the story of the princess who makes dinner for the Messiah, we still see a fairly reverential attitude, whereas the beggar's story seems more openly defiant. After all, the princess does not seek the destruction of the Messiah, she anticipates their arrival eagerly. The beggar, in contrast, does seem to possess a kind of irreverence for the higher figure with whom he briefly identifies. He does not care about the king at all except as a pathway to getting his shirt. He sees the illusion of kingship and works through it to return to material reality. As previously noted, while the first passage still seems quite theistic, the second one seems to break with any concept of God or any kind of hierarchy altogether.

My wager is that rather than choose between these attitudes we can find Benjamin's actual attitude toward messianism between these two passages. We must, in effect, offer the reverence of the princess along with the dismissal of the beggar. If our attitude is just reverence, we risk, of course, returning to the mythic violence that we have only just (presumably) shaken off. Reverence without distance is a dangerous thing for both Kafka and Benjamin. We are always faced with the seduction of mythic violence (as well as its threat) so we cannot afford to simply say that the divine (or some other iteration of it) is all-powerful and leave it at that.

At the same time, we also cannot afford to have distance without reverence (like the beggar). To take this attitude is to forsake in effect the precise basis that motivates us to be political creatures in the first place. If we see a phantasm as only that, as a pure chimera, then we cannot learn from or be drawn to its example, even as we betray or turn against what we think it has to tell us. We become more rather than less susceptible to its allures when we think we have dismissed or defeated them altogether; indeed, that is the problem with secularism in its current form.

To help explain this better let me return to Benjamin's consideration of the commandment "Thou Shalt not Kill." Recall that he tells us that it "exists not as a standard of judgment, but as a guideline of action for the agent or community who have to confront it in solitude and, in terrible cases, take on the responsibility of disregarding it" (*TC*, 58; See too *SW1*, 250). This is perhaps the clearest expression of our proper attitude toward the divine that I can find in Benjamin's writing (made clearer, of course, via the intercession of Kafka himself). To study the commandment and then, at times, to turn your back on it does not lessen the reverence that we feel for a commandment. We know it is correct, even as we don't know what it means. The obscurity (even in a sentence that seems so perfectly clear as the commandment) of our charge is what gets us to think and ponder, to "wrestle with it in solitude," and to come to our own conclusions.

Thus, we must be both the princess and the beggar at once and this indicates both the proper attitude to messianism as well as suggesting a way toward an anarchist politics. In terms of messianism, there is ample evidence in Benjamin to find that for him the coming of revolution is also and simultaneously the coming of the Messiah. It is tempting then to say that "we are our own Messiah," and that is not exactly wrong but there must be an element for Benjamin in that messianism that is not entirely of our own devising. We require some modicum of externality, which gets us to reach past what we think is possible insofar as the sense of what is possible is itself an artifact of mythic violence. We must, therefore, use the very mechanisms that help to bind and order us to undo our servitude, to turn the blankness of externality into a weapon against those who use it for mythic purposes.

This may sound like "atheism light," insofar as it retains an element of theism after all. Wouldn't a truly "untrammeled" atheism dispense with God and divinity altogether? But this wish is itself a product of mythic violence in a way because it assumes that such total control over externality is possible. This is the mistake of ordinary atheism or secularism, to think that it is within the power of human beings to declare that there is no God and be done with it. Given, as I have shown, that theism structures our very reality whether we like it or not, Benjamin's stance, I would argue, is much *more* atheistic than this kind of endeavor. Benjamin is effectively saying "I acknowledge that there may well be a God and that this God stands for truth and justice but I also acknowledge that I can never know the slightest thing about this deity and for that reason, I must turn not towards but away from God to find out what I myself and those who are in my community may deem best. Any human sense of what God wants is inherently mythic and so, while acknowledging the power of God, I use that turning away to grant myself and my community a power and authority of our own."

This also helps to indicate, finally, what kind of anarchism could come out of this sort of atheism. Insofar as divine violence serves the living, we must strive, like the princess, to find what we ourselves deem best, not worthy of a God or a Messiah but worthy of one another even as we hold in contempt, like the beggar, all the false trappings of such a divine source of power. Anarchism too is constantly under threat from mythic violence. The Spanish anarchists of the 1930s were forever vigilant against something that could be called "leaderism" (with the concomitant disease of "followerism"), a tendency to become corrupted by the trappings of power (or, in the case of followerism, the tendency to defer to those in power) (Mintz 2013: 56). Benjamin (via Kafka) offers a way to keep one's eye on the source of authority without succumbing to the seductive powers of that source (as well as to stave off the seductive lies, which others will attribute to that source).

If we recall yet again Benjamin's claim that divine violence works on behalf of the living, then we can see that an atheistic anarchism in the terms that I have spelled out as follows is really a way to return our gaze to our own ordinary lives. But rather than seeing life as dull and insipid (as the term ordinary tends to suggest), we see it as full of possibility, radical and valuable in itself. Ordinary life becomes, as it were, its own goal, akin to what Benjamin calls "pure means" (*TC*, 51; see too *SW*1, 245), that is, means which have been liberated (untrammeled!) from their own ends, not by willing those ends out of existence (that cannot be done), but rather by looking those ends squarely in the face and turning the other way (*absuzehen*).

In both cases, in atheism and anarchism, the "a" (or "an") in question is not purely a negative concept. These terms do not just mean "not theistic" and "not archist." Rather the "a" stands for a positive; the ability to make collective decisions. More precisely, the "a" in question *is* negative but perhaps more in the sense of being a negation of the negation. It undoes all of the false power systems that are attributed to theism and archism alike and, in so doing, allows the positive expression of those forms to be visible and legible to the human beings that are otherwise subjected to them. Thus the "negative" of the "a" is the bridge to a positive, which is itself as broad and diverse as the living in all of their complexity and possibility.

## References

Benjamin, Andrew. (2013), *Working with Walter Benjamin: Recovering a Political Philosophy*, Edinburgh: Edinburgh University Press.
Botwinick, Aryeh. (1997), *Skepticism, Belief, and the Modern: Maimonides to Nietzsche*, Ithaca: Cornell University Press.
Kafka, Franz. (1998), *The Castle*, trans. Mark Harman, New York: Schocken Books.
Kafka, Franz. (2007), "Building the Great Wall of China," in Stanley Corngold (ed.), *Kafka's Selected Stories*, 113–24, New York: W.W. Norton and Co.
Kafka, Franz. (2006), *The Zürau Aphorisms of Franz Kafka*, trans. Geoffrey Brock and Michael Hofmann, New York: Schocken Books.
Mintz, Frank. (2013), *Anarchism and Worker's Self-Management in Revolutionary Spain*, trans. Paul Sharkey, Oakland: AK Press.
Moran, Brendan. (2018), *Politics of Benjamin's Kafka: Philosophy as Renegade*, New York: Palgrave Macmillan.
Schmitt, Carl. (1976), *The Concept of the Political*, trans. George Schwab, New Brunswick: Rutgers University Press.
Žižek, Slavoj. (2000), *The Ticklish Subject: The Absent Centre of Political Ontology*, New York: Verso.

# 6

# Study, Sovereignty, and Justice

## Benjamin, Scholem, and Agamben

Brendan Moran

Anyone with even a modicum of institutional power finds themselves in a Schmittian situation.[1] Carl Schmitt himself surmises: "[S]overeignty . . . resides . . . in determining definitively what constitutes public order and security, in determining when they are disturbed, and so on" (Schmitt 1985: 9, 1990 [1934]: 15). Notwithstanding reservations about identifying with it, many of us exercise such sovereignty in our daily institutional roles as well as in a myriad of other roles. We decide what must disappear—that is, what must be eliminated—for certain institutional contexts to survive if not thrive, and the grounds for such disappearance might often be ones that our more scrutinizing or studious selves could not accept as particularly compelling. The grounds for our decisions unravel.

Walter Benjamin, Gershom Scholem, and Giorgio Agamben are less complacent than most about the pervasive predicament—in so-called everyday politics—of voluntary or involuntary opposition to study. Benjamin and Agamben, in particular, associate messianism with the potentiality—the inexhaustible potential—for study. Messianism is the pressure to persist in studying—especially when and where complacency and comfort instill a reluctance to study. Messianism is the pressure of time to go beyond whatever is regarded as settled. Time has not settled anything. The settled is an implausible presumption to halt time, however provisionally. Life demands further study. The justice of time is its registration of this demand that recognizes the domination of no settled space over time.

Study attempts to do justice to life. Study frees what is studied from conclusions hitherto drawn about it. How does life *demand* study? Life interpellates us by appearing distorted in relation to existing conclusions. It interpellates us so that we study further or study again.

For Benjamin and Agamben, whatever exceeds law, or exceeds other human constructions, appears distorted in relation to those constructions. Distortion complements study by accentuating the incompleteness of study, an incompleteness that includes the independence of distortion from law. In seeming awry, distortion shows itself to be independent of law, somehow lawless.

Agamben claims that Scholem unwittingly becomes Schmittian in invoking a fundamental law, albeit a very unclear law, as sacredly valid. Agamben contends that Benjamin ultimately does not recognize such validity, for Benjamin emphasizes all that is not sublated by any law or any representative of law. Agamben shares Benjamin's emphasis—an emphasis that, more than some of Scholem's relevant remarks, can be construed as unSchmittian in its regard for whatever is excluded by sovereignty associated with law and its representatives. This line of consideration could, nonetheless, give rise to further questions, including the question of whether Benjamin ever indulges a Schmittian notion of sovereignty.

## Law, Secret, and Validity

In an early text, Scholem formulates the precept that *"[j]ustice eliminates fate"*—*Die Gerechtigkeit eliminiert das Schicksal*.[2] Scholem reportedly read this statement, along with others, aloud to Benjamin and Benjamin's wife, Dora, on October 30, 1918.[3] As a verdict imposed on existence, fate is the antithesis of justice. Hence, Scholem's remark concerning "the messianic centre of justice," whereby "in truth there is indeed no sinner whatsoever."[4] This perhaps disconcerting exemption of all from verdicts is also evident in Benjamin's critique of legal justice. Even in cases where egregious deeds must be halted, the perpetrators are not entirely identifiable with those deeds.

In his 1916-essay on language, Benjamin says that the story of Adam and Eve conveys a condition in which "the question of good and evil" is simply, in Kierkegaard's terminology, "'empty prattle' [*Geschwätz*]." "The tree of knowledge stood in the garden of God not on account of information [*Aufschlüsse*] about good and evil but as emblem [*Wahrzeichen*] of the court," emblem of divine judgment, "over the questioner." Non-paradisial law, which is mythic law, conceals this irony of its judgment about questions over which it has no certain prerogative. "Law" (*Recht*) cannot concede its own "immense [*ungeheure*] irony": its "mythic origin" in judging as though it could provide what it cannot possibly provide—true knowledge of good and evil (*SW*1, 71–72/ GSII:1, 153–54).

Benjamin's "Fate and Character" (1919) elaborates: a judge might see "fate," but with "every punishment" proclaimed, the judge "must blindly dictate fate. It is never the human but only the mere life [*das bloße Leben*] in the human that it strikes—the part involved in natural guilt and misfortune by virtue of semblance [*des Scheins*]" (*SW*1, 204/ *GS*II:1, *175*).[5] The "natural guilt" is nature that instils acquiescence to semblance; the natural guilt is not the messianic nature that treats such guilt as something other than necessary, as not equivalent to time itself.[6] Messianic time cannot rest with a semblance of guilt. Whether law is *Recht* or *Gesetz* might be irrelevant, for—in Benjamin's accounts—both German terms pertain to human constructions that cannot ultimately ensure they are divinely constituted or created. This, for instance, is the case for *Recht* in "On Language as Such and on the Language of the Human" (1916). In "Toward the Critique of Violence" of 1921 (*TC*, 39–61/GSII:1, 179–203) and in his writings on Kafka, *Recht* and *Gesetz* are both discussed critically.

The divine court suspends humanly constituted worlds and is perpetually on call. Franz Kafka says that the Last Judgment is actually "a summary court in perpetual session [*ein Standrecht*]."[7] This statement has attracted many different interpretations—most of them sharing Scholem's view that it is an "overwhelming statement."[8] Benjamin's reading is relatively unique in regarding the "*Standrecht*" as something that judges against judgments. It pressures us to reconsider judgments we have hitherto made. Benjamin might be recalling Scholem's statement that "[j]ustice is the indifference of the last judgment."[9]

A draft for Benjamin's 1934 essay on Kafka paraphrases Kafka's remark on the Last Judgment as a "summary court in perpetual session" (*GSII*:3, 1216). A note for Benjamin's "On the Concept of History" (1940) also cites Kafka's statement on the Last Judgment as "a summary court in perpetual session" (*SW*4, 407/ *GSI*:3, *1245/ WuN19, 135*). In both of these texts by Benjamin, it is claimed that "an apocryphal gospel" proposes the Day of Judgment "would not be distinguishable from other days." The Day of Judgment is already a pressure in every day, in every moment (whatever "moment" means). According to the note for the 1940-text: "[e]very moment is a moment of judgment concerning certain moments that preceded it" (*SW*4, 407/ *GSI*:3, *1245/ WuN19, 135*).[10] The Day of Judgment is the reality that eludes judgment and suspends it.

In a statement that clearly echoes, but does not mention, texts by Benjamin, an essay by Jacob Taubes of 1983 remarks: "Revelation in the strict sense happens ... only at the beginning and at the end of history, which are in secret agreement [*in geheimer Verabredung*]. The course of history itself is a summary court in perpetual session [*Standrecht in Permanenz*]."[11]

Taubes's remark might be about human history and the relentless judgment that it often entails. There is, however, some hope in Benjamin's adaptation of Kafka's remark about the Last Judgment as a summary court in perpetual session. The pressure of the Day of Judgment is that it renders all other judgments transient and provisory. This pressure is hopeful in depriving those judgments of complete control; it is shown that they do not extinguish secret. The secret agreement, for Benjamin, is the basis for recognizing secret as something that underlies history. It is a secret that cannot be told, for it is known only as secret, as something unmalleable for pretenses to sovereign control.

In this sense, there is something secret in messianic time. In an interview of 1973 or 1974, Scholem says: "If the feeling that the world holds a secret ever vanishes from humanity, then it's all over" (Scholem 2002: 109). This feeling is at least part of the "*geheime Verabredung*" that Benjamin describes in "On the Concept of History"; Benjamin refers to "*eine geheime Verabredung zwischen den gewesenen Geschlechtern und unserem*"—"a secret agreement between past generations and ours." We "were expected on earth" in the sense that, "like every generation before us, we have been endowed with a *weak* messianic force [*Kraft*], a force on which the past has a claim. This claim cannot be settled cheaply" (*SW*4, 390/ *GS*1:2, 694/ *WuN*19, 70; see too: *WuN*19, 16–17, 31, 60, 83, 94). Our agreement with the past is secret, for its pressure exceeds any attempt to respond to it. Our expressions are inadequate to its pressure. The claim of the past is thus secret, somehow inexplicable, even though it might feel utterly compelling. Benjamin articulates this secret agreement, for it is threatened, always threatened, by an "enemy" from which "even the dead will not be safe" if the enemy "is victorious"—and this enemy "has never ceased to be victorious" (SW4, 391/ GSI:2, 695/ WuN19, 72; see too: WuN19, 18–19, 33, 62, 85, 96). Preserving the secret involves not only keeping the agreement with the past effective by trying to prevent the enemy from dominating the past entirely. Preserving the secret also means making sure that there is never a presumption to extinguish it. According to Benjamin's *Elective Affinities*-essay (1922), "[a]ll mythic significance seeks secret [*Geheimnis*]," whereas art presents secret as always already there: a "true artwork . . . presents itself ineluctably as secret [*Geheimnis*]" (SW1, 351/ GSI:1, 195). This secret includes nature "incapable of being unveiled," nature "that keeps safe a secret [*ein Geheimnis verwahrt*] as long as God allows this nature to exist" (353/ 197). In the *Trauerspiel* book, this theme is specifically developed with respect to philosophy. Loved and not pursued, truth is no "unveiling" that destroys "the secret [*Geheimnis*]" but a "revelation [*Offenbarung*] that does justice to it [*die ihm gerecht wird*]" (OT, 7/ OGT, 31/ GSI:1, 211). Even as Benjamin in the Surrealism-essay (1929) decries "pathetic or fanatical stress on the enigmatic side of the enigmatic [*die rätselhafte Seite am Rätselhaften*]," he adds: we "penetrate the secret [*durchdringen . . . das Geheimnis*] only to the degree that we retrieve [*wiederfinden*] it in the everyday by dint of a dialectic optic that perceives the everyday as impenetrable, the impenetrable as everyday" (SW2, 216/ GSII:1, 307).

The inherent secret is retrieved if lives are no longer regarded as that which the victorious might have made them seem or continue to make them seem. This retrieval requires recognition of the temporality that eludes judgments denying inextinguishable secret—judgments claiming to resolve history into fate and into ostensible annulment of the open potentiality inherent in time. This messianic time has implications for law.

Much discussion has been occasioned by the aforementioned note toward "On the Concept of History"—the note about the Last Judgment as a court in perpetual session and about every moment as judgment about what preceded it. In an essay of 1992–8 titled "The Messiah and the Sovereign: The Problem of Law in Walter Benjamin," Agamben concludes that the passage refers to "judgment pronounced in the state of exception," whereby philosophy is "*always . . . a* decision *on*" its "*relationship*" with "the entire codified text of tradition, whether it be Islamic *shari'a*, Jewish *halakhah*, or Christian dogma" (PO, 160–61/ 257–58).[12] Evidently reworking the same passage, Agamben's *Homo Sacer* (1995) refers to the "legitimation crisis" experienced by "[a]ll societies and all cultures today" with regard to "law." By "law" Agamben says that he means "the entire text of tradition in its regulative form, whether the Jewish *Torah* or the Islamic *shari'a*, Christian dogma or"—he adds this time—"the profane *nomos*" (HS, 51/ 59).

In the essay of 1992–98, Agamben observes that Scholem—in a letter of September 20, 1934 to Benjamin (CS, 140–43/ BS, 173–77)—contends there is, for Kafka, a revelatory force in holy texts and in the law borne, however obscurely, by those texts (PO, 169–71/ 268–72). The law is addressed in earlier letters of 1934 from Scholem to Benjamin. Scholem thinks that Benjamin neglects the standing and the importance of a "secret," hidden "law" (*Gesetz*) in Kafka's works. Scholem refers to the "*existence* of secret law" in Kafka (CS, 123/ BS, 154) and claims that Benjamin disregards this while interpreting Kafka's "terminology of the law . . . only from its *most profane* side" (127/ 158). In the letter of September 20, 1934, Scholem does not think that the "*Schrift*" is lost and insists on its ongoing validity in a "nothingness of revelation." Revelation "appears to be without meaning [*bedeutungsleer erscheint*]," but in this condition revelation "still maintains itself." Revelation "*has validity* but no *significance* [sie *gilt*, aber nicht *bedeutet*]." To this now well-known formulation, Scholem adds a description of the relevant condition: "[w]here the wealth of significance [*Bedeutung*] falls away, and what appears [*das Erscheinende*], as if reduced to the null point of its own content, nonetheless does not disappear (and revelation is something that appears [*etwas Erscheinendes*]), there the nothingness of the appearing becomes evident" (142/ 175).[13] After discussing this statement by Scholem, Agamben reiterates that—for Scholem—"Law" (*Legge*) "maintains itself 'in the zero point of its own content'" (*PO*, 169/ 268). Scholem mentions Law and makes it clear that the holy text, its law, is the revelation that appears, but does so as if reduced to the null point of its own content; its revelatory force appears without meaning.

Agamben modifies Scholem's formulation, "sie [*Offenbarung*] *gilt*, aber nicht *bedeutet*," into the German syntagm "*Geltung ohne Bedeutung*"—in Italian, "*vigenza senza significato*." In English, the German syntagm is usually rendered as "being in force without significance" and it could be rendered as "being in force without meaning" or simply as "validity without meaning," whereby there is validity but a validity without clear meaning. Agamben even suggests that Scholem's notion, which was developed to express disagreement with Benjamin, is compatible with Benjamin's "absolutization" in "On the Concept of History" of the condition of exception as the "legitimation crisis" that can include taking exception to law as well as taking exception to sovereigns who seek to dominate such possibility of independence from law (*PO*, 169–70/ 269–70). In *Homo Sacer*, Agamben adds: All tradition in its regulative forms is in a legitimation crisis whereby "law . . . is in force as the pure 'nothingness of revelation'"; "this is precisely the original structure of the sovereign relation, and the nihilism in which we are living is, from this perspective, nothing other than the coming to light of this relation as such" (*HS*, 51/ 59). The coming to light of the sovereign relation is the emergence of questioning about its validity.

"Validity" is one of the most obvious translations of "*Geltung*," whereas Agamben's Italian formulation "*vigenza*" pertains to "validity" in a much more obviously legal sense (*PO*, 169/ 269). "*Geltung*" could be translated by "*validità*," "*evidenza*," or "*risalto*" (in English, "emphasis"). Scholem is indeed more insistent than Agamben on the specific validity of a law, especially in Kafka's works. Like Agamben, Benjamin is much less certain than Scholem concerning this validity. For Scholem, of course, the relevant law in its revelatory force has no meaning—that is, no significance in the sense of a tangible meaning. It is a law for which revelation is nothing, the paradoxical meaning or significance of nothing. This could recall Benjamin's *éloge* (in 1921) of "the holy text" as that in which "meaning [*Sinn*] has ceased to be the watershed for flowing language and flowing revelation" (*SW1*, 262/ *GSIV*:1, 21). This view of the holy text undergoes permutations, however, in some of Benjamin's later work—even to the point where there are no texts of sacred validity.

Particularly striking are Benjamin's remarks as developed in his Kafka-analyses. "Kafka does not dare attach to this study the promises which tradition has attached to the study of the Torah. His assistants are sextons who have lost their house of prayer, his students are pupils who have lost the Holy Writ [*die Schrift*]" (*SW2*, 815/ *GSII*:2, 437). Lacking any holy text as various traditions conceive it, study does not assuredly have a law about which, or from which, there could be assured *Geltung*. As Benjamin says in one of his notes toward a letter of August 8, 1934 to Scholem:

> I consider Kafka's constant insistence on the law [*Drängen auf das Gesetz*], of which nothing is ever proclaimed [*verlautbart*], to be the dead point [*den toten Punkt*] of his work, something for the drawer of the mystery-monger [*Geheimniskrämers*]. Precisely with this concept [of the law] I do not want to involve myself. If it [this concept of the law] were, nonetheless, to have a function in Kafka's work— something I want to leave open—an interpretation such as mine, which takes images as its point of departure, will lead to this function. (*GSII*:3, 1245)

There seems to be a contradiction in this statement. On the one hand, Kafka insists on the existence of the barely elaborated law; Benjamin does not wish to involve himself with this insistence and its mystery-mongering. On the other hand, Benjamin wants to leave open whether this concept of the law *has a function* in Kafka's work. Has Benjamin not already said that this concept of law has a function in Kafka's work? Perhaps one should not expect too much precision from an informal note. In any case, if such a concept of law has a function in Kafka's work, Benjamin's image-oriented interpretation will lead to it, Benjamin's note tells us. The dismissive reference to mystery-mongering is somehow repeated in Benjamin's diary entry of August 31, 1934, where he records Bertolt Brecht's criticism that Benjamin's Kafka essay contains "a lot of mystery-mongering [*Geheimniskrämerei*]." Even Brecht, however, says Kafka's "images" are "good" (*SW2*, 786/*GSVI*, 527). In other words, Benjamin takes at least some solace in thinking his image-oriented reading will show Kafka to be beyond the mystery-mongering that invokes a barely elaborated law. In the actual letter of August 11, 1934 to Scholem, Benjamin says simply that he does not "wish to go into explicit detail on this concept [of law as the dead point of Kafka's work]." He considers "Kafka's constant insistence on the Law [*das Gesetz*] to be the dead point of his work, by which I want to say only that, on the basis of this dead point, the work does not seem to move interpretatively" (*CS*, 135–36/ *BS*, 167–68/ *C*, 453/ *GBIV*, 479). Law is a dead point in setting interpretative parameters that unduly constrain readings of Kafka's works; those works can be read in terms of their independence from law.

In his 1980 annotations to Benjamin's letter, Scholem seems to suggest that aspects of Benjamin's notes on Kafka might indulge, more than does the actual letter, Kafka's invocation of an otherwise unelaborated Law (*CS*, 134–36 n1, n2, and n4/ *BS* 168 n1-3).[14]

Agamben too mentions both Benjamin's letter of August 11, 1934, and Benjamin's notes toward the letter. With regard to this material by Benjamin and with regard to Scholem's aforementioned comments on nothingness of revelation, Agamben—in his essay of 1992–98—detects an "equivalence between messianism and nihilism" in both

Benjamin and Scholem. He also detects, however, two distinct "forms of messianism or nihilism"—evidently a Scholemian one and a Benjaminian one. Apparently referring to Scholem, Agamben cites "a first form (which we may call imperfect nihilism) that nullifies the law but maintains the Nothing in a perpetual and infinitely deferred state of validity." In Scholem's rendering, the nullified law still has validity notwithstanding its unfulfilled and meaningless condition. The "second form" of "messianism or nihilism" is Benjamin's—"a perfect nihilism that does not even let validity survive beyond its meaning" (*PO*, 171/ 272). In other words, any validity associated with meaning passes away, for the meaning itself passes away or is at least modified.

Scholem's form of nihilism is particularly indicative of a condition under which almost everyone suffers: law has validity that is not quite identifiable with any particular meaning. Agamben refers to "the whole text of tradition, the whole law," as involving "*Geltung ohne Bedeutung*," even though the upshot of this involvement is that all and everything are "outside law"—including law itself, for its exercise entails forces not specified in law. This point is Agamben's explicit move toward Benjamin, for whom all and everything are not bound by law. All and everything are in the condition where the presumed *Geltung* of law is indeed only a presumption and not a condition whose "ban" reaches entirely into anything. There is, accordingly, a kind of panic among those most fervently perpetrating the ban: "The entire planet has now become the exception that law must contain in its ban" (*PO*, 170/ 270–71). Benjamin registers doubts about whether tradition and law have "*Geltung*" of the sort advocated by Scholem. Elaborating on Benjamin, Agamben says the "Messiah's task" entails the difficulty that the Messiah "must confront not simply a law that commands and forbids but a law that, like the original Torah, is in force without significance [*vige senza significare*]." Insofar as we experience, or can conceive of, any independence from such law, we are confronted with the messianic task—a task defined by ultimate time in its independence from validity of law and tradition. Agamben says we "who live in a state of exception that has become the rule must reckon" with the messianic task. We are confronted by persistent exception in relation to forces that would like to eliminate exception. Living in a state of exception that has become the rule means we are simultaneously subject to law "that, like the original Torah, is in force without significance," and yet are also dissociated from law—living in a condition of exception in relation to it (*PO*, 171/ 272). In a condition of exception in relation to law, we find ourselves thrown into, or opened to, the time without law. The messianic—the time without law—can be felt.

In *Homo Sacer* (1995), Agamben distinguishes Benjamin and Scholem even more clearly. "Benjamin . . . writes, . . . objecting to Scholem's notion of being in force without significance, that a law that has lost its content ceases to exist and becomes indistinguishable from life" (*HS*, 53/ 62). This notion of life might seem to pertain to life in its independence from law. In a way, it does indeed pertain to such life. Agamben is, however, a perceptive reader in noticing that the life at issue, at least initially, is bare life—life subordinate to law, a law that has validity even though it is without content or significance. In *The Castle*, K. lives in subordination to a law that he does not otherwise know: "in Kafka's village the empty potentiality of law is so much in force as to become indistinguishable from life" (*HS*, 53/ 61). The law converges with bare life.[15] Yet Agamben recognizes there is something that Benjamin "opposes to law's being in force without significance" (*HS*, 54/ 63). Agamben alludes to this by saying that bare life and the form of law eventually "abolish each other and enter into a new dimension" (*HS*, 55/ 64).

In Benjamin's terms, it could be said that messianic life breaks through mere life and its form of law. With this breakthrough, writing releases itself from the law that is without significance. "[W]ithout the key that belongs to it, writing [*Schrift*] is not Scripture [*Schrift*] but life." On the one hand, as Benjamin immediately adds, this life is life subordinate to the law without significance: "life as it is lived in the village on the castle hill." On the other hand, "[i]n the attempt at transformation [*Verwandlung*] of life into scripture [*Schrift*]," Benjamin detects "the meaning of 'reversal' [*den Sinn der Umkehr*']" that is sought in many of Kafka's "parables [*Gleichnisse*]." This meaning of reversal is effectively a reversal of meaning; it is evident in the "existence" of Kafka's Sancho Panza, an existence that "actually consists in rereading [*Nachlesen*] one's own existence" (*CS*,135/ *BS*,*167*; *C*, 453/ *GBIV*, *479*; see too GSII:3, 1246).[16] The life of study, as we shall see, somehow seeps through, indeed breaks through, the life of subordination.

Indicating a continued interest in his earlier debates on Kafka, Scholem in 1960 provides an implicit rejoinder to Benjamin: "mystical exegesis . . . has the essential character of a key. The key itself might even be lost, but the infinite drive to look for it still remains." Even though "the mystical impulses" seem to have dwindled to a "vanishing point [*Nullpunkt*]," those impulses show themselves to be "infinitely effective" in "the writings of Franz Kafka."[17]

Benjamin recognizes this drive in Kafka's writings but considers it to be outweighed by other tendencies in those writings—tendencies that question the impetus or drive itself. In the letter of August 11, 1934 to Scholem, he says—as noted twice above —that he considers "Kafka's constant insistence on the Law [*Drängen auf das Gesetz*]" to be "the dead point [*den toten Punkt*]" of Kafka's work (*CS*, 135/ *BS*, 167–68; *C*, 453/ *GBIV*, 479; see too: *GSII*:3, 1245). Study is somehow annulled if blocked by this insistence. Like time, study is ultimately lawless. Study deals with, but is not bound by, claims to law or to a drive toward a key.

## Justice as Study Avoids a Schmittian Law

Agamben's *Homo Sacer* continues with a point that adapts Benjamin's "Toward the Critique of Violence" (1921). Be it secular or religious (or both at once, as political theology often detects), law is the force without significance or meaning as it implicates everyone while, and even though, its ultimate legitimacy is not clear. As force without significance (*Bedeutung*), law renders life as something dominated by law and does so beyond anything specific that is stated in law. In this domination by law, life is bare life—life as subordinate adaptation. As force without significance, law lets bare life "subsist before it." Bare life is produced as a life that sovereign power can control and neglect, as is portrayed in Kafka's *The Castle* (*HS*, 55/64). For Agamben, of course, there is life—form of life—that frees itself somewhat from bare life. "It is important," Agamben says in *The Use of Bodies* (2014), "not to confuse bare life with natural life.

Through its division and its capture in the apparatus of the exception, life assumes the form of bare life, which is to say, that of a life that has been cut off and separated from its form" (*UB*, 263/ 333). The latter form can at least sometimes be an uprising. The anarchy of life, anarchy of the form in which life is uncontainable, frees itself somewhat from, renders "destitute," the anarchy of power—power exercised as though it conclusively grounds validity even though it does not. Mentioning Benjamin, and perhaps referring to Benjamin's expressly Brechtian comment in the late 1930s that "[t]he anarchy of bourgeois society is an infernal anarchy" (*SW*4, 222/ *GS*II:2, 546), Agamben extrapolates: "Anarchy is what becomes thinkable only at the point where we grasp and render destitute the anarchy of power" (*UB*, 275/ 347–48). Anarchy of life is the form of life that cannot abide reduction to mere life (or bare life) and the latter's anarchy of assertion over life.[18]

Benjamin's Kafka essay thus characterizes study, in its respite from legal practice, as "[t]he gate of justice" (*SW*2, 815/ *GS*II:2, *437*). Study for Agamben, as for Benjamin, will be shown to concern law in its removal from any semblance of dominative force. There is, however, something that might seem overly aggressive in Agamben's attendant conclusion, in *State of Exception* (2003), that Scholem, unlike Benjamin and Agamben himself, is Schmittian. Whereas Benjamin reads Kafka "as having shown that" law "ceases to be law and blurs at all points with life," Scholem suggests that Kafka has "maintained a law that no longer has any meaning." Scholem's Kafka-reading entails a notion of "Scripture (the Torah) without its key" as "the cipher of the law in the state of exception, which is in force but is not applied or is applied without being in force." "[N]ot at all suspecting that he shares this thesis with Schmitt," Scholem "believes" it "is still law" that prevails albeit not in terms of any specific contents or meanings (*SE*, 63/ 81–82). According to this aside by Agamben, Scholem conceives law in terms that parallel those in which Schmitt characterizes and defends sovereign power.

Of course, Scholem is not *expressly* invoking (as does Schmitt) the necessity for a sovereign ruler based on mythic devices of domination.[19] Scholem does not say, as does Schmitt, that "all great historical activity . . . lies in the aptitude for myth [*Fähigkeit zum Mythos*]" (Schmitt 1923, 1939: 11). It is possible, however, that there is some overlap between Scholem's conception of law and the following claim by Schmitt: "For a legal order to make sense, order must be produced. A normal situation must be created, and sovereign is the one who definitively decides whether this normal situation actually exists" (Schmitt 1985: 13, 1990: 20).

What could this statement possibly have in common with Scholem's statements concerning law in Kafka's works? It has in common only that law is conceived by Scholem as having an authority that is independent of its contents, and (although Agamben does not mention this) that there is someone in the prevailing order who exercises correlative authority. In a letter of July 17, 1934, Scholem complains that Benjamin neglects the prevalence of Halakhah, the law that teaches, in Kafka: "The moral world of the Halakhah and its abysses and dialectic lay there right before you: in Kafka" (*CS*, 127/ *BS*, *158*). With the 1980 publication of this letter, an editorial note by Scholem mentions "the contradictory interpretations given by the 'religious man' in the cathedral of the parable 'Before the Law' in Kafka's *The Trial*." Concerning this religious man, who is associated with the sovereign power in *The Trial* (he is a prison chaplain), Scholem continues:

> I was of the opinion that the religious man in the cathedral was an encoded halakhist, a rabbi, who knows how to transmit—if not the "Law [*Gesetz*]" itself—at least the traditions circulating about the law in the form of a parable. He is not an official of the "court" by accident, even if only with the rank of a prison chaplain, for that court is somehow linked to the "Law," no matter how one interprets these concepts. (*CS*,127n3/ *BS*,159n3)

Scholem acknowledges that Benjamin does not share this emphasis on a prevailing law (without meaning) and on a correlative authority figure (the prison chaplain as halakhist). It has been mentioned above how Benjamin's 1934 essay detects in Kafka a *Schrift* that has dissolved into life to a point at which the *Schrift* is simply something to study—whereby study is no longer bound to a view of the text as divine teaching. Kafka fails in the attempt "to convert poetry into teaching [*Lehre*]" (*SW*2, 808/ *GS*II:2, *427*). Benjamin does not grant the prison chaplain the prerogative detected by Scholem. Kafka could not, moreover, be "founder" of a religion or have a pretense to divination—he was no "mantic" (*SW*2, 805–6/ *GS*II:2, 424–25). In an outline for the essay, Benjamin seems to suggest that Kafka avoids the "shamelessness of theology" and might recognize no God (*GS*II:3, 1210). Benjamin notes that Werner Kraft, in his interpretation of Kafka's "The Bucket Rider," "found an image that emphatically pinpoints [*festlegt*] the place of the divine in Kafka's world." The bucket rider's ascent "'is a becoming-raised [*Gehobenwerden*]—like that of the weighing-scale when the full weight is on the other side.'" The divine is something someone has pushed up—somehow pumped up. Justice shows that this is a merely human elevation. Hence Benjamin's reference to "[t]he full weight of justice . . . that so degrades everything divine" (*GS*II:3, 1220).[20]

Partly because it is past, law no longer practiced registers the transience of law. Law is an historical, not a transcendent, accomplishment.[21] Kafka's Dr. Bucephalus is a horse who is no longer the steed of Alexander of Macedonia. Bucephalus has further distanced himself from myth by studying law that is no longer practiced. Kraft proposes that Bucephalus's study of law is an exercise of justice against myth. Kraft effuses: "Nowhere else in literature is there such a forceful [*gewaltige*], such an effective [*durchschlagende*], critique of myth in its full scope" (Kraft 1933: 569).[22] Benjamin's 1934 essay cites Kraft in this regard and adds: "The law [*Recht*] . . . no longer practiced and . . . only studied . . . is the gate of justice [*Pforte der Gerechtigkeit*]./ The gate of justice is study [*das Studium*]" (*SW*2, 815/ *GS*II:2, *437*; see too: *GS*II:3, 1244–45). Unnoted by Benjamin is that Kraft is particularly responsive to the modesty evoked in Kafka's account: "Through a 'perhaps,' the human observer [of Bucephalus's study] introduces, in unswerving modesty, his hymn to justice" (Kraft 1933: 569).[23] Kafka says: "Perhaps, therefore, it is really best, as Bucephalus has done, to immerse oneself in law books."[24] As Kraft and Benjamin observe, the laws in these books are no longer applied. Concerning the modesty, Kraft adds that the observer in Kafka's text "does not use the word 'justice [*Gerechtigkeit*]'; it is really too grand [*groß*]." The interpreter, who "must magnify [*vergrößern*] in order to understand," has less "responsibility [*Verantwortung*]" (Kraft 1933: 569).[25] Both Kraft and Benjamin seem conscious, nonetheless, of responsibility to the modesty of Kafka's text; it is a modesty that is just with regard to law. Modesty about law is justice. Wrenching us out of the time of applied law, the unpracticed law is the gate of justice and the study is the gate of justice. The existing English translation says "gate to justice," as though the gate has been opened but no more than that. If the formulation were "gate to justice," however, the German would likely be "*die Pforte zur Gerechtigkeit*" and not "*die Pforte der Gerechtigkeit*," which is the formulation used twice in Benjamin's remarks on study in the 1934 essay and once in a related note (*GS*II:3, 1245).[26] The gate, as indicated, is twofold: it is both the law studied but no longer applied, and it is the exercise of study itself. What happens with this twofold gate of justice? There ensues the aforementioned reversal. "Reversal is the direction of study, the direction that transforms existence into writing" (*SW*2, 815/ *GS*II:2, *437*). As writing, the *Heilige Schrift* emphasizes its own mediate character; it points to a withholding in any conveying. To be more specific: the writing disempowers projections of the unstudious upon it—including even ascriptions of divinity to it.[27] It disempowers the prison chaplain's verbal bullying and intimidation of K. on behalf of a law that is not known.[28]

Agamben detects the profanation in Benjamin's reading of Kafka, and he associates this with profanation of law. In *State of Exception*, Agamben comments: "In the Kafka-essay [by Benjamin], the enigmatic image of a law that is studied but no longer practiced corresponds . . . to the unmasking of mythico-juridical violence." Study releases from the latter violence. Agamben refers to "law after its nexus with violence and power has been deposed." It is "law that no longer has force or application, like the one in which [according to Kafka's story] the 'new attorney' leafing through 'our old books,' buries himself in study, or like the one Foucault may have had in mind when he spoke of a 'new law' that has been freed from all discipline and all relation to sovereignty." Agamben extrapolates: "the law—no longer practiced, but studied—is not justice, but only the gate that leads to it [*la porta che conduce ad essa*]." Whereas Benjamin characterizes both unapplied law *and* study as the gate *of* justice, Agamben seems here to address deactivated law as only the gate leading *to* justice. Agamben continues, however, with a statement somewhat closer to Benjamin: "What opens a passage toward justice [*verso la giustizia*] is not the erasure of law, but its deactivation and inactivity [*inoperosità*]—that is, another use of law. . . . Kafka's characters . . . seek, each one following his or her own strategy, to 'study' and deactivate it, to 'play' with it" (*SE*, 63–64/ 82–83).

It has been argued that the commandment against idolatry, including against idolatrous approaches to law, is paradoxically Benjamin's law—his one and only law.[29] Of Kafka, Benjamin proclaims: "[n]o writer [*Dichter*] so exactly followed" the commandment 'You should make yourself no graven image [*Bildnis*]'" (*SW*2, 808/ *GS*II:2, *428*). Perhaps even that prohibition could be questioned, whereby anti-idolatry might occasionally turn on itself, for the very notion of law—including the law of anti-idolatry—can be an object of critical regard. No law, including the anti-idolatrous one, is a fate. Perhaps this can be illustrated by the possibility that love of someone can help one find the freedom to withstand, even oppose, the pressures to relate idolatrously—fatefully—to other aspects of life. "In your arms, fate would stop forever," says Benjamin in a drafted letter of 1933 to the painter Anna Maria Blaupot (*GB*IV, 278).[30] It is unlikely such love would stop fate forever, but love—as a force keeping fate in abeyance—seems to underlie Benjamin's regret concerning the missed possibility of love among the main characters in Goethe's *Elective Affinities* (*SW*1,297–360/ *GS*I:1, 123–201). There is no recognizable law of existence besides the law, if it is really a law at all, that paradoxically recognizes no law—no fate—of existence. This is the law of study, which cannot abide any Schmittian sovereign. Study is, therefore, the challenge that can barely be tolerated—including in institutions nominally devoted to study (Moran 2019).

## Justice Restitutes Study, Study Restitutes Justice

*In Profanations* (2005), Agamben reformulates Benjamin's comments on Kafka's "The New Lawyer": "the law that is no longer applied but only studied is the gate of justice [*è la porta della giustizia*]" (*PR* 76/ 87). Agamben does indeed refer now to the gate *of* justice and not the gate *to* justice. He adds, moreover, a statement about the use and even the happiness that might be possible once various questionable constraints are deactivated. "Just as the *religio* that is played with but no longer observed opens the gate of use, so the powers [*le potenze*] of economics, law, and politics, deactivated in play, can become the gateway of a new happiness [*la porta di una nuova felicità*]" (76/ 87). For Benjamin, it is in transience that happiness and justice converge.

Benjamin's so-called "Theological-Political Fragment" (dated variously at 1920–21, 1922–23, or 1937–38 [Hamacher 2006: 175]) proposes that happiness is reliant on transience. In that sense, every happiness is a new happiness and "all that is earthly seeks its downfall [*Untergang*]" (*SW*3, 305/ GSII:1, *204*). On the one hand, "[t]he profane" is "no category of the messianic realm." In other words, the profane is not the messianic realized. On the other hand, the profane "is . . . a category—indeed the most pertinent one"—of the "quietest approach" of the messianic (305/ *204*). The messianic is quiet in its constancy; it is always there—in misfortune and in release from misfortune. In the draft-letter of 1933 to Anna Maria Blaupot, Benjamin identifies fate with "horror" and "happiness" that simply surprise (*GB*IV, 279). For the theological-political fragment, neither misfortune nor release from misfortune is irrevocably necessary, but precisely the transience underlying those experiences binds the profane with happiness. The profane as downfall brings the "unhappiness" of "suffering" and yet it also brings "happiness" as release. With regard to suffering, Benjamin remarks: "the immediate messianic intensity of the heart, of the particular human being, passes through misfortune [*Unglück*] as suffering." This intense experience of unhappiness is messianic in its recognition that the suffering does not have to be. "[J]ust as a force can, through its way, promote another going in the opposite direction, so the order of the profane, through being profane, can promote the coming of the messianic realm" (*SW*3, 305/ GSII:1, *204*). In rendering transient, profanation bears the promise of release from ostensibly necessary suffering. Regardless of what happens in life, there is this capacity to think that a specific suffering is somehow unnecessary even if happiness itself is also unnecessary.

In Benjamin's words, "a spiritual *restitutio in integrum* . . . introduces immortality." Immortality is a *restitutio in integrum* in the literal sense that it pertains to the possibility of an uninjured condition—the possibility of returning, so to speak, to the permanent condition in which legitimacy is withdrawn from suffering. This possibility is a twofold recognition: first, the suffering is not necessary; second, we thereby recognize time's independence from closure, not least from mortality itself (we can imagine that a death did not have to happen—that it is necessary only according to transient, or conceivably transient, criteria). To the "spiritual *restitutio in integrum*," moreover, there "corresponds a worldly" *restitutio in integrum* "that leads to the eternity of a downfall." In other words, "the rhythm of this eternally transient worldly condition" is "transient in its totality, in its spatial and temporal totality." The eternally transient worldly condition is "the rhythm of messianic nature," the nature that resists all attempts to lock space and time (*SW*3, 306/ *GS*II:1, *204*).

As messianic nature, the eternally transient worldly condition is "happiness." Happiness is possible by virtue of spatiotemporal transience; happiness is possible because space and time are never entirely locked, never entirely closed. First, "nature is messianic by reason of its eternal and total passing away"; second, there is a correlation of transience and happiness (306/ *204*).

A striving for "transience" (*Vergängnis*) is so fundamental that Benjamin's theological-political fragment associates the striving with "the task of world politics, whose method is to be called nihilism" (306/ *204*). This nihilism is simply the recognition that time passes, and that even nature itself might pass away in the human. "To strive for this passing away," this "transience [*Vergängnis*]," "even the passing away of those stages of the human that are nature," is the nihilistic task of world politics (306/ *204*). There might be anthropocentrism in Benjamin's conception of nature that itself passes away in the human, as though the human is a culmination and an overcoming of nature. This does not entirely disqualify, however, the association of world politics with the happiness immanent in transience. In *world-political* nihilism, transience and its prospective happiness pertain to questions of justice.

In messianic happiness, we *return* to our transient self that eludes all fates, even the fate of death—for death in its specific circumstances, as noted, is a fate whose necessity can be questioned. Time heals not so much in enabling us to forget old wounds, but rather in freeing us from purported fates.

A recapitulation of the relationship of happiness and justice may now be attempted. For Agamben, the deactivation of powers of law, as well as other deactivations, such as that of religion or religious scruples, could become gateways of happiness. Such deactivation—such study—would make us less subordinate to the injuries inflicted by aggressions of religion, politics, economics, and law. Agamben regards some of these deactivated aggressions as themselves the gate of happiness and he regards deactivated law as the gate of justice. Benjamin says law no longer practiced and only studied is the gateway of justice, and then he says more broadly that the gate of justice is study. Justice entails happiness, for both are aided by study entering transience to find protection from the forces that are injurious in refusing to acknowledge *their* transience.[31] Justice is acknowledgment of transience. Study is the conduit of this justice. Study is the conduit of justice *tout court*—notwithstanding the seeming immodesty of such a claim. In rendering us modest about all other claims, study is the conduit of justice.

The study is a *restitutio in integrum*. Agamben's essay of 1992–8 rejects what it presents as Scholem's bifurcation of two opposed antinomian tendencies in messianism: first, "the restorative tendency aiming at the *restitutio in integrum* of the origin"; second, "a utopian impulse turned instead toward the future and renewal" (*PO*, 166/ 265). Irrespective of whether this is a correct interpretation of Scholem, the word "renewal" (*rinnovamento*) is already indicative of the convergence that Agamben proposes between these two messianic tendencies. In an essay of 1993 on Hermann Melville's "Bartleby, the Scrivener," Agamben says there can be a "*restitutio in integrum* of possibility" so that no occurrence is regarded as exhaustive and possibility is instead "suspended between occurrence and nonoccurence, between the capacity to be and the capacity not to be" (*PO*, 267/ "Bartleby," in Agamben 2012: 83). This is obviously the *restitutio in integrum* that Agamben detects in Benjamin. In *The Open* of 2002, Agamben cites a few texts by Benjamin, including some of the aforementioned passages from Benjamin's "Theological–Political Fragment" that refer to spiritual and worldly *restitutio in integrum*. Agamben even reiterates the anthropocentrism noted above regarding a passage of the "Theological-Political Fragment." Agamben extrapolates that the human "is the sieve in which creaturely life and the spiritual, creation and redemption, nature and history are continually discerned and separated, yet nevertheless continue to conspire toward their own salvation" (*O*, 82/*84*). Agamben reiterates Benjamin's assumption that the human is this salvatory axis, an assumption that is perhaps a somewhat dangerous aggrandizement of the human (Salzani 2022). Despite this, it is still possible to maintain the notion that study facilitates a *restitutio in integrum* of transience—and thereby a dissociation from fate as closure of possibility.

Study enacts such dissociation. In *The Idea of Prose* (1985), Agamben recalls that "Talmud means study." He contends that "study, the Talmud, has become the real temple of Israel." A transition from worship to a greater emphasis on study is, for Agamben, messianic. The "figure of the scholar [*studioso*], respected in every tradition, . . . acquired a messianic significance" (*IP*, 63/ 43). The reference to respect sometimes garnered by study should not mislead; study is messianic in being interminable, and it will offend those who wish to terminate it. "Study . . . is per se interminable." It "not only can . . . have no rightful end, [it] does not even desire one" (64/44), or—at least—"[t]he end to study may never come" (65/ 45). Its termination might, after all, be the ultimate victory of those who do not wish to study.

Justice restitutes study. For Benjamin's 1934 essay on Kafka, there is a happiness of study. Without a house of prayer or an unequivocally holy text, the relevant students have "nothing to support them on their 'untrammeled, happy journey [*leere fröhliche Fahrt*]'" (*SW2*, 815/ GSII:2, 437; see too GSII:3, 1209). With the formulation "'untrammeled happy journey,'" Benjamin is quoting from an aphorism by Kafka that identifies the untrammeled happy journey with a horse ride in which there is a tearing of the harness (Kafka 2006: 146, 2002b: *123*). Such a ride might seem potentially dangerous or potentially fatal for the rider, and of course study is potentially dangerous and fatal in the face of those who oppose it. For Benjamin, however, if there is happiness in unfettered study, it is happiness in breaking normal constraints, in rendering them transient. There is happiness in freeing us for the condition that we always already are: the world before those constraints, before the constitution of worlds (Moran 2018: chapter 11, "In the Epic *Vorwelt*"). Study restitutes to transience, which prevails over norm and law.

Even more clearly than Agamben, Benjamin characterizes both non-applied law and study itself as the gate of justice. Study is the very activity of justice. Study disengages from prevailing practices in order to examine anew all that is or was subjected to those practices. "*Je n'ai rien négligé*," quotes Benjamin—perhaps quoting French baroque painter Nicolas Poussin (*GSII*:3, 1211).[32] There is, of course, always a risk that the studier has neglected something. Justice is the gate that study opens and keeps open. Justice cannot content itself with unstudied and unstudious existence—the subordination and the complacency that are opposed to study, the subordination and the complacency that are hostile to life's inherent insubordination, which is life's transience. Life's insubordination, its transience, demands to be studied for it is repressed and oppressed by all else. In this sense, the justice of study is that it opposes everything else.

## Study and the "Hunchback" Who Is to Disappear

Study finds no reason to desist. Hence the rejection that study often incurs. In its relentlessness, study is a perpetual capacity to be cast aside. The time of study is messianic in pushing beyond what has hitherto been established, which can always be subject to the scrutiny of study. In the essay of 1992–8, Agamben refers to "the event of the Messiah" that coincides "with historical time yet at the same time [can]not be identified with it, effecting in the *eskhaton* that 'small adjustment' in which . . . the messianic reign [*regno*] consists" (*PO*, 174/ *276*).

In light of Scholem's celebration of the prison chaplain in *The Trial*, it might be asked whether this bullying interlocutor of Josef K. is not symptomatic of a potential problem with the notion of messianic small adjustment. The prison chaplain is, after all, representative of a system whose adjustment requires the execution—the disappearance—of K.

Does Benjamin anywhere manifest a relevant zeal of messianic adjustment? Of obvious pertinence is the mockingly laughing "little hunchbacked man" from an old German folksong whom Benjamin discusses as somehow prototypical of the distortion pervading Kafka's work. This man, Benjamin writes, will "disappear with the coming of the Messiah, who . . . will not wish to change the world by force but will merely make a slight adjustment in it [*nur um ein Geringes sie zurechtstellen werde*]" (*SW2*, 811/ *GSII*:2, 432). As "occupant" (*Insasse*) of "distorted life," "the little hunchbacked man [*bucklicht Männlein*]" "will disappear [*wird verschwinden*] if the Messiah comes." That will be the slight adjustment made by Messianic time (*SW2*, 811/ *GSII*:2, 432).[33] Are there problems with the specific notion, developed in Benjamin's Kafka essay, that the little hunchbacked man *will disappear* with the coming of the

Messiah? In a draft for the 1934 essay, Benjamin summarizes: various Kafkan figures "are distorted [*sind enstellt*], just as the world was distorted for the rabbi who taught that the coming of the messiah does not change" the distorted figures "through and through" but "'only sets them aright'"—"'*rückt sie nur zurecht*'" (*GS*II:3, 1239). In the 1934 essay, Benjamin says the adjustment to be undergone by the little hunchbacked man indicates the condition in which the Messiah "will someday appear in order to set aright [*zurechtzurücken einst erscheinen werde*]" (*SW*2, 811/*GS*II:2, 432). That the hunchback in this text is to *disappear*, however, might bring the motif into conflict with a passage of "In the Sun" (1932), where Benjamin recounts the purportedly Hasidic saying that concerns what would be different in the world to come: "nothing remains and nothing disappears" (*SW*2, 664/ *GS*II:1, 420). In the 1934 essay, the little hunchbacked man is to disappear. There seems thereby to be a risk that Benjamin enters a Schmittian mode of deciding "whether there is an extreme emergency as well as about what should happen to eliminate [*beseitigen*] it" (Schmitt 1985: 7, 1990: 12–13). If there were not this risk, the hunchbacked man would not have to disappear.

The justice of study *is not*, of course, a prohibition on all adjustments that—in some way or other—might relieve conditions called "hunchbacked," disfigured, or distorted. To regard such conditions as simply fate would be another variation of what Benjamin criticizes as myth. So-called distortions might *want* to be altered or even eliminated, or such alteration or elimination might simply happen. The justice of study is, after all, the refusal to treat life-conditions as fated.

Study concerns itself with what has been dismissed, disregarded, treated as lost. In *The Time that Remains* (2000), Agamben refers to a Benjaminian view that "the messianic subject" "contemplates salvation only to the extent that" it "loses" itself "in what cannot be saved" (*TR*, 42/ 45; see too 56–57/ 58). Elaborating on some statements by Benjamin, Agamben's *The Open* also refers to the "salvation" that concerns what is irretrievably lost and forgotten—"that is, something unsavable" (*O*, 82/ 84). To lose oneself in what cannot be saved is to reject any fate that deems something unsavable—*nicht zu retten*. Agamben recuperates something of Benjamin's notion of the justice of study—the justice of attention to all that seems hopeless to criteria of alleged non-distortion, or hopeless to calls for the disappearance of what seems distorted in relation to those criteria. This justice of study is perhaps implied in Benjamin's maxim from the end of the *Elective Affinities*-essay: "Only for the sake of those without hope is hope given to us" (*SW*1, 356/ *GS*I:1, *201*). Study does not happen where there is disregard for whatever seems hopeless. In his Kafka essay and elsewhere, Benjamin cites Kafka's alleged remark that there is "'plenty of hope, an infinite amount of hope—but not for us'" (*SW*2, 798/ *GS*II:2, 413–14; *GS*II:3, 1218, 1246, 1262. Citing Brod 1921: 1213). If we are indeed hopeless, this occasions considerable study on Kafka's part. For Benjamin, moreover, Kafka also creates figures, such as certain assistants, for whom there is "an infinite amount of hope." There is hope for them precisely because they do not attach themselves as much as the rest of us to societal constructs that make us hopeless in making us negligent of others and ourselves. The relative detachment of the assistants recalls all that we abandon in our hopelessness (*GS*II:3, 1262).

# Notes

1. Many thanks to Paula Schwebel and Carlo Salzani for their attentive and insightful comments and suggestions on an earlier version of this chapter.
2. Scholem, "Über Jona und den Begriff der Gerechtigkeit" (1919) in Scholem 2000: 529. See too the same statement in "Zwölf Thesen über die Ordnung der Gerechtigkeit," 534 (thesis 8) and in a diary entry, 359.
3. See Scholem's diary entry for October 30, 1918 in Scholem 2000: 401.
4. Scholem, "Über Jona und den Begriff der Gerechtigkeit," in Scholem 2000: 529. See too: Scholem 2000: 359–60.
5. If a translation has been modified, the pagination for the text in its original language is italicized (e.g., *SW*1, 204/ *GS*II:1, *175*).
6. On these two distinct natures, see Moran 2015.
7. This is the translation in Kafka 1970: 169. For the German, see Kafka 2002b: 122.
8. Scholem, Letter of August 1, 1931 to Benjamin, in Scholem 1981: 171/ 1990: 213.
9. Scholem, "Zwolf Thesen über die Ordnung der Gerechtigkeit," in Scholem 2000: 533.
10. Gérard Raulet's editorial comments (*WuN*19, 292–93) note that the statement of the apocryphal gospel is transmitted in St. Justin Martyr's *Dialogue with Trypho* (Martyr 2003, chapter 47:5, p. 72). Raulet also provides information about the echo of the statement in Augustine and other "Church fathers" as well as critically in Ernst Bloch (who might have learned of it through Benjamin) (Bloch 1985: 363). It has sometimes been thought that Benjamin's formula from the "apocryphal gospel"—"'That over which I meet anyone, about that I want to judge him [*ihn*]'"—refers to a similar formulation that is repeated in the "Apocalypse of Paul," part of the *New Testament Apocrypha*: "my patience bears with them until they convert and repent. But if they do not return to me, I will judge them." Variations of this statement appear in paragraphs 4, 5, and 6 of the Apocalypse of Paul (Schneemelcher 1992: 717–18/ 1989: 648–49).
11. Taubes, "On the Current State of Polytheism," trans. Charlotte Elisheva Fonrobert and Amir Engel with William Rauscher, in Taubes 2010: 312/ 2007: 349.
12. Abbreviations for works by Agamben: **PO** = *Potentialities*/ *La potenza del pensiero*; **HS** = *Homo Sacer*/ *Homo Sacer*; **IP** =*The Idea of Prose*/ *Idea della prosa*; **O** = *The Open*/ *L'aperto*; **PR** = *Profanations*/ *Profanazioni*; **SE** = *State of Exception*/ *Stato di eccezione*; **TR** = *The Time that Remains*/ *Il tempo che resta*; **UB** = *The Use of Bodies*/ *L'uso dei corpi*.
13. The German is quite different from the translation given in *CS*.
14. Some of Benjamin's relevant notes are discussed in more detail in Moran 2018; see, for instance, 127.
15. For elaboration of this point, see Bielik-Robson 2017, especially 266–67.
16. See Kafka 2002b: 38.
17. See the elaboration in Scholem, "Religious Authority and Mysticism," in Scholem 1969: 12/ "Religiöse Autorität und Mystik," in Scholem 1989: 22–3.
18. On mere life for Benjamin and bare life for Agamben, see Salzani 2015. On anarchy in Agamben's works, see Malabou 2002, 265–324.
19. At least partly along these lines, Agamben's reading of Scholem has been criticized in Vatter 2021: 150. See too: 174.
20. Citing Kraft, "Geld und Güte. Der Kübelreiter," in Kraft 1968:32. See Kafka, "The Bucket Rider," trans. Willa and Edwin Muir in Kafka 1976: 412–14/ "Der Kübelreiter," in Kafka 2002b: 313–16.

21 Compare this with Levinas's citation of the Gemara (as "the living Torah") "that teaches us and puts us on guard against that ultimate contempt for the Torah, that final contesting of its celestial origin" (Levinas 1988, 63/ 2007, *88*).
22 For Kraft's rewrite of this brief article, see Kraft, "Mythos und Gerechtigkeit: *Der neue Advokat*," in Kraft 1968: 13–15.
23 In perhaps even heightened modesty, Kraft's rewrite over thirty years later does not presume that it is a "human" observer; reference is only to "[t]he observer" (Kraft 1968: 15).
24 Kafka, "The New Lawyer," in Kafka 2007: 60/ "Der neue Advokat," in Kafka 2002a: 252.
25 This formulation about the interpreter and the responsibility are not in Kraft's later version.
26 This elaboration refines a statement in Moran 2018: 168.
27 Benjamin develops such a notion of writing in the *Trauerspielbuch* of the mid-1920s: see especially, *OT*, 230–33/ *GSI*:1, 387–89. For elaboration, see Rrenban 2005, 121–37.
28 For relevant remarks on the lower-level officials of the court, see Sagnol 2011: 212–13.
29 James Martel notes that Agamben does not seek "to do away with law entirely," but "simply seeks to do away with mythic law"—"as does Benjamin himself." Benjamin and Agamben present the prospect for non-idolatrous law (Martel 2014: 37; see too: 113, 115, 168, 172). This "one law becomes the source of our autonomy vis-à-vis all other law" (198; see too: 199). This law we must "decide" to "follow . . . anew" (186), for otherwise we succumb to phantasm, and will be unable to break "from the dictates of fate" (199).
30 Cited by Howard Eiland in this volume.
31 Fate is culpability, while "justice" entails "revocation of culpability" (Birnbaum 2008: 176).
32 Regarding Poussin, see Rosenberg and Temperini 1994.
33 In their respective essays in this volume, Sami Khatib and Carlo Salzani provide analyses of this figure, particularly in relation to the expressly hunchbacked theology discussed in "On the Concept of History."

# References

Agamben, Giorgio. (1995a), *The Idea of Prose*, trans. Michael Sullivan and Sam Whisitt, Albany: State University of New York Press.
Agamben, Giorgio. (1995b), *Homo Sacer. Il potere sovrano e la nuda vita*, Turin: Einaudi.
Agamben, Giorgio. (1998), *Homo Sacer. Sovereign Power and Bare Life*, trans. Daniel Heller-Roazen, Stanford: Stanford University Press.
Agamben, Giorgio. (1999), *Potentialities: Collected Essays in Philosophy*, trans. Daniel Heller-Roazen, Stanford: Stanford University Press.
Agamben, Giorgio. (2000), *Il tempo che resta. Un commento alla Lettera ai Romani*, Turin: Bollati Boringhieri editore.
Agamben, Giorgio. (2002), *L'aperto. L'uomo e l'animale*, Turin: Bollati Boringhieri.
Agamben, Giorgio. ([2002] 1985), *Idea della prosa*, Macerata: Quodlibet.
Agamben, Giorgio. (2003), *Stato di eccezione*, Turin: Bollati Boringhieri editore.
Agamben, Giorgio. (2004), *The Open: Man and Animal*, trans. Kevin Attell, Stanford: Stanford University Press.

Agamben, Giogio. (2005a), *State of Exception*, trans. Kevin Attell, Chicago: University of Chicago Press.
Agamben, Giorgio. (2005b), *The Time that Remains: A Commentary on the Letter to the Romans*, trans. Patricia Dailey, Stanford: Stanford University Press.
Agamben, Giorgio. (2005c), *Profanazioni*, Milan: Nottetempo.
Agamben, Giorgio. (2007), *Profanations*, trans. Jeff Fort, New York: Zone Books.
Agamben, Giorgio. (2012), "Bartleby o della contingenza," in Giorgio Agamben and Gilles Deleuze (eds.), *Bartleby. La formula della creazione*, 45–89, Macerata: Quodlibet.
Agamben, Giorgio. ([2012] 2005), *La potenza del pensiero. Saggie e conferenze*, Vicenza: Neri Pozza Editore.
Agamben, Giorgio. (2014), *L'uso dei corpi*, Turin: Neri Pozza Editore.
Agamben, Giorgio. (2015), *The Use of Bodies*, trans. Adam Kotsko, Stanford: Stanford University Press.
Bielik-Robson, Agata. (2017), "Mysteries of the Promise: Negative Theology in Benjamin and Scholem," in Michael Fagenblatt (ed.), *Jewish Modernity as Negative Theology*, 258–81, Bloomington: Indiana University Press.
Birnbaum, Antonia. (2008), *Bonheur Justice. Walter Benjamin. Le detour grec*, Paris: Éditions Payot & Rivages.
Bloch, Ernst. (1985), *Neuzeitliche Philosophie II: Deutscher Idealismus. Die Philosoophie des 19. Jahrhunderts. Leipziger Vorlesungen zur Geschichte der Philosophie*, Vol. 4, eds. Eberhard Braun and Hanna Gekle, Frankfurt/M.: Suhrkamp.
Brod, Max. (1921), "Der Dichter Franz Kafka," *Die neue Rundschau*, 32 (1 November): 1210–16.
Hamacher, Werner. (2006), "Das Theologische-politische Fragment," Burkhardt Lindner with Thomas Küpper and Timo Skrandies (eds.), *Benjamin-Handbuch: Leben—Werk—Wirkung*, 175–92, Stuttgart: Verlag J.B. Metzler.
Kafka, Franz. (1970), *The Great Wall of China: Stories and Reflections*, trans. Willa and Edwin Muir, New York: Schocken Books.
Kafka, Franz. (1976), *The Complete Stories*, ed. Nahum N. Glatzer, New York: Schocken Books.
Kafka, Franz. (2002a), *Drucke zu Lebzeiten*, eds. Wolf Kittler, Hans-Gerd Koch, and Gerhard Neumann, *Kritische Ausgabe*, eds. Jürgen Born, Gerhard Neumann, Malcolm Pasley, and Jost Schillemeit, Frankfurt/M.: Fischer.
Kafka, Franz. (2002b), *Nachgelassene Schriften und Fragmente II*, ed. Jost Schillemeit, *Kritische Ausgabe*, eds. Jürgen Born, Gerhard Neumann, Malcolm Pasley, and Jost Schillemeit, Frankfurt/M.: Fischer.
Kafka, Franz. (2006), *The Zürau Aphorisms*, trans. Michael Hofmann, New York: Schocken Books.
Kafka, Franz. (2007), *Kafka's Selected Stories*, trans. and ed. Stanley Corngold, New York: W.W. Norton and Company.
Kraft, Werner. (1933), "'Positive Ironie.' Zu einer Erzählung Franz Kafkas," *Jüdische Rundschau*, September 20, 569.
Kraft, Werner. (1968), *Franz Kafka. Durchdringung und Geheimnis*, Frankfurt/M.: Suhrkamp.
Levinas, Emmanuel. (1988), *A l'heure des nations*, Paris: Les Éditions de Minuit.
Levinas, Emmanuel. (2007), *In the Time of Nations*, trans. Michael B. Smith, London: Continuum.
Malabou, Catherine. (2022), *Au voleur! Anarchisme et philosophie*, Paris: Presses universitaires de France.

Martel, James R. (2014), *The One and Only Law: Walter Benjamin and the Second Commandment*, Ann Arbor: University of Michigan Press.
Martyr, St. Justin. (2003), *Dialogue with Trypho*, trans. Thomas B. Falls and Thomas P. Halton, ed. Michael Slusser, Washington, DC: Catholic University of America Press.
Moran, Brendan. (2015), "Nature, Decision, and Muteness," in Brendan Moran and Carlo Salzani (eds.), *Towards the Critique of Violence: Walter Benjamin and Giorgio Agamben*, 73–90, London: Bloomsbury.
Moran, Brendan. (2018), *Politics of Benjamin's Kafka: Philosophy as Renegade*, London: Palgrave Macmillan.
Moran, Brendan. (2019), "A Murmur of Indifference to Authorial Identity in Intellectual Life," in Cornelia Wächter and Robert Wirth (eds.), *Complicity and the Politics of Representation*, 139–57, London: Rowman and Littlefield International.
Rosenberg, Pierre and Renaud Temperini. (1994), *Poussin: "Je n'ai rien négligé,"* Paris: Gallimard.
Rrenban, Monad. (2005), *Wild, Unforgettable Philosophy in Early Works of Walter Benjamin*, Lanham: Lexington Books.
Sagnol, Marc. (2011), "Das Gesetz als Konvergenzpunkt von Archaik und Moderne," in Ashraf Noor (ed.), *Walter Benjamin: Moderne und Gesetz*, 199–213, Munich: Wilhelm Fink Verlag (Makom).
Salzani, Carlo. (2015), "From Benjamin's '*bloßes Leben*' to Agamben's '*nuda vita.*' A Genealogy," in Moran and Salzani (eds.), *Towards the Critique of Violence: Walter Benjamin and Giorgio Agamben*, 109–23, London: Bloomsbury Academic.
Salzani, Carlo. (2022), *Agamben and the Animal*, Cambridge: Cambridge Scholars Press.
Schmitt, Carl. ([1923] 1939), "Die Politische Theorie des Mythus," in *Positionen und Begriffe im Kampf mit Weimar-Genf-Versailles. 1923–1939*, 9–18, Hamburg: Hanseatische Verlagsanstalt.
Schmitt, Carl. (1985 [based on 1934 German edition]), *Political Theology: Four Chapters on the Concept of Sovereignty*, trans. George Schwab. Cambridge: The MIT Press.
Schmitt, Carl. (1990 [1934 edition]), *Politische Theologie. Vier Kapitel zur Lehre von der Souveränität*. Berlin: Duncker & Humblot.
Schneemelcher, Wilhelm and Edgar Hennecke, eds. (1989), *Neutestamentliche Apokryphen in deutscher Übersetzung, vol. II: Apostolisches. Apokalypsen und Verwandtes*, Tübingen: J.C.B. Mohr.
Schneemelcher, Wilhelm and Edgar Hennecke, eds. (1992), *New Testament Apocrypha, vol. II: Writings related to the apostles; apocalypses and related literature*, trans. R. McL. Wilson, Cambridge: James Clarke and Co.
Scholem, Gershom. (1969), *On Kabbalah and its Symbolism*, trans. Ralph Manheim, New York: Schocken Books.
Scholem, Gershom. (1981), *Walter Benjamin: The Story of a Friendship*, trans. Harry Zohn, Philadelphia: The Jewish Publication Society of America.
Scholem, Gershom. (1989), *Zur Kabbala und ihrer Symbolik*, Frankfurt/M.: Suhrkamp.
Scholem, Gershom. (1990), *Walter Benjamin: Die Geschichte einer Freundschaft*, Frankfurt/M.: Suhrkamp.
Scholem, Gershom. (2000), *Tagebücher nebst Aufsätzen und Entwürften bis 1923. 2 Halbband 1917–23*, eds. Karlfried Gründer, Herbert Kopp-Oberstebrink, and Friedrich Niewöhner with Karl E. Grözinger, Frankfurt/M.: Jüdischer Verlag.
Scholem, Gershom. (2002), *"Es gibt ein Geheimnis in der Welt." Tradition und Säkularisation*, ed. Itta Shedletzky, Frankfurt/M.: Jüdischer Verlag im Suhrkamp Verlag.

Taubes, Jacob. (2010), *From Cult to Culture: Fragments Toward a Critique of Historical Reason*, eds. Charlotte Elisheva Fonrobert and Amir Engel, Stanford: Stanford University Press.

Taubes, Jacob. (2007), *Vom Kult zur Kultur. Bausteine zu einer Kritik der historischen Vernunft*, eds. Aleida and Jan Assmann, Wolf-Daniel Hartwich, and Winfried Menninghaus, Munich: Wilhelm Fink Verlag.

Vatter, Miguel. (2021), *Living Law: Jewish Political Theology from Hermann Cohen to Hannah Arendt*, Oxford: Oxford University Press.

# Part III

# Fate, Messianic Time, and Messianic Adjustment

7

# Benjamin's Concept of Fate

Howard Eiland

Drafting a letter in August 1933 to a woman he met on the island of Ibiza that summer of incipient exile, Walter Benjamin wrote: "In your arms I would forever cease to be accosted by fate. Never again could it surprise me with fear or with happiness" (*GBIV*, 279). These ardent lines, insofar as they form part of a larger textual network, bespeak not only a conception of fate as something surreptitiously at work in human life and its contingencies, but also, in contrast to certain passages in Benjamin's writings discussed in this chapter, an association of fate with good fortune as well as bad.[1] They point to a concept of fate as an incalculable conjuncture whose working recurrently takes one unawares, although it can be eluded or overcome through the way one lives. Given the concept's manifold literary-philosophic provenance, in which the decree of fate usually entails an intricately intertwined sequence of events, it becomes a question for Benjamin, in large part, of working through the opposition between proximity and distance where experience of time is concerned. At stake in the seemingly outdated *topos* of fate are possibilities not only of a physiognomic, divinatory critical reading[2] but also of a dialectical experience of freedom and redemption in the face of ultimately indeterminable determinacies. It is then a political no less than a theological matter, and with Benjamin the convergence of such ostensible opposites as politics and theology generally shatters their customary signification. In the context of a Benjaminian political theology, which must be distinguished from the brute decisionism of Carl Schmitt's political theology, the idea of fate dictates neither predetermination nor free agency conceived as opposites.

Benjamin's profane theology finds expression, early on in his career, in the problematic of human selfhood—that is, of the self's immanent otherness, self as constitutive aporia. In proverbially theological terms: one has to lose oneself to find oneself.[3] It is a practice clearly distinguished from what has been called armed self-interest.[4] Rather, the wakened self will *open itself*—resolutely and critically—to a given fate so as to appropriate and transform it. Redemption of the mortal self, as of "that dream we name the past" (*AP*, 389/*GSV*:1, 491), depends on this resolute immersion, gathering in dispersion, and on what Benjamin calls dialectical reflection. One wakens from the dream through waking *to* it, doing it justice by bringing to light its often labyrinthine import. And this, in turn, depends on a transformed experience of time, making possible, on each particular occasion, the communication of past and present moments. Such continually renewed educational awakening will emerge, in the course of this chapter, as the nucleus of a Benjaminian political theology. From the early writings on, education—the fostering of conscience in a global or planetary perspective—is understood to be the key to social justice. The latter would hinge on the dialectical process of a relentlessly self-questioning community of individual consciences, a federated collectivity instituting the "world politics" of a "free humanity."[5] Theological and political, "immediate messianic intensity of the heart" and integral "worldly restitution," interpenetrate solely by virtue of their reciprocity in difference, as two opposed forces may augment each other. The political-theological is grounded in paradox, and only through a paradoxical comportment of spatial and temporal nearness in distance can it enter into, so as to countervail, the natural-historical annunciation of a fate. Insofar as conscience, working at a distance from the "I," and almost as an alien force within the self, nevertheless intimately animates the "I," it furnishes a model of this charged comportment. Being vigilantly and vulnerably "beside itself," such detached intimacy—the transcendence of egology in attentiveness—makes the state of freedom possible and is a condition for doing justice. If personal fate (as discussed here) can articulate a "dramatic truth" of history, then it will simultaneously adumbrate a manifold burden and task, beginning with the political-theological imperative of remembrance as grounding all hope—remembrance inseparable from lament for the barbarisms of history. What "fate" itself says—*fatum*, like *mythos*, is literally something spoken—remains a mystery to be plumbed rather than resolved.[6]

Words for fate—primarily, the common German term *Schicksal*—are in fact attested at every phase of Benjamin's writing career, though less frequently in the 1930s. It is during the period of emigration that the theory of fate, based in the recurring claim of the past on the present, yields to a conception of historical time as ever-new citation of what has been. The notion of fate is invoked casually and idiomatically, as a term needing no particular glossing, in letters to correspondents and throughout the journalism of the Weimar years, while, especially in the period 1913–25, it is developed in essays and surviving fragments as a principal literary-philosophical concern. It should be added that this development of the concept of fate in Benjamin's writings is by no means systematic or even always theoretically consistent, although it does unfailingly presuppose a mode of revelation that aligns it with the ontological theory of language first annunciated in 1916. At the same time, this thematic development neither prevents Benjamin from recognizing a self-deluding "hunger for destiny" (*SW*2, 303/*GS*III, 235) nor blinds him to the way the idea of fate has been deployed to mask despotism and every sort of machination.

Keeping in mind, then, the many-sided and at times contradictory development of Benjamin's concept of fate over the course of three decades, we can retrace his thinking on the subject as documented in a series of longer and shorter texts. Fundamental to every phase in the sounding of this theme is encounter with an elusive temporal possibility—that of nearness in distance—antithetical to the model of chronological continuum and to what he calls the epical manner of history writing. It is the intimate interplay of temporal stations, the communication of moments widely separated in time, that turns the fate theme, each time newly improvised upon, into something like a "touchstone of [Benjamin's] thinking."[7]

## Immortal Time

In what time, then, does the human being live? This question arises at the midpoint of Benjamin's posthumously published essay of 1913–14, "The Metaphysics of Youth," in which the concept of fate is first expounded. The different times of time will become his abiding subject. In this early, adventurous three-part "cycle," clearly marked by his reading of Henri Bergson in a seminar of 1913, the question of time already necessitates paradox: "That [man] lives in no time is something thinkers have always known. The immortality of thoughts and deeds banishes him to a . . . timelessness at whose heart . . . inscrutable death lies in wait" (*EW*, 150/*GS*II:1, 96–97). The essay pivots on a distinction between two temporal spheres. The realm of "calendar time, clock time, and stock-exchange time," "developmental time" in its "everyday reality," is distinguished from "youthful time" or "immortal time" in its purity, as two different possibilities of experience (*EW*, 150–51/*GS*II:1, 97–98).[8] What first divides these two ways of being is the intimate transformation Benjamin here identifies with diary writing. Of course, the term *Tagebuch*, literally daybook or book of days, with its echo of the biblical "book of life," carries considerable allegorical significance (though the essay does not employ the term "allegory" or exploit its connection to language theory); at issue is the "book of a life in whose time everything we experienced inadequately is transformed and perfected" (*EW*, 150/*GS*II:1, 97).[9] The key to this liberating transformation is attention (a Bergsonian theme) to "the unnameable despair that flows in every soul" (*EW*, 150/*GS*II:1, 96). The one who thus despairs—in what will become a defining Benjaminian gesture of dialectical reversal—"gazes down and down into the current whence he has emerged [from childhood]" (*EW*, 150/*GS*II:1, 97) and, in this vertiginous, almost oblivious immersion in the depths of what has been, is discovered anew. Which is to say, the diary begins. Linear developmental time, with its regimented "chain of experiences," is each time absorbed in the emergent vortex of a resonating "immortality," while through the discontinuous moment of reflection the day is distilled: "the self that acts in time" is purified and overcome in writing itself (*EW*, 151/*GS*II:1, 98). With its experience reflected at intervals (*Abständen*) in the diary, the everyday self can witness and study itself from a distance (*Abstand*), and it is precisely such being-at-a-distance from oneself—miming the great distancer, death—that allows proximity to the otherwise concealed, sleeping, and ultimately anonymous ownmost.

The interval in time, then, discloses a threshold and passage into the historical dimension of the now. In the deep time of the diary's inscribed distance, in that decisive clearance and spacing of the self which Benjamin likens to the pregnant silence that is condition and fruit of conversation, the self is gathered to itself from out of its everyday (unreflected and unintegrated) diffusion. Through such concentration it gains "the strength to befall things, to draw them into itself" as they impinge upon it; this fundamental dialectic of diary writing constitutes a "rite of purification" in which, by means of reciprocal gathering and dissemination of itself, the self is "entirely transposed into time," agitated and irradiated by it (*EW*, 151, 156/*GS*II:1, 98, 103). As the diarist attains the inner anonymity—utter attentiveness—necessary for writing, the diary writes itself.[10] The daily self is transcended in opening itself to the immanent nocturnal, which awakens its mortal immortality.

> In that self to which events occur and which encounters human beings—friends, enemies, and lovers—in that self courses immortal time . . . [That self] is time's radiation and nothing else. (*EW*, 151/*GSII*:1, 97-98)

This is an immortality *in* time, however precariously, not beyond or after it; the tension-filled critical moment transforms chronological happening kairologically, through expansive concentration. Moreover, it is an immortality inseparable from, predicated upon, the experience of transience and despair—as educative.[11] Here is the political-theological cue for the invocation of fate. With the interpenetration of subject and object occasioned by diary writing, the self can "disregard its own fate"; which is to say, "our fate declares its faith in us because we have long since ceased to relate it to ourselves" (*EW*, 151–52/*GSII*:1, 98–99). Broken through is the everyday egoistic self that assumes the "I," its murky inwardness rendered transparent to something in itself other and older than itself, collectively unfolding here and now. "Time, which has radiated as the self we are now, befalls [*widerfährt*] all things around us as our fate" (*EW*, 152/*GSII*:1, 98 translation modified). A radically open, dialectical subjectivity emerges, made possible by the ever-renewed reflexive entry—an entry that simultaneously withdraws and keeps its distance—into the radiating of this temporal deep. Subjectivity becomes the focus of divergent theological and political energies.

Fate is accordingly defined by a recurrent countermovement (*Gegenbewegung*) in which the "I" encounters its immanent alterity: "fate is: this countermovement of things in the time of the self" (*EW*, 156/*GSII*:1, 102). Under the aegis of the neo-romantic youth movement, with its educationalist ethic of conversation (the object of scorn in Carl Schmitt's political theology[12]), Benjamin revolutionizes the terms of inherited oppositions, ensuring that self and world, both in crisis, are interarticulated in the emancipatory—indeed, redemptive (*erlösend*)—distillation of the daybook. In that "book *of* time" (*EW*, 151/*GSII*:1, 98), the self recurrently dies to itself, dies daily, and, thus critically mortified, is at intervals resurrected in the writing of it all. Emancipated from the rigid sovereignty of the "I," the self is redeemed through suddenly waking to itself as sent forth in the midst of things. In other words, the self is fulfilled in attaining to nearness in distance.

> There is, however, a place of those resurrections of the self, when time sends it forth in ever-widening waves. This is the landscape. All that happens surrounds us as landscape, for we, the time of things, know no time. Nothing but the leaning of the trees, the horizon and the sharply etched mountain ridges, which suddenly awake full of meaning insofar as they position us in their midst, at the center . . . We, their midpoint, befall these things. (*EW*, 152-53/*GSII*:1, 99)

Benjamin characterizes the interpenetration of self and things—made manifest through the diary's distillation of daily life—in terms derived from Bergson's *Matter and Memory*.[13] At issue is not so much our posing questions to nature as a mutual interrogation: things "delimit the human essence [*Wesen*] through their questioning existence and deepen time; and as time itself happens to things at their outermost, there vibrates within it a slight insecurity which, questioning, gives answer to the questions posed by things. In the interchange of such vibrations, the self has its life" (*EW*, 152/GSII:1, 99). Such living discourse makes for the content of the diary, in which a texture of fates woven of time is intermittently propagated. In this vibratory or tidal "rhythm of time"—time deepened—far and near auratically mingle: "Things see us; their gaze propels us into the future . . . [W]e could feel time, which sent us forth, flooding back toward us" (*EW*, 153–54/GSII:1, 99–100). Across the dynamic landscape of a life opened up by the diary and radiating time, "past things become futural. They send forth the time of the self anew"; the time of things is overcome in the time of the self that befalls them, as "fate is overcome in greatness" (*EW*, 156/GSII:1, 102). In keeping with the essay's striking, if evidently involuntary, congruence with Hegelian vocabulary, Benjamin writes here *aufgehoben*: overcome in being taken up.

It is on this note of historical indebtedness, waking to the fatality and futurity of past within present, that "The Metaphysics of Youth" so strikingly opens: "Each day, like sleepers, we use unmeasured energies. What we do and think is filled with the being of our . . . ancestors. An uncomprehended symbolism unceremoniously enslaves us" (*EW*, 144/GSII:1, 91). Just as the diary articulates time-woven fate, breaking its spell in witness and in questioning, the conversation (in the essay's first, Hölderlinian section) takes as its content "knowledge of the past . . . The conversation laments lost greatness" (*EW*, 144/GSII:1, 91). In such resounding lament, the conversation "gravitates toward silence," which is its generative "inner frontier," for it is in the silence born from conversation that energy is renewed and the possibility of further conversation prepared (*EW*, 145/GSII:1, 91–92).[14] Benjamin can thus go on, at the end of the first section, to evoke the conversation of Sappho and her women friends as a discourse of unspoken words, language yet "inchoate" (*ungeschaffen*) that in silent delight turns to greatness. And in the essay's central section there is the characterization of the diary's interval and distance as its silence. This all bears on the thesis of fate's overcoming in "greatness"—which, contrary to reactionary abuse of the term, signifies a spiritual and moral power of profane resurrection, of remembrance and inauguration.

As the "sovereignty of the 'I'" withdraws into silence, and the ever-greater expansion of attention "weaves the ever nearer mythos of things" (*EW*, 155/GSII:1, 102), the encounter with alterity plays out in the vibrating abyssal temporality of the self. But the time of the self has now, in the allegory of writing as simultaneous shattering and redemption, become the time of death. Inscrutable death makes evident "the great interval" from whose vantage point is manifest the fateful play-character of mortal life—something important to the later development of Benjamin's fate concept and reflected here in the figure of the dance that organizes the essay's third section.

> Redeemed, we become aware of the fulfillment of the game; the time of death was the time of our diary; death was the last interval, death the first loving enemy, death, which bears us with all our greatness and the destinies [*Schicksalen*] of our wide plain into the unnameable midpoint of times. And which for a single moment

gives us immortality. Manifold and simple, this is the content of our diaries. (*EW*, 156/*GS*II:1, 103)

Instrumental in the fulfillment of this momentary death-borne summons to immortal time—the term anticipates Benjamin's watchword "eternal transience" (*ewige Vergängnis*)—is the other "loving enemy" aiding in the confrontation with fate. This is "the tireless, courageous conscience that pricks and spurs us on" (*EW*, 154/*GS*II:1, 101). At issue is not so much a faculty as a reflexive activity. The moral process of conscience is conceived as an active expression of the mortifying and saving distance generated in the "interval," that vital caesura out of which both the conversation of self as other and the conversation of selves each time arise. With an eye always to the unnameable midpoint condition of mortality and historical transitivity, conscience at a distance furthers its interrogation of and in the daybook of the self. Through the reflexivity of the reading that is a writing, we are fruitfully, if uncomfortably, beside ourselves: "We ourselves are the reader, or our own enemy . . . After every sight and every flight from death, we return home to ourselves as our enemy. The diary never speaks of any other" (*EW*, 154/*GS*II:1, 100–01). The return home is imaged in the essay's third section, "The Ball," as day pours into night and night becomes radiant, and as the many solitudes—each with its own dreams and each concealing "something monstrous" (*EW*, 157/*GS*II:1, 103)—are joined together in a round dance, suggesting the federated collectivity that, as indicated earlier, is a Benjaminian constant. The field-oriented constellatory working of the modern monadology central to Benjamin's later work is already evident here in the immanent, socially articulated rhythm of gravitation and radiation and in the figure of the music-filled windowless house to which "all the merciless realities" keep returning for conscience to brood upon (*EW*, 158/*GS*II:1, 104). It is through the intimate conversation of conscience, in deepening time, that political and theological energies come together to countervail fate's accosting.

The discourse of conscience is central to a text explicated at a key moment in Benjamin's *Origin of the German Trauerspiel* (published 1928): namely, Shakespeare's *Hamlet*. There are several interlocking steps on the way to this climactic moment.

## Guilt Context

In the political-theological speculations of Benjamin's youth metaphysics, the possibility of redemption bespeaks interpenetration of an intimated mythos of fate; it is inseparable from the sublimation of despair.[15] In the war years following the composition of "The Metaphysics of Youth" and the companion essay "Two Poems by Friedrich Hölderlin,"[16] the contradictory moral content of the concept of fate comes newly to expression in the guise of guilt, functioning within a dialectic of destruction and renewal. The texts discussed below conceive the *topos* of fate as an elemental pattern of historical tiding—an "entelechy"[17] of occurrence—within the field of guilt, *Schuld*, the latter understood first in the context of archaic demonology, then in that of early modern Christianity and the doctrine of original sin.

In fragmentary notations from the period 1918–19, at a moment when the ethical rationalism of Hermann Cohen was on his mind, Benjamin addresses the enigmatic temporality of fate in its determining guilt context. Fragment 64, "On the Problem of Physiognomics and Foretelling," closely resembles a passage in the well-known essay of 1919, "Fate and Character," source of the bracketed phrase "with another" in the following translation of the fragment:

> The time of fate is the time that at each time can be made *simultaneous* [with another] (not present). It is subject to the order of guilt, which in it determines the context. It is a dependent [*unselbständige*] time, and there is in it neither present nor past nor future (*GSVI*, 91).

In the essay, not without having first invoked the fortuneteller and palm reader who make acausal connections in time, Benjamin more precisely qualifies the time of fate as "parasitically dependent on the time of a higher, less natural life" (*SW*1, 204/*GS*II:1, 176); having no immediate present, it knows past and future only in singular inflections (*eigentümlichen Abwandlungen*). It follows that fate itself is perceived only indirectly, mediated through "signs." Both essay and fragment conceive fate in terms of context, a virtual convergence of divergent times, as opposed to a continuous time line. Fateful temporality, as experiential, bespeaks a meaningful *simultaneity* of chronologically distinct moments that, within a context of guilt-transmission, would each time "parasitically" articulate the time of a higher life, which I take to be the living, changing matrix and medium of meaning Benjamin soon will be calling "natural-historical."[18] Precipitated discontinuously, the time of fate is legible only as veiled or hinted, announcing itself in withdrawing. As we shall see, it is not in the realm of causality but in that of teleology—Benjamin speaks of a teleology without goal (*GB*II, 109)—that the entelechy of fate may be said to operate.[19]

This operation, he argues in the post-war years, is subject not to the mechanical order of cause and effect but to the order of *Schuld*, denoting, in its "demonic ambiguity," both "guilt" and "debt" (*SW*1, 289/*GSV*I, 102). Palpable here is the influence of Hermann Cohen, who likewise detects *Schuld* at the core of *Schicksal*, and who derives the concept of myth itself from that of fate.[20] The idea of guilt-history—history as a "process by which guilt is incurred"[21]—is broached in fragment 65, from 1918, before being more specifically developed in "Fate and Character."[22] In the fragment, guilt is said to constitute the decisive link in world history:

> The highest category of world history, that which best guarantees the connectedness of what happens [*Einsinnigkeit des Geschehens*], is guilt. Every world-historical moment encumbered and encumbering... It is an error of rationalistic conceptions of history to look upon a historical totality (that is, a world-state [*Weltzustand*]) as cause or effect. A world-state is always only guilt (in relation to a later state). (*GSVI*, 92)

In "Fate and Character," the guilt-relation functions as both inherited and self-propagating. Fate, in its punctuated connectedness, is formally defined by Benjamin as "the guilt context of the living [*Schuldzusammenhang des Lebendigen*]" (*SW*1, 204/*GS*II:1, 175). A veiled "nexus of meaning" (*Bedeutungszusammenhang*) never to be founded causally, fate is now construed—insofar as it can be thought at all in the contemporary world—from a comprehensive historical perspective (*SW*1, 202/*GS*II:1, 172). Presupposed in "Fate and Character" is the divide between an ancient cult of demonic powers and a modern emancipating genius. It is in Athenian tragedy (as Cohen had argued [1904: 345]) that demonic fate, casting its spell of inherited guilt, is first broken through, as pagan man recognizes his moral superiority to the god; the seemingly inexorable cycle of guilt and atonement spreading over generations gives way before the new moral sublimity of the individual's unreconciled tragic heroism. The concept of fate, then, is rooted in a primordial "demonic stage of human existence" (*SW*1, 203/*GS*II:1, 174), as Goethe likewise understood.[23] Thus its untoward manifestation in contradiction, in context without continuity, in contracting-and-expanding time and space. And thus, the mythic enslavement of whatever is fated: "insofar as something is fate, it is misfortune and guilt" (*SW*1, 203/*GS*II:1, 174). Happiness is what releases from fate, in the classic acceptation of the concept.

But the fatal dogma of natural guilt, argues Benjamin in "Fate and Character," is not yet dispelled. It shadows the customary appearance of things, lending a persistent semblance of guilt to the very existence of what lives and thereby occasioning a pernicious split between the *seeming* bare life of humanity and humanity's "best part" (its idea of the good, its greatness), which is repressed under fate's rule.[24] Given the endemic "mist of guilt," the subject of fate proves indeterminable; never the human being as spiritual-physical complex but only "the part involved in natural guilt and misfortune by virtue of semblance" can be struck by fate (*SW*1, 203–04/*GS*II:1, 174–75). It is this reduced body of creaturely life as inherently condemned that is then subject to positive law, the institution that Benjamin depicts, here and in the 1921 "Critique of Violence," as a sclerotic administrative survival of the ambiguous archaic order of fate. Critical reflection, however, with a historical understanding animated by the promise of both freedom and justice, can transform an oppressive inheritance, deconstructing and neutralizing its terms in order to awaken dormant possibilities of practice. Reflectively confronting the myth of primal guilt, the theologically and politically individualizing genius can disclose alternative prospects of "natural innocence," originary openness, so that where *fatum* prevailed there can be freedom as a potential, and instead of *mere* life a more integral actuality (*SW*1, 206/*GS*II:1, 178). For the guilt context is only inauthentically temporal, "very different in its kind and measure from the time of redemption, or of music, or of truth" (*SW*1, 204/*GS*II:1, 176). To be more clearly determined is "the particular nature of time in fate"; and it is at this point in the argument of "Fate and Character" that Benjamin adapts fragments 64 and 65 concerning the temporality of fate, its virtuality of inscription without graspable presence and its peculiar inflection of elements past and future.[25] The genuine (*echte*) conception of fate in terms of veiled but portentous synchronicity[26] applies equally, he concludes, to the demonic fate broken through in tragedy and to the commodified fate conjured up and marketed by the fortuneteller. Archaic and modern currents converge, pointing beyond the antinomy of guilt and innocence, in disclosure of the underlying "anonymity of human being and human morality" (*SW*1, 205/*GS*II:1, 178 translation modified)—which is to say, the underlying "situation of groundlessness [*verfehlbaren Grundlage*]" (*EW*, 110/*GS*II:1, 51 [1913]).

## Dramatic Tension

Some four years after the composition of "Fate and Character," fate as a literary theme reappears in Benjamin's posthumously published essay "Calderón's *El Mayor Monstruo, Los Celos* and Hebbel's *Herodes und Mariamne*: Comments on the Problem of Historical Drama" (spring 1923) and in the closely related dissertation *Origin of the German Trauerspiel* (written 1923–5). It also appears prominently, in relation to the theme of nature, in the fragmentary "Schemata concerning the Psychophysical Problem" (1922–3) and somewhat more marginally, in connection with the theme of the demonic and of eternal return, in the celebrated essay of the early 1920s, "Goethe's Elective Affinities." The question of temporal inauthenticity does not resurface in these works, but the association of fate with a death-haunted—indeed, annihilating—guilt context exceeding the measure of mechanical causality largely persists, as does the idea of fate's overcoming, which again involves transformation of the relation to space and time. The concern with spatiotemporal reorientation and regeneration remains pressing, of course, even after the notion of guilt context, associated with destructive love relationships in the literary texts Benjamin is treating, recedes.[27]

In delineating the operativity of fate according to parameters of bodily-spiritual existence—above all, those of distance and proximity—the speculative "Schemata concerning the Psychophysical Problem" make use of categories in part reminiscent of Benjamin's youth metaphysics, itself in part anticipatory of the latest stages of his thought. To be determined exclusively by what lies near, he writes here, is to be caught in the bonds of fate. The emancipated self, like the purified "I" of the diarist, necessarily comes to itself from afar, from out of frontiers and horizons, and only thereby breaks the spell of nearness so as to appropriate the present in its historically mediated and usually repressed depth. The self realizes itself by vigilantly opening itself to the burden of an uncircumscribable but navigable historical nature *coming to pass* in its midst. Through this self-awakening in the opening moment, nocturnal and diurnal energies interact.

> The less a man is entangled in bonds of fate, the less he is determined by *what lies nearest*, whether it be circumstances or people. By contrast, a free human being has his immediate environment entirely to himself; it is he who determines it. As for the determinateness belonging to his life in virtue of his fate, it comes to the free human being from afar.... For that which at a distance determines the human being should be nature itself, and nature does this determining all the more undividedly the purer this being is... [It does this], however, not in regard to one's actions [*Handeln*] but in regard to one's life, which alone can be fateful. And it is here, not in the realm of action, that freedom has its place. (*SW*1, 398/*GS*VI, 84 translation modified)

The conventional opposition between freedom and necessity, such as informs the Schmittian voluntarism, is overturned in paradox. The function of freedom, Benjamin continues, dialectically conjoining freedom-from and freedom-for, is to deliver the human being from determination by particular natural occurrences so as to be guided, insofar as one is sufficiently open and attentive, by the *existence* of nature, by its rhythms. Released from the influence of individual events through this interfused attentiveness, the human being is "guided, but like a sleeper" (*SW*1, 398/*GS*VI, 84). The more consummate the human being, the deeper the element of sleep. The primal "sea of sleep" (*Meer von Schlaf*) flows in the depths of *all* human nature; the living being is continually reborn from this dream-filled "womb of the depths [*Schoße dieser Tiefen*]" (*SW*1, 398–99/*GS*VI, 85).[28] Attunement to the oceanic *Urgrund*—only in such attunement can there be freedom in human life—is conditioned on the purification and consummation of that life in its radiating natural-historical moment. The thought-imagery here recalls that of the "surging sea" (*wogendes Meer*) of inherited teachings evoked in Benjamin's letter of September 6, 1917, to Gershom Scholem, on the subject of education as sea change (*C*, 94/*GB*I, 382). If tradition, he tells Scholem, is the medium through which a learner is continually transformed into a teacher, and if knowledge is transmissible solely through those who understand their own knowledge to have been transmitted, then only the one who knowingly surrenders to the tidal surge of teachings, as it emerges "precipitously like a wave from living abundance" (*C*, 94/*GB*I, 382), becomes truly free. Again, in contrast to a sovereignty-based decisionism, it is resolute immersion, it is the resolve to live by learning, that makes for freedom—freedom as the ground and fruit of education. The theological paradigm underlying this idea of the teachings (*Lehre*), and of the educational awakening fundamental to Benjaminian political theology, is made somewhat more explicit in the "Schemata." There the working of natural history is defined in terms of "the two great processes of dissolution and resurrection" (*SW*1, 395/*GS*VI, 81). These processes determine the cyclic "daybook" of metaphysical youth, as we noted, no less than the complementary "rhythm" of worldly existence, according to the "Theological-Political Fragment" (*SW*3, 306/*GS*II:1, 204). In the problematic of the psychophysical, this natural-historical dialectic entails the interdependence of fate and art. Movement into the creative and destructive vitality of nature, in Benjamin's scheme, is fate; the resultant movement outward from these depths—in other words, the emancipatory intention, the deconstruction of madness—is art, the psychophysical work site of truths.[29]

The representation of fate in art is at issue in texts coming in the wake of "Fate and Character." The essay on Calderón and Hebbel is occupied not only with the relation of "dramatic fate" to history, that is, to the chronological narrative of conventional historiography, but also with the "dramatic truth" to be traced within historical narrative insofar as it makes evident the shadowy inscription of a fate.[30] Bearing the stamp of a teleology without linear causality, fate in historical drama is understood, once again, in terms of "resistance to the never-ending flow of historical development" (*SW*1, 365/*GS*II:1, 249). As the darkly legible entelechy of a passional-moral process unfolding in guilt and atonement, it lends a pattern—as though immanently inscribed and rhythmed—to bare facticity: "Wherever there is fate, a piece of history has become nature" (*SW*1, 365/*GS*II:1, 249–50). Fate is invoked in these literary works where data of historical narratives are felt to intimate elemental affinities. In contrast to the colorless historicist inventory of deeds, the fatefully articulated stormy natural life in history formulates *dramatic* truth—"if history can lay claim to dramatic truth only as fate" (SW1, 384/GSII:1, 276). Such presentational truth in drama will of course differ from propositional truth. What is decisive for "the authentic idea of fate" (*der echte Schicksalsgedanke*)—in this respect recalling "immortal time" and "eternal transience"—is the assumption of something eternal, if not necessarily static, in its finite determinateness; it need not operate according to established laws of nature (SW1, 377/GSII:1, 266). The nature of fate in these works is therefore meta-natural; in the face of its baleful and irresistible manifestations, only "never-ending dialectical reflection" avails, taking up from different sides what seems fated so as to interpenetrate it (SW1, 380/GSII:1, 270). For these reasons it can be argued that the genre of drama, rather than the novel or epic, remains best suited to the literary treatment of fate. The task of the *modern* dramatist—no longer directly tied to cultic mythology—is then to mine the fields of history, letting emerge a "figuration of the fateful" (*Gestaltung des Schicksalhaften*) from out of the plausible details the historical source may provide; for there are subjects that allow "forms of a fateful cast" (*Formen schicksalhafter Bildung*) to be divined in them, and the older the motif, the more intimately tinged with fate (SW1, 365/GSII:1, 250 translation modified).

In the fate dramas of Calderón and Hebbel, permeated as they are with inherited material creatively adapted, the incalculable "law of fate" (*Gesetz des Schicksals*) recurrently finds expression through the working of passion in human nature and of chance in the nature of things bearing upon humans.[31] Through unrelenting reflection, however, Calderón's heroes can set the engine of fate turning like a plaything in their hands, just as, at the end of *One-Way Street*, the wakeful moment, arching between past and future, becomes a "Caudine Yoke beneath which fate must bow to . . . bodily presence of mind"; such integral comportment can turn a looming burden into a fulfilled "now" (SW1, 483/GSIV:1, 142). It is only inferior, unromantic fate tragedies, comments Benjamin, that represent fate as purely and simply real. The dramatist will give expression to dramatic truth, then, by formally and substantively doing justice to the manifoldly ambiguous virtual play of a dramatic fate,[32] a matter not so much of linear development—since fate concerns a way of life more than a sequence of deeds—as of subtle conjuncture and dramatic tension.

## Princely Life

That fate should speak through chance may seem surprising, and Benjamin himself appears to waver on this point.[33] The point is reiterated in *Origin of the German Trauerspiel*, however, which incorporates several passages from the essay on historical drama. It is in this semi-hermetic "tractatus" with its political-theological aesthetic—its investigation of a "theology of history" and "theology of evil"[34] informing the literature of an epoch riven by contradictions—that Benjamin's theory of fate as such effectively culminates. Expounding the concept of fate as it figures in the Baroque drama of fate, he gives definitive formulation to themes from his earlier work:

> [F]ate is no purely natural occurrence, any more than it is purely historical. However it may disguise itself in pagan, mythological guise,[35] fate is meaningful only as a natural-historical category in the spirit of the restoration theology of the Counter-Reformation. It is the elemental natural force in historical occurrence, . . . not the ineluctable causal nexus in itself . . . [but] the entelechy of occurrence [*Entelechie des Geschehens*] in the field of guilt. (*OT*, 128-9/*GSI*:1, 308)

Notwithstanding this emphatic restriction of its meaning to the spirit of Counter-Reformational theology (which Calderón is said to reflect), the fateful entelechy of occurrence—the emergent constellation of divergent moments—is again understood in terms of field dynamics and action at a distance. Its figuration is evinced, in the course of a Baroque trauerspiel, as disparate things—elements of the scene and action—are unexpectedly entangled: "Fate . . . is distinguished by just such an isolated field of force [*Kraftfeld*], in which everything of material and incidental importance is so heightened that the entanglements . . . betray through their paradoxical vehemence one thing: a fate has galvanized this play" (*OT*, 129/*GSI*:1, 308-9). The collective self-heightening and spin into salience, the galvanizing of individual moments interarticulated in all their particularity, is the signature of the fatal entanglement.

Reciprocal determination of fatality and contingency is at issue in Benjamin's packed remarks on Shakespeare's *Hamlet* as a consummate trauerspiel and drama of fate. I have referred to the law of fate that, in such literary works, governs both human passion and chance occurrence. In the *Trauerspiel* book, Benjamin conceives the motif of chance in seventeenth-century trauerspiels in terms of a consequential apportioning of occurrence into discontinuous but communicating elements or stations: "chance, as the dissolution of occurrence into elements parceled out like things [*dinghaft abgestückte*], corresponds entirely to the meaning of the stage property" (*OT*, 133/*GSI*:1, 312). In a manner that marks it as distinctively modern, the hybrid open-form mourning play orchestrates what is irreparably dismembered; the profane world of things burdens the action like a nightmare "loom[ing] oppressively over the horizon of the trauerspiel" (*OT*, 134/*GSI*:1, 312). As a result of this burden, the very air tastes of fate. Benjamin quotes a German critic's complaint of the "entirely external contingency" determining Hamlet's death scene; that the Prince should die in consequence of a poisoned rapier—not to mention the three or four other deaths he accidentally occasions, in which other objects are singularly involved—is said to undermine the tragic character of the drama.[36] Indeed! counters Benjamin: such blatant externality marks the play as a trauerspiel.

> The death of Hamlet, which has no more in common with tragic death than the Prince himself has with Ajax, is, in its vehement externality, characteristic of the trauerspiel . . . Hamlet wants to imbibe the fate-saturated air, like a poisonous substance, in one deep breath. He wants to die by chance, and as the fateful stage properties gather around him, as around their lord and master, there flashes up

at the conclusion of this trauerspiel, as though contained within it and, naturally, overcome, the drama of fate. (*OT*, 137-38/*GSI*:1, 315)

Whether or not the death of Hamlet should be considered tragic in an exemplary sense surely remains debatable; Benjamin dismisses the question rather too cavalierly.[37] In the section of the *Trauerspiel* book entitled "Hamlet," which caps the discussion of Shakespeare's play as a Baroque trauerspiel comprising both a fate- and martyr-drama, the emphasis is again on the figure of princely *life*, characterized, in the conflicted perspective of the period, by suddenly changeful, high-minded acedia. What distinguishes the figure of Hamlet from protagonists of German Baroque trauerspiel is not only richer humanity but "the bright gaze of self-reflection" in an "empty world"—enlightened awareness of the existential abyss opened up by the withering of eschatology (*OT*, 164, 141/*GSI*:1, 335, 317). Hamlet attests to having "that within which passes show" in a world of "seems."[38] If the mystery of his person—Benjamin's language itself becomes especially mysterious here—involves an initiatory passage through ever more challenging "stations," a *Via Crucis* at once measured and playful (measured *because* playful, writes Benjamin), then the "mystery of his fate" (*Geheimnis seines Schicksals*) resides in a happening "entirely homogeneous with this his gaze" (*OT*, 163/*GSI*:1, 334). Which might suggest a close correspondence between the trauerspiel of Hamlet's fate and his undisguised, if strangely playful, melancholy. As in Calderón, it is only through *continually renewed* reflection that melancholy can ever be redeemed. With his studious, allegorizing gaze, which gives him critical distance on himself and on a world of semblance wherein wisdom haunts only equivocally, Hamlet is "spectator by grace of God" (*OT*, 163/*GSI*:1, 335—a phrase singled out for criticism in Schmitt 2009: 60). Uppermost in Hamlet's reflections is his own mysterious fate, the articulated broken life and legacy that in his eyes bespeaks a providential womb of occurrence, just as, according to Benjamin's "Schemata," human nature bespeaks a womb (*Schoß*) of deep-sea sleep. It will be recalled that, in Shakespeare, Hamlet's revenge takes place in the aftermath of a perilous sea journey, one in which contingency unfolds fatality, while the fatal objects converge as though magnetized:

> It is not ... what a man might play for him but only his own fate that can satisfy him. His life, as the exemplary object of his mourning, points, before its extinction, to the Christian providence[39] in whose bosom [*Schoß*] his mournful images turn into blessed existence. Only in a life of this princely sort is melancholy, on being confronted with itself, redeemed. (*OT*, 163/*GSI*:1, 335)

As with the elegiac rhapsody of Youth (in which a sick-at-heart Hamlet already figures: *EW*, 27/*GSII*:1, 9–10), *Trauer*, exposed in its depths to reflection, intimates *Spiel—Weltspiel* at once elemental and allegorical, shattering and providential: theology of evil. The section "Hamlet" ends with an allusion to the *winged* melancholy iconically rendered in Dürer's engraving, *Melencolia I*; in the dialectic of the saturnine temperament, wisdom—hearkening to the deep—dawns mournfully "from the night of brooding" (*OT*, 157/*GSI*:1, 330). Whereas for Carl Schmitt, in his 1956 monograph *Hamlet or Hecuba*, the incursion of historical reality into the play turns the figure of

Hamlet into "a true myth,"[40] in Benjamin it is as allegory, not myth, that trauerspiels assimilate what accrues to them from historical conditions (*OT*, 234/*GSI*:1, 390). Integral to the allegorical design of the Baroque trauerspiel is the political-theological "image of apotheosis," melancholy transfigured. By dialectical reversal out of "the empty abyss of evil," the emergent image of apotheosis *interrupts* "the images of succession," affording "both entry and exit to mourning" (*OT*, 252, 258/*GSI*:1, 404, 409). It is the brooding and elusive figure of princely life in its readiness for the untoward (a comportment befitting actor and fencer as much as Christian martyr) that is finally determinative in overcoming, while fulfilling, the equivocal tidings of fate. "My fate cries out," exclaims Hamlet unhesitatingly on first encountering the ghost of his father, that grim apparition through which directives from the past and future seemingly speak together.[41] He will answer the singular summons—without ceasing, in his shame and despair, to serve the good enemy conscience—by enlisting art to dispel semblance: in the mortal wager he will "frankly," that is, freely and rigorously, "play."[42]

In Benjamin's late work one rarely comes upon the question of fate as such. The question had generally receded in all its undecidability by the time his own fate, if you will, began closing in on him. But key structural principles of the multifaceted and problematic concept of fate, with its roots in biblical and classical antiquity as well as early modernity, are carried over into his later philosophy of historical existence. From the start, Benjamin's concept of fate is determined by a philosophical field theory that, as we have seen, works in antithesis to the model of linear causality. Its working is experienced discontinuously, usually at unpredictable moments suddenly constellating with, or superimposed upon, moments from the past. This field-theoretical principle of virtual synchronicity, which conditions the oblique legibility of fate's allegorical inscription, leaves its stamp on Benjamin's historical-materialist conception of historical time.[43] In creatively citing, that is, animating and summoning, elements of what has been, the dialectical image ruptures (without erasing) the chronological framework of historicism, adumbrating a vibratory field of dramatic tension between often widely separated historical occurrences. The interplay of fore- and after-histories that, each time, newly constitutes the oscillating "now of recognizability"—doing so in accordance with a "secret index" of the past's subterranean claim upon the present (*SW*4, 390/*GSI*:2, 693/*WuN*19, 17)—thus itself recalls features of the intimately, spectrally relayed manifestation of fate across stations of an individual life-form or historical object. At issue in such spatiotemporal citation and intimation is always a dark, if not demonic, oceanic dimension, a surging womb of dream energies primed to awaken to acts of attention. If truth is revelation that does justice to mystery rather than expunging it (*OT*, 7/*GSI*:1, 211), then truth will not lack a pregnant negativity, necessitating allegory; and freedom will be won through studious, vigilant openness. Operative in both cases is political-theological nearness in distance to what remains unspoken in time's "large discourse."[44]

# Notes

1 My thanks to Brendan Moran and Paula Schwebel for expert advice. Regarding fate and good fortune, see also *GB*III, 78 and *GB*IV, 46.

2   See Bahti 1988: 65–73.
3   Alternately: "a care of self that should lead to a letting go of self" (Agamben 2004: 117).
4   Cohen 1904: 582 (*gewappnete Selbstsucht*).
5   Citing, here and in the following sentence, "Theological-Political Fragment" (ca. 1920–1), so named by Theodor Adorno. See *SW*3, 305–06/*GS*II:1, 203–4.
6   See Fenves 1991: 1–12, 97–8, 218–23.
7   Jäger 2000: 737–8 (*Probierstein seines Denkens*).
8   On the term "pure" (*rein*) in Benjamin, implying both "generative" and "expressionless," see Andrew Benjamin (2013: 122–25).
9   Compare, from 1940: "The historical method is a philological method grounded in the book of life [*Buch des Lebens*]" (*SW*4, 405/*GS*I:3, 1238); and from *The Arcades Project* (N4,2): "one can read the real like a text . . . We open the book of what happened [*Buch des Geschehenen*]" (*AP*, 464/*GS*V:1, 580).
10  On inner anonymity as precondition for writing: *C*, 125/*GBI*, 456 (May 1918).
11  See Steizinger 2013: 71–3.
12  "A class that shifts all political activity onto the plane of conversation in the press and in the parliament is no match for social conflict . . . Dictatorship is the opposite of discussion. . . . The core of the political idea, the exacting moral decision, is evaded in [everlasting discussion]" (Schmitt 1985: 59, 63, 65). Such decisionism would seem to presuppose the sovereign egology that Benjamin calls into question.
13  Bergson 1991: 45–6. Compare *SW*1, 143–48/*GS*I:1, 53–61.
14  Compare *TC*, 50/*GS*II:1, 192, on discussion (*Unterredung*) as a technique of civil accord. (Thanks to Brendan Moran for this reference.)
15  Compare *C*, 34/*GBI*, 127: "redemption of the unredeemable" (1913). On the inseparability of downfall and salvation in all phases of Benjamin's work, see Adorno 1981: 231.
16  In the Hölderlin essay (1914–15), the poet's fate unfolds a death-haunted spatiotemporal order wherein "every function of life is destiny [*Schicksal*];" for "the activity of the poet always reaches into orders determined by destiny" (*EW*, 191–92, 182/*GS*II:1, 124, 114).
17  The Aristotelian term refers here not to a causal nexus but to an obliquely manifest constellation of divergent moments. See note 19.
18  "[N]atural history [*Naturgeschichte*], as primal history [*Urgeschichte*] of meaning or intention, [is] dialectical in character" (*OT*, 173/*GS*I:1, 342).
19  On "entelechy" as synonymous with "monad," see Adorno 1997: 179.
20  See Cohen 1904: 343–7.
21  Hamacher 2002: 84. "[G]uilt is not only a category of provenance but also a category of moral and, more precisely, legal relations" (83).
22  "Fate and Character" proposes to disentangle the concept of fate from that of character—both connected to interpretive practices—and thereby sound the "original life" of these two hackneyed terms, beyond traditional religious and ethical frameworks (*C*, 229/*GBII*, 409). This aim is pursued in Agamben 2018: 49, 103–4, 106.
23  See *SW*1, 316/*GS*I:1, 149–50.
24  See *SW*1, 204/*GS*II:1, 175. Compare, from "Goethe's Elective Affinities": "With the disappearance of supernatural life in man, his natural life turns into guilt, even without his committing an act contrary to ethics. For now it is in league with mere life [*bloßen Lebens*], which manifests itself in man as guilt" (*SW*1, 308/*GS*I:1, 139).
25  Benjamin writes here: "this time [of fate] . . . has no present, for fateful moments exist only in bad novels" (*SW*1, 204/*GS*II,1, 176). But in an essay of 1930 on the novelist

Julien Green, a "great interpreter of fate," the latter is expounded precisely in terms of "fateful moments" and "lightning flashes" (*SW*2, 333–35/*GS*II:1, 331–33). See also *SW*2, 159/*GS*III, 154–55 and *GS*IV:2, 860.
26  To be distinguished from the transhistorical Jungian conception.
27  Adorno sees Benjamin's theory of fate transitioning from guilt context of the living to guilt context of society (1981: 233).
28  Compare "sea of the soul," from "Ibizan Sequence" (*SW*2, 592/*GS*IV:1, 408).
29  See *SW*1, 396, 278/*GS*VI, 81, 47.
30  See *SW*1, 376, 384/*GS*II:1, 264, 276. On Benjamin's concept of "the dramatic," see Moran 2015: 79–86.
31  *SW*1, 378/*GS*II:1, 267. See Birnbaum 2015: 100.
32  Concerning fate as play in Calderón, see *SW*1, 372–73, 381/*GS*II:1, 259–60, 272.
33  "Chance is the figure of Necessity abandoned by God" (*SW*2, 332/*GS*II:1, 330). On the simultaneity of fate and chance in book collecting: *SW*2, 486/*GS*IV:1, 388. On the mutual exclusion of fate and chance: *SW*2, 797/*GS*II:2, 412 and *GS*VI, 247 (1911).
34  Sharing the presupposition of infinite fall, *Geschichtstheologie* and *Theologie des Bösen* typify the Lutheran Baroque (*OT*, 134, 251–52/*GS*I:1, 390, 404). "[The death's head] is the core of the allegorical vision, of the Baroque profane exposition of history as the Passion of the world [*Leidensgeschichte der Welt*]" (*OT*, 174/*GS*I:1, 343).
35  "Fate and Character" invokes "the Greek classical development of the idea of fate" (*SW*1, 203/*GS*II:1, 174).
36  Leopold Ziegler's *Zur Metaphysik des Tragischen* (1902) is representative of a "lax concept of tragedy" (*OT*, 137/*GS*I:1, 315). Compare A. W. Schlegel, from 1808, on *Hamlet* as a tragedy of thought (*Gedankentrauerspiel*): "the criminals are at last punished, but as it were by an accidental blow, and not in a manner requisite to announce, with solemnity, a warning example of justice to the world" (1840: 199, 202–03).
37  See Jameson 2019: 110, 115, and Eiland 2022: 59–60.
38  Shakespeare 1982: 183–84 (1.2.85, 76). "Passes" in the sense of surpasses: that which is within him *exceeds* the possibility of outward appearance in the world.
39  Schmitt argues, contra Benjamin's theological emphasis, that Shakespearean drama is "no longer Christian" (2009: 39, 60–62).
40  Schmitt 2009: 44. Benjamin's modernist conception of play contrasts with Schmitt's pietistic conception (2009: 38–9).
41  "Here again what seems to be out front, the future, comes back in advance: from the past, from the back. 'Something is rotten in the state of Denmark,' declares Marcellus at the point at which Hamlet is preparing . . . to *follow* the ghost" (Derrida 1994: 10). Hamlet's fate does not just speak (*fatum* derives from *fari*, to speak) but "cries out."
42  Shakespeare 1982: 409 (5.2.249).
43  Concerning "simultaneity of the non-simultaneous" in Benjamin's late work, see Hamacher 2001: 182.
44  Shakespeare 1982: 345 (4.4.36–7).

# References

Adorno, Theodor W. (1981), "A Portrait of Walter Benjamin," in *Prisms*, trans. Samuel and Shierry Weber, 227–41, Cambridge: MIT Press.
Adorno, Theodor W. (1997), *Aesthetic Theory*, trans. Robert Hullot-Kentor, Minneapolis: University of Minnesota Press.

Agamben, Giorgio. (2004), "'I am Sure That You Are More Pessimistic than I am…': An Interview with Giorgio Agamben," *Rethinking Marxism*, 16 (2): 115–24.
Agamben, Giorgio. (2018), *Pulcinella*, trans. Kevin Attell, London: Seagull.
Bahti, Timothy. (1988), "Theories of Knowledge: Fate and Forgetting in the Early Works of Walter Benjamin," in Rainer Nägele (ed.), *Benjamin's Ground: New Readings of Walter Benjamin*, 61–82, Detroit: Wayne State University Press.
Benjamin, Andrew. (2013), *Working with Walter Benjamin: Recovering a Political Philosophy*, Edinburgh: Edinburgh University Press.
Bergson, Henri. (1991), *Matter and Memory*, trans. N. M. Paul and W. S. Palmer, New York: Zone.
Birnbaum, Antonia. (2015), "Variations of Fate," in Brendan Moran and Carlo Salzani (eds.), *Towards the Critique of Violence: Walter Benjamin and Giorgio Agamben*, trans. Carlo Salzani and Brendan Moran, 91–105, London: Bloomsbury.
Cohen, Hermann. (1904), *Ethik des reinen Willens*, Berlin: Cassirer.
Derrida, Jacques. (1994), *Specters of Marx*, trans. Peggy Kamuf, London: Routledge.
Eiland, Howard. (2022), "Hamlet as Trauerspiel?" *Berlin Journal of Critical Theory*, 6 (3): 43–61.
Fenves, Peter D. (1991), *A Peculiar Fate: Metaphysics and World-History in Kant*, Ithaca: Cornell University Press.
Hamacher, Werner. (2001), "'NOW': Walter Benjamin on Historical Time," in Heidrun Friese (ed.), *The Moment: Time and Rupture in Modern Thought*, 161–96, Liverpool: Liverpool University Press.
Hamacher, Werner. (2002), "Guilt History: Benjamin's Sketch 'Capitalism as Religion,'" trans. Kirk Wetters, *Diacritics*, 32 (3/4): 81–106.
Jäger, Lorenz. (2000), "Schicksal," in Michael Opitz and Erdmut Wizisla (eds.), *Benjamins Begriffe*, vol. 2, 725–39, Frankfurt: Suhrkamp.
Jameson, Fredric. (2019), *Allegory and Ideology*, London: Verso.
Moran, Brendan. (2015), "Nature, Decision and Muteness," in Brendan Moran and Carlo Salzani (eds.), *Towards the Critique of Violence: Walter Benjamin and Giorgio Agamben*, 73–90, London: Bloomsbury.
Schlegel, A. W. (1840), *Course of Lectures on Dramatic Art and Literature*, Vol. 2, trans. John Black, London: Templeman and Smith.
Schmitt, Carl. (1985), *Political Theology: Four Chapters on the Concept of Sovereignty*, trans. George Schwab, Cambridge: MIT Press.
Schmitt, Carl. (2009), *Hamlet or Hecuba*, trans. David Pan and Jennifer Rust, New York: Telos.
Shakespeare, William. (1982), *Hamlet*, ed. Harold Jenkins, London: Methuen.
Steizinger, Johannes. (2013), *Revolte, Eros und Sprache*, Berlin: Kadmos.

# 8

# Fulfilled Time

## Benjamin's Reception of Hermann Cohen's Idea of Messianism

Tamara Tagliacozzo

Walter Benjamin's idea of messianism has a clear connection to both Gershom Scholem's and Hermann Cohen's ideas of messianism, despite important differences between the three. In what overlaps within their ideas of messianism, the relation between politics and theology is fundamental. This is because of the role of the Judaic religion in connection to human ethics and politics, the mosaic institutions and the messianic ideals of the Prophets (peace, justice, a New Kingdom of David). In both Benjamin and Cohen, we see a secularization of the messianic idea, which plays a strong role in ethical and political theory. According to this idea of messianism, humankind acts within history to achieve the realization of the ideals of the Prophets and of reason. In Benjamin, unlike Cohen, however, there is not a progressive advancement of history toward this goal, but rather a connection to the past, and a vision of the interruption of history within history in every messianic event. Scholem, who will not be a main interlocutor in this chapter, theorizes a separation between Zionism (politics) and messianism (theology), and has an apocalyptic idea of messianism. Unlike Scholem, Benjamin's concept of messianism approximates Cohen's in that it is neither apocalyptic nor eschatological. For Benjamin, theology (messianism) and politics (the theory of revolution) have a close bond which is not visible and direct, but must remain hidden.

Although it appears that Benjamin is critical of the Neo-Kantian approach to progress, he actually appropriates an idea of fulfilled time from his reading of Cohen. This chapter intends to flesh out what Benjamin finds compelling in Cohen's account. To that end, I will describe the concepts of messianic time in Benjamin and Cohen respectively, and their convergences and divergences. I will end with an *excursus* on ethics and religion in Cohen and a conclusion about Benjamin's debt to Cohen's Judaic-messianic conception of history, his ethical anti-ontologism and anti-eschatologism.

## Messianic Time in Benjamin and Cohen: Past, Remembrance, Future

Benjamin's first reflections on history and messianism emerge in 1914–15 and are linked to the biblical concept of messianism. The connection between messianism and Judaism appears in full force in the *incipit* to "The Life of Students" (*Das Leben der Studenten*, 1914–15),[1] the most important essay Benjamin would write from within the student movement (and the last he would dedicate to that subject):

> There is a view of history that puts its faith in the infinite extent of time and thus concerns itself only with the speed, or lack of it, with which people and epochs advance along the path of progress. This corresponds to a certain absence of coherence and rigor in the demands it makes on the present. The following remarks, in contrast, delineate a particular condition in which history appears to be concentrated in a single focal point, like those that have traditionally been found in the utopian images of the philosophers. (*SW*1, 37/ *GS*II:1, 75)

The image of history Benjamin presents to us is that of time fulfilled and gathered into a momentaneous illumination, a time he will later call *Jetztzeit*.[2] In the immanence of the present, this "now" captures from the past an image of the state of moral perfection, a redemption to come upon the arrival of the Messiah at the end of history—an ending that interrupts history even while remaining within it, with the building of a reign of God, of justice, on earth.[3] Messianism is not passive waiting for the beginning of another world beyond history itself, but an active possibility of changing and redeeming the historical world "now." This messianic time reveals itself in images of utopian thought; that is, in the representation by thinkers and philosophers of the metaphysical idea of a new and perfect political, ethical, and epistemic reality to be achieved in the future.

The concept of messianic time stands opposed to the physical-mathematic concept of a homogeneous, empty time, in which physical phenomena take place according to a model of infinite progress. A description in Benjamin's 1916 essay, "Trauerspiel und Tragödie," exemplifies the contrast between the two opposed visions:

> For empirical events time is nothing but a form, but, what is more important, as a form it is unfulfilled [*unerfüllt*] ... Historical time, however, differs from this mechanical time ... [T]he determining force of historical time cannot be fully grasped by, or wholly concentrated in, any empirical process. Rather, a process that is perfect [*vollkommen*] in historical terms is quite indeterminate empirically; it is in fact an idea. This idea of fulfilled time [*der erfüllten Zeit*] is the dominant historical idea of the Bible: it is the idea of messianic time. (*SW*I, 55–6/ *GS*II:1, 134)

Benjamin conceives the state of moral perfection and justice as a final state. In this he follows the Judaic-Kabbalistic doctrine of the "breaking of the vessels" (*Shevirat haKelim*), a messianic recuperation and re-composition (*Tikkun*) of the broken shards.

This kabbalistic doctrine is used by him as a basis to build a conception of ethics and politics where the accomplishment of the idea of justice on earth, as perfection, is seen as a messianic redemption and a reconstruction of the vessels, which contained the divine emanations (*Sefirot*) whose rupture was caused by the strength of the divine light itself in the Creation. Human beings can and must help in the reconstruction of these vessels with their good actions (*mitzvot*), looking for the sparks of divine light in the fragments (*quelipot*) of these vessels, which are mixed up with evil and which lie deeply hidden in the imperfect world.[4] The final state of ethical and political perfection manifests itself in reality in immanent, but often denigrated fragments, such as works of art or philosophical reflections, which can be recognized for what they are and "saved," set aside to be recomposed in a newly pristine future, a perfect state of the world. This salvation can be achieved solely through a historical and critical recuperation and symbolic exhibition that positions the fragments, "in a pure way [*rein*]" (*SW*1, 37/ *GS*II:1, 75 translation modified), within the metaphysical structure of the final state—an idea in which history and the state of the world come to fulfillment. This anticipates Benjamin's epistemology (developed between 1918 and 1925), in which the relation between phenomenon, concept, and idea is linked to presentation (*Darstellung*), that is, to the symbolic exhibition of the unconditional idea in the already-conceptualized phenomena. He maintains this same epistemological structure in the 1930s in his concept of the dialectic image.

Benjamin's interpretation of *Shevirat haKelim* also draws on a Cohenian background (i.e., Cohen's logic, ethics, and philosophy of religion), in bringing together an idea of redemption and an idea of the symbolic exhibition *in* the fragments—as pure concepts—of a metaphysical idea. We don't find an interpretation of *Shevirat haKelim* in Cohen,[5] but there is a concept of purity (an independence from empirical knowledge), which we also find in Benjamin's conception of the reconstruction of the shards. The concept of purity is crucial for Cohen throughout his *System der Philosophie*.[6] He writes in the *Logic of Pure Knowledge*: "We begin with thought. Thought must have no other origin than itself . . . Pure thought in itself and only itself must exclusively produce all pure knowledge" ([1914] 1977: 13). Cohen thus eliminates the Kantian distinction between pure thought and pure intuition, between the forms of space and time and the categories, by positing the foundation of thought and logic, and thus of all pure knowledge, and of reality, in the principle of the origin developed from the idea of the hypothesis (cf. [1914] 1977: 601). Cohen's idea of the hypothesis institutes the task of the constitution of the system of concepts, which remains forever open-ended. The two other parts of Cohen's *System der Philosophie*, his *Ethics of Pure Will* and *Aesthetics of Pure Feeling* ([1907] 1981; [1912] 1982), are founded on the principle of purity. Common to all three works is the transcendental method, retracing from the "facts" of science, law, and the work of art, the pure principles which, starting from the concept of the idea as "task," are at their foundation.

In Benjamin, who is thinking of Cohen's System, reflection on the concept of "purity" develops into his critical encounter with Kant in the essay "On the Program of the Coming Philosophy" (*SW*1, 100–10/ *GS*II:1, 157–71). Benjamin's essay points out the need for the philosophical system to be founded (even in the contents of its future "experience") on completely *a priori* concepts and ideas, and on the independence (like Cohen) from anything empirical, in both the theoretical and practical realms. This renders concepts, in relation to ideas, forms of knowledge capable of taking on a "deep" meaning that is ideal, religious, and metaphysical. Concepts and ideas are always differentiated for Benjamin; concepts are limited; they select the phenomena and bring these, through a process of abstraction, to knowledge and to purity, not to truth (*Wahrheit*). They can however be loaded with a symbolic charge that expresses (or presents, [*darstellt*]) the idea (related to truth and totality) in a limited image, which Benjamin characterizes as a constellation of concepts. Purity is in this case fundamental because it saves the phenomena from their empirical status (cf. Tagliacozzo 2018: 11–59). The fragments, that is, must be pure concepts, which restore and represent, in immanence, the final state as a metaphysical idea:

> The elements of the ultimate condition do not manifest themselves as formless progressive tendencies, but are deeply rooted in every present in the form of the most endangered, excoriated, and ridiculed ideas and products of the creative mind. The historical task [*geschichtliche Aufgabe*] is to disclose this immanent state of perfection and make it absolute in a pure way, to make it visible and dominant in the present . . . [T]he task is to grasp its metaphysical structure, as with the messianic domain or the idea of the French Revolution. (*SW*1, 37/ *GS*II:1, 75 translation modified)

As examples of the metaphysical structure of the state of perfection, Benjamin holds up the conception of the Messianic Kingdom and the idea of the French Revolution—an idea that will turn up again in 1940 in the theses "On the Concept of History" (*Über den Begriff der Geschichte*, *SW*4, 395/ *WuN*19, 102, thesis XIV). He establishes a parallel between these two ideas and identifies in them a common denominator, the idea of justice, as the fulfillment of the Kantian idea of liberty.[7] The *Theses* create an indissoluble link between the historical task of restoring the past in remembrance and the redemptive/messianic idea of the achievement of the final condition, the reign of justice. Starting in the early 1920s, the new idea (*Vorstellung*) of felicity/good fortune (*Glück*)—alongside the dimension of contingency—emerges in Benjamin's thought. This dimension, in the messianic "now" (*Jetztzeit*), binds us to remembrance and its salvation, and thus to its potential redemption in political action. There is a strong connection between the ideas of felicity and redemption in political action in the *Theses* of 1940:

> In other words, the idea of happiness is indissolubly bound up with the idea of redemption. The same applies to the idea of the past, which is the concern of history. The past carries with it a secret index by which it is referred to redemption . . . Then, like every generation that preceded us, we have been endowed with a *weak* messianic power, a power on which the past has a claim [thesis II]. (*SW*4, 389/ *WuN*19, 93-4)[8]

History is the subject of a construction whose site is not homogeneous, empty time, but time filled full by now-time [*Jetztzeit*]. Thus, to Robespierre ancient Rome was a past charged with now-time, a past which he blasted out of the continuum of history. The French Revolution viewed itself as Rome reincarnate. It cited ancient Rome exactly the way fashion cites a bygone mode of dress ... [I]t is the tiger's leap into the past. Such a leap, however, takes place in an arena where the ruling class gives the commands. The same leap in the open air of history is the dialectical leap Marx understood as revolution. ([thesis XIV], *SW*4, 395/ *WuN*19, 102)

Twenty-five years after utilizing the image of the French Revolution in "The Life of Students," Benjamin revisits this image in thesis XIV. Here, the image refers to the past of republican Rome as a historical event to be re-actualized. For the French revolutionaries, republican Rome yields an idea of the final state of redemption. In this thesis, he explains the concept of the fulfillment of messianic time, *Jetztzeit*, in opposition to the empty, homogeneous times of science and the idea of progress.

In the *Theses*, Benjamin criticizes the social democratic and historicist concept of progress, and the Neo-Kantian concept of politics at its base: the idea of an infinite progress of society and of history as an "infinite task," which transforms the representation of the messianic idea of breakthrough to a kingdom of justice into an "ideal"—that is, a forever unattainable goal.[9] However, despite Benjamin's critique of Hermann Cohen and their obvious differences, it is possible to discover the influence of Cohen's messianism on Walter Benjamin's ethical-messianic thought.[10]

It is noteworthy that Benjamin does not name Cohen among those he attacks in the *Theses*.[11] This is perhaps because Benjamin is not entirely opposed to Cohen's conception of history, which does not perceive historical time simply as that of science and mathematics (namely, as "homogenous and empty," exactly measured and not filled with a spiritual content), but as a time charged with redemptive moments.[12] Furthermore, Benjamin esteemed Cohen as a person and admired his *Die Religion der Vernunft aus den Quellen des Judentums* (1919, 1929), which he had read in 1920. By contrast, he was quite critical of the thought of August Stadler, Paul Natorp, and Karl Vorländer, whose ideas constituted the theoretical basis of social democracy:[13]

> In the idea of the classless society, Marx secularized the idea [*Vorstellung*] of messianic time. And that was a good thing. It was only when the Social Democrats elevated this idea to an "ideal" that the trouble began. The ideal was defined in Neo-Kantian doctrine as an "infinite [*unendlich*] task." And this doctrine was the school philosophy of the Social Democratic party—from Schmidt and Stadler through Natorp and Vorländer. Once the classless society had been defined as an infinite task, the empty and homogeneous time was transformed into an anteroom, so to speak, in which one could wait for the emergence of the revolutionary situation with more or less equanimity. In reality, there is not a moment that would not carry with it *its* revolutionary chance—provided only that it is defined in a specific way, namely as the chance for a completely new resolution of a completely new problem [*Aufgabe*]. For the revolutionary thinker, the peculiar revolutionary chance offered by every historical moment gets its warrant from the political situation. But it is equally grounded, for this thinker, in the "power of the keys" [*Schlüsselgewalt*][14] which the historical moment enjoys vis-à-vis a quite distinct chamber of the past, one which up to that point has been

closed and locked. The entrance into this chamber coincides in a strict sense with political action, and it is by means of such entry that political action, however destructive, reveals itself as messianic. (Classless society is not the final goal of historical progress but its frequently miscarried, ultimately [*endlich*] achieved interruption.)[15]

Benjamin's view does not consider time as a process, but rather as an ideal dimension (comparable to the biblical idea of history), wherein a sudden flash reveals a dimension of totality, eternity, and fulfillment. Jewish messianism implicates a restorative dimension of history, conceived as a return to a kingdom of justice and peace, presented as a new Kingdom of David. But this restoration is also utopian, since the Kingdom of David never actually existed in Jewish history, but represents a new utopian state (cf. Scholem 1995). In Benjamin, the materialist conception of history (preceded in Benjamin's thought by an anarchistic, nihilistic phase)[16] is strictly connected to the theological idea of time as *Jetztzeit*, an intensive, redemptive time. Through the redemptive actualization of the past, and with a critique of the concept of progress, the historian exercises a "*weak* messianic power" and provides direction to political action.[17] This is a revolutionary action aimed at founding a classless society—an idea which secularizes the Judaic realm of justice, namely, by transposing it into a political rather than a theocratic idea.

In Cohen, messianism is a guiding idea for the achievement of justice on Earth, rather than in a world beyond, since the immortality of the individual soul is conceivable only within human history as it progresses toward sanctity. This idea is conceived as a necessary effort with respect to a law seen as real. In Kant also, the will, determined by the moral law, is characterized by the "incessant effort of exact and continuous observance of a strict, inflexible natural law which is not ideal, but real" (Kant 2002: 156, 1900–: 221).[18] According to the biblical-Talmudic tradition that Cohen follows in *Religion der Vernunft*, justice is equal to sanctity, that is, to the realization of morality, and is an attribute of the Messiah, while peace is the distinctive negative sign of the messianic era:

> Justice is the second virtue of the first rank. It is first among God's characteristics: "The Eternal is just in all His ways and gracious in all His works . . . Thy justice is everlasting justice" (Ps. 145:17; 119:137, 142). Justice is equal to holiness: "And God the Holy One is sanctified through justice" [righteousness] (Isa. 5:16). Justice is the attribute of the Messiah: "And justice shall be the girdle of his loins" (Isa. 11:5). The cessation of wars is the negative sign of the Messianic Age; the positive sign, however, is one's learning of, and habituation to, justice. "Neither shall they learn war any more" (Mic. 4:3). It says positively: "The inhabitants of the world learn justice" (Isa. 26:9) Thus, justice becomes the sign of the Messianic Age. (Cohen 1995: 429, [1929] 1988: 506)

For Cohen, the Messiah has meaning as a metaphysical and moral idea, an ideal projected onto the dimension of the future of history (and not toward a life beyond) in the face of which the individual existence of human beings vanishes:

> The ideality of the Messiah, his significance as an idea, is shown in the overcoming of the person of the Messiah and in the dissolution of the personal image in the pure notion of time, in the concept of the *age*. Time becomes future and only future. Past and present submerge in this time of the future. This return to time is the purest idealization. All existence sinks into insignificance in the presence of the point of view of this idea, and man's existence is preserved and elevated into this being of the future. Thus, the thought of *history* comes into being for human life and for the life of the peoples . . . // Mankind did not live in any past and did not become alive in any present; only the future can bring about its bright and beautiful form. This form is an idea, not a shadowy image of the beyond. (Cohen 1995: 249–50, [1929] 1988: 293–94)

Since the immortality of the individual soul is conceivable only within the story of humanity as it proceeds toward sanctity, messianism is Cohen's guiding idea toward the achievement of justice on Earth rather than in a world beyond, and it is conceived as a necessary labor to be carried out with regard to a law seen as real.

Cohen's messianic vision comes close to the aforementioned Neo-Kantian conception of socialism, which Benjamin criticized in "The Life of Students" and the theses "On the Concept of History." This is because it posits an idea of progress as one of infinite development, to which humankind must contribute (because the Creator is not enough). It suggests, namely, progress toward an *idea* of humanity. According to this vision, the end of history falls inside history itself, since it demands perfection in an earthly future. Thus, this idea of messianism stands against an eschatological conception of history: there is not an *eschaton*, a "strong" and ontological goal of history; "the end is here" (Cohen 1877: 270), on earth, where humankind must progress toward the idea of humanity; this is Cohen's "weak" and idealistic messianism:

> An important moment already comes to the fore, which lays down the bridge between the root of monotheism and its peak formed by Messianism; *the distinction between eschatology and Messianism*. The dignity of man is not grounded merely in the individual man but in the idea of humanity. (Cohen 1995: 49, [1929] 1988: 57)[19]

> The concept of God's being, too, becomes different under the impact of this idea. The creator of heaven and earth is not sufficient for this being of the future. He must create "a new heaven and a new earth" [Isa. 65:17]. The being of previous history is inadequate even for nature, for *development* is required for the course of things, and development presupposes a goal to which it strives. Thus progress is required in the history of human race. // This is the meaning of the future as the establishment of true being, that is, God's being on earth; the future, this idea of existence, represents exclusively the *ideal* of history . . . The future, in opposition to all these myths about the past, makes another transformation: the "Day of the Lord" comes to be "the End of Days." With this prospect, in this perspective of an infinite plateau of mankind,[20] the notion of man is raised to that of mankind, as

the concept of God is to the "Lord of the whole Earth." (Cohen 1995: 250, [1929] 1988: 292)

According to Cohen, therefore, messianism is created out of a conception of history—that of the Prophets—which refers back not to the origins of Greek culture, nor to a Christian world beyond, but to the real world, which must accommodate the ethical-religious idea of humanity (an idea produced by prophetic messianism): "Messianism must be considered as a creation of ideas brought about by the prophetic concept of history. *The concept of history is a creation of the prophetic idea*" (Cohen 1995: 261, [1929] 1988: 305). History is a dimension of the future in which every individual is lifted, in his/her moral autonomy, to the level of humanity, becoming a member of humanity as it proceeds on its path toward sanctity.

## Convergences and Divergences

The question of the influence of Cohen's messianism on Benjamin remains open, but alongside the differences between the two thinkers, and beyond Benjamin's great esteem for Cohen, we cannot fail to recognize indisputable affinities.[21] In *Religion der Vernunft* Cohen opposes the Christian vision of the kingdom of God, as an eschatological concept, setting aside the question as to whether the request in the Lord's Prayer, "let kingdom come," refers only to a heavenly beyond or may also evoke a moral becoming within the historical world. For Cohen, in the Jewish Kaddish Prayer "confidence is directed to the 'Kingdom of God,' the express prayer is for the earthly days, for the historical days of the people which, in the messianic sense, means the whole mankind" (Cohen 1995: 310, [1929] 1988: 360). The duty to adore God in practice, through prayer and by obeying God's precepts in preparation for taking on the yoke of the kingdom of God, brings on the moment in which the messianic future becomes real and present, rather than being forever deferred toward an infinite dimension:

> [The duty of worship] does not wait for the future, but fills my whole life and every moment of my existence. And the same must also hold for the messianic future //. . . *For my personal worship the Kingdom of God is not to be in a future advent, but must be a permanent actuality* . . . I do not wait for the "Kingdom of God" to come and merely pray for its advent but bring it about through my own preparedness [*Kawwanà*], through my own will I bring it about. // Thus, the Kingdom of God is present to me and is a personal actuality for my consciousness of duty. Therefore it is more than just an object of hope and confidence. This realization and actualization of the messianic future was made possible through the abovementioned distinction between the messianic future and the beyond, which, in spite of all connection, remained alive in the Jewish consciousness, particularly because it was maintained by the idea of resurrection. (Cohen 1995: 310, [1929] 1988: 360–61)

In a recent monograph on Walter Benjamin, Fabrizio Desideri has indicated points of convergence between Benjamin and Cohen, with regard to Cohen's messianism, the reception of the Prophets, a shared resistance to eschatology, and the conviction of both thinkers that the messianic idea implicates a connection between ethics and religion, prophecy and history, and a continuum from Platonism to Kant to Judaism.[22] According to Desideri, and this is also my view, Cohen himself does not conceive of time as homogeneous and empty, but as filled up, charged with the messianic-ethical idea, from the moment the individual enters history and becomes a member of a humanity, aspiring to the redemptive potentialities of sanctity and justice. At the same time, however, Desideri identifies divergences between the two authors' concepts of messianism. Among these, Benjamin regards the present as actuality and remembrance, in contrast to Cohen's orientation toward the future. Their perceptions of "origin" also differ: Cohen's is logical while Benjamin's is historical, an expression of the dialectical unity of catastrophe (the mythical condition of humankind) and redemption. The infinitesimal which, in Cohen, creates being from nothingness in the judgment of the origin, becomes, in Benjamin, infinitesimal time, gathered within the messianic time of *Jetztzeit*:[23]

> The originality of Benjamin's position consists, in fact, in his reversing the time perspective of prophecy, making of remembrance [*Eingedenken*] the hinge of the "small door [or narrow gate]" (the infinitesimal time) through which might enter, at every instant, the Messiah . . . For Benjamin, as for Cohen, the Messianic understanding of historical time produces a crisis in the traditional image of history as a homogeneous course of events and in the perception of time as a pure flow. Certainly—in the case of Benjamin—this crisis takes the form of an arrest and of an interruption, not of time as such, but of its apparent continuity . . . We can gather the subtlest philosophical difference between Benjamin and Cohen at the point of their greatest proximity. I mean here indeed the conceptual figure of origin, which—as we know—Benjamin proposed to be understood in a historical sense rather than in a logical one . . . [T]he notion of origin that Benjamin defines means both a criticism of Cohen's idealism and the dialectic that is inherent to the constitutive incompleteness of what emerges as *Ursprung* . . . Consequently, Benjamin transforms, in the dialectic between incompleteness and revelation that is inherent to the origin, the Cohenian idea of an infinite task into the infinitely intensive process of a *restitutio in integrum* . . . In this idea of the origin, which is related with the unfulfillable character of Justice, consists then the theological and philosophical peculiarity of Walter Benjamin. (Desideri 2015: 139–43)

As we have already seen, in *Über den Begriff der Geschichte* in 1940 (thesis XVIIa), Benjamin speaks of an "entirely new task," different from the Neo-Kantian infinite task, directed at recuperating a past threatened with oblivion and re-actualized in the moment of revolutionary *chance*. This envisions a restoration bound to praxis, including even destructive revolutionary action. In Cohen, too, the "moment" has a fundamental importance for the individual, who in the redemptive moment enters into relation with the origin and becomes part of the messianic history of humanity.[24] Messianism is not, for Cohen, a dimension of waiting, but a political force for the transformation of today. It is in this sense that in his discussion *Die Messiaidee* (1892), he cites the Talmudic passage (*Sanh.* 98a) that says the Messiah comes *today*, provided we hear its voice:

> The difference between "one day" and "today" consists in virtue. And it is in effect virtue, pure morality, that is conceived in these passages of the Talmud as the content of messianic religiosity . . . Thus the Talmud has compelled us to an appreciation of the idea of the Messiah in ethical terms. (Cohen [1892] 1924: 120)[25]

The not-conditional, the *focus imaginarius*, is, in Cohen, eternity, which is the regulative idea of ethics, the "perspective point for a trend forward, without respite or end, of pure will" (Cohen [1907] 1981: 410). Eternity, according to Pierfrancesco Fiorato,

> [as a] "temporal condition," without being actually a "determination of time," on the one hand "transcends" the latter, while, on the other, it supplies the present with its orientation criteria and in this does not only appear structurally analogous to the "days of the Messiah" [Cohen (1907, 1981): 406], but plays a methodological role for the ethical problem which is similar to that which, in the *Logik*, belonged to the principle of infinitesimal reality. (Fiorato 2005: 157)

As the principle of the infinitesimal creates reality from thought and "nothing," eternity is what creates the reality of ethics, in the future, where the end is never reached but is already always "here." In the concept of eternity, which is the same as the concept of future, we find the idea of an "end in itself." In Cohen's words, "the end is here, the moral law is the final law" (Cohen 1877: 270). This pertains to the liberty and autonomy of reason, and the idea of humanity itself, understood to be a community of autonomous ends, acting within history, and striving toward sanctity and justice. The fulfillment is both "now" and in an infinite future:

> One can understand the meaning of the transformation of time into pure future dealt with in the *Religion der Vernunft*. The pathos worthy of true messianic fulfillment of the times with which this transformation is described—a justified pathos, since a true *Erfüllung* is involved, a fulfillment of time, in the sense of the restoration of its most apt, originary nature—does not refer back to any *consummatio saeculi*, but rather announces its definite negation. As restoration to time of its risky, open nature, its "fulfillment" is only thinkable as taking up that radical "incompleteness" which only ethical life can make its own. This taking up inaugurates the "being of the future" that the *Religion der Vernunft* immediately identifies specifically with the open dimension of history. (Fiorato 2005: 156)

We can say that Cohen's messianic idea culminates in a notion of the "now" that anticipates Benjamin's idea of *Jetztzeit*, although in Benjamin the fulfillment of the *Jetzt* is given intensively in the relation between past and present rather than between past, present, and future.

## Ethics and Religion in Cohen

Cohen's concept of ethics is linked to the fundamental relationship between history and eternity. Eternity—as an "unconditioned focal point [*Blickpunkt*] for the advancement, without respite or end, of pure will" (Cohen [1907] 1981: 410)—furnishes the conditions and the ideal, immanent criteria for the ethical task, the infinity of which was already familiar to Benjamin in 1917–18 and after.[26] In Cohen, along with the transcendental method, and within that setting, the reference of each member of the system itself to a limit-idea, formulated as a task, provides unity to the system (and constitutes the possibility of truth as a systematic unity). "If the 'being true' of the law constitutes the foundation of the being of the existent, the duty-to-be of the ethical idea constitutes the limit of being, and truth consists solely in the infinite task of logic and ethics" (Poma 1997: 67). Cohen's essay *On Perpetual Peace* (*Vom ewigen Frieden*) explains:

> The truth, as we comprehend this fundamental idea of critical idealism, consists in the *distinction* of the *idea* as infinite *task* for all moral purposes, both for the human race and the single individual, in the distinction of this *ethical* meaning of the *idea* from any existent reality of nature and any historical experience. Both these things are necessary: the distinction, but also the *preservation of both elements* in their equal logical value, just as existent reality maintains its value before the idea, and the idea founds its own meaning in the admonition and guidance it proffers to existent reality. This truth of idealism, which simultaneously renders honor to existent reality, guarantees us personal veracity in all our thought, investigation, and action. (Cohen [1914] 2012: 314–15)

Time, as an anticipation of the future, is for Cohen the fundamental category of ethics. Thus, in *The Ethics of Pure Will* (*Ethik des reinen Willens*), against the infinity of space as a totality, he proposes an *analogon* of the infinity of time, opposing totality with the "*concept of eternity*" (Cohen [1907] 1981: 400). Eternity is the guiding concept of the will, which posits the infinite task of morality, in which the ideal is never reached on an individual level, but is present as an infinitely distant point:

> Thus eternity means nothing other than the *focal point* [*Blickpunkt*] of the incessant, infinite tendency to proceed forward on the part of pure will. *In itself, it does not at all mean an eternal time and an eternal place, but only an eternal effort* . . . Each individual level includes the infinitely distant point to which, conceptually, it intrinsically refers. *Eternity is, for every single point, this infinitely distant point* . . . They must be taken together if one wishes to understand that eternity is the effectual reality of the ethical, and that the finite point of realization does not represent a contradiction. (Cohen [1907] 1981: 410–11)

The concept of eternity, as a reality produced by pure will, establishes the methodical autonomy of ethics from the religious messianism of the Prophets. Cohen ([1907] 1981: 406) considers the latter almost a philosophy of history, which envisions the beginning of a new time and a new world, a "new humanity on Earth," distinguished by peace among peoples and the justice of "the days of the Messiah." Despite the fundamental ethical value of its reference to the concept of the future, and despite being the most instructive example of the "indissoluble historical nexus between ethics and religion" (Cohen [1907] 1981: 407), this is still not sufficient for ethics. Its ethical value consists in its political significance, expressed in a poetic language with images of perfection that could lead to stasis, in foreseeing a future that can become the present: "This is the poetic limitation of the idea of the Prophets, the difference from the ethical concept. The future cannot be reduced to an image of peace. Humanity must be oriented toward the future, but the future can never become present, not even a present completely different from any historical past" (Cohen [1907] 1981: 408).[27] In ethics, instead, the progression of ethical labor is eternal, and has nothing in common with scientific thought. Together with the ethical "ideal," eternity—as an image and model of perfection—forms the reality of ethics. For Cohen, the ideal, immanent in being, "indicates the perfection of being; it represents it in itself." In the ideal, "eternity is put into relation with temporality" (Cohen [1907] 1981: 424). Infinity is manifest down to the smallest element in the world: "infinity resides [and is actualized] in every walnut shell," but at one and the same time, every "level of immanence simultaneously demonstrates the distance," the incompleteness of the ideal (Cohen [1907] 1981: 424). The will creates an authentic being; it creates humanity as eternity, as an ideal of ethical self-awareness. This sense of eternity "does not exhaust itself in the apparent self-awareness of the individual, not even if the individual is considered immortal." Rather, "the being of the ideal lasts well beyond the individual" (Cohen [1907] 1981: 426), rendering explicit the "*superiority of history*, of universal history, of the history of humanity," a history of the human race in the progress of its ethical labor "with respect to nature and all the greatness and strength of its being" (Cohen [1907] 1981: 426). It is not the immortality of the individual, but the "eternity of the moral conscience, the eternity of humanity as bearer of this self-awareness: this is the ideal. This is the being of will, the highest idealism" (Cohen [1907] 1981: 427).

> That such a future may not be understood as a mere "not-yet," lined up in order, read in time as a sequence of events, is made clear by the short circuit established between the exigency brought forth in the *Ethics*, according to which "the future can never transform itself into a present"[28] and the affirmation [in the] *opus postumum*, that the "messianic future" must fill up every moment of existence, without "awaiting the future." (Fiorato 1996: 315; cf. Cohen 1995: 310, [1929] 1988: 360)

Appearing at the end of the *Ethics*, the "panoramic gaze of consideration [*Rücksicht*]" (Cohen [1907] 1981: 361) brings about, without yet being able to find adequate expression, the "reversal of the prohibition against making the future a present, in the imperative of conferring on the present the profundity of the messianic future" (Fiorato 2008: 64). This consideration does not fear looking back at the past, at the present, and at specific cases; it is thus that "the 'collapse' of past and present into the messianic future will be understood:[29] with reference to a messianic age which will always be in the future, but which is (must be) already here" (Fiorato 2008: 64). In

*Religion der Vernunft*, Cohen sees this realized, in the virtue of peace as an emblem of eternity, in messianic humanity's mission of peace, fulfilled in eternity and historical survival.[30]

## A Partial Proximity

It thus seems possible to perceive a continuity between the concept of the ideal in the *Ethics* and in the *Religion of Reason*. In the same way, there is a possible, although partial, proximity of the ethical and messianic temporality that characterizes these concepts to Benjamin's *Jetztzeit*. In Benjamin, the ethical and "historical task" pertaining to the conscious subject and collective agent—the generations, the oppressed masses, in the *Theses*—is founded on a conception of time that is not empty and mechanical, but that is full, intensive, and redemptive. This latter is the time of the Bible and prophecy, where historical contingency and the eternity of the idea coincide and mirror one another, as in the idea of happiness and downfall (*Untergang*) referred to in Benjamin's "Theological-Political Fragment" (*SW*4, 306–7/ *GS*II: 1, 203–4). The infinity of the "new" cognitive, ethical, and political task is intensive and comes to fruition in "actuality," in which the concept of historical consciousness redeems the past and provides instruction for praxis. This owes a great deal—even granted Benjamin's inversion of Cohen's idea of ethics bound to the future in the actuality of remembrance and the political interruption of the course of history—to Cohen's Judaic-messianic conception of ethics and his concept of temporality and eternity, his concepts of sanctity, humanity, justice, and peace bound to history, and to his ethical anti-ontologism and anti-eschatologism.

Benjamin reads Cohen's Messianism as an ethical ideal in history, which even if seen as an unreachable goal in an unreachable future, fulfills every "now" with the presence of its totality. In Cohen, past and present fall into the future—in his logic with the method of anticipation, in his ethics with the concept of eternity: "Cohen contrasts, as more originary, the 'per-spective' of anticipation with the extrinsic retrospectiveness of the ordinary conception of time as a given succession. The correlation of future and past within which theological determination of 'plurality' [*Mehrheit*] finds its originary formulation, replaces the 'correlation of past and present'" (Fiorato 2005: 148).

In Benjamin, the fulfillment is given in the relation between past and present, in the historical monad. The concept of history is a construction where the messianic idea, the perfect world, is present in every "now of knowability" in which the monadological "dialectical image" presents itself as the actualization of moments of an unredeemed past that is redeemed in knowledge and afterward in political action. Benjamin presents the Jewish conception of the future in Thesis B, not as homogeneous and empty time (empty of spiritual values), like in the mechanical time-conception of the sciences, but as fulfilled time, full with the messianic ideals of peace, moral and theoretical perfection, and justice. Every second of this time of the future is seen by Judaism as the "small gateway" though which the Messiah arrives (cf. *SW*4, 397/ *WuN*19, 106).

# Notes

1 "The Life of Students" was published in *Der neue Merkur*, April-September 1915, and successively in *Das Ziel. Aufrufe zu tätigem Geist*, and was composed between May 1914 and September 1915. It originated in two talks given by Benjamin in May and June 1914—the first in Berlin upon his election as president of Berlin's *Freie Studentenschaft*, the second in Weimar on the occasion of the fourteenth Day of the Free Student Movement. Benjamin had taken an active part in the Student Movement (*Jugendbewegung*), which was inspired and led by Gustav Wyneken. The movement fought for a libertarian reform of secondary schools and the university system, but split due to schisms in 1914; Benjamin was elected president of one of the factions. On *Das Leben der Studenten* and Benjamin's ethical-philosophical thought during the period 1913–15 in general, cf. Hartung (1992).

2 As early as 1920–1, Benjamin spoke of the "now of knowability (*Jetzt der Erkennbarkeit*)" as a time logically opposed to the conception of the atemporal validity of knowledge. The *Jetzt der Erkennbarkeit* is the temporal messianic-redemptive moment of the perfect world and the self-offering of truth. Cf. Benjamin's fragment "Theory of Knowledge" (*SW*1, 276–7/ *GSV*:1, 46).

3 Cf. "On the Concept of History" (1940): "The Messiah comes not only as redeemer; he comes as the victor over the Antichrist" (*SW*4, 391/ *WuN*19, 96).

4 Benjamin probably learned of this doctrine through conversations with Gershom Scholem, whom he had met in July 1915, but he may have already known of it from other sources. Cf. Scholem (2012: 233, 1983: 66): "At the same time, however, Benjamin's meaning includes the kabbalistic concept of *tikkun*, the messianic restoration and repair which mends and restores the original being of things, and of history as well, after they have been smashed and corrupted by the 'breaking of the vessels.'" According to Scholem, Benjamin learned of this concept from Scholem himself and from the work of Franz-Joseph Molitor (cf. Molitor, 1827–53); cf. Scholem ([1946] 1995, 1967); see also Scholem (1971, 1997). For the concept of *Tikkun*, cf. also Consigli (1986). Consigli also makes reference to *Shevirat haKelim*, which Franz Rosenzweig discusses in *Der Stern der Erlösung* (1988).

5 We don't find any mention of *Shevirat ha Kelim*, but a conception of *Teshuvah*, conversion and individual redemption (cf. Cohen 1995: 194, [1929] 1988: 227).

6 Cf. Cohen ([1902 & 1914] 1977); "On the Program of the Coming Philosophy" (*SW*1, 100–10/ *GSII*:1, 157–71); Tagliacozzo ([2003] 2013: 333–4).

7 For Kant, the French Revolution aroused enthusiasm even in those who did not participate directly because it was a manifestation of the idea of right. Cf. Kant ([1798] 1902–/ 1992: 5–116).

8 The idea of a messianic reference toward an earthly redemption, in relation to the idea of happiness, is fundamental to Benjamin's text of 1920–1, the "Theological-Political Fragment" ("Theologisch-politisches Fragment," in *GSII*:1, 203–4). For an interpretation of the "Fragment" as a critique of Bloch's eschatological conception (of Christian origin), see Deuber-Mankowsky (2002). Cf. also Guerra and Tagliacozzo (2019).

9 In "On the Concept of History" (*Über den Begriff der Geschichte*), Benjamin criticizes both historicism and the politics of social democracy, which was supported and theorized by the Neo-Kantians. This is because he sees in the conception of "homogeneous and empty" time the opposite of the concept of *Jetztzeit*, as fulfilled and messianic time, which must, he argues, inhere in historical materialism and

revolution. Cf. "On the Concept of History," thesis XIII and the beginning of thesis XIV (*SW4*, 394-5/ *WuN*19, 101-2): "Social democratic theory, and still more its practice, was determined by a concept of progress out of touch with reality, but derived from dogma . . . History is the object of a construction not constituted by homogeneous and empty time, but by time filled by the *now* [*Jetztzeit*]." On Benjamin's conception of time, linked to the new mathematics of the twentieth century, cf. Ng (2019, 2017).

10  For a comparison between Cohen's and Benjamin's messianism, see Günther (1974) and Fiorato (1996, 2005). See also Fiorato (1993) and Desideri (2018: 128-39 in particular); Tagliacozzo (2018); Khatib (2013), who dedicates part of his book to Benjamin's messianism and Cohen's part in it. For a broader comparison of Benjamin and Cohen, cf. Deuber-Mankowsky (2000)—on ethics, pp. 129-64 in particular—and Tagliacozzo ([2003] 2013). See also the 2012 issue of *Modern Language Notes* (Ng and Tobias 2012), which contains previously unpublished texts by Scholem on Kant and Cohen. See Fenves (2011), an important text that studies the influence of Cohen and Husserl on the young Benjamin. Lastly, see Homburg (2018), a text that identifies, at the base of Benjamin's materialism, the critique of empiricism and idealism of early Romanticism and the Post-Kantian tradition.

11  A possible influence of Cohen's messianic thought on Benjamin, as early as 1913-15, may have been the essay "Das Gottesreich," published by Cohen in 1913 in *Soziale Ethik im Judentum*, and *Die Messiaidee* (1892, in *Jüdische Schriften*, vol. I). *Der Begriff der Religion im System der Philosophie* was published in 1915, while the *Ethik* is cited in Benjamin's 1919 essay "Fate and Character" (*SW*1, 201-6/ *GSII*:1, 171-9), and the *Logik* in the "Epistemo-Critical Foreword" in Benjamin's *The Origin of the German Trauerspiel* (*OT*, 1-39/ *OGT*, 27-56/ *GSI*:1, 207-237). After his return to Berlin, Benjamin had frequented lessons and talks by Cohen (in Freiburg he had followed Rickert in 1912-13), and read in 1920 *Die Religion der Vernunft aus den Quellen des Judentums* (cf. Benjamin's letter to Scholem of Dec. 1, 1920 [*GBII*, 107, 110n.]). He also wrote to Scholem from Bern in 1918, asking him to order for him Cohen's entire four-volume *System der Philosophie* (cf. *GBI*, 429). In a January 7, 1913 letter to Ludwig Strauss, Benjamin mentions Cohen's works *Logik der reinen Erkenntnis* and *Ethik des reinen Willens* (cf. *GBI*, 82). With Scholem, he read *Kants Theorie der Erfahrung* in 1918, but found it disappointing (cf. Scholem 1975: 78-9).

12  Cf. Ng (2017: 41-60). Julia Ng considers Cohen's concept of time to be limited by its still-Newtonian vision and links Benjamin's vision of history instead to Scholem's mathematical studies and to his knowledge of some notions in new mathematics and twentieth-century physics.

13  Paul Natorp had written *Sozialidealismus. Neue Richtlinien sozialer Erziehung* (Berlin, 1920), while Karl Vorländer sought to unify Neo-Kantian theory with a Marxist approach to socialism. See Vorländer (1900; [1911] 1962). For a panoramic view of Neo-Kantian socialism, cf. Holzhey's (1994) edited volume and Sandkühler's and de la Vega's (1970) anthology.

14  It is possible here to identify in this expression a Christian theological concept which originally referred to the power bestowed by Christ on Peter (cf. *Gospel of Matthew*, 16:18-19: "the keys of the kingdom of heaven") which Benjamin utilizes to indicate the possibility of an operation that breaks the un-modifiability of the past.

15  Thesis XVIIa from "Paralipomena to "On the Concept of History"" (*SW4*, 401-2/ *WuN*19, 152 translation modified). The concept of "infinite task" can be considered a development of the Kantian doctrine of sanctity, or perfect conformation of the will to

moral law (cf. Kant (1902–: 3–163, 220–2). The immortality of the soul is a postulate of pure practical reason.
16  On the "romantic" and messianic anarchism of Benjamin, cf. Löwy (1983). On the *Theses*, see Gentili ([2002] 2019).
17  Cf. "On the Concept of History" (*SW*4, 390/ *WuN*19, 94).
18  Cf. Kant's concepts of sanctity and justice in the section "The immortality of the soul as a postulate of pure practical reason" in Kant (2002: 156, 1900–: 221–2): "For a rational but finite being, only the progression *ad infinitum* from the lower to the higher levels of moral perfection is possible. The *infinite one*, for whom the time condition is nothing, sees in this series—which for us is endless—the whole of adequacy to the moral law; and the holiness, which his command unremittingly demands in order [for one] to conform to his justice [*Gerechtigkeit*] in the same share that he determines for each in the highest good, is to be found whole in a single intellectual intuition of the existence of rational beings." Benjamin had read the *Critique of Practical Reason* in 1918 (cf. Benjamin's letter to E. Schoen, May 1918, in *GB*I, 455).
19  Cf. Cohen (1995: 289, [1929] 1988: 336): "If one surveys the entire collection of messianic references in the Bible, in which nothing indubitably messianic should be omitted, then it first of all follows that the understanding of Messianism as *eschatology* is wrong. For, if one disregards the one reference in Isaiah, in which 'death shall forever be swallowed up' [Isa. 25:8], then all other instances indicate an earthly future, be it of Israel or of all the peoples." Pierfrancesco Fiorato concentrates especially on Cohen's critique of the eschatological interpretation of history and messianism. Fiorato wishes to demonstrate a similarity between Cohen's and Benjamin's conceptions of messianism. Fiorato (1996: 310–11) posits Karl Löwith as an example of a "strong" eschatological vision of history in contrast to the "weak," radically anti-ontological version of Cohen, who sees in messianism a systematic philosophical principle (identified with the ethical theme of humanity) that bears comparison with Benjamin's conception of the philosophy of history and the system of philosophy: "It is with respect to such a model [that of Löwith] that we can specify how Cohen's philosophy pursues a systematic devaluation of the *eschaton* as such, prohibiting any speculation on where history is leading. In reality, Cohen . . . turns to messianism precisely to perform this devaluation . . . On the basis of such premises, the value of messianism as a *philosophical* principle becomes clear . . . It is within the dimension of truth of the system itself [cf. Cohen (1907) 1981: chs 1 & 9], that is, in the course of a definition of the reciprocal relations among diverse *Systemglieder*, that the question of messianism as a unifying principle of reason can be adequately hypothesized." Cf. also Fiorato (2005).
20  On the expression "infinite plane of humanity," cf. Benjamin's critique as early as 1917–18 of the Neo-Kantian concept of "infinite task" in the fragment "Ambiguity of the concept of 'infinite task' in the Neo-Kantian school" ("Zweideutigkeit des Begriffs der 'unendlichen Aufgabe' in der kantischen Schule") (*GS*VI, 53; fragment 32, dated by the editors 1918). Benjamin sees in the Neo-Kantians a prevalent notion of infinite task which is empty and not *a priori*, that is, exclusively linked to the physical-mathematical sciences and connoted as empirical. What may derive from Cohen is the meaning, considered more positively despite being empirical, of "infinite task" as an *ideal* whose goal lays an infinite distance away, "in the sense that the entire extension of its distance is progressively measured from every point along its path" (*GS*VI, 53). Cf. Fiorato (1997: 367 n.32).

21 Not to be neglected is the great influence of Cohen's philosophy of Judaism in the Germany of his era, especially among Jewish intellectuals (secular and not) and on Scholem, Benjamin's principal source for Jewish thought. In addition to following Cohen's courses and conferences in Berlin, Scholem had read, in July 1918, *Der Begriff der Religion im System der Philosophie* (cf. Scholem 1994: 152, 159 n.3), and slightly earlier, half of *Logik der reinen Erkenntnis*, which he received as a gift in 1915. In that same July 1918, however, Scholem found himself disappointed, as did Benjamin, by the third edition of *Kants Theorie der Erfahrung* (cf. Scholem 1975: 78–9). Scholem held Cohen's conception of the philosophy of religion in the highest regard; about Cohen he wrote to Werner Kraft in April, 1918 from Bern, shortly after learning of Cohen's death and after having written in his diary a *Nachruf*, 'Dem Andenken Hermann Cohens' (cf. Scholem 1994: 152, 379 n.3): "in Germany, Judaism has expressed itself in greatness and truth for the last time . . . For me, it was as though after his death the Day of Judgment should come to German Jews . . . I realized only last winter *to what degree* Cohen was Jewish . . . In a very high sense, Cohen will be my model [*Vorbild*]" (Scholem 1994: 152).

22 Cf. Desideri (2018: 132–4). Cf. also Desideri (2015). Desideri (2015: 140) writes about Cohen's and Benjamin's anti-eschatology: "Despite of this divergent direction of the Messianic time (toward the future, for Cohen and toward the past, for Benjamin), the idea of a non-eschatological messianism, which is so evident in Cohen's perspective, applies also to the author of the *Theses on the concept of history*. In so far as he shares the criticism of the myth, which is implied in Cohen's connection between rationalism and monotheism, Benjamin shares also his consequent criticism of eschatology as a mythology of the end of time."

23 Cf. Poma (1997: 96): "Therefore, judgment of origin is infinite or limitative. The importance of this judgment, often misinterpreted in philosophy, was understood both by ancient (Democritus) and by modern (Leibniz) science, which has extensively built upon the principle of infinity as the origin of the finite" Cf. also Fiorato (1993: 163–78).

24 Cf. Cohen (1995: 230–1, [1929] 1988: 269): "But since we have now set up, beyond the fellowman, the man as I, we need for the concept of his redemption from sin the limit determining the moment of redemption. Redemption is to be thought of only for one moment's duration. Only for one moment, which may be followed by moments of sin. No matter! They also will again be relieved by the moment of redemption."

25 Cf. Cohen ([1907] 1924: 142–8), where Cohen sees the ethical idea, humanity, as an infinite but real, non-utopian task to be accomplished in the future: "Not only what the present offers in nature and the human world must be real [*wirklich*], but in a pronounced sense that which is not yet real, but anticipated in hope *is real*, requested as reality in the *vision of hope. Hope, future, and humanity go together*: they constitute the protest against the exclusive reality of the present in nature and history . . . The profoundly deep, irremovable foundation of the ethics of humanity can no longer reside in the prophetic *hope* of the future but, according to its method, in the *reality of the future*. This reality is idea, ethical idea; the idea in which the idealism of ethics distinguishes itself from the utopia of a bucolic transcendental world, just as Jean Paul once called the beyond . . . If ethical reality is an idea, then it is founded upon idealism, and thus on conscious knowing. *The consciousness of morality requires security, the certainty of that future of humanity*." On these passages (and for their translation) see Poma (1997: 67 translation slightly modified).

26  Cf. the 1917 fragment "The Infinite Task" ("Die unendliche Aufgabe," in *GSVI*, 51–2, fragment 30). In December 1917 Benjamin planned to dedicate his doctoral dissertation to the theme "what does it mean that science is an infinite task?" (Benjamin to G. Scholem, Dec. 12, 1917, in *GBI*, 409). He saw the autonomy and unity of science and the system of philosophy as founded on the fact that in regard to its form, science is the infinite task; that is, it cannot be a task imposed from outside, nor "the answer to a finite question" ("Die unendliche Aufgabe," in *GSVI*, 51), but it is the "solution dominated by its task" (*GSVI*, 52), the methodical dimension of the autonomous progress of thought and ethical action pursuant to its internal guiding idea. For logic, this is the idea of the scientific hypothesis that leads toward a totality never achieved by categorical determinants. For ethics, it is the idea of freedom, the idea of autonomy and humanity.

27  Cf. the subsequent passage: "The peace of the messianic kingdom of God . . . can enthusiastically affirm and paint with luminous images a better, purer, higher ethical quality. But there can be no doubt that all historical existence, even that of the future, therefore, must absolutely continue to progress and develop, and cannot be equated with the idea of perpetual peace, if it must mean something more than the redemption of the world's peoples from war" (Cohen [1907] 1981: 408).

28  Fiorato here cites Cohen ([1907] 1981: 408).

29  Cf. Cohen (1995: 249, [1929] 1988: 291).

30  Cf. Cohen (1995: 462, [1929] 1988: 533): "Death is peace. The grave is 'the House of Eternity.' This eternity is the true end of the world, the goal of earthy existence. It is to this eternity that peace as a way of virtue leads. But this eternity is only the continuation of the earthly life—the same root of the world comprises both sides of existence; hence, peace, as it leads to eternity, is also the guide to earthly life, to the beginning of all historical survival, which lies in it. Peace is the sign of eternity and also the watchword for human life, in its individual conduct as well as in the eternity of the historical calling. In the historical eternity the mission of peace of messianic mankind is completed."

# References

Cohen, H. (1877), *Kants Begründung der Ethik*, Berlin: Dümmler.
Cohen, H. ([1892] 1924), *Die Messiaidee*, in H. Cohen, *Jüdische Schriften*, vol. 1, ed. B. Strauß, Berlin: Schwetschke.
Cohen, H. ([1907] 1924), *Religion und Sittlichkeit. Eine Betrachtung zur Grundlegung der Religionsphilosophie*, in H. Cohen, *Jüdische Schriften*, vol. 3, ed. B. Strauß, Berlin: Schwetschke.
Cohen, H. ([1907] 1981), *Ethik des reinen Willens*, in H. Cohen, *Werke*, vol. 7, ed. H. Holzhey and the Hermann-Cohen-Archiv, Hildesheim: Georg Olms Verlag.
Cohen, H. ([1912] 1982), *Ästhetik des reinen Gefühls*, in H. Cohen, *Werke*, vol. 8/9, ed. H. Holzhey and the Hermann-Cohen-Archiv, Hildesheim, Zürich, and New York: Georg Olms Verlag.
Cohen, H. (1913), *Soziale Ethik im Judentum*, Frankfurt/M.: Kaufmann.
Cohen, H. ([1914] 1977), *Logik der reinen Erkenntnis*, in H. Cohen, *Werke*, vol. 6, ed. H. Holzhey and the Hermann-Cohen-Archiv, Hildesheim: Georg Olms Verlag.
Cohen, H. ([1914] 2012), *Vom ewigen Frieden*, in *Kleine Schriften V 1913–1915*, in *Werke*, vol. 16, ed. H. Holzhey and the Hermann-Cohen-Archiv, Hildesheim: Georg Olms Verlag.

Cohen, H. (1915), *Der Begriff der Religion im System der Philosophie*, Giessen: Töpelmann.
Cohen, H. ([1929] 1988), *Die Religion der Vernunft aus den Quellen des Judentums*, 2nd edn. (1st ed. 1919), Frankfurt a./M.: J. Kaufmann 1929; anastatic reprint Wiesbaden: Fourier Verlag 1988.
Cohen, H. (1995), *Religion of Reason Out of the Sources of Judaism*, trans. S. Kaplan, Atlanta, Georgia: Scholar's Press.
Consigli, P. (1986), "Ricomporre l'infranto. Walter Benjamin e il messianesimo ebraico," *Aut Aut*, 36 (211–212): 151–74.
Desideri, F. (2015), "Messianica Ratio: Affinities and Differences in Cohen's and Benjamin's Messianic Rationalism," *Aisthesis*, 8 (2): 133–45.
Desideri, F. (2018), *Walter Benjamin e la percezione dell'arte. Estetica, storia, teologia*, Brescia: Morcelliana.
Deuber-Mankowsky, A. (2000), *Der frühe Walter Benjamin und Hermann Cohen. Jüdische Werte. Kritische Philosophie. Vergängliche Erfahrung*, Berlin: Verlag Vorwerk 8.
Deuber-Mankowsky, A. (2002), "Walter Benjamin's Theological-Political Fragment as a Response to Ernst Bloch's Spirit of Utopia," *The Leo Baeck Institute Yearbook*, 47 (1): 3–19.
Fenves, P. (2011), *The Messianic Reduction: Walter Benjamin and the Shape of Time*, Stanford: Stanford University Press.
Fiorato, P. (1993), "Unendliche Aufgabe und System der Wahrheit. Die Auseinandersetzung des jungen Walter Benjamin mit der Philosophie Hermann Cohens," in R. Brandt and F. Orlik (eds.), *Philosophisches Denken—Politisches Wirken. Hermann-Cohen-Kolloquium*, Marburg 1992, Hildesheim, Zürich, and New York: Georg Olms Verlag.
Fiorato, P. (1993), *Geschichtliche Ewigkeit. Ursprung und Zeitlichkeit in der Philosophie Hermann Cohens*, Würzburg: Königshausen & Neumann.
Fiorato, P. (1996), "Una *debole* forza messianica. Sul messianismo antiescatologico di Hermann Cohen," *Annuario filosofico*, 12: 299–327.
Fiorato, P. (1997), "L'ideale del problema. Sopravvivenza e metamorfosi di un tema neokantiano nella filosofia del giovane Benjamin," in S. Besoli and L. Guidetti (eds.), *Conoscenza, valori, cultura: Orizzonti e problemi del neocriticismo*, 361–86, Firenze.
Fiorato, P. (2005), "Notes on Future and History in Hermann Cohen's Anti-Eschatological Messianism," in R. Munk (ed.), *Hermann Cohen's Critical Idealism*, 133–60, Dordrecht: Springer.
Fiorato, P. (2008), "Al di là del sublime. Hermann Cohen sulla virtù messianica della pace," *B@belonline*, 4: 51–65.
Gentili, D. ([2002] 2019), *Il tempo della storia. Le tesi sul concetto di storia di Walter Benjamin*, Macerata: Quodlibet.
Guerra, G., and T. Tagliacozzo, eds (2019), *Felicità e tramonto. Sul Frammento teologico-politico di Walter Benjamin*, Macerata: Quodlibet.
Günther, H. (1974), "Der Messianismus von Hermann Cohen und Walter Benjamin," *Emuna. Horizonte zur Diskussion über Israel und das Judentum*, 5/6: 352–9.
Hartung, G. (1992), "Das Ethos philosophischer Forschung," in M. Opitz and E. Wizisla (eds.), *Aber ein Sturm weht vom Paradiese her. Texte zu Walter Benjamin*, 14–51, Leipzig: Reclam-Verlag.
Holzhey, H. (1994), *Ethischer Sozialismus. Zur politischen Philosophie des Neukantianismus*, Frankfurt/M.: Suhrkamp.
Homburg, P. (2018), *Walter Benjamin and the Post-Kantian Tradition*, London and New York: Rowman & Littlefield.

Kant, I. ([1788] 1900–), *Kritik der praktischen Vernunft*, in I. Kant, *Kants Gesammelte Schriften*, vol. V, Berlin: Königlich Preussischen Akademie der Wissenschaften.
Kant, I. ([1798] 1900–), *Der Streit der Fakultäten*, in I. Kant, *Kants Gesammelte Schriften*, vol. VII, Berlin: Königlich Preussischen Akademie der Wissenschaften.
Kant, I. (1992), *The Conflict of the Faculties*, trans. M. J. Gregor, Lincoln: University of Nebraska Press.
Kant, I. (2002), *Critique of Practical Reason*, trans. W. S. Pluhar, Indianapolis and Cambridge: Hackett.
Khatib, S. R. (2013), *"Teleologie ohne Endzweck." Walter Benjamins Ent-stellung des Messianischen*, Marburg: Tectum Verlag.
Löwy, M. (1983), "L'anarchisme messianique de Walter Benjamin," *Les Temps Modernes*, 40: 772–94.
Molitor, F. -J. (1827–53), *Philosophie der Geschichte, oder über die Tradition in dem alten Bunden und ihre Beziehung zur Kirche des Neuen Bundes mit vorzüglicher Rücksicht auf die Kabbala*, 4 vols, Münster: Theissingschen Buchhandlung.
Ng, J. (2017), "Acts of Time: Cohen and Benjamin on Mathematics and History," *Paradigmi*, Special Issue: "Critical Idealism and Messianism. From Hermann Cohen to Walter Benjamin and Beyond," ed. T. Tagliacozzo, R. Monk, and A Poma, 35 (1): 41–60.
Ng, J. (2019), "La matematicità di un'esperienza transitoria: A proposito di due espressioni del *Frammento teologico-politico*," in G. Guerra and T. Tagliacozzo (eds), *Felicità e tramonto. Sul Frammento teologico-politico di Walter Benjamin*, 33–54, Macerata: Quodlibet.
Ng, J., and R. Tobias, eds. (2012), *Modern Language Notes*, Special Issue: "Walter Benjamin, Gershom Scholem and the Marburg School," 127 (3): 440–680.
Poma, A. (1997), *The Critical Philosophy of Hermann Cohen*, trans. J. Denton, Albany: SUNY Press.
Rosenzweig, F. (1988), *Der Stern der Erlösung*, Frankfurt/M.: Suhrkamp.
Sandkühler, H. J., and R. de la Vega, eds (1970), *Marxismus und Ethik. Texte zum neukantianischen Sozialismus*, Frankfurt/M.: Suhrkamp.
Scholem, G. ([1946] 1995), *Major Trends in Jewish Mysticism*, New York: Schocken Books.
Scholem, G. (1967), *Die Jüdische Mystik in ihren Hauptströmungen*, Frankfurt/M.: Suhrkamp.
Scholem, G. (1971), "Toward an Understanding of the Messianic Idea in Judaism," in G. Scholem (ed.), *The Messianic Idea in Judaism and other Essays on Jewish Spirituality*, 1–36, New York: Schocken Books.
Scholem, G. (1975), *Walter Benjamin—Die Geschichte einer Freundschaft*, Frankfurt/M.: Suhrkamp.
Scholem, G. (1983), "Walter Benjamin und sein Engel," in G. Scholem (ed.), *Walter Benjamin und sein Engel. Vierzehn Aufsätze und kleine Beiträge*, Frankfurt/M.: Suhrkamp.
Scholem, G. (1994), *Briefe. Band I. 1914–1947*, ed. I. Shedletzky, München: C. H. Beck.
Scholem, G. (1995), "Toward an Understanding of the Messianic Idea in Judaism," in G. Scholem (ed.), *The Messianic Idea in Judaism and Other Essays in Jewish Spirituality*, 1–36, New York: Schocken Books.
Scholem, G. (1997), "Zum Verständnis der messianische Idee im Judentum," in G. Scholem (ed.), *Über einige Grundbergriffe des Judentums*, 7–74, Frankfurt/M.: Suhrkamp.

Scholem, G. (2012), *Walter Benjamin and his Angel*, in G. Scholem, *On Jews and Judaism in Crisis. Selected Essays*, ed. W. J. Dannhauser, Philadelphia: Paul Dry Books.

Tagliacozzo, T. ([2003] 2013), *Esperienza e compito infinito nella filosofia del primo Benjamin*, Macerata: Quodlibet.

Tagliacozzo, T. (2018), *Experience and Infinite Task: Knowledge, Language and Messianism in the Philosophy of Walter Benjamin*, London and New York: Rowman & Littlefield.

Vorländer, K. (1900), "Kant und der Sozialismus," *Kant-Studien*, 4 (1–3): 361–412.

Vorländer, K. ([1911] 1962), *Kant und Marx. Ein Beitrag zur Philosophie des Sozialismus*, Tübingen: J. C. B. Mohr.

9

# Beyond Mysticism and the Apocalypse

## Benjamin's Dislocation of the Messianic[1]

Sami Khatib

Benjamin's figure of the messianic stands at the crossroads of conflicting traditions of messianic thought. This chapter argues that for Benjamin the messianic neither presents a contribution to the discourse of political theology nor designates a certain *theological* strand of messianic thought. Rather, the messianic models a third domain, in which politics and theology enter a (non-)relation of analogy, the elements of which never collapse into one another. Throughout Benjamin's *œuvre*, at least two strands of messianic thought can be identified in various combinations and transvaluations: (1) the mystical idea of a minimal messianic transformation or "adjustment" (*Zurechtstellung*) and (2) the apocalyptic rupture and intrusion of a radically heterogeneous dimension of transcendence (the Messiah) in human events. Both traditions of messianic thought inform some of the best-known figurative images of Benjamin's later work, particularly the figurative images in the theses "On the Concept of History" (1940). The physiognomies and the epistemological function of Benjamin's messianic figures—angel, puppet, dwarf, and the little hunchback—can be traced to revolutionary-apocalyptic and adjusting-transformative currents of the messianic. The scenes and images evoked in these figures have, as Stéphane Mosès notes, an "epistemological function": "These images do not serve to illustrate an idea that also exists outside of themselves. They are the form or the medium through which two conceptions of history are 'telescoped' to give birth to a new vision" (Mosès 2009: 69). Benjamin's "image thinking" ("Bilddenken," cf. Weigel 1997: 15–16) does not involve supplementary illustration of a preexisting meaning but a conceptual presentation that unfolds in the medium of these images and figures themselves. The intricacies and the layers of meaning of these "thought images" (*Denkbilder*) cannot be disentangled in terms of actual (primary) speech and signifying (secondary) image.

## Redemption and Destruction

The mystical-transformative dimension of the Messianic is inscribed above all in the emblematic figure of the little "hunchback," who stands for both the coming and the inhibition of the Messianic. This "little man," we are told in Benjamin's *Kafka* essay, "is the inmate of disfigured life; he will disappear with the coming of the Messiah, who (a great rabbi once said) will not wish to change the world by force but will merely make a slight adjustment in it" (*SW*2:2, 811/*GS*II:2, 432 translation modified). This "great rabbi with the profound dictum on the messianic kingdom" is none other than Gershom Scholem: "[W]hat a way to achieve fame!! It was one of my first ideas about Kabbalah" (*CS*, 123/*BSB*, 154), as Scholem clarifies in the letter from July 9, 1934 to Benjamin. From Scholem, the motif of a minimal messianic shift travels via Benjamin to Bloch. Bloch, too, knows a rabbi, "a true Kabbalist," who is believed to have once said:

> To bring about the kingdom of freedom, it is not necessary that everything be destroyed, and a new world begin; rather, this cup, or that bush, or that stone, and so all things must only be shifted a little. Because this "a little" is hard to do, and its measure so hard to find, humanity cannot do it in this world; instead this is why the Messiah comes. Thereby this wise rabbi too, with his saying, spoke out not for creeping progress but completely for the leap of the lucky glimpse and the invisible hand. (Bloch 2006: 59)

This "wise rabbi" from Bloch's *Spuren* (*Traces,* 1930) maintains a close relationship not only to Scholem's mystical idea of the Messianic but also to Benjaminian figures of thought. Two years after Bloch's *Traces*, Benjamin employs the motif of the small messianic *Zurechtstellung* (adjustment) in the thought image "*In der Sonne*" ("In the Sun," 1932).

> The Hasidim have a saying about the world to come. Everything there will be arranged just as it is with us. The room we have now will be just the same in the world to come; where our child lies sleeping, it will sleep in the world to come. The clothes we are wearing we shall also wear in the next world. Everything will be the same as here—only a little bit different. Thus it is with imagination. It merely draws a veil over the distance. Everything remains just as it is, but the veil flutters and everything changes imperceptibly beneath it. (*SW*2:2, 664/*GS*IV:1, 419-20)[2]

Going beyond Bloch and Scholem, Benjamin illuminates the transformative role of imagination. Imagination as a veil does not constructively change what it imperceptibly conceals. In contrast to some strands of modern utopian thought, it modifies the imaginative distance to that coming world without positively envisioning this world.

In his late writings, Benjamin brought the motif of the small messianic adjustment to fruition for his concept of history. In Benjamin's posthumously published work, among the drafts of the theses "On the Concept of History,"[3] there is a short handwritten note that reads: "sets things in it aright, similar to what is said of the

Messianic period, that it is basically only a slight displacement of things" (*WuN*19, 127 translation mine). The missing subject of this note is presumably the Benjaminian historian, whose task, as we know from Theses IV and VII, is to "brush history against the grain" (*SW*4, 392/*GS*I:2, 696) as a "historical materialist" or as a "historian schooled in Marx" (*SW*4, 390/*GS*I:2, 694). The eminently political commitment of the historian, however, consists not only in the destructive movement of opening up the ideologically closed and supposedly completed text of official historiography and blasting out the fragments enclosed in it, but at the same time in "setting this text aright"—which is analogous to the task of the Messiah. Benjamin, however, does not identify the historian's task with that of the Messiah. The inward displacement, adjustment of history—the virtual displacement of the things in it—has here an epistemological function.

The "*dérangement de l'axe*" (*GS*II:3, 1200), a quotation of Félix Bertaux mentioned in the notes to the Kafka essay, relates, as a minimal change in the axis of vision, to the "Copernican turn of historical perception" elaborated in the first drafts of the *Arcades Project* (*AP*, 941/*GS*V:2, 1057). In the motif of the parallactic shift,[4] which reflects a change in both the subject and object of cognition, different strands of Benjamin's thought converge. The task of the rectifying historian does not apply to the facts of historiography, but to the depository of collective dream images whose distortion he deciphers. In this sense, the historian takes on "the task of dream interpretation" (*AP*, 464/*GS*V:1, 580). The political adjustment of history by the historian concerns not only the historical text, but also the subjects of history themselves. With *historia rerum gestarum*, historiography, the Benjaminian historian also sets *res gestae*, the things in it, aright. Turning away from the historian's contemplative attitude, that is, the historicist approximation and understanding of the historical object, Benjamin weaves historiography and history inseparably into one another. Whereas historiography perpetuates history as the history of domination, the Benjaminian historian, who is affected by and involved in history, grasps the present in which he stands in constellation with the past. The "true image of the past" is unique, it "flits by," it "flashes up at the moment of its recognizability, and is never seen again" (*SW*4, 390/*GS*I:2, 695)—only "at the moment of its recognizability" (ibid), and thus cannot assume a stable identity. But it is precisely in its utmost transience that it is eternal. If "the eternal, in any case, is far more the ruffle on a dress than some idea" (*AP*, 463/*GS*V:1, 578), eternity is contained in transient particles and not in idealistically immortalized images of victorious history. The way eternity is addressed here is reminiscent of the idea of "eternal transience" of the earlier "Theological-Political Fragment" (*SW*3, 306/*GS*II:1, 204). Accordingly, a note on the theses of history reads: "To hold fast the eternity of historical incidents is actually to hold fast to the eternity of their transience" (*GS*I:3, 1246 translation mine). This eternity can never be captured in narrative, but only in true images. In their radical transience, these images escape any closed narrative that seeks to represent itself in historical images.

The mystical-transforming adjustment of things in history is the counterpart of the destructive-blasting citation of history, which is bound to a revolutionary act, a "tiger's leap into the past" (*SW*4, 395/*GS*I, 701). The famous Thesis XIV is about the latter.

> History is the subject of a construction whose site is not homogeneous, empty time, but time filled full by now-time [*Jetztzeit*]. Thus, to Robespierre ancient Rome was a past charged with now-time, a past which he blasted out of the continuum of history. The French Revolution viewed itself as Rome reincarnate. It cited ancient Rome exactly the way fashion cites a bygone mode of dress. Fashion has a nose for the topical, no matter where it stirs in the thickets of long ago; it is the tiger's leap into the past. Such a leap, however, takes place in an arena where the ruling class gives the commands. The same leap in the open air of history is the dialectical leap Marx understood as revolution. (*SW*4, 395/*GS*I:2, 701)

This explosive, interrupting citation of the past in the present as "now-time" corresponds to a messianic countermovement from the past, which Benjamin called "*weak* messianic power" (*SW*4, 390/*GS*I, 694) in Thesis II. The unredeemed past "carries with it a secret index by which it is referred to redemption" (*SW*4, 390/*GS*I:2, 693). It is this unredeemed past that demands the historian's rectifying task. The mystical-transformative redemption of the past, which in Benjamin scholarship is often filed under the keyword "redemptive criticism" (Habermas 1979: 30–59), should thus never be separated from its destructive side. The complementary notion to this supposition, purporting that the past addresses the present, is that of the destruction of the idea of a historical continuum, brought about by nineteenth-century historicism, the Enlightenment idea of progress, and its later socialist versions (socialism as guaranteed progress and end goal of history).

From the complementary entanglement of political action and historiography follows the political demand to "entangle revolutionary destruction with the idea of redemption" (*GS*I:3, 1241 translation mine). With this entanglement, no identity of politics and messianism is indicated, but rather a relation of correspondence of the apocalyptic and mystical forces in the field of messianism as well as of revolutionary-destructive and adjusting-transformative energies in the field of politics. In an alternative draft of "On the Concept of History," Benjamin formulated this relationship of correspondence as follows:

> He [the historian] grasps the constellation into which his own era has entered, along with a very specific earlier one. Thus, he establishes a conception of the present as now-time shot through with splinters of messianic time. This conception provides a link between historiography and politics, which is identical with the theological one between remembrance [*Eingedenken*] and redemption. The present articulates itself in images that can be called dialectical. They represent a "redemptive idea" ["*rettenden Einfall*"] of humanity. (*GS*I, 1248 translation mine)

Here, the political and the theological are by no means identical; rather, the relations within the political are equal to relations within the theological. Historiography (rectifying) and politics (destructive revolutionary) relate to each other like remembrance and redemption.

## There Is No Messianic Relation

In the allegory of the puppet and the dwarf from Thesis I of "On the Concept of History," the intricate relationship between messianism and historical materialism can be studied best.

> There was once, we know, an automaton constructed in such a way that it could respond to every move by a chess player with a countermove that would ensure the winning of the game. A puppet wearing Turkish attire and with a hookah in its mouth sat before a chessboard placed on a large table. A system of mirrors created the illusion that this table was transparent on all sides. Actually, a hunchbacked dwarf—a master at chess—sat inside and guided the puppet's hand by means of strings. One can imagine a philosophic counterpart to this apparatus. The puppet, called "historical materialism," is to win all the time. It can easily be a match for anyone if it enlists the services of theology, which today, as we know, is small and ugly and has to keep out of sight. (*SW*4, 389/*GSI*:2, 693)

The chess automaton, disguised as a puppet, can only answer every move of its opponent with a countermove because it enlists into its service a "hunchbacked dwarf" who sits invisibly inside it. The illusion of transparency of the chess automaton's apparatus, created by an arrangement of mirrors and hinged compartments, reads as an ironic commentary on the supposed scientific infallibility of "historical materialism," which during Stalinism ossified into a doctrinal worldview: the appearance of invincible self-activity must first be established by a sophisticated system of optical and mechanical illusions under the chess table.

In Benjamin scholarship, the allegory of the chess automaton would become the most discussed scheme for interpreting his thought on the relationship between theology and historical materialism. Its decoding always proved to be tricky, since allegory and meaning conspicuously fall apart. Indeed, Benjamin's interpretation ("to take into service") contradicts the image of the chess player ("to pull by strings"): image and interpretation owe themselves to different, conflicting perspectives. Consequently, according to Thesis I of "On the Concept of History," it cannot be concluded unambiguously whether historical materialism has to function as *ancilla theologiae* or theology as *ancilla philosophiae*.

With regard to the German secularization debate, Gerhard Kaiser argued "that Benjamin does not belong in the intellectual history of secularization, but rather carries out a countermovement in his thought that sharply distinguishes between the profane and the messianic" (Kaiser 1975: 74 translation mine). However, this distinction is not symmetrical, but split in itself: The Messianic itself divides profane history from its messianic end. In light of this "division of divisions," which separates and connects the messianic and profane aeon (cf. Agamben 2005b: 49–53), the figure of the messianic can be understood as a liminal (non-)relation. As such it cannot be ascribed exclusively either to theology or to the profane world of historical materialism. The attempt to split up the thought image of Thesis I along the lines of an uncontaminated division into the actual (meaning) and the inauthentic (image, metaphor) falls short. In the Messianic neither a secularization of theology nor a theologization of politics is articulated. Kaiser's objection to a Marxist reading of Benjamin therefore remains a mirror-image of his structurally identical counter-position. "Benjamin does not thereby secularize theology, he theologizes Marxism, so that the very true historical materialism to which the first thesis ["On the Concept of History," S. K.] points and which presents itself in the 'Theses' is in truth the true theology" (Kaiser 1975: 74 translation mine). In the context of this reading, it should be mentioned that neither historical materialism nor theology can make use of the other as instrumental devices of speech. The discrepancy between the image (the directed puppet and the dwarf pulling the strings) and its meaning (putting theology at the service of historical materialism), which is the subject of critical analysis in many commentaries, rather points to the symptomatic impossibility of distinguishing between actual and inauthentic speech.

> This contradiction [between theology and historical materialism, S.K.] is of course the very contradiction between allegory and its meaning, ultimately between signifier and the signified, which pretends to "enlist the services" of the signifier as its instrument but finds itself quickly entangled in its network. The two different levels thus traverse one another: the formal structure of Benjamin's allegory functions in exactly the same way as its "content," theology in its relationship to historical materialism, which pretends simply to enlist its services but becomes more and more entangled in its strings[.] (Žižek 1989: 137)

The formal structure of Benjamin's allegory affects its communicated content too: historical materialism and theology are not externally opposed to each other in Benjamin's thought image, so that the complementary movements of theologization and secularization would produce two distinct theoretical objects. Rather, Benjamin revealed the messianic structure of historical materialism precisely in working out a materialist core in theology and, vice versa, a theological one in materialism. Theology and historical materialism are therefore not identical. The point is rather to conceive of their relationship as "entangled" and to consider the nature of this relationship, assessing what is revealed *in* these very relations. Benjamin was concerned with this insight—an insight on the level of form that is always missed from the standpoint of content, which assumes the exclusivity of theology and historical materialism and their respective (reversible) patterns of interpretation of theologization or secularization. This does not mean that historical materialism and theology are actually the same or signify the same object, which they then merely express in different registers. The non-identical object, which Benjamin's Thesis I thematizes, consists precisely in a relation that is split in itself, the paradoxical structure of which comes to light in the thought image of the puppet and the dwarf.

If one looks at the allegory of the chess automaton more closely, the relationship between the pictorial and the interpretive level becomes complicated, since Benjamin works with ironizing references to an allegedly ("famously") shared knowledge about the origin of the chess automaton and the distribution of roles between theology and historical materialism. What is striking is the change of quotation marks when employing the terms "historical materialist" and "historical materialism." While in

Thesis I, Benjamin places historical materialism in quotation marks, in Thesis II, he begins to assume the position of the first-person narrator of the historical materialist without distancing punctuation. From Thesis V onward, the perspective ultimately turns into the political standpoint of a new Benjaminian historical materialism, whose politics of history is developed in the following theses without a distancing gesture or the use of quotation marks.

Benjamin's argumentation unfolds in keeping with this change from distancing to affirmation. It frames Thesis I with two ironizing gestures ("known"), which he opposes in the center with the antithesis of a standpoint of truth ("in truth").[5] The figurative level ("to pull the strings"), however, still contradicts the level of meaning ("enlists the services"). The question remains whose "truth" is revealed here. In fact, in Baron von Kempelen's historical chess automaton (cf. Racknitz 1789), a servant sat below the board in what appeared to be a transparent under-table. Edgar Allan Poe "famously" dedicated the essay on "Maelzel's Chess Player" (1836) to this fact. With the elucidation of the historical factual content of this apparatus, however, nothing has yet been said about its truth content in its "counterpart in philosophy."

So what does it mean that "in truth" a little dwarf pulled the puppet on strings?—Certainly not that the dwarf could "in truth" win the game just as well without the puppet. The attempt to grasp the factual content—that is, the actually chess-playing dwarf pulling the puppet on strings—misses the truth content according to which the dwarf can win the chess game only by staying veiled, hidden. The illusion of the transparency of the automaton belongs to the dwarf's kind of winning. It is true that every materialistic criticism of the chess automaton will lead to the insight of the illusory nature of its transparency and self-activity; however, this goal itself cannot be taken as the starting point of the analysis of the functioning of the automaton. The most important aspect escapes such a critique reduced to factual content: namely, that "in truth" the secret interplay of puppet and dwarf, historical materialism and theology, requires the appearance of self-activity and transparency. In the "*Wahlverwandtschaften*" essay, Benjamin captured the relationship between factual content and truth content in the literary work with a famous image, which can also be related to the functioning of the chess automaton:

> If... one views the growing work as a burning funeral pyre, then the commentator stands before it like a chemist, the critic like an alchemist. Whereas, for the former, wood and ash remain the sole objects of his analysis, for the latter only the flame itself preserves an enigma: that of what is alive. Thus, the critic inquires into the truth, whose living flame continues to burn over the heavy logs of what is past and the light ashes of what has been experienced. (*SW*1, 298/*GS*I:1, 126)

Thus, if the historical materialist as a critic wishes to ask for the truth of the image of the chess automaton, he must, like the alchemist, recognize the riddle of this image stored in the flame. The flame's relation to wood and ashes is the equivalent to the relation between the secret and hidden interaction of puppet and dwarf to the factual apparatus consisting of playing table, chessboard, puppet in Turkish costume, and the transmission apparatus made of strings. The truth of the relationship between puppet and dwarf lies in the physiognomy of the dwarf, more precisely in his hump. This distortion—the hump—forces the dwarf "in truth" into his hiding place under the chessboard, where no one can see him.

It is true that Benjamin based the physiognomy of the dwarf figure on Poe's essay "Maelzel's Chess Player." Joshua Robert Gold has pointed out, however, that Benjamin decisively modified the image of "Maelzel's Chess Player" (Gold 2006: 1225). While in Poe it is said of the character of the hidden chess player that "this man is about the medium size, and has a remarkable stoop in the shoulders" (Poe 1836: 325), in Benjamin he not only has a stoop, but is described as a small and ugly dwarf. In "Maelzel's Chess Player" there is no mention of this disfigurement—Poe even explicitly rejects this hypothesis (ibid., 321). Gold infers from this modification a connection to the hunchback of the hunchbacked man, of whom it is said in the Kafka essay that he is "the inmate of deformed life; it will disappear when the Messiah comes" (SW2:2, 811/GSII:2, 432 translation modified). If one combines the figure of the dwarf with the figure of the hunchbacked little man and merges these figures and their meanings in a hunchbacked "dwarf-man," we get this picture: Instead of bringing about the Messiah directly, the dwarf-like theology would rather have to disappear at the exact moment of the Messiah's arrival. The small and ugly feature of the dwarf-like theology stems from the fact that theology, far from embodying a merely transcendent dimension, is itself the disfigured ("hunchbacked") occupant of a disfigured life. But the game—the historical-political chess game—can be won only if this deformed inmate's services are enlisted. With the arrival of the Messiah, this inmate would lose his hunch and hence his ability to finish the game victoriously. In other words, the disfigured theology can only play out its striking game as an "*entstellte*"—disfigured and displaced—theology so that the puppet can "take on anyone" (SW4, 389/GSI:1, 693).

It follows from such a reading that the "victory" on the profane battlefield of history is not identical with the actual intrusion of the Messiah into human events. For the messianic horizon of expectation of the Jews, as Benjamin writes in Appendix B of the Theses, "every second was the small gateway in time through which the Messiah might enter" (SW4, 397/GSI:2, 704). Three moments are to be distinguished here: first, the "homogeneous, empty time" (SW4, 395/GSI:2, 704) of waiting for a future event; second, the messianic transformation of every second into a second in which the Messiah could enter; and third, the end of time as the Messianic Kingdom, after the Messiah will have entered through the gate and thus the gate will have ceased to exist.

In a diary entry from December 1917, Kafka mentions an enigmatic conception of the Messiah that, on a formal level, comes quite close to Benjamin and the aforementioned distinction between the event of passing through the gate and messianic time as the time the Messiah needs to step through the gate: "The Messiah will come only when he is no longer needed, he will come only one day after his arrival, he will come not on the last day, but on the very last" (Kafka 1980: 67). With this postponement, Kafka rejects any expectation of the Messiah projected into the future. If the Messiah comes only when he is no longer needed, the messianic time no longer needs to be directed toward the eschatological *end of time*. Waiting is no longer necessary. The Messiah will come only when his interrupting work has been completed—by us. He will come only after the *eschaton* of historical time. In this way, with Kafka, an intermediate realm can be conceived between the last day and the very last, between the uttermost *eschaton* of this aeon and the very last day, which already belongs to the new aeon. When the last day and the coming of the Messiah fall apart, the share of tasks and responsibilities between politics and theology change. Theology is relieved of its task to contribute to salvation; politics has to accomplish by political means what theology cannot project as its telos: a slight adjustment of *this* world.

In Bloch's *Spirit of Utopia* we can find a related idea in which the Messiah can only come after the "real" work of redemption has already been completed by humanity.

> It is thus, as Baalschem would say, that the Messiah can only come when all guests have sat down at the table; the latter is initially the table of work and only then it is the table of the Lord—the worldly organization possesses in the secret of the Kingdom its immediately effective, immediately deducible metaphysics. (Bloch 1918: 411 translation mine)

Here, too, the coming of the Messiah is postponed to the very last day: only when humanity has "sat down at the table" can the Messiah come. However, this "table of work" is not completed on the very last day, but in profane everyday life. Here, Kafka's earlier distinction of the last and the very last day is shifted to the distinction between the Messianic Kingdom and the human world. But the work of the Messiah is similarly transferred: from the Messiah to humanity, for the Messiah can only sit down at the table, when, in Kafka's words, "he is no longer needed." Unlike in Bloch, however, in Benjamin the organization of the profane does not possess a "directly effective, directly deducible metaphysics" (Bloch) in the Messianic Kingdom, since the order of the profane, as the "Theological-Political Fragment" states, has only an indirect, counteracting influence on the coming of the Messianic Kingdom (*SW3*, 305–6/*GSII*:1, 203–4).

The shift of the messianic work of redemption from the Messiah to the activity of humanity corresponds with Friedrich Schlegel's "revolutionary desire to realize the kingdom of God" (Schlegel 1967: 201). Echoing Schlegel, Franz Rosenzweig writes:

> Without this anticipation and the inner pressure to realize it, without "the desire to make the Messiah arrive before his time" and the attempt "to do violence to the heavenly Kingdom," the future is not a future, but only a past drawn out to an infinite length, a past projected forward. For, without this anticipation, the moment is not eternal but something that interminably crawls along the long strategic roadway of time. (Rosenzweig 2005: 244)

If one confronts Kafka's note with the tradition of a "romantic messianism" (*SW1*,168/*GSI*:1, 12) that found its readers in both Benjamin and Rosenzweig, a complementary picture emerges in which the worldly anticipation of the Messiah in the profane world, constituting the driving force of the political, is combined with the postponement of the coming of the Messiah *after* his worldly anticipation. That political desire that wishes to realize the Messianic Kingdom before its time, in the here and now, saves the Messiah from accomplishing humanity's revolutionary work. The tension between the Messianic and the profane world, however, is not dissipated. As little as it is God's work that humanity accomplishes in its revolutions, the urgency of humanity's work forbids a postponement of the arrival of the Messiah. Rather, the revolutionary work of humanity is the precondition for the very event that "every second" can become the "small gate" for the coming of the Messiah. Rosenzweig goes so far as to characterize the modern age of revolution as the turning of "the demands of the Kingdom of God . . . into demands of time" (Rozenzweig 2005: 305). "Only since then were all those great works of liberation undertaken, which, as little as they already constitute the Kingdom of God, are yet the necessary conditions for its coming" (ibid.).

Such a counter-polar movement is not so far from Benjamin's "Theological-Political Fragment," with its image of two opposing, yet mutually promoting forces and its repudiation of "the political significance of theocracy" (SW3, 305/GSII:1, 203). The Messiah must not be politically anticipated *as* Messiah; his conception as an individual personality is nothing other than, to use Scholem's words, "political irony" (Scholem 2003: 177). Reading "On the Concept of History" in line with the earlier "Theological-Political Fragment," only the profane and *glückliche* (happy and fortunate) interaction of the puppet and the dwarf on the battleground of history announces the "quietest approach" (SW3, 305/GSII:1, 204) of the Messianic Kingdom, without being identical with this Kingdom. From this perspective it also becomes clear why the Messiah, according to the mystical-transforming tradition of messianic thought, does not "wish to change the world by force" (SW2:2, 811/GSII:2, 432): He simply does not have to do it anymore. The task of changing the world is incumbent on the striving for happiness of a free humanity and a politics of the profane. It is in this profane arena where the striking interplay of the puppet and the dwarf take place. The task of the dwarf-theology as a small, ugly, and hidden "player" is thus to be distinguished from the apocalyptic intrusion of the Messiah and the actual coming of the Messianic Kingdom.

Benjamin's materialistic deployment of theology is very consistent in conceiving the relation of the messianic and the political as a relation of non-relation. For theology in the age of modernity can only maintain its (non-)relation to the messianic as a hunchbacked and hidden one: it is *entstellt*—disfigured and displaced to a different scene. If one follows Benjamin's assumption of a "connection exist[ing] between the secularization of time in space and the allegorical mode of perception" (AP, 472/GSV:1, 590), the spatial allegory of the chess automaton can no longer be translated back into the binary of a sacral time of messianic theology and an "empty, homogenous time" of the secular progress of history. With the dawn of modernity, theology falls irrevocably under the gaming table of history. Only there hidden "under the table," it maintains a relation to the messianic, embodied in the figure of the dwarf, whose non-instrumental incognito is historical materialism.

## State of Exception

The task of the dwarf-theology consists in keeping open the small gate through which the Messiah may enter. This gate does not exist as such, but only opens up from the perspective of the chess players of history. The opening of this gate in the profane sphere is thus to be distinguished from the actual entrance of the Messiah through this gate. The time of true political action is the time of keeping this gate open. Giorgio Agamben calls this time "messianic time," that is, the "time of the end" in contradistinction to the apocalyptic end-time (Agamben 2005b: 83).[6] Politically speaking, this time of keeping the gate open can be both mystical or revolutionary, a slight adjustment or a violent interruption. When speaking about actually existing fascism, however, Benjamin seems to revert to a plain apocalyptic tone. Thesis VI reads: "The Messiah comes not only as the redeemer; he comes as the victor over the Antichrist" (*SW*4, 391/*GSI*:2, 695). As we shall see, here Benjamin also adds an important complication to the apocalyptic imaginary of end-times.

The Christian concept of the Christos-Messiah as the redeemer from Anti-Christos alludes to the apocalyptic tradition of the New Testament in John. "Dear children, this is the last hour; and as you have heard that the antichrist is coming, even now many antichrists have come. This is how we know it is the last hour" (1 Jn 2: 18). The historically current "Antichrist" in Benjamin's "On the Concept of History" is fascism and a political conformism that paves the way for fascism. This Antichrist threatens the tradition of the oppressed, for "*even the dead* will not be safe from the enemy if he is victorious" (*SW*4, 391/*GSI*:2, 695). The task of Benjamin's historian as historical politician is thus twofold: averting the deadly danger from the living and preventing the "second death" of the dead in the historical text. Benjamin has inseparably interwoven both aspects in the expression of the "tradition of the oppressed." The addressee of this tradition is by no means humanity and its cultural heritage, but "the struggling, oppressed class itself" (*SW*4, 394/*GSI*:2, 700). Only in the struggle of the oppressed can their tradition be saved from the enemy who "has never ceased to be victorious" (*SW*4, 391/*GSI*:2, 695). Benjamin goes so far as to state that even the act of forgetting is preferable to enacting a wrong form of tradition.

> What are phenomena rescued from? Not only, and not in the main, from the discredit and neglect into which they have fallen, but from the catastrophe represented very often by a certain strain in their dissemination, their "enshrinement as heritage."—They are saved through the exhibition of the fissure within them.—There is a tradition that is catastrophe. (*AP*, 473/*GSV*:1, 591)

Against this catastrophic appreciation as cultural heritage Benjamin highlights the "exhibition of the fissure," the oppressive nature of a tradition that it inherited as cultural treasury. The kindling of the spark in the past by the historian does not nourish the warming embers of tradition as cultural heritage, but the hope of its explosion as a charged "now" in the present. It is the unconditional urgency of this explosive "tiger's leap" (*SW*4, 395/*GSI*:2, 701) that Benjamin addressed in the apocalyptic image of the Antichrist.

Against this historical-political background, the fascist "Antichrist" of the late 1930s, in contrast to the apocalyptic tradition of Christianity, is not the one with whose coming the end-times begin to dawn, but the one who has already come and has not ceased to be victorious. "That things are 'status quo' *is* the catastrophe. It is not an ever-present possibility but what in each case is given" (*AP*, 473/*GSV*:1, 592). This "status quo" owes itself to having failed to interrupt the "always–continuing." The catastrophe of the ever-persisting status quo, then, is always also the catastrophe of having "missed the opportunity" (*AP*, 474/*GSV*:1, 593). If "the critical moment," the moment of *krisis*, of decision, is missed, "the status quo threatens to be preserved" (ibid.). Benjamin radicalizes these considerations from Konvolut N of the *Passagenwerk* in his "On the Concept of History" by relating them to the catastrophic state of exception ("state of emergency"), which is established as the normal state. The ever-so-continuing catastrophe of the status quo, the missing of all opportunities to politically interrupt the course of events, prepares the ground for the fascist antichrist, whose own normal state coincides with the state of exception. "The tradition of the oppressed teaches us that the 'state of emergency' in which we live is not the exception but the rule" (*SW*4, 392/*GSI*:2, 697), states Thesis VIII. Benjamin contrasts the political-theological justification of the "state of exception," whose theory was spelled out by Carl Schmitt (Schmitt 2004: 13), with "the bringing about of the real state of exception" (*SW*4, 395/*GSI*:2, 697 translation modified). The "first revolutionary measure" (*AP*, 474/*GSV*:1, 593) consists in the substitution of the Schmittian "state of exception," which Benjamin puts here deliberately into quotation marks, with the revolutionary real state of exception. The latter coincides with the overcoming of the Antichrist: anti-fascism is revolution, revolution is anti-fascism—there is no way back to the pre-fascist "normal" state of affairs.

The Schmittian state of exception represents the extreme contrast to what Benjamin called "divine violence" in his essay on the "Critique of Violence" (1921). While "divine violence" deposes (*entsetzt*) law and its constitutive dialectic of "mythic violence" (*SW*1, 251–252/*GSII*:1, 202–203), Schmitt's theory of the state of exception designates the paradoxical attempt to inscribe the suspension of law—the anomic zone of its suspension while being in force—into the law as its presumable grounding in the state of exception. "The modern state of exception," Agamben argues, is "an attempt to include the exception itself within the juridical order by creating a zone of indistinction in which fact and law coincide" (Agamben 2005a: 26). Thus, in order to guarantee the applicability of a legal norm to reality, the state of exception creates a zone of anomie, "in which application is suspended, but the law . . . as such, remains in force" (ibid.). Schmitt attempts to ground this seemingly paradoxical guarantee of the applicability of law in its own suspension, so that only the force of law without the law remains effective in a fictitious zone whose "decisionist" figure is the sovereign who decides on the state of exception. By creating this zone of indeterminacy in which inside and outside do not exclude each other, the state of exception creates an anomic space "in which what is at stake is a force of law without law (which should therefore be written: force-of-~~law~~)" (ibid., 39). Agamben rejects this constitutive (in)determination of law, zone of anomie, which is asserted in the state of exception as the prelegal enactment of law. "Far from being a response to a normative lacuna, the state of exception appears as the opening of a fictitious lacuna in the order for the purpose of safeguarding the existence of the norm and its applicability to the normal situation" (ibid., 31). In this way, the state of exception presents the paradoxical grounding of the normal case of legality in the latter's exceptional suspension. The state of exception, however, does not precede, either logically or historically, the "normal" case of the modern bourgeois state and its constitutive *Staatsgewalt,* state power and violence; rather, it is a result of the impossibility of grounding the state's legal order in a prelegal power relation. In this way, the theory of the state of exception "solves" a fictitious problem by inscribing what is outside the law into the law and by reframing this outside and its political potentialities (i.e., human relations beyond the paradigm of the state and legal violence) as an internal problem *of* the law. Sovereign violence, however, is not the source of the political but, rather, a reaction to this political zone of indetermination and potentiality. Turning this causality upside down, Schmitt theorized this reaction as a distinctive "decision," supposedly constitutive of the entire sphere of the political and its "normal" functioning. With regard to Benjamin's Thesis VIII, we can conclude that fascism enacts such a "state of exception" of "normal" modern bourgeois capitalism in order to secure the latter's "normal" functioning. This is what is meant when in fascism the state of exception becomes the rule: The fascist disclosure of the separation of law and the force-of-law, norm and its applicability, serves the "normal" preservation of the ruling class by "exceptional" means.[7]

In this respect, the struggle against fascism does not refer to an imminent final battle between the Messiah and the Antichrist, communism and fascism, but to the daily struggle against the extremism of the normal capitalist state of affairs, which fascism— as a radical form of anti-communism—aimed to preserve. Already in 1932 Benjamin approvingly quotes Brecht, according to whom "communism is not the extreme."[8] "'[C]apitalism is radical'" (*SW*2:1, 559/*GS*II:2, 511 translation modified). This radicalism expressed itself in the final phase of the Weimar Republic in the establishment of a permanent state of exception in order to maintain a presidential rule. In this context, Benjamin also speaks of an "anarchy of bourgeois society" as an "infernal" one (*SW*4, 222/*GS*II, 546). In such an anarchy of hell, exception and rule are no longer clearly separated. In Germany, this constitutive conflation of rule and exception, inside and outside, normal state and state of emergency, did not establish itself with the fascist dictatorship of National Socialism, but already began in 1930 with the government of Heinrich Brüning, which, with the help of Article 48 of the Weimar Constitution, ruled de facto by presidential emergency decree (cf. Blomeyer 1999: 62–80; 121–91).

The extremism of the normal state is also at stake in Benjamin's early fragment "Capitalism as Religion" from 1921, where capitalism, as a purely practical cult religion, persists without a "real" state of exception: "There are no 'weekdays'[,] . . . no day that is not a feast day, in the terrible sense that all its sacred pomp is unfolded before us; each day commands the utter fealty of each worshiper" (*SW*1, 288/*GS*VI, 100). Festive and everyday life collapse into one. Without the separation of festive day and workday, capitalism no longer knows resting days: "Capitalism is the celebration of a cult *sans [t]rêve et sans merci* [without rest or mercy]" (*SW*1, 288/*GS*VI, 100 translation modified, cf. Steiner 2003: 285). However, for a world in which "God's transcendence has fallen" and "he has been incorporated into human existence" (*SW*1, 289/*GS*VI, 101 translation modified), God has become part of capital's religion of culpability and debt (*Verschuldung*)—a world that celebrates its end-times, its "time of hell" (*AP*: 842/*GS*V:2, 1010) on a daily basis. From a political point of view, the apocalyptic image of the coming of the fascist "Antichrist" fails to recognize the already-catastrophic "normalcy" of capitalism. Benjamin's concept of history aims precisely at this bourgeois normalcy of capitalism and the "amazement that the things we are experiencing are 'still' possible in the twentieth century" (*SW*4, 392/*GSI*:2, 697). This amazement owes itself to a perspective that is unable to grasp fascism as an extreme defense-mechanism of capitalist normality. Put differently, from Benjamin's Marxian perspective fascism is always an internal possibility of capitalism to keep the latter intact—there is no room for amazement here. The advent of the fascist "Antichrist" is thus not the historical sign of a sudden urgency in the now, but a consequence of the political failure, as Benjamin prophetically foresaw in the mid-1920s, to cut "the lighted fuse" of fascism "before the spark reaches the dynamite" (*SW*1, 470/*GSIV*:1, 122). In 1940, it is already burning and an end to the explosions is not in sight.

If, in theological terms, the Messiah comes as the victor over the Antichrist, he comes, in political terms, as the one who suspends a state in which the state of exception is the rule. This analogy, equality of relations, does not equate or identify the sphere of the political with the theological. The relata at stake are non-identical. The failed revolutions of the past are catastrophic, yet catastrophe is not an impending apocalypse but the status quo of the ever-continuing. Hence, the "real" state of emergency and thus the first revolutionary measure is reversal, standstill. Genuine revolution in the face of catastrophe promises only the pulling of "the emergency brake" (*SW*4, 402/*GSI*:3, 1232). But who is the one to pull it? Whose arm reaches so far?

Only the "true historian" (*SW*4, 405/*GSI*:3, 1238) as "the true politician" (*SW*1, 470/*GSIV*:1, 122) has the presence of mind, in the moment of danger, to explode the destructive energies of the past in the now, in order to suspend and derail the catastrophic status quo. "The destructive or critical momentum of materialist historiography is registered in that blasting of historical continuity with which the historical object first constitutes itself" (*AP*, 475/*GSV*:1, 594). In an alternative Thesis XVIII (also called "XVIIa"), Benjamin gives the destructive moment of materialist historiography another twist by linking knowledge of the past directly to political action in the present.

> For the revolutionary thinker, the peculiar revolutionary chance offered by every historical moment gets its warrant from the political situation. But it is equally grounded, for this thinker, in the right of entry which the historical moment enjoys vis-a-vis a quite distinct chamber of the past, one which up to that point has been closed and locked. The entrance into this chamber coincides in a strict sense with political action, and it is by means of such entry that political action, however destructive, reveals itself as messianic. (*SW*4, 402/*GSI*:3, 1231)

Here, too, Benjamin upholds his relational separation of politics and theology; there is no messianic politics of liberation. The coincidence of political and destructive action does not place the series of "revolutionary thinker," "historical materialist," "true politician," "true historian," "historian" in the position of Messiah as the redeemer and victor over the Antichrist. Rather, Benjamin's historical subject of action keeps the empty place of the Messiah free for His (belated) coming. Political action itself can never be messianic, there is no messianic predication. Politics can only assume the character of a violent messianic manifestation without becoming identical with the messianic. In the vicissitudes of the profane, political action aims at revolutionary interruptions, not at final goals or programs. The struggle for the classless society does not take place as an apocalyptic endgame but is carried out on the existing battlefield of history.

In this battlefield, a messianic *analogon* can be named: the struggle for the classless society. This *analogon*, however, remains paradoxical; it expresses a relation of non-relation. Political action, without becoming messianic itself, can be conceived as an interruptive struggle that opens a gateway to a different time—a time in between the time of revolution and the catastrophic status quo. The profane name of this kairological time, in which the possibility of the occurrence of the fortunate moment, of the kairos, suddenly opens up, is the "[n]ow-time, which, as a model of messianic time, comprises the entire history of mankind in a tremendous abbreviation" (*SW*4, 396/*GSI*:2, 703). The messianic can provide here a model for the profane. Agamben points out that messianic time cannot be understood along the lines of the traditional opposition of chronological and kairological time. Messianic time, which is not actual in the now, is in its absence nevertheless present—in a condensed, abbreviatory form. For "what we take hold of when we seize *kairos* is not another time," Agamben comments, "but a contracted and abridged *chronos*" (Agamben 2005b: 69). The now-time as anticipating and abbreviating "time within time" maintains the tension of the separation of two temporal orders without relapsing to an apocalyptic conception of two-world ages. In terms of Thesis I, we are not dealing with a chess game, which is headed for final checkmate (revolution as apocalypse) or eternal stalemate (bad infinity of political reformism), but with a striking interplay, which can open a kairological time within chronological time. The time of this interplay is the time of the struggle for the classless society "as now-time shot through with splinters of messianic time" (*SW*4, 397/*GSI*:2, 704).

## Notes

1 This chapter contains translated and reworked passages of chapter III.1 of the author's book *"Teleologie ohne Endzweck"* (Cf. Khatib 2013). Translation of the text is by the author in collaboration with Alina Khatib.
2 See too the remarks on this text in the respective chapters by Moran and Salzani in this volume.
3 Benjamin's eighteen theses "On the Concept of History" are subsequently referred to as Thesis I – XVIII.
4 This use of parallax does not distinguish between its epistemological and ontological function. It thereby follows a Hegelian-Lacanian understanding of parallax, introduced by Slavoj Žižek: "The standard definition of parallax is: the apparent displacement of an object (the shift of its position against a background), caused by a change in observational position that provides a new line of sight. The philosophical twist to be added, of course, is that the observed difference is not simply 'subjective', due to the fact that the same object which exists 'out there' is seen from two different stances, points of view. It is rather that, as Hegel would have put it, subject and object are inherently 'mediated', so that an 'epistemological' shift in the subject's

point of view always reflects an 'ontological' shift in the object itself" (Žižek 2006: 17).

5   I owe the insight into the formal structure of Thesis I to Massimiliano Tomba and his seminar "Benjamin's Theses 'On the Concept of History': A Political-Philosophical Commentary" at Goldsmiths, University of London, October 27, 2010.

6   In *The Time That Remains* (2005b), Agamben argued that "messianic time is the time that time takes to come to an end, or, more precisely, the time we take to bring to an end, to achieve our presentation of time. This is not the line of chronological time . . . , nor the instant of its end . . . ; nor is it a segment cut from chronological time; rather, it is operational time pressing within the chronological time, working and transforming it from within; it is the time we need to make time end: *the time that is left us*" (ibid., 67f.). Agamben's term "operational time" is borrowed from the French linguist Gustave Guillaume and used here to introduce a non-contemplative and non-idealist concept of time in which we would only be impotent "spectators who look at the time that flies without any time left" (ibid., 68).

7   I have elaborated on the difference between Benjamin and Schmitt elsewhere (cf. Khatib 2016: 41–65).

8   Cf. Brecht's poem *Der Kommunismus ist das Mittlere* (Brecht 1967: 503f.). The English translation is taken from Brecht [2015] 2019.

# References

Agamben, G. (2005a), *State of Exception*, trans. K. Attell, Chicago: University of Chicago Press.

Agamben, G. (2005b), *The Time that Remains: A Commentary on the Letter to the Romans*, trans. P. Dailey, Stanford: Stanford University Press.

Bloch, E. (1918), *Geist der Utopie*, Munich, Leipzig: Duncker & Humblot.

Bloch, E. (2006), *Traces*, trans. A. A. Nassar, Stanford: Stanford University Press.

Blomeyer, P. (1999), *Der Notstand in den letzten Jahren von Weimar. Die Bedeutung von Recht, Lehre und Praxis der Notstandsgewalt für den Untergang der Weimarer Republik und die Machtübernahme durch die Nationalsozialisten*, Berlin: Duncker & Humblot.

Brecht, B. (1967), *Gesammelte Werke*, Vol. 9, Frankfurt/Main: Suhrkamp.

Brecht, B. ([2015] 2019), *The Collected Poems of Bertolt Brecht*, trans. T. Kuhn and D. Constantine, New York: W. W. Norton, E-book.

Gold, J. R. (2006), "The Dwarf in the Machine: A Theological Figure and Its Sources," *MLN*, 121 (5): 1220–36.

Habermas, J. (1979), "Consciousness-Raising or Redemptive Criticism: The Contemporaneity of Walter Benjamin," *New German Critique, Special Walter Benjamin Issue*, 17: 30–59.

Kafka, F. (1980), *"Die acht Oktavhefte," Hochzeitsvorbereitungen auf dem Lande und andere Prosa aus dem Nachlaß*, in M. Brod (ed.), *Gesammelte Werke*, 30–118, Frankfurt/Main: Fischer.

Kaiser, G. (1975), "Walter Benjamins 'Geschichtsphilosophische Thesen," in P. Bulthaup (ed.), *Materialien zu Benjamins Thesen "Über den Begriff der Geschichte"*, 43–76, Frankfurt/Main: Suhrkamp.

Khatib, S. (2013), *"Teleologie ohne Endzweck": Walter Benjamins Ent-stellung des Messianischen*, Marburg: Tectum.

Khatib, S. (2016) "Towards a Politics of 'Pure Means': Walter Benjamin and the Question of Violence," in E. E. Arrieta Burgos (ed.), *Conflicto armado, justicia y memoria, 1: "Teoría crítica de la violencia y prácticas de memoria y resistencia,"* 41–65, Medellín: Editorial de la Universidad Pontificia Bolivariana.

Mosès, S. (2009), *The Angel of History: Rosenzweig, Benjamin, Scholem*, Stanford: Stanford University Press.

Poe, E. A. (1836, April), "Maelzel's Chess-Player," *Southern Literary Messenger*, 2: 318–26.

Racknitz, J. F. (1789), *Ueber den Schachspieler des Herrn von Kempelen und dessen Nachbildung*, Leipzig, Dresden: Breitkopf.

Rosenzweig, F. (2005), *Star of Redemption*, trans. B. E. Galli, Madison: University of Wisconsin Press.

Schlegel, F. (1967), "Athenäums-Fragmente," in E. Behler (ed.), *Kritische Friedrich-Schlegel-Ausgabe*, Vol. 2, 165–255, Munich: Schöningh.

Schmitt, C. ( 2004), *Politische Theologie: Vier Kapitel zur Lehre von der Souveränität*, Berlin: Duncker & Humblot.

Scholem, G. (2003), "Theses on the Concept of Justice," in E. Jacobson (ed.), *Metaphysics of the Profane: The Political Theology of Walter Benjamin and Gershom Scholem*, 174–77, New York: Columbia University Press.

Steiner, U. (2003), "Die Grenzen des Kapitalismus," in D. Baecker (ed.), *Kapitalismus als Religion*, 35–59, Berlin: Kadmos.

Weigel, S. (1997), *Entstellte Ähnlichkeit: Walter Benjamins theoretische Schreibweise*, Frankfurt/Main: Fischer.

Žižek, S. (1989), *The Sublime Object of Ideology*, London: Verso.

Žižek, S. (2006), *The Parallax View*, London: Verso.

# 10

# A Hunchbacked Political Theology

## Creaturely Biopolitics as the Self-Sublation of Distorted Life

Carlo Salzani

## A Theology of Hunchbacked Possibilities

The theology famously enlisted by Benjamin to political ends in the first thesis of "On the Concept of History" presents some peculiar features: it is "small and ugly," like the "hunchbacked dwarf" representing it, and for this very reason "has to keep out of sight" (*SW4*, 389/*GSI*:2, 693).[1] Not only reduced to a dwarfish dimension in contrast with its ancient dominance, but also crooked, deformed, and distorted like a hunched back, Benjamin's peculiar brand of theology cannot show its face (*darf sich nicht blicken lassen*) in the political struggle, not even as a diminished sidekick of historical materialism, but must hide inside the automaton of an unusual form of political theology, where it must remain, as it were, *sous rature*.[2] Another famous image expresses this relation in an entry of the *Arcades Project*: "My thinking is related to theology as blotting pad is related to ink. It is saturated with it. Were one to go by the blotter, however, nothing of what is written would remain" (*AP*, 471/*GSV*:1, 588, entry N7a,7). Though saturating the blotter of thought (and of the political) as a most powerful catalyst, the ink of theology must remain invisible.

The form of this exclusion (from view) is not what Agamben (1998: 7 and *passim*) has called "inclusive exclusion," an exclusion that includes something as excluded or rejected, since Benjamin's theology *sous rature* remains invisible as merely hidden and retains a form of power that, although "weak," would allow its collaboration with historical materialism to "be a match for anyone" and "win all the time" (*SW4*, 389–90/*GSI*.2, 693–94). This theology stands actually in opposition to the very logic of the exception that is articulated around the *dispositif* of inclusive exclusion: it does not aim at ruling through exclusion, but rather at redeeming through inclusion. This is another way of saying that Benjamin's strategy, as Sigrid Weigel puts it (2009: 107), is a rejection of all appropriations of theology to legitimize a political mandate, and is therefore a critique of (Schmittian) political theology. Werner Hamacher captured the essence of this structure in a powerful insight:

Redemption, as Benjamin here talks about it, is meant most prosaically: a redeeming (*Einlösung*) of possibilities, which are opened with every life and are missed in every life. If the concept of redemption points towards a theology—and it does so without doubt and *a fortiori* in the context of the first thesis, which mentions the "little hunchback" of theology—then this is not straightforwardly Judeo-Christian theology, but rather a theology of the missed or the distorted—hunchbacked—possibilities, a theology of missed, distorted or hunchbacked time. (2005: 40)

The form of this theology is in fact the inverted version of the inclusive exclusion since it aims at re-including the missed and hunchbacked possibilities. And the "real state of emergency" (*wirklichen Ausnahmezustands*) it should help to bring about, as a counter-articulation of the sovereign exception (*SW*4, 392/*GSI*.2, 697), retains the distortion—the hunchback—as a distinctive mark, rejecting its normalization and rectification. The mechanisms of exclusion inherent in the model of the sovereign exception work through apparatuses of normalization and rectification that determine what is crooked and distorted and eventually rectify or reject it as abnormal. A theology of hunchbacked possibilities is instead a theology that does not eliminate (normalize) the distortion but rather retains and redeems it.

In this chapter I will articulate this thesis through an analysis of the famous little hunchback in all his reincarnations in Benjamin's *œuvre* and in his relationships to politics and theology. This analysis will progressively open up its scope, starting from the distortion of memories and lost possibilities and passing then to the distortion of life itself. It will thereby propose a fundamental contraposition between two approaches to life: on the one hand, a politics of life that is based on the apparatus of the exception and the inclusive exclusion and aims thus at the "rectification" of life; on the other, a politics of life that refuses instead the logic of the exception and "redeems" life and its distortion by a fundamental inclusion. The little hunchback becomes therefore the point of contention between what I will call a "biopolitics of rectitude," which considers him an exception (a freak) and will want to straighten him up, and a "creaturely biopolitics," which deactivates instead the very apparatus that deems him an exception.

## The Hump of Inattentiveness

As Burkhardt Lindner notes (1992: 237), thesis I involves a reconfiguration of the little hunchback who previously was used to represent the sphere of myth, whereas in "On the Concept of History," the hunchback is upgraded to a figure of theology. This by-now emblematic figure of Benjamin's iconography appears, as is well-known, in three main locations in Benjamin's *œuvre*: "On the Concept of History" (as *buckliger Zwerg*, hunchbacked dwarf), "Berlin Childhood around 1900" and "Franz Kafka" (in both as *bucklichte Männlein*, little hunchback)—plus a minor appearance in the 1935 journalistic piece "Rastelli's Story," where he is already a dwarf hidden within a sort of fake automaton, a juggler's ball (cf. *SW*3, 96–98/*GSI*V, 777–80). The origins of this figure have been thoroughly researched in Benjamin scholarship: Benjamin was acquainted with it already in his childhood, since the little hunchback inhabits famous childhood rhymes that were common patrimony of German folklore. In "Berlin Childhood," Benjamin gives as his source Georg Scherer's *Das Deutsche Kinderbuch* (1865), which "revealed" to him as a child the identity of the malicious, mischief-making creatures haunting his days and nights (SW3, 385/GSIV:1, 303). But these verses were originally collected (and often re-invented) by the Heidelberg Romantics, Achim von Armin and Clemens Brentano, in their famous edition of folk poems and songs *Des Knaben Wunderhorn: Alte deutsche Lieder* (1805–8; specifically in the section "Kinderlieder" in volume 3, 54–55). This folkloric figure finally merged with the dwarf character of Poe's story "Maelzel's Chess-Player" (1965), which provides the model for the automaton in thesis I.[3]

In "Berlin Childhood," the little hunchback (placed in all reworkings of the text at the end of the collection) plays a double role. On the one hand, as his avatar "Mr. Clumsy," he creates disorder by distracting the child who thus ends up breaking things or falling down: "Whoever is looked at by this little man pays no attention. Either to himself or to the little man. He stands dazed before a heap of fragments." He is thus a figure of the inattentiveness that envelops the child and his world.[4] This inattentiveness, on the other hand, has also a temporal dimension and pushes things into oblivion (*Vergessenheit*), as the world of childhood slips into the past. Before the hunchback's look, "things receded—until, in a year's time, the garden had become a little garden, my room a little room, and the bench a little bench: they shrank, and it was as if they grew a hump, which made them the little man's own." With the passing of time, things become small and distorted, since the little hunchback has exacted from them "the half part of oblivion." However, the character's mythic role seems to be invoking its own overcoming or sublation into a redeemed dimension, just like the hunchbacked possibilities of the past in "On the Concept of History" call for their redemption. In fact, the piece on the hunchback thus ends: "He has long since abdicated. Yet his voice, which is like the hum of the gas burner, whispers to me over the threshold of the century: 'Dear little child, I beg of you, / Pray for the little hunchback too'" (SW3, 385/GSIV:1, 303–4).

The half-forgotten world of childhood, like the missed or distorted possibilities of a life, invokes the redeeming work of remembrance. And this is what allows for the transformation of the little hunchback of oblivion in "Berlin Childhood" into the hunchbacked dwarf of theology in "On the Concept of History." As Joshua Robert Gold argues (2006: 1122), what the small and ugly theology of "On the Concept of History" signifies is ultimately a "vigilant orientation towards the past" set against the emphasis on progress and future typical of (Social-democratic) historicism and progressivism that is criticized throughout the text. The hunchbacked dwarf reverses the little hunchback's inattentiveness into a vigilant orientation, whereby the redeeming work of theology is equated to that of remembrance.

## *Entstellung*

The little hunchback is related to forgetfulness also in the 1934 Kafka essay. Here the hunched back (which is never explicitly thematized as such in Kafka's *œuvre*) is taken by Benjamin as the "prototype" of all those Kafkan creatures whose form is in some way "distorted," and this distortion is in turn equated with oblivion. Among the distorted creatures are Odradek from "The Cares of a Family Man," which epitomizes "the form which things assume in oblivion," as well as "the bug, which we know all too well represents Gregor Samsa" from *The Metamorphosis*, and the half-lamb, half-kitten from "A Crossbreed," "for which 'the butcher's knife' might be 'a release.'" Also distorted are the human figures:

> Among the images in Kafka's stories, none is more frequent than that of the man who bows his head far down on his chest: the fatigue of the court officials, the noise affecting the doormen in the hotel, the low ceiling facing the visitors in the gallery. In the penal colony, those in power use an archaic apparatus which engraves letters with curlicues on the back of every guilty man, multiplying the stabs and piling up the ornaments to the point where the back of the guilty man becomes clairvoyant and is able to decipher the script from which he must derive the nature of his unknown guilt. It is the back on which this is incumbent. (*SW*2, 811/*GS*II:2, 431-32)[5]

Kafka presents to the reader a world deformed by some distortive lens, and that is why the little hunchback of the folktale is "at home" in this world as "in distorted life" (he is *der Insasse*—the inhabitant—*des entstellten Lebens*). This distortion is also the very deformation imposed upon all that is forgotten and lost to the past. And this forgotten, whose presence the hunchback signifies, is, just as in "Berlin Childhood," not simply an issue of singular individualities, but rather (also) a desubjectified presence: "What has been forgotten ... is never something purely individual. Everything forgotten mingles with what has been forgotten of the prehistoric world, forms countless uncertain and changing compounds, yielding a constant flow of new, strange products" (*SW*2, 809–10/*GS*II:2, 430).

The Freudian roots of this notion of distortion (*Entstellung*) have been duly stressed (e.g., Wohlfarth 1988; Comay 1993; Khatib 2013a; Bielik-Robson 2017). Etymologically, *Entstellung* derives from the verb *stellen*, which means "to place something so that it stands upright," to put something on its feet (*Stellung*, position), and what the negative prefix *Ent-* denotes is thus that something is not "*an seiner Stelle*," in its place—also in the sense of (up)right posture (*Stellung*). In ordinary language the term has two main meanings: deformation (the distortion in something's form) and falsification (the distortion in something's truth). Freud uses it, from as early as *The Interpretation of Dreams* (1899) and up to *Moses and Monotheism* (1939), to refer to the effects of repression and denial. In a nutshell, repression produces a deformation of the contents of memory in a number of guises (lacunae, chronological disorder, unintelligibility, etc.), which also result in a resistance to recollection (and thus in further distortion). This distortion is also a displacement, a transposition whereby the signifier ends up in another place, thus masking the signified (in memory, dream), and becoming a falsification (cf. Rabinovitch 2014).[6] Sami Khatib (2013a: 44) notes that Benjamin must have been acquainted with this constellation of meaning from at least 1919, when he read Freud's *Introductory Lectures on Psycho-Analysis* (1916–17); however, where it takes a central place is in his interpretation of Kafka more than a decade later.

The structure of *Entstellung* makes for the fact that the little hunchback is never where we direct our gaze; he always eludes our grasp. "I never saw him. It was he who always saw me," writes Benjamin in "Berlin Childhood" (*SW*3, 385/*GS*IV:1, 304), though he is a sort of *Hausgeist* and lives intimately with us (Khatib 2013a: 472). It also explains, however, the relevance of the *back* as primary site of physical distortion: the back, Irving Wohlfarth notes (1988: 128), is the body part we are unable to attend to and which slips away from our attention and memory; but it is most of all the part metaphorically burdened and bent over by the metaphysical guilt of creatureliness, the mark of the fallen, sinful nature of creation, which in the Kafka essay is equated to a guilty forgetfulness. The forgotten stands for a mysterious, metaphysical guilt that burdens and bends down Kafka's characters (cf. *SW*2, 810/*GS*II:2, 430). Kafka's constellation of guilt and forgetfulness is best exemplified in the apparatus of "In the Penal Colony," which bloodily inscribes the sentence and/as the punishment for an unknown guilt on the back of the guilty subject until, in the sixth hour, it is the back itself that finally deciphers the script and identifies the guilt. But this feature can be generalized as a mark of Kafka's *œuvre* as a whole, where guilt (as a burden on the back) physically deforms the subject and enigmatically displaces/represses meaning and understanding, masking them under a distortion/falsification (Khatib 2013a: 473; Asman 1995).[7]

## Distortion and/as the Messianic

In a classic instance of Kafkan reversal,[8] however, the double structure of distortion (as deformation and displacement) also makes for its redeeming potential: in the Kafka essay Benjamin writes that "forgetting [i.e., distortion] always involves the best, for it involves the possibility of redemption" (*SW*2, 813/*GS*II:2, 434), and a tenet of his reading of Kafka (and of the messianic more generally) is that distortion *as such* is a harbinger of the messianic. In a famous letter to Scholem from August 11, 1934, discussing his Kafka essay and Scholem's response to it (and in particular the latter's thesis of the "nothing of revelation" in Kafka), Benjamin writes: "That I do not deny the component of revelation in Kafka's work already follows from my appreciation— by declaring his work to be 'distorted'—of its messianic aspect" (*C* 453/*GB*IV, 479). In the words of Sigrid Weigel (1996: 129), "the remoteness from revelation reverses into a Messianic figure: into redemption."[9] That happens insofar as this remoteness denies any claim to somehow being able to attain revelation (which is distorted/ displaced/falsified), but also insofar as it challenges the norms that deem it a distortion (cf. Moran 2018: 282). Distortion is thus also revelatory, and this is its redemptive role.

The section titled "The Little Hunchback" both in "Berlin Childhood" and "Franz Kafka" closes tellingly with the evocation of the prayer the little hunchback himself begs of the child in the folksong: "My dear child, I beg of you, / Pray for the little hunchback too." This prayer denotes the redemptive role, and the redemption itself, of distortion, which Benjamin equates to attention. The section in fact ends with this famous passage:

> Even if Kafka did not pray—and this we do not know—he still possessed in the highest degree what Malebranche called "the natural prayer of the soul": attentiveness. And in this attentiveness he included all creatures, as saints include them in their prayers. (SW2, 812/GSII:2, 432)

Distortion, which manifests itself as the hump of inattentiveness and forgetting, calls precisely for the countermeasure of attentiveness, i.e., for remembrance and for care, and the great merit of Kafka's work is to pay attention, to imply the need for remembering and caring. The nature of this care, however, is a contested point, and the rest of this chapter will be devoted to an examination of it.

If a classic motif of messianic literature is the messianic as figure of a de-figuration and structural dis-placement that can be expressed only through distortion and parody (cf. Khatib 2013a: 487[10]; Hamacher 2005: 67[11]; but also e.g., Agamben 2007: 33–34[12]), another classic point is the disappearing of this distortion with the coming of the Messiah. Of the little hunchback Benjamin writes in the Kafka essay: "he will disappear with the coming of the Messiah, who (a great rabbi once said) will not wish to change the world by force but will merely make a slight adjustment in it [*nur um ein Geringes sie zurechtstellen*]" (SW2, 811/GSII:2, 432). The issue is precisely the meaning of this disappearance and/as the "slight adjustment" the Messiah will make.

## *Nur ein klein wenig anders*

The parable about the coming of the Messiah is told by Benjamin with some more details (though with no reference to the hunchback) in the 1932 journalistic piece "In the Sun":

> The Hasidim have a saying about the world to come. Everything there will be arranged just as it is with us. The room we have now will be just the same in the world to come; where our child lies sleeping, it will sleep in the world to come. The clothes we are wearing we shall also wear in the next world. Everything will be the same as here—only a little bit different [*nur ein klein wenig anders*]. (SW2, 664/GSIV:1, 419)[13]

This story circulated in Benjamin's circle of friends and, two years earlier, Ernst Bloch had already published it, with a slight variation, in *Traces*:

> Another rabbi, a true Kabbalist, once said: To bring about the kingdom of freedom, it is not necessary that everything be destroyed, and a new world begin; rather, this cup, or that bush, or that stone, and so all things must only be shifted a little [*ein wenig*]. Because this "a little" is hard to do, and its measure so hard to find, humanity cannot do it in this world; instead this is why the Messiah comes. (2006: 158)

The "great rabbi" of the Kafka essay is diluted into the collective noun "The Hasidim" in "In the Sun" and becomes "a true Kabbalist" in *Traces*. However, another difference is more relevant: whereas for Bloch the little measure is impossible to find for humans, who therefore need the coming of the Messiah, Benjamin still retains the possibility of changing the world, even if only a little. For Andrew Benjamin (2013: 23), this "a little" spells out a yet to be actualized possibility in the present, and for Agamben (1993: 54) it "does not refer to the state of things, but to their sense and their limits" and introduces the possibility of an "otherwise" in the world. The whole point, however, is the very form of this possibility and of this "otherwise."

The source of the story seems to be Scholem, who perhaps told it to Benjamin, and from him it was passed on to Bloch, though the direction of the "debt" is not certain. In a letter from July 9, 1934, Scholem writes to Benjamin:

> Who is actually the source of all those stories? Does Ernst Bloch have them from you or you from him? The great rabbi with the profound dictum on the messianic kingdom who appears in Bloch is none other than *I* myself; what a way to achieve fame!! It was one of my first ideas about the Kabbalah. (*CS*, 123)

As Brendan Moran points out (2018: 303n62), Scholem's own "Theses on the Concept of Justice"[14] contain a strikingly similar formulation: "To allow the messianic world to break through, the perspective of redemption needs only a *virtual* shift. 'The messianic world will look exactly like this one, just a little different [*nur ein ganz klein wenig anders*]'" (available in Jacobson 2003, 177, 180). The quotation marks signal the phrase as, precisely, a quotation, and Eric Jacobson (2003: 312n99) reveals the source as Maimonides (1138-1204), who in the *Commentary on the Sanhedrin* wrote that "there is no difference between this world and the days of the Messiah except the subjugation of foreign Powers alone" (qtd. in Starr 2020: 200).

Michael Brocke (1991: 284), however, points to another source (with a little ironic rebuke to Scholem's claim to originality and fame): Rabbi Nachman of Breslov (1772-1810), the great-grandson of the Baal Shem Tov (Rabbi Israel ben Eliezer), the founder of Hasidic Judaism—which would clarify Benjamin's citing the Hasidim as the source of the story. Like Maimonides (and other messianic thinkers), Nachman of Breslov claimed that the coming of the Messiah "will change nothing, except that the fools will suddenly be ashamed of their foolishness" (qtd. in Mandel 1963: 7). What is interesting in this reference for my analysis is that this "change that will not change anything" can be related to one of the main teachings of Rabbi Nachman, the *Tikkun HaKlali*, usually translated as "general rectification": it is an analysis of the *tikkun* as the meaning of the "little bit different" and "slight adjustment" that will allow for a clarification of Benjamin's strategy with regard to the little hunchback.

## Orthopedics of Redemption

Traces of a kabbalistic notion of *tikkun* abound in Benjamin's *œuvre*, from the reference to the fragments of a broken vessel "that are to be glued together" in "The Task of the Translator" (*SW*1, 260/*GS*IV:1, 18)[15] to the angel in thesis IX of "On the Concept of History," who would like to "make whole what has been smashed" (*SW*4, 392/*GS*I:2,

697). In Lurianic Kabbalah, according to Scholem's interpretation, the *tikkun* is precisely salvation as reintegration of the original whole, as "making whole" the world (the vessel) that "has been smashed,"[16] and the term in Hebrew means "restoration," "fixing," "rectification." Though etymologically *tikkun* has no relation to metaphors of verticality,[17] it is this last translation, "*rect*ification" (as in Rabbi Nachman's *Tikkun HaKlali*, "general rectification"), that becomes relevant for the discussion of Benjamin's little hunchback, since in the Kafka essay his disappearance at the coming of the Messiah is equated to a "slight adjustment" that in German is rendered with the verb *zurechtstellen*, to put (up)right. The question is thus whether redemption means the straightening out of the hump, of the distortion and deformity that the hunchback represents.

When the distortion of the hunchback stands for forgetting and/as guilt, then, in its contraposition to *Ent-stellung*, *Zurecht-stellen* amounts to the redemptive attentiveness/remembrance evoked at the end of the section on the little hunchback. In Wohlfarth's words, "what forgetting distorts [*entstellt*], remembrance will put right [*wird . . . zurechtstellen*]. The messianic world would then be a restored state in which everything would have again its "'right place' [*seine 'bestimmte Stelle'*]" (1988: 128: cf. also Khatib 2013a: 476–77). The right *Stelle* is, however, also a right *Stellung*, a right position/posture, and Wohlfarth spells this out by pointing to the very last sentence of the Kafka essay, where Benjamin, blending together his analysis of the horse Bucephalus from Kafka's story "The New Lawyer" and Sancho Panza from "The Truth about Sancho Panza," concludes: "Whether it is a man or a horse is no longer so important, if only the burden is taken off the back" (*SW2*, 816/*GSII*:2, 438). This removal of the burden of forgetting/guilt from the back is equated to a straightening out of the back, of what is crooked, and the very notion of justice, which in German is Gerecht*igkeit* (etymologically closer to "*rect*itude" than justice), is ultimately equated to a putting (up)right what is bent and twisted (Wohlfarth 1988: 145).[18]

In German as in many other languages the "verticalization" of justice is linguistically evident: *Recht*, *Gerechtigkeit*, *Rechtschaffenheit* express the same positioning as "right," "righteousness" and "rectitude," a positioning that takes the upright posture as the "just" norm and that, as Adriana Cavarero (2016) has shown, is far from neutral and rather plays a strong "normalizing" function. "Right" is precisely what is not bowed, what does not deviate from the straight line of justice, from the "rule" and the "norm," where the former comes from the Latin term for "ruler" and the latter comes from the set square to measure right angles—all very vertical metaphors. The obvious reference here is Foucault and his discussion of the "orthopedics" of individuality in *Discipline and Punish* (e.g., 1995: 294) and of the *dispositifs* of "normalization" in *Security, Territory, Population* (2007: especially 55–86). And Rebecca Comay (1993, 259) emphasizes how Benjamin's political strategy is set against this "orthopaedia of the upright posture," against bourgeois idealism celebrating the "classical ideal of humanity."

However, Moran (2018: 296–97, 307) points out a fundamental ambiguity with regard to the redemption of the distortion represented by the little hunchback—an ambiguity that inherently belongs to the very notion of distortion as presented in Kafka, as Benjamin himself remarks in a preparatory note for the Kafka essay ("the concept of distortion in Kafka's representation has a double function"; *GSII*:3, 1200).

Distortion as a mark of forgetfulness and guilt is mythic; but at times it also signifies a violation of the (mythic) vertical norm and as such it represents the excluded exception and an opposition to myth. This very ambiguity informs the messianic attitude toward the little hunchback, whose disappearance, when seen as *Zurechtstellen*, definitely marks, at times, not the Kafkan redemptive attentiveness but rather a (very traditional) intolerance of distortion and a patronizing and cavalier approach to it.

## Play and the Self-sublation of Distortion

At other times, however, the rectification of the *Zurechtstellen* is given a different meaning, and the primary places for this interpretation are Benjamin's references to "the Nature Theater of Oklahoma," the last chapter of Kafka's unfinished novel *The Missing Person* (*Der Verschollene*, formerly titled *Amerika* by Max Brod). In Kafka's intentions, the chapter would have constituted the *happy ending* of Karl Rossman's adventures (Arendt 2007: 108), and in the Kafka essay Benjamin notes indeed that "happiness awaits him [Rossman] at the Nature Theater of Oklahoma," where he "attains the object of his desire" (*SW2*, 800–1/*GSII*:2, 417). The peculiarity of this theater is that everyone is hired by it: there are no standards for admission and "all that is expected of the applicants is the ability to play themselves." This constitutes their final redemption. Nobody is excluded from this theater of redemption, there are no exceptions, no inclusive exclusions. At the same time, however, "[i]t is no longer within the realm of possibility that [the applicants] could, if necessary, be what they claim to be" (*SW2*, 804, 14/*GSII*:2, 422–23, 435). As Moran notes (2018: 285), acceptance and inclusion do not mean that everyone plays one's wishes or what one really is (which is unknown and unknowable), but rather implies the defiance of established and complacent norms (of inclusion/exclusion).

Some preparatory notes for the Kafka essay clarify this point in relation to distortion. A note connects precisely the coming of the Messiah to the Nature Theater of Oklahoma: just as the Messiah, as the great rabbi said, will not change completely the world (*durch und durch verändere*) but only "set it aright" (*rückt sie nur zurecht*), so also the Nature Theater of Oklahoma "does not change people completely. It sets them aright by letting them play" (*verändert die Menschen nicht durch und durch. Es rückt sie nur zurecht, indem es sie spielen läßt*) (*GSII*:3, 1239). Here the "slight adjustment" the Messiah will bring about still has a vertical connotation (*zurecht*), but this "uprightness" seems to be deactivated by the "free rein" which is given to play (expressed by the verb *lassen*), which is moreover an activity not denoted by verticality (it is not specified here that play signifies the theatrical playing of roles—or of oneself; it seems just to mean playing as such).

Another important note again relates this playing to the theme of *Entstellung* in Kafka's creatures: "The distortion will sublate itself [*sich selber aufheben*] by making its way unto redemption. This displacement of axis [*Axenverschiebung*] in the redemption manifests itself in that it becomes play (the nature theater of Oklahoma)" (*GSII*:3,

1201). Here the orthopedics of "setting aright" disappear and are replaced by play as a "displacement of axis," a change of perspective. In another note, quoting from Felix Bertaux's 1928 book *Panorama de la litterature allemande contemporaine*, Benjamin defines *Entsellung* itself as a *"derangement de l'axe"* (GSII:3, 1200). Distortion and its disappearance seem to revolve around the positioning with respect to an axis. The Hegelian *Aufhebung* does indeed lead to the disappearance of distortion, but in a dialectical movement that is at the same time also a preservation and a salvation. Moreover, this redemption is not an external imposition (a rectification, a normalization) on a passive "subject,"[19] but rather a *self*-sublation as a mere geometrical displacement of the axis that "will not change anything" (cf. also Wohlfarth 1988: 152–53). Developing Moran's insight, we could say that the self-sublation of distortion here is that change of perspective (a "parallax shift," writes Khatib [2013a: 407 and his essay in this volume] with a Žižekian wink[20]) that shows the complete arbitrariness of the norm that declares something as distorted.

In this sense, Khatib (2013a: 46, 477–78) adds a fundamental point with respect to Freud's notion of *Enstellung*: the redemption of distortion through memory and redemptive attentiveness does not mean the restoration of an original, undistorted state, since *there never was such an undistorted state in the first place*. For Freud, distortion itself is the only means to try to access the distorted and forgotten truth of the unconscious (Rabinovitch 2014: 269). The redemption of distortion is thus the setting aright (if we want to keep using this vertical metaphor) of what was actually never aright, or it is, for the redeeming historian, to read in the book of the past what was never written;[21] it is in fact the creation of an entirely new *Stelle/Stellung*, of a new state and of a new positioning not construed through the exclusion, rejection, submission, and normalization of what is deemed distorted.

## Creaturely Biopolitics

The politics that captures and manages life through apparatuses of exclusion, rejection, submission, and normalization is the bio-politics of the sovereign exception. According to Agamben (1998), the sovereign posits himself as exception outside the law and, in so doing, establishes, through a decision, the "norm" by which he will rule: by establishing the exception through a decision, the sovereign sets the criteria of inclusion and exclusion through which he captures, controls, and manages life. To this politics Benjamin opposes the need to bring about a "real state of emergency" that would deactivate the apparatuses of exception. Since this politics of exception is fundamentally based on apparatuses of verticality (cf. e.g., Cavarero 2016), we could name it a *biopolitics of rectitude*, and Benjamin's countermove, the messianic self-sublation of the hunched back, is thus the proposal of a different politics of life, a *biopolitics of distorted life*. The exemplarity of Kafka's creatures for strategies to combat the various forms and instances of the biopolitics of rectitude have been identified and developed not only by Benjamin but also by a number of contemporary critical voices[22]—though with important exceptions.

Peter Sloterdijk (2013: 61–72), for example, enlists Kafka as one of the main examples of his anthropotechnical thesis about the vertical orientation of humans, arguing that he is "part of the great unscrewing of the moderns from a system of religiously coded vertical tensions that had been in force for millennia" (2013: 64): even when, with the death of God, the world above disappears, the vertical tension persists as the main orientation of the human, and this can be also detected, according to Sloterdijk, in the love for tightropes and acrobatics that mark Kafka's work as a whole.[23] More tricky is the case of Eric Santner, who developed a compelling theory of "creaturely life" that takes as one of its emblems Benjamin's little hunchback and his Kafka readings (2006: 130). The "creaturely" is defined by Santner as "life abandoned to the state of exception/emergency" (2006: 22) and thus exposed to the biopolitics of exclusion and normalization; however, Santner not only sees the sole possibility for redemption in the "interruption" (i.e., rectification) of this creaturely exposure (2006: 86; cf. Moran 2018: 308) but also transforms the creaturely itself in yet another apparatus of exclusion, submission, and normalization, since he defines it as a "distinctly human dimension," whereby "human beings are not just creatures among other creatures but are in some sense *more creaturely* than other creatures by virtue of an excess that is produced in the space of the political and that, paradoxically, accounts for their 'humanity'" (2006: 26).[24]

Against such biopolitical accounts of verticalization or exception, Benjamin's Kafkan distortion is instead what disrupts the very logic of exceptionality.[25] The creaturely in Benjamin's Kafka marks not human exceptionality but rather a challenge to hierarchization and exclusion, and this challenge is a challenge to humanity itself as construed through the biopolitics of rectitude: a challenge implied by the redemptive attentiveness toward the creaturely in Kafka's many distorted characters, but also in the very human (bent) body, which for Benjamin is "the most forgotten source of strangeness" (*SW2*, 810/*GSII*:2, 431). This challenge to the biopolitics of rectitude is perhaps best expressed in a famous passage of a letter Kafka sent to Felice Bauer on March 3, 1915. Here he interprets a dream that Felice related to him in a previous letter (which is unknown to us):

> Had you not been lying on the ground among the animals, you would have been unable to see the sky and the stars and wouldn't have been set free. Perhaps you wouldn't have survived the terror of standing upright [*Angst des Aufrechtstehens*]. I feel much the same; it is a mutual dream that you have dreamed for us both. (Kafka 1973: 447)

The upright posture—which is a source of *Angst!*—is the first, perhaps archetypical, biopolitical apparatus of inclusion/exclusion; it is what defines and discriminates the human as "right" and the rest of creation as wrong (because "crooked"); it is the standard that informs, from time immemorial, the biopolitics of rectitude.[26] Freedom/redemption is therefore the (merely perspectival, postural) abdication of this sovereign exclusivity by "lying on the ground among the animals." This is the self-sublation of distorted life; this is the creaturely biopolitics that does not "wish to change the world by force" but promises instead the disappearing of exception and exclusion when the Messiah comes—that is, every second of every day.

## Coda: The Double Hump of Pulcinella

Distortion is comic (it is the comic in Kafka) and the challenge to sovereign exclusion is epitomized by the mocking laughter of the little hunchback ("When I come into my room, / My little bed to make, / A little hunchback is in there, / With laughter he does shake"), which is the same laughter of Odradek sounding "something like the rustling of falling leaves" (*SW*2, 811/*GS*II:2, 432). Another famous comic hunchback, Pulcinella—a classic character of Italian *commedia dell'arte* who even has two humps, one on the back and another on the chest—has recently been analyzed by Agamben in a peculiar book (2019). Agamben's own challenge to the exclusion by the biopolitics of rectitude may be quoted here, as a final gloss:

> *Pulcinella's teaching: I am not to blame for the features of my body, my nose, my belly, my hump. I am innocent of all of it. Ethics begins right after this, but not somewhere else: given this—my?—body, what is ethical is the way in which I live the affection that I receive from being in relation to it, how I renounce or make mine this nose, this belly, the hump. In a word: how I smile at them.* (2019: 115, emphasis in the original)

Pulcinella's smile, like the laughter of the little hunchback and of Odradek, deactivates and deposes the logic of exception that judges him responsible for, and redeemable from, his crookedness. Ethics—which in Agamben's ontology is also immediately politics—begins precisely in this smile ("not elsewhere"), in the very gesture that simultaneously disowns and appropriates his distorted creatureliness.

## Notes

1  I warmly thank Benjamin Lewis Robinson, Paula Schwebel, and Brendan Moran for their comments and suggestions on a first draft of this chapter.
2  For our times, Žižek (2003: 3) proposed to invert the roles between theology, which enjoys a new lease on life in our "postsecular" age, and a by-now wizened historical materialism, which cannot show its face anymore. It is perhaps precisely the ominous entanglement of politics, religion, and violence characterizing our postsecular times that brings Benjamin's brand of political theology to a new legibility (cf. Critchley 2012; Weigel 2010).
3  See also Vardoulakis (2010: 192–202).
4  In her introductory essay on Benjamin, Hannah Arendt named a whole section after the little hunchback and suggested that Benjamin's whole life could be placed under the sign of the hunchback ("Wherever one looks in Benjamin's life, one will find the little hunchback"; 1968: 168). This attitude, which Arendt shares with a number of other interpreters (from Adorno to Scholem and up to Susan Sontag) was very successful in Benjamin's posthumous reception. Such interpretations, however, tend to emphasize Benjamin's melancholic side and Saturnian disposition, according to the worn-out stereotype of the intellectual as impractical, clumsy, and melancholic. In the specific case of the little hunchback, this attitude works however to deactivate

his philosophical and political functions and relegates him to the realm of aesthetic tropes.

5  Deleuze and Guattari (1986: 3–4) similarly identify the "bent head" as a paradigmatic image in Kafka's *œuvre* (including the diaries and letters).

6  Just one example from chapter IV, "Distortion in Dreams," of *The Interpretation of Dreams*: "We may therefore suppose that dreams are given their shape in individual human beings by the operation of two psychical forces (or we may describe them as currents or systems); and that one of these forces constructs the wish which is expressed by the dream, while the other exercises a censorship upon this dream-wish and, by the use of that censorship, forcibly brings about a distortion in the expression of the wish" (Freud 2010: 168).

7  Khatib (2013a: 473n116) points out that Benjamin thematized the connection of back and guilt already in the 1931 Kraus essay, where he describes "the experience and the name of that nameless power toward which the backs of people bent: guilt" (*SW*2, 445/*GS*II:1, 351).

8  In a letter to Scholem, Benjamin famously identified the "reversal" (*Umkehr*) as the kernel of Kafka's messianism ("Kafka's messianic category is the 'reversal' or the 'studying'" [*C* 453/*GB*IV, 479]), an insight that was then appropriated by Agamben ("One of the peculiar traits of the Kafkan allegories is that they contain right at the end a possibility of reversal which overturns completely their meaning" [1998: 58]).

9  Weigel's study (1996) amplifies the scope of distortion and makes it into a sort of paradigm of Benjamin's thinking, including his peculiar form of dialectics and his writing style, a point that cannot however be examined in depth here.

10  "The messianic does not allude to a radical alterity or a mystical secret but bears witness to a lack, an incompleteness that prevents the order of the profane from ultimately being closed as a self-totalizing sphere" (Khatib 2013b: 2).

11  "The Messiah only comes in a time that is distorted, however slightly, against any linear course. And only as distorted in such a way, as an always leaped time (*ersprungene Zeit*), can the messianic time come; it can only come as the distortion of time, distortion of the conditions of experience, distortion of its very possibility" (Hamacher 2005: 67).

12  "The idea that the Kingdom is present in profane time in sinister and distorted forms, that the elements of the final state are hidden precisely in what today appears despicable and derisory, that shame, in sum, secretly has something to do with glory, is a profound messianic theme. Everything that now appears debased and worthless to us is the currency we will have to redeem on the last day. And we will be guided toward salvation precisely by the companion who has lost his way" (Agamben 2007: 34).

13  See too the remarks on this text in the respective chapters by Moran and Khatib in this volume.

14  Scholem's text is uncertainly dated between 1919 and 1925, thus much earlier than both Bloch and Benjamin's re-telling. At some point, Scholem himself probably read this text to Benjamin and his wife Dora (Scholem 1981: 72).

15  "Fragments of a vessel that are to be glued together must match one another in the smallest details, although they need not be like one another. In the same way a translation, instead of imitating the sense of the original, must lovingly and in detail incorporate the original's way of meaning, thus making both the original and the translation recognizable as fragments of a greater language."

16  The complex details of the Lurianic Kabbalah and of its notion of *tikkun* exceed the scope of this chapter. For an overview of Scholem's view see, for example, chapter 7 ("Isaak Luria and his School") in Scholem (1974). For a more recent interpretation (which often contests and corrects Scholem) see Moshe Idel (1990).
17  I owe this information to Ilit Ferber.
18  It must be pointed out, against Wohlfarth's reading, that Sancho Panza is no hunchback and the burden that must be taken off Bucephalus's (straight) back is the weight of Alexander the Great as the "onrushing conqueror," as the weight is for Sancho that of another rider, Don Quixote, with the burden of his folly. I have analyzed these issues in Salzani (2019: 401–7).
19  Here the concept of subject must be understood in the passive sense of "subjected to" a (sovereign) subjectification (as normalization). Moreover, this very subjectification is strongly marked by the verticality of the upright posture that marks out the "proper" human subject and excludes the distorted creature. (I owe this insight to Benjamin Lewis Robinson.)
20  On the parallax shift see Žižek (2006).
21  In a preparatory note for "On the Concept of History," Benjamin famously used a line from Hugo von Hofmannsthal's 1893 play *Der Tor und der Tod* (*Death and the Fool*), "to read what was never written," to define the task of the materialist historian (*SW*4, 405/*GS*I:3, 1238).
22  I'm thinking in particular of critiques of anthropocentrism and human exceptionalism, where the bibliography is by now too rich to allow for some exemplary mentions.
23  Chris Danta has convincingly demonstrated, *contra* Sloterdijk, that "the lowering of the vertical to the point of its virtual collapse is one of Kafka's characteristic rhetorical tricks—a technique he uses to generate both comedy and pathos in his writing" (2015: 76).
24  I have explored Kafka's creaturely life against Santner's exclusionary logic in Salzani (2019).
25  The logic of exceptionality is ultimately a theory of the state of exception, insofar as what is "exceptional" is precisely what is *excepted* from a certain norm/normality and placed above it. This is made clear in the posture of human exceptionality, where human beings are extracted/excepted from, and placed above, the rest of creation, and in particular above the other, nonhuman animals as their "sovereign." If we follow Agamben's theorization, human exceptionalism is properly a theory of sovereignty.
26  Freud's hypothesis of an "organic repression" at the origin of human civilization, as developed more specifically in *Civilization and Its Discontents* (Freud 1962: 46–47n1, 52-54n3) and which is precisely linked to the adoption of the upright posture, can be given a biopolitical twist and be considered as the archetypical biopolitical *dispositif*. This argument cannot be developed here, but I explored it in relation to Kafka's quotation in Salzani (2019: 394–7).

# References

Agamben, Giorgio. (1993), *The Coming Community*, trans. Michael Hardt, Minneapolis: University of Minnesota Press.

Agamben, Giorgio. (1998), *Homo Sacer: Sovereign Power and Bare Life*, trans. Daniel Heller-Roazen, Stanford: Stanford University Press.

Agamben, Giorgio. (2007), "The Assistants," in Agamben, *Profanations*, trans. Jeff Fort, 29–36, New York: Zone Books.
Agamben, Giorgio. (2019), *Pulcinella: Or Entertainment for Children*, trans. Kevin Attell, Kolkata: Seagull Books.
Arendt, Hannah. (1968), "Walter Benjamin: 1892–1940," in Hannah Arendt, *Men in Dark Times*, trans. Harry Zohn, 153–206, New York: Harvest Books.
Arendt, Hannah. (2007), "Franz Kafka, Appreciated Anew," in Hannah Arendt, *Reflections on Literature and Culture*, ed. Susannah Young-ah Gottlieb, 94–109, Stanford: Stanford University Press.
Asman, Carrie L. (1995), "The Language of Defamiliarization: Benjamin's Kafka," in Richard T. Gray (ed.), *Approaches to Teaching Kafka's Short Fiction*, 76–83, New York: The Modern Language Association of America.
Benjamin, Andrew. (2013), *Working with Walter Benjamin: Recovering a Political Philosophy*, Edinburgh: Edinburgh University Press.
Bielik-Robson, Agata. (2017), "Mysteries of the Promise: Negative Theology in Benjamin and Scholem," in Michael Fagenblat (ed.), *Negative Theology as Jewish Modernity*, 258–81, Bloomington: Indiana University Press.
Bloch, Ernst. (2006), *Traces*, trans. Anthony A. Nassar, Stanford: Stanford University Press.
Brocke, Michael. (1991), *Die Erzählungen des Rabbi Nachman von Bratzlaw*, Hamburg: Rowohlt.
Cavarero, Adriana. (2016), *Inclinations: A Critique of Rectitude*, trans. Amanda Minervini and Adam Sitze, Stanford: Stanford University Press.
Comay, Rebecca. (1993), "Benjamin's Endgame," in Andrew Benjamin and Peter Osborne (eds.), *Walter Benjamin's Philosophy: Destruction and Experience*, 251–91, London: Routledge.
Critchley, Simon. (2012), *The Faith of the Faithless: Experiments in Political Theology*, London: Verso.
Danta, Chris. (2015), "Acrobats and Ascetics: Peter Sloterdijk and the Aesthetics of Verticality," *European Journal of English Studies*, 19 (1): 66–80.
Deleuze, Gilles, and Félix Guattari. (1986), *Kafka: Toward a Minor Literature*, trans. Dana Polan, Minneapolis: University of Minnesota Press.
Foucault, Michel. (1995), *Discipline and Punish: The Birth of the Prison*, trans. Alan Sheridan, New York: Vintage.
Foucault, Michel. (2007), *Security, Territory, Population. Lectures at the Collège de France 1977–78*, trans. Graham Burchell, Basingstoke: Palgrave Macmillan.
Freud, Sigmund. (1962), *Civilization and Its Discontents*, trans. and ed. James Strachey, New York: Norton and Company.
Freud, Sigmund. (2010), *The Interpretation of Dreams*, the complete and definitive text, trans. and ed. James Strachey, New York: Basic Books.
Gold, Joshua Robert. (2006), "The Dwarf in the Machine: A Theological Figure and Its Sources," *MLN*, 121 (5): 1220–36.
Hamacher, Werner. (2005), "'Now': Walter Benjamin on Historical Time," trans. N. Rosenthal, in Andrew Benjamin (ed.), *Walter Benjamin and History*, 38–68, London: Continuum.
Idel, Moshe. (1990), *Kabbalah: New Perspectives*, New Haven: Yale University Press.
Jacobson, Eric. (2003), *Metaphysics of the Profane: The Political Theology of Walter Benjamin and Gershom Scholem*, New York: Columbia University Press.
Kafka, Franz. (1973), *Letters to Felice*, trans. James Stern and Elisabeth Duckworth, New York: Schoken.

Khatib, Sami R. (2013a), *Teleologie ohne Endzweck: Walter Benjamins Ent-stellung des Messianischen*, Marburg: Tectum.

Khatib, Sami R. (2013b), "The Messianic Without Messianism: Walter Benjamin's Materialist Theology," *Anthropology & Materialism: A Journal of Social Research*, 1: 1–17.

Lindner, Burkhardt. (1992), "Engel und Zwerg, Benjamins geschichtsphilosophische Rätselfiguren und die Herausforderung des Mythos," in Lorenz Jäger and Thomas Regehly (eds.), *Was nie geschrieben wurde, lessen*, 235–65, Bielefeld: Aisthesis.

Mandel, Arnold. (1963), *La voie du hassidisme*, Paris: Calmann-Lévy.

Moran, Brendan. (2018), *Politics of Benjamin's Kafka: Philosophy as Renegade*, Basingstoke: Palgrave Macmillan.

Poe, Edgar Allan. (1965), "Maelzel's Chess-Player," in *The Complete Tales and Poems of Edgar Allan Poe*, 421–39, London: Penguin.

Rabinovitch, Solal. (2014), "Entstellung," in Barbara Cassin (Ed.), *Dictionary of Untranslatables: A Philosophical Lexicon*, trans. Steven Rendall et al., 268–69, Princeton: Princeton University Press.

Salzani, Carlo. (2019) "Kafka's Creaturely Life," in Günther Ortmann and Marianne Schuller (eds.), *Kafka: Organisation, Recht und Schrift*, 394–407, Weilerswist-Metternich: Velbrück Wissenschaft.

Santner, Eric L. (2006), *On Creaturely Life: Rilke – Benjamin – Sebald*, Chicago: The University of Chicago Press.

Scholem, Gershom. (1974), *Major Trends in Jewish Mysticism*, New York: Schocken Books.

Scholem, Gershom. (1981), *Walter Benjamin: The Story of a Friendship*, trans. Harry Zohn, Philadelphia: The Jewish Publication Society of America.

Sloterdijk, Peter. (2013), *You Must Change Your Life: On Anthropotechnics*, trans. Wieland Hoban, Cambridge: Polity Press.

Starr, Zachary Alan. (2020), *Toward a History of Jewish Thought: The Soul, Resurrection, and the Afterlife*, Eugene: Wipf and Stock.

Vardoulakis, Dimitris. (2010), *The Doppelgänger: Literature's Philosophy*, New York: Fordham University Press.

Weigel, Sigrid. (1996), *Body-and Image-Space: Re-Reading Walter Benjamin*, trans. Georgina Paul with Rachel McNicholl and Jeremy Gaines, London: Routledge.

Weigel, Sigrid. (2009), "The Sovereign, the Martyr and 'Just War' beyond the *Jus Publicum Europaeum*: The Dilemma of Political Theology, Discussed via Carl Schmitt and Walter Benjamin," in Esperanza Bielsa and Christopher W. Hughes (eds.), *Globalization, Political Violence and Translation*, trans. Georgina Paul, 88–113, Basingstoke: Palgrave Macmillan.

Weigel, Sigrid. (2010), "'In ungeheuren Fällen' – Benjamin's *Critique of Violence* and Constitutional Law," in Vittoria Borsò et al. (eds.), *Benjamin – Agamben: Politik, Messianismus, Kabbala*, 229–41, Würzburg: Königshausen and Neumann.

Wohlfarth, Irving. (1988), "'Märchen für Dialektiker.' Walter Benjamin und sein bucklicht Männlein," in Klaus Doderer (ed.), *Walter Benjamin und die Kinderliteratur: Aspekte der Kinderkultur in den zwanziger Jahren*, 121–76, Weinheim: Juventa.

Žižek, Slavoj. (2003), *The Puppet and the Dwarf: The Perverse Core of Christianity*, Cambridge: MIT Press.

Žižek, Slavoj. (2006), *The Parallax View*, Cambridge: The MIT Press.

# Contributors

**Leora Batnitzky** is Perelman Professor of Jewish Studies and Professor of Religion at Princeton University. She is the author of *How Judaism Became a Religion* and several other books on modern Jewish philosophers, hermeneutics, and political and legal theory. She is currently writing two books, the first a biography of the book of Ecclesiastes, and the second a study of the Jewish apostate and Catholic Saint Edith Stein.

**Agata Bielik-Robson** is Professor of Jewish Studies at the University of Nottingham and Professor of Philosophy at the Polish Academy of Sciences. She is interested in modern Jewish thought, philosophical theology of Judaism and psychoanalytic theory. Her publications include the books: *The Saving Lie: Harold Bloom and Deconstruction* (2011), *Judaism in Contemporary Thought: Traces and Influence* (coedited with Adam Lipszyc, 2014), *Philosophical Marranos: Jewish Cryptotheologies of Late Modernity* (2014), *Another Finitude: Messianic Vitalism and Philosophy* (2019), and *Derrida's Marrano Passover: Exile, Survival, Betrayal and the Metaphysics of Non-Identity* (2023).

**Howard Eiland** taught literature at MIT from 1983 to 2014. He is author, with Michael W. Jennings, of *Walter Benjamin: A Critical Life* (2014), and translator of such Benjamin works as *A Berlin Childhood around 1900*, *Origin of the German Trauerspiel*, and, with Kevin McLaughlin, *The Arcades Project*. He has published articles on modern literature and philosophy as well as *Notes on Literature, Film, and Jazz* (2019).

**Sami Khatib** was a Visiting Professor at the Karlsruhe University of Arts and Design (HfG) and is a founding member of the Beirut Institute for Critical Analysis and Research (BICAR). His publications include the co-edited volume *Critique: The Stakes of Form* (2020) and the book *'Teleologie ohne Endzweck': Walter Benjamins Ent-stellung des Messianischen* (2013).

**Vivian Liska** is Professor of German literature and Director of the Institute of Jewish Studies at the University of Antwerp as well as Distinguished Visiting Professor in the Faculty of the Humanities at The Hebrew University of Jerusalem. She is the (co-) editor of many books on Modernism, German Literature and German-Jewish Thought and the editing director of the book series *Perspectives on Jewish Texts and Contexts* (De Gruyter). Her books include *When Kafka Says We: Uncommon Communities in German-Jewish Literature* (2009) translated into German and Hebrew, *Giorgio Agamben's Empty Messianism* (2011), and *German-Jewish Thought and its Afterlife: A Tenuous Legacy* (2017).

**James Martel** is Professor of Political Science at San Francisco State University, USA. His books include: most recently *Anarchist Prophets: Disappointing Vision and the Power of Collective Sight* (2022); *Unburied Bodies: Subversive Corpses and the Authority of the Dead* (2018); and *The Misinterpellated Subject* (2018).

**Brendan Moran** is Professor of Philosophy at the University of Calgary. Publications include the books *Politics of Benjamin's Kafka. Philosophy as Renegade* and *Wild, Unforgettable Philosophy in Early Works of Walter Benjamin*, as well as the co-edited books *Towards the Critique of Violence: Walter Benjamin and Giorgio Agamben* and *Philosophy and Kafka*. He has also published many book chapters and articles on Benjamin, Agamben, Foucault, Laruelle, Heidegger, Levinas, Kafka, Salomo Friedlaender, and Seloua Luste Boulbina. Much of his writing focuses on philosophy and literature, political philosophy, and questions of complicity.

**Carlo Salzani** is Research Fellow in the Department of Philosophy of Innsbruck University and Guest Scholar at the Messerli Research Institute of Vienna, Austria, and Faculty Member of the Paris Institute of Critical Thinking (PICT). His research interests focus on animal studies, biopolitics and posthumanism. His recent publications include the books *Agamben and the Animal* (2022) and *Walter Benjamin and the Actuality of Critique: Essays on Violence and Experience* (2021), and the edited volumes *The Biopolitical Animal* (2024) and *Animality in Contemporary Italian Philosophy* (2020).

**Paula Schwebel** is Associate Professor of Philosophy at Toronto Metropolitan University. Her research focuses on Benjamin, twentieth-century readings of early modern political philosophy, and modern Jewish thought, subjects about which she has published several chapters and articles. She is co-editor, with Ilit Ferber, of *Lament in Jewish Thought: Philosophical, Theological and Literary Perspectives* (2014), and translator, with Sebastian Truskolaski, of the Correspondence of Theodor Adorno and Gershom Scholem (2021).

**Tamara Tagliacozzo** is Associate Professor of Moral Philosophy at the Università di Roma Tre. Her interests focus on the philosophy of Benjamin and German neo-criticism, about which she wrote her doctoral thesis, *Esperienza e compito infinito nella filosofia del primo Benjamin* (2003, 2013). She translated Benjamin's Fragments on knowledge and language into Italian (W. Benjamin, *Frammenti II. Conoscenza e linguaggio*, 2013). She co-edited with Reinier Munk and Andrea Poma the volume "Critical Idealism and Messianism: From Hermann Cohen to Walter Benjamin and Beyond," in "Paradigmi," I/2017, and she is the author of *Experience and Infinite Task: Knowledge, Language and Messianism in the Philosophy of Walter Benjamin* (2018).

**Miguel Vatter** is Professor of Politics at the Alfred Deakin Institute of Citizenship and Globalisation, Deakin University, Australia. His most recent books are *Living Law. Jewish Political Theology from Hermann Cohen to Hannah Arendt* (2021) and *Divine Democracy: Political Theology After Carl Schmitt* (2021). He is co-editor with Vanessa Lemm of *The Viral Politics of COVID-19: Nature, Home and Planetary Health* (2022).

# Index

absolute   4, 53, 95, 97, 100, 102, 106, 119, 137, 177
  decision   75, 80, 85–6
  power   27, 32, 34, 63, 65, 127
absolutism   1, 27, 31, 34, 43 nn.7–8
acedia
  Baroque concept of   45 n.26, 46 nn.31 and 34, 47 n.38
  medieval/monastic concept of   27, 34, 45 nn.25–6, 46 nn.31 and 33, 58
  and sin   7, 34
  and sovereignty   28, 30, 39
  and trauerspiel   33–5, 37–8, 169
Adam
  language of   39–42, 47 nn.40 and 42, 134
  original sin and   28–30, 32–6, 39–40, 43 n.10, 44 nn.17 and 19, 46 n.32, 58, 134
Adorno, Gretel   7
Adorno, Theodor W.   7, 19 n.21, 20 n.25, 94, 109 n.9, 112 n.22, 171 nn.5, 15 and 19, 172 n.27, 223 n.4
Agamben, Giorgio
  and adjustment   147, 218
  and anarchy   141, 149 n.18
  and Augustine   43 nn. 10–11, 44 n.19
  and bare life   2–3, 149 n.18, 139–41
  and baroque   53
  and Benjamin   2–3, 53, 99–100, 104, 107, 109 n.10, 110 nn.13–14, 136–41, 143–8, 150 n.29
  on Benjamin and Schmitt   6, 19 n.20, 20 n.23, 82, 84, 107
  on Benjamin and Scholem   133–4, 136–9, 141, 146, 149 n.19
  and biopolitics   101, 223
  and distortion   133, 217, 223
  and exception   53, 136, 139, 206, 225 n.25
  and happiness   144–5
  and inclusive exclusion   212, 223
  and justice   143–8
  and law   13, 136–7, 139–41, 143, 145, 147, 150 n.29, 206, 221
  and messianism   88 n.4, 146–8, 199, 205, 209, 210 n.6, 224 n.8, 217
  and nihilism   138–40
  and Schmitt   13, 20 n.23, 67 n.21, 53, 73, 80, 141
  and sovereign   221
  and study   13, 133, 141, 145–7
  and time   205, 209, 210 n.6, 224
  works of
    *Bartleby*   146
    *The Coming Community*   218
    *Homo Sacer*   136–7, 139–40, 212, 221
    "I am Sure That You Are More Pessimistic Than I am"   171 n.3
    *The Idea of Prose*   146
    "A Jurist Confronting Himself: Carl Schmitt's Jurisprudential Thought"   80
    *The Kingdom and the Garden*   43 nn.10–11, 44 n.19
    *The Open*   99–100, 104, 146, 148
    *Potentialities*   136–7, 139, 146–7
    *Profanations*   144, 217, 224
    *Pulcinella*   171 n.22, 223
    *State of Exception*   6, 19 n.20, 20 n.23, 53, 66 n.4, 84, 141, 143, 206
    *The Time that Remains*   3, 82, 109 n.10, 110 n.13, 148, 199, 205, 209, 210 n.6
    *The Use of Bodies*   104, 140–1
allegory   45 n.23, 59, 224 n.8
  in baroque drama   33–9, 52, 172 n.34
  in "The Metaphysics of Youth"   159, 161
  in the theses "On History"   199–200, 204

in the *Trauerspiel* book   33–9,
    45 nn.28–9, 47 nn.37 and 40, 61,
    169–70
alterity   103, 160–1, 224 n.10
ambivalence   5, 31, 52, 75–6, 79, 81–2,
    86, 104, 112 n.22
anarchism   3, 11, 114 n.34, 117–18
    Benjamin's concept of   6, 11, 13, 120,
        124, 126–7, 129–31, 179, 207
    of life   141
    Schmitt and   4
angel   36, 45 n.29, 121, 195, *see also* Satan
    fall of   34, 45 n.29
    of history   17, 218–19
    new angel   12
animal   36, 59, 61–2, 101, 222, 225 n.25
Antichrist   82, 87, 114 n.35, 205, 208
    and fascism   205–8
antinomianism   52, 61, 94, 101, 146, 164
antiquity   16, 45 n.26, 46 n.31, 66, 170
anxiety   30, 37, 65, 120
apocalypse   5, 17, 82, 107, 149 n.10,
    208–9, *see also* messianic
apocalyptic   17, 87, 99, 101, 110 n.13,
    112 n.22, 174, 195, 198, 204–5,
    207, 209
archism   13, 117–20, 123–7, 129, 131–2
Arendt, Hannah   80–1, 109 n.9, 220,
    223 n.4
Aristotle   29, 98, 109 n.11
Armin, Achim von   214
art   19 n.19, 42 n.2, 51, 136, 166, 170,
    176
astral   52, 54, 56–8, 60, 66, *see also* stars
Atger, Frédéric   42 n.2, 55
atheism   10, 13, 117–18, 120, 123–4, 126,
    131
Athens   15, 75–6, 86, 164
attentiveness   4, 5, 11–12, 83, 86, 105,
    123, 158–9, 161, 166, 170,
    213–14, 216–17, 219–22
Augustine, St.   38, 46 n.35, 47 n.37,
    149 n.10
    and acedia   34–6, 45 n.25, 46 nn.31–4
    and *felix lapsus* (fortunate fall)   99,
        106
    Genesis interpretation of   8, 39–41,
        45 nn.24 and 29, 46 n.32
    and Judaism   77–8

and original sin   28, 33–6, 43 n.10,
    44 nn.17 and 19
and politics   7–8, 28–30, 43 n.11,
    44 n.18
and psychology   34–5, 45 nn.26–7,
    46 n.30
and time   102
aura   101–3, 161
authoritarianism   1, 2, 9–10, 12, 28, 32,
    39–40, 43 n.8
authority   1–2, 5, 8, 13, 28, 30, 32–3,
    43 n.8, 73–4, 84, 108 n.7,
    118–19, 122, 127–8, 131, 141,
    142
autonomy   82, 84, 109 n.10, 150 n.29,
    181, 183–4
awakening   16, 33, 38, 47 n.38, 51, 62–3,
    65, 85, 158, 160, 164–6, 170

Baal Shem Tov (Baalschem; Rabbi Israel
    ben Eliezer)   203, 218, *see also*
    Hasidism, founder of
Babel   47 n.42, 127
Bachofen, Johann Jakob   94, 96–9, 103,
    106, 108 nn.6–8
Baer, Yitzhak Fritz   76, 78–9
baroque   7, 29, 31, 34, 37, 45 n.26,
    46 nn.31 and 34, 50, 52–5, 58,
    61, 63, 65, 87, 147, 172 n.34,
    *see also* trauerspiel
    plays   7–8, 18 n.5, 27–9, 31–3, 36–9,
        42 n.2, 47 n.37, 50–2, 54–5, 57,
        62, 67 n.23, 84, 168–70
Barth, Karl   97–9, 102, 105, 107, 108 n.5,
    109 n.9
Basilides   99–104, 107, 110 nn.14–15
Benjamin, Dora (Dora Sophie
    Kellner)   134, 224 n.14
Benjamin, Walter
    correspondence of
        with Blaupot, Anna Maria (draft
            letter of 1933)   143–4, 157
        with Rang, Florens Christian
            (December 9, 1923)   104
        with Schmitt (1930)   6–7,
            19 nn.19–21, 20 n.23, 42 n.2, 82,
            84, 88 n.9
        with Scholem (August 11,
            1934)   138, 140, 216, 224 n.8

with Scholem (of general
significance)   66 n.5, 85, 136,
166, 188 n.11, 191 n.26
with Strauss, Ludwig (1913)   188
with Thieme, Karl (1939)   109 n.9
and Schmitt
on decisionism   6, 16, 27, 73, 82,
85–6, 157, 166, 171 n.12
on exception   6–9, 17, 27, 32,
50–1, 53, 55, 65, 73, 82, 86–7,
148, 206–7, 213, 221–3
relationship to and differences
from   1–9, 13–14, 17, 19 n.19,
20 n.23, 42 n.2, 73–4, 81–3, 88,
133–4, 160
on sovereignty   7–8, 27–8, 31–2,
34–5, 39, 41–2, 42 n.2, 50, 53,
82, 84–5, 128
on trauerspiel and tragedy   54–6,
60, 64, 169–70, 172 nn.39–40
writings of
*Arcades Project*   14, 66 n.7, 157,
171 n.9, 197, 204–8, 212
"Berlin Childhood
around   1900"   213–16
on Brecht   10, 94, 101, 112 n.20,
141, 207
"Calderón's *El Mayor Monstruo, Los
Celos* and Hebbel's *Herodes und
Mariamne*"   165–7
"Capitalism as Religion"   2, 82,
207
*The Concept of Art Criticism in
German Romanticism*   203
"On the Concept of History"   9–
11, 14, 17, 61, 83, 87, 135–7,
170, 177–80, 182, 186, 187 n.9,
195–202, 204–9, 212–13
"The Crisis of the Novel"   158
"Curriculum Vitae (III)"
(1928)   19 n.19, 42 n.2
"Epistemo-Critical Foreword"   5,
47 n.40, 188 n.11
"Fate and Character"   134, 163–6,
171 nn.22 and 25, 172 n.35,
188 n.11
"Franz Kafka" (1934)   18, 51,
86, 94, 107, 107 n.2, 113 n.27,
118–20, 122–4, 126, 130, 134,
138, 141–3, 146–8, 196–7,
214–17, 219–20, 222
"Goethe's Elective Affinities"   136,
144, 148, 165, 171 n.24, 201
"Ibiza Sequence"   172 n.28
"The Infinite Task"   191 n.26
"Johann Jakob Bachofen"   94, 96,
103, 106
"Julian Green"   171 n.25, 172 n.33
Kafka (Benjamin's other writings
on)   135, 142–3, 146–8, 197,
219–20, 222
"Karl Kraus"   12, 224 n.7
"On Language as Such and on the
Language of the Human"   5,
40–1, 47 nn.39–40 and 42, 134
"The Life of Students"   14, 175,
178, 180, 187 n.1
"On Love and Related
Matters"   107, 113 n.24
"The Metaphysics of Youth"   159–
62, 165
"Moral Education"   164–5
"Notes (IV)"   82
Notes on "the category of justice"
(1916)   11
*One-Way Street*   66, 167, 208
*Origin of the German
Trauerspiel*   5–6, 8, 12, 15,
19 n.22, 27–9, 31–42, 44 nn.19
and 21, 45 nn.26 and 28–29,
46 nn.31 and 33–6, 47 nn.37
and 40, 50–8, 61, 65, 68 nn.34
and 45, 69 n.52, 84, 86–7, 128,
136, 150 n.27, 162, 165, 167–70,
172 n.34
Paralipomena to the theses "On the
Concept of History"   111 n.17,
171 n.9, 225 n.21
*Politik*   9
"On the Problem of Physiognomics
and Foretelling"   163
"On the Program of the Coming
Philosophy"   176
"Rastelli's Story"   213
Review of Bernoulli's
*Bachofen*   108 n.6
Review of Green's *Adrienne
Mesurat*   171 n.25

"The Role of Language in Trauerspiel and Tragedy" 41, 47 n.40
"Schemata concerning the Psychophysical Problem" 165–6, 169
"Sleeping Beauty" 169
"In the Sun" ["In der Sonne"] (1932) 148, 196, 217
"Surrealism" 136
"The Task of the Translator" 137, 218
"Theological-Political Fragment" 4–5, 11–12, 43 n.12, 61, 83, 93–4, 96, 98–102, 107, 109 n.10, 112 n.22, 144–6, 166, 186, 187 n.8, 197, 203–4
"Theory of Knowledge" 187 n.2
"Toward the Critique of Violence" 2, 9–11, 15, 84–5, 88 n.11, 105, 111 n.17, 114 n.31, 119–21, 125–6, 130–1, 134, 140, 164, 206
"*Trauerspiel* and Tragedy" 175
"Two Poems by Friedrich Hölderlin" 112 n.18, 162, 171 n.16
"Unpacking my Library" 172 n.33
"World and Time" 101, 107, 108 nn.3–4
"Zweideutigkeit des Begriffs der 'unendlichen Aufgabe' in der kantischen Schule" 89 n.12, 189 n.20
Bergson, Henri 54–5, 159–60
Bertaux, Félix 197, 221
Bible/biblical 16, 47 n.42, 63, 84, 95, 109 n.12, 159, 170, 175, 179, 186, 189 n.19
biopolitics 12, 17, 74, 101, 107, 212–13, 221–3, 225 n.26
Bloch, Ernst 51, 96, 98, 107, 107 n.2, 108 n.5, 109 n.9, 149 n.10, 187 n.8, 224 n.14
and messianic adjustment 196, 217–18
*Spirit of Utopia* 11–12, 93–5, 101, 105, 203

Blumenberg, Hans 19 n.15
bodily presence of mind (*leibhaftige Geistesgegenwart*) 86, 167
body 32, 37, 46 n.34, 51, 94, 98, 103, 112 n.22, 120, 125, 164–5, 216, 222–3
Brecht, Bertolt 10, 81, 94, 101, 112 n.20, 138, 141, 207
Brentano, Clemens 214
Brod, Max 148, 220
Buber, Martin 12, 107
Butler, Judith 3, 18 n.10

Cain 37, 77, 110 n.12
Calderón, de la Barca Pedro 7–8, 51–2, 54, 56, 58–65, 165–9
Calvinism 52, 59
capitalism 2, 11, 67 n.23, 82, 118–19, 125, 207–8
Carnot, Sadi 105
Cassian, John 45 n.25
catastrophe 51, 53–4, 127, 182, 205–9
Catholicism 55, 57, 76, 82
Causality 57, 163–6, 168, 170, 171 n.17, 207
Cavarero, Adriana 219, 221
chaos 4–5, 29, 40, 103, 108
  *tohu va-vohu* 103
chess automaton 83–4, 199–202, 204–5, 209, *see also* Poe, Edgar Allan
  in "Maelzel's Chess Player" 201–2, 214
childhood 159, 214
Christ 9, 29, 36–7, 43 n.14, 47 n.37, 76–7, 188 n.14, 205
Christian 30, 45 n.29, 52, 58, 60, 78, 80, 99, 169, 188 n.14, 205
  dogma 136
  eschatology 15, 18 n.5, 181, 187 n.8
  love and mercy 36, 38–9, 64, 77
  martyrdom 9, 37, 78–9, 170
  political theology 3, 79–80
  sin, concept of 15, 18 n.5, 57
  triumphalism 3, 6, 9, 76–8, 80–2
Christianity 4, 58, 64, 68 n.33, 77, 79, 97, 108 n.5, 162, 205
Church 29–30, 36, 52, 76–7, 117, 122
class 171
  classless society 14, 111 n.17, 178–9, 209

conflict 11
  and hierarchy 111 n.17
  oppressed 64, 205
  ruling 178, 198, 207
  struggle 111 n.17
Clausius, Rudolf 105, 113 n.29
Cohen, Hermann 3, 15
  death of 190 n.21
  ethics 16–17, 163, 174, 176, 180, 182–6, 190 n.25
  infinite task, concept of 178, 182, 184, 189 n.20
  influence on Benjamin 15–17, 163, 174, 176–8, 181–2, 188 n.11, 189 n.19, 190 n.22
  Judaism of 15–16, 174, 181, 183, 186, 190 n.21
  logic 176, 182, 188 n.11, 190 n.21
  philosophy of religion 178–9, 185, 188 n.11, 190 n.21
  system of philosophy 176–7, 189 n.19
command/commandment 1, 5, 29, 35, 39–41, 125–6, 130, 139, 143, 178, 207
communism 51–2, 66, 96, 106, 207
  Communist Party 85
  Marxist-Leninist 108 n.7
  primitive 96, 99, 103, 106, 108 n.7
conscience 60, 158, 162, 170, 185
constellation 37–8, 77, 96–7, 102, 162, 168, 170, 171 n.17, 177, 197–8, 215–16
contingency 4, 10, 15, 63, 109 n.12, 112 n.21, 157, 168–9, 177, 186
conversation 73–4, 159–62, 171 n.12
cosmology 3, 8, 51, 53–7, 99, 108 n.5
Counter-Reformation 3, 8, 52, 168
court
  divine 134–6, 142
  of law 142, 215
  royal 28, 33, 45 n.28, 55–6, 60, 62, 65, 129
  summary 135–6
covenant, covenantal 77, 84
creation 4, 45 n.26, 55, 95, 97–8, 103, 105–6, 110 nn.13 and 15, 111 n.17, 146, 176, 181, 221, 225 n.25

fallen 8, 28, 30–5, 37–8, 40–1, 45 n.29, 46 n.35, 56, 99, 105–6, 109 n.10, 146, 216, 222
  Genesis story of 29, 32–3, 35–6, 39–41, 45 n.29
  innocence of 8, 28, 31–2, 35, 38–9, 41–2, 44 n.20, 56
  order of 28–9, 32, 35, 39–42
  state of 8, 31–2, 35, 38, 45 n.26, 54, 56, 58
creature 31, 33–6, 40–1, 44 n.19, 81, 84, 104, 108 n.8, 130, 214–15, 217, 220–2, 225 n.19
  sovereign as 31, 84
creaturely 15, 31, 33, 35, 38–9, 44 nn.16 and 19, 50, 57, 84, 95–7, 99, 105, 146, 164, 213, 216, 221–3

damnation 29–30, 43 n.11, 44 n.17
danger 43 n.9, 85–6, 101, 112 n.18, 130, 146, 205
  moment of 82, 87, 208
death 51, 87, 97–8, 101–2, 106, 112 nn.18 and 22, 113 n.27, 119, 125, 189 n.19, 190 n.21, 191 n.30, 205
  Christ's 9, 36–7
  and entropy 104–5
  and expiation/redemption 35–8
  and fate 145, 159, 161–2, 165, 168–9, 171 n.16
  of God 222
  and martyrdom 78–9
  not to be lamented 97, 106, 112 n.22
  and sin 29, 31, 36, 39, 43 n.10, 44 nn.17 and 19
  sovereign's 36–8, 67 n.22
debt 15, 84, 161, 163, 207, 218
decision 65, 81, 129, 131, 133, 136, 171 n.12, 206, 221
  and Schmitt 3, 5, 7–8, 16, 27, 43 n.6, 50, 67 n.23, 75–7, 79–81, 85–6, 207
  sovereign's incapability of 7, 27, 35, 50, 84–6
  and Strauss (Leo) 75–6, 79–80
decisionism 6, 27, 42 n.4, 73, 81, 82, 85–6, 157, 166, 171 n.12
deconstruction 16, 74, 164, 166

deferral 74, 80, 86, 95
democracy 1, 3, 14, 73-4, 108 n.7,
    113 n.25, 118, 178, 187 n.9, 214
Democritus 190 n.23
demon 12, 34, 45 n.29, 47 n.38
    demonic 15, 34, 37-8, 45 n.26,
        46 n.31, 163-5, 170
    demonology 162
Derrida, Jacques 2, 74, 85, 88 n.4,
    113 n.25, 172 n.41
Descartes, René 55
destruction 13, 51, 106, 108 n.3, 110 n.15,
    112 n.21, 130, 162, 165-6, 182
    and justice 11-12
    and mortality 96-7
    and nihilism 6, 12
    and political action 182, 196-8, 208
    and transience 102-4, 109 n.10
devil 34, 37, 57, see also Satan
dialectic 51, 81-2, 95, 136, 141, 159, 162,
    166, 169, 176, 182, 206, 224 n.9
dialectical 16, 51, 63, 65, 68 n.34, 73, 81-
    3, 86, 95, 99, 109 n.9, 114 n.31,
    157-60, 170, 182, 221
    image 16, 28, 34-6, 39, 170, 186,
        198
    leap 178, 198
    reflection 51, 60-1, 64, 157, 167
diary 159-62
    as daybook (*Tagebuch*) 159
dictatorship 7, 18 n.3, 32-3, 87,
    171 n.12, 207
distortion (*Entstellung*) 13, 17, 80,
    124-5, 133, 147-8, 197, 202,
    212-17, 219-22, 224 n.9
    disappearance of 18, 148, 221,
        225 n.19
    etymology of 215, 219
    Freudian roots of 215, 221, 224 n.6
        (*see also* Freud)
    redemptive role of 13, 133, 213,
        216-17, 219-23, 224 nn.11-12
divination 167
divine 10, 38, 50, 55, 57, 59, 61, 75, 94-6,
    98, 106-7, 108 n.4, 110 n.13,
    121, 126, 128-30, 142, 176
    and atheism 13, 131
    justice/judgment 12, 31, 33, 39, 84,
        134-5

madness 45 n.26, 46 n.31 (*see also*
    melancholy)
power 38, 108 n.3, 131
providence 32, 57
punishment 28, 30, 38
and sovereignty 8, 31, 83-4
violence 64, 84-5, 88 n.11, 119-21,
    123-5, 128, 131, 206 (*see also*
    "Critique of Violence")
and writing 61, 143
domination 7, 10, 12-14, 28-9, 33,
    42, 57, 108 n.3, 117, 119, 133,
    136-7, 140-1, 197
dominion 29-30, 33-4, 36, 40-1,
    43 n.14
downfall 61, 95, 97-100, 102, 107,
    144-5, 171 n.15, 186
drama 35, 37, 50-2, 54-5, 64, 95, 124,
    158, 165-70
dream 37, 47 n.38, 51, 124, 162, 166,
    170, 222
    and *Arcades Project* 66 n.7, 157, 197
    and Calderón 51, 60-5
    demonic 34, 37, 46 n.31
    Freud's theory of 68 n.45, 215,
        224 n.6
    interpretation of 68 n.46, 197
    Marx and 51
    prophetic 36, 63
Dürer, Albrecht 58, 169
"dwarf" 17, 83, 195, 213-14, *see also*
    "hunchback"
    "dwarf"-like theology 17, 83, 195,
        199-202, 204, 212-14
    hump of 202, 213-14, 217, 219, 223

early modern 16, 28, 52, 58, 162, 170
earth 30, 46 n.34, 53, 56, 59, 66, 77, 98,
    102, 104, 112 n.22, 113 n.29,
    119, 135, 181
    heaven on 52, 82, 175-6
    justice on 83, 175-6, 179-80, 184-5
earthly 38, 57, 128, 180-1, 187 n.8,
    189 n.19, 191 n.30, *see also*
    profane, temporal, worldly
    city 29-30
    desires 34, 45 n.26
    downfall of 97, 144
    things 34-5, 45 n.26, 46 n.35

emergency, state of  1, 9, 17, 18 n.3, 27,
    86–7, 111 n.17, 148, 206–8, 213,
    221–2, *see also* exception
  real  18, 111 n.17, 213, 221
  revolution and  85, 111 n.17, 208
  sovereignty and  207
enemy  43 n.9, 81, 103, 124, 136, 161–2,
    170, 205
enlightenment  82, 84, 125, 198
entelechy  57, 162–3, 166, 168, 171 n.19
entropy  3, 10, 12, 93, 99–101, 104–5,
    107, 113 n.29, 114 n.30
eschatology  3, 15, 17, 18 n.5, 51–4, 58,
    87, 96, 169, 174, 180–2, 186,
    187 n.8, 189 n.19, 190 n.22, 202
eschaton  180, 189 n.19, 202–3
eternal  15, 29, 34, 97, 99, 102, 129, 167,
    184–5, 203, 209
  forms  103
  God as  34–5, 179
  life  36, 38
  peace  106
  punishment  29, 36, 38–9
  return  59, 165
  transience  12, 61, 94–6, 98–9, 107,
    109 n.10, 145, 162, 167, 197
eternity  61, 95, 99–100, 102–3, 145, 179,
    183–6, 191 n.30, 197
ethics/ethical  5, 8, 11, 56, 80, 160,
    171 nn.22 and 24, 223
  and Cohen  16, 163, 174–6, 178, 181–
    6, 187 n.1, 188 n.10, 189 n.19,
    190 n.25, 191 nn.26–7
Evagrius, Ponticus  45 n.25, 46 nn.31 and
    33
Eve  33, 35, 39–40, 46 n.32, 134, *see also*
    Adam
evil  33–4, 38, 40–1, 43 nn.8–9, 47 n.39,
    50, 98, 100, 105, 113 n.26, 134,
    170, 176
  theology of  167, 169
exception  11, 32, 40, 77, 87, 111 n.17,
    122–4, 137, 139, 207, 213, 220–2
  logic of  212–13, 222–3, 225 n.25
  permanent  114, 139
  real  51, 206–7
  sovereign  17, 128, 141, 213, 221
  state of  62, 222, 225 n.25 (*see also*
    emergency, state of)

and Agamben  3, 53, 136, 139,
    141, 206
and Benjamin  3, 51, 53, 65, 82,
    206–8
and Schmitt  1, 3–8, 18 n.3, 27, 32,
    43 n.6, 50, 53, 55, 73, 82, 87, 206
exile  76–80, 88 n.5, 120, 157, *see also*
    *galut*
Exodus  95, 97, 105, 113 n.29
expression  17, 40–1, 47 n.41, 53, 78, 87,
    118, 123, 131–2, 135, 162, 167,
    171 n.8, 185, 224 n.6
  and art  19 n.19, 112 n.22, 167
  blocked  30, 33, 39–42, 44 n.16
  of creation  33, 39–42
  of God  39, 45 n.26, 105
  of suffering  41–2
externality  119, 122–3, 125, 129–31, 168

faith  15, 29–30, 33, 38, 50, 52–3, 56–7,
    74–7, 79, 113 n.29, 160, 175
fall/fallen  8, 28–42, 44 n.19, 46 n.35,
    47 n.38, 82, 94, 97, 99, 101, 103–
    4, 106–7, 110 n.13, 172 n.34, 207
  angelic  34, 45 n.29 (*see also* Satan)
  creation  8, 28, 30–5, 37–8, 40–1,
    45 n.29, 46 n.35, 56, 99, 105–6,
    109 n.10, 146, 216, 222
  happy (*felix lapsus*)  99, 102–3, 106,
    144, 186
  of language  39–41, 47 nn.40 and 42
fantasy  123, 125–6, *see also* phantasm;
    phantasmagoria
fascism  9, 84, 108 n.7, 118–19, 205–8
fate  157–70, 171 n.22, 172 nn.33 and 35
  astral determinism and  56–60, 63
  demonic  15, 164
  drama of  35, 50–2, 54–5, 57, 166–9,
    172 n.32
  and guilt  16, 35, 54, 57, 150 n.31,
    164, 172 n.27
  of the Jewish people  75, 77, 79, 82
  and myth  10–12, 129, 148
  overcoming of  134, 143–4, 148,
    150 n.29
  and sin  68 n.27
  and time  6, 15–16, 136, 145–6, 157,
    160–1, 163–4, 171 nn.16 and 25,
    172 n.41

Ficino, Marsilio  46 n.34, 58
finitude  96–7, 102–3, 112 n.18, 113 n.27, see also death; mortality
Fitzralph, Richard  29, 43 n.13
flesh  29, 35–8, 97–8, 103–4, 125
force  5, 11, 17, 74, 100, 106, 110 n.13, 142, 145, 147, 168, 175, 202–3, 217, 224 n.6
 coercive  5, 12, 59–60
 and law  2, 137, 139–41, 143, 206–7
 and love  35, 45 n.26, 144
 messianic  82, 86, 135, 147, 183, 196, 198, 204, 217, 222
 opposed  98, 106, 144, 158, 204 (see also "Theological-Political Fragment")
 revelatory  136–7
 revolutionary  64
 and theology  83–4
 and violence  84, 114 n.31, 119
forgetting  77, 103, 123, 145, 205, 214, 216, 217, 219, 220, see also guilt; inattentiveness; oblivion
forgiveness  64, 65, 110 n.13
Foucault, Michel  101, 143, 219
freedom  5, 12, 38, 52, 60, 63–4, 80, 83, 101, 113 n.29, 147, 166, 191 n.26, 217, 220
 Adam's  29, 35, 43 n.14, 44 n.19
 and anarchy  127, 129, 140–1
 and fate  15–16, 50, 143, 145, 157–8, 164–6
 and happiness  96, 98–9, 102–3, 147, 204
 and love  96, 102–3, 106, 143
 and messianism  196, 208, 217, 222
 and play  170, 220
 and sovereignty  27, 32
 and study  13, 133, 143, 147, 170
Freud, Sigmund  215, 221
 and dreams  68 n.45, 224 n.6
 and melancholy  44 n.21, 52
 and repression  225 n.26
future  2, 60, 63, 81, 105, 113 n.24, 118, 125, 146
 and eternity  184–5
 and hope  190 n.25
 and messianism  16, 83, 175–6, 179–83, 185–6, 189 n.19, 190 n.22, 191 n.27, 202–3
 and progress  214
 and time of fate  161, 163–4, 167, 170, 172 n.41

*galut*  76–8, 88 n.5, see also exile
gateway  120, 122
 of justice  127, 141–5, 147
 of a new happiness  144–5
 through which the Messiah enters  182, 186, 202, 204–5, 209
Genesis  14, 43, 45 n.29
 Augustine's interpretation of  8, 34, 39–41, 45 n.24
 Benjamin's interpretation of  8, 39, 41, 45 n.29, 82
 creation story  8, 34, 40, 43 n.14, 45 n.29
 symbolism of the tree of knowledge  33, 39, 41, 134
German
 folklore  214
 folksong  147, 216
 German-Jewish  9, 73, 76, 88
Giehlow, Karl  46 n.33
Gnosticism  95, 98–100, 104–5, 107, 108 n.5, 110 n.14, 111 n.17, 113 n.29
God  52, 61, 80, 81, 85, 109 n.12, 110 n.15, 119, 125, 134, 136, 207
 and archism  120
 and atheism  117–18, 123, 126, 131
 and Augustine  29–30, 33–6, 38–41, 44 nn.17–19, 46 nn.30 and 32–5, 47 n.37, 102
 and Barth  97, 108 n.5, 109 n.9
 and Bloch  95, 108 n.5, 109 n.9
 and Cohen  179, 181
 and expression  39, 41, 47 n.42
 and hierarchy  10, 13, 118, 130
 and incarnation  36, 76, 84
 and justice  8, 11, 32
 and Kafka  123, 125, 127–8, 142, 222
 kingdom of  83, 94, 181, 203–4
 and Luther  30, 44 n.18, 47 n.37, 52
 and Mainländer  105–6
 and Marcion  95, 113 n.29
 and messianism  96, 112 n.19, 175, 203–4

and miracles   32, 43 n.6, 54
pagan   58, 164 (*see also* gods)
and Paul   44 n.18, 46 n.32
and sin   8, 28, 30–1, 33–5, 39, 44 n.17
and sovereignty   1, 4, 7, 28, 31–2,
    34–5, 38, 39, 43 n.6, 53, 55, 63, 84
and trauerspiel   37–8, 47 n.37, 50, 169
gods   15, 45 n.29, 81, 100, 104, 107 n.1,
    119, 164
Goethe, Johann Wolfgang von   164
Golden Age   58, 96–7
good   8, 11, 16, 29, 39, 44 n.19, 59–60,
    62, 106, 164, 189 n.18
and evil   33, 40–1, 43 nn.8–9, 44 n.18,
    134
fortune   97–9, 102, 157, 170 n.1, 177
and happiness   109 n.11
and material   125
Platonic idea of   34
will   60, 157
works   50, 52, 57, 60, 64, 68 n.28, 94,
    107, 176
grace   8, 36
fall from   8, 33–4, 45 n.29, 54, 56
God's   29, 34–5, 38–40, 44 n.17,
    47 n.37, 50, 57–8, 62, 86, 169
Gregory the Great   45 n.25
Gryphius, Andreas   36–7, 47 n.38
guilt   45 n.21, 80, 215, 224 n.7
and atonement   15, 37–8, 166
creation and   8, 28, 31–5, 37–9
creaturely   33, 44 n.19, 57, 216
forgetfulness and   216, 219–20 (*see also* inattentiveness; oblivion)
guilt-context   15–16, 18 n.5, 162–5,
    172 n.27
history and   54 (*see also* history)
inherited   15–16, 164
and life   35–6, 50, 52
natural   44 n.19, 134, 164, 168,
    171 n.24
original sin and   31, 33, 57, 60

Haggadah   86
Halakhah   86, 136, 141–2
Hamlet (and *Hamlet*)   12, 50, 55–6, 64,
    66 n.2, 67 nn.22 and 25, 162,
    168–70, 172 nn.36 and 41,
    *see also* Shakespeare

happiness (*Glück*)   220
and fate   144, 157, 164
and justice   12, 83, 144–6
paradisiacal   29–30
and politics   29, 98, 107, 109 n.11,
    145, 204
and redemption   177, 187 n.8
and study   144–7
in the "Theologico-Political
    Fragment"   43 n.12, 61, 83,
    93–100, 102, 107, 144–5, 186,
    187 n.8
and transience   11, 61, 94, 96, 99–100,
    107, 109 n.10, 144–5
Harnack, Adolf von   108 n.5, 114 n.29
Hasidim   124, 218, *see also* Baal Shem
    Tov
in Benjamin's "In the Sun"   148, 196,
    217
founder, Baal Shem Tov (Rabbi Israel
    ben Eliezer)   218
heaven   38, 44 n.15, 51–3, 82, 180–1,
    188 n.14, 203
Hebbel, Christian Friedrich   165–7
Hegel, G. W. F.   81, 93, 96–9, 101–3,
    108 n.5, 111 n.17, 112 n.21, 161,
    209 n.4, 221
hell   29, 34, 38, 45 nn.28–9, 207
Helmholtz, Hermann von   105, 114 n.29
hierarchy, hierarchical   10, 13, 40–1,
    47 n.42, 52, 108 n.8, 111 n.17,
    117–19, 121, 128, 130, 222
Hindenburg, Paul von   1, 18 n.3
historian   78, 83, 179, 197–8, 205, 208,
    225 n.21
task of   197–8, 205, 221
historiography
conventional   15, 166, 197
drama   166–7
epic   158
event   54, 178
historical   29, 36, 50, 66 n.7, 67 nn.15
    and 17, 73, 77, 99, 114 n.31, 118,
    119, 141, 142, 161–4, 171 n.9,
    182, 185–6, 191 nn.27 and 30,
    197–8, 205, 208
historicist   167, 170, 178, 187 n.9, 197,
    198, 214
justice   5, 164

materialist   14, 16, 51, 84, 170, 179,
    187 n.9, 197, 199–201, 204, 208,
    212, 223 n.2
official   114 n.31, 197
perception/understanding   51, 61,
    164, 197, 201, 204
process   55, 179
progress   54, 56, 58, 61, 83, 99,
    107 n.2, 111 n.17, 178, 198
reality   51, 55–6, 60, 76, 169–70
relation to the messianic of the   83,
    94–6, 98, 101, 175–6, 181
situation   10, 14
task   177, 182, 186, 197–8, 205,
    225 n.21
time   14, 16, 58, 147, 158–9, 178,
    188 n.12, 202
history   1, 7, 118, 123
    adjustment of   196–7
    and allegory   61, 172 n.34, 199–201
    battlefield of   202, 204, 209
    biblical, prophetic   175, 179, 181–2
    and catastrophe   51, 54, 205–6
    citation of   197–8
    claim of   2
    continuum of   158, 182, 188 n.9, 198,
        208
    and danger   87, 208
    end of   4, 82–3, 87, 96–8, 101, 135,
        180, 189 n.19, 198
    errancy of   95, 103–4, 111 n.17
    and eternity   184–5
    and fate   50–1, 55–6, 136, 158, 167
    fulfilment of   175–7, 179
    God's action in   31–2
    guilt and   16, 44 n.19, 163
    human action in   183
    Judaism and   9, 17, 74–5, 77–9, 83,
        174–5, 179, 186, 196
    messianic and   14–15, 17, 31–2, 82–3,
        94–5, 104, 108 n.5, 135, 174–5,
        179, 182, 184, 186, 187 nn.3–4,
        189 n.19, 199, 209
    natural   5, 16, 44 n.19, 54–5, 61,
        67 n.18, 95, 99, 158, 163, 165–8,
        171 n.18, 180, 190 n.25
    philosophy of   3, 184, 189 n.19
    politics of   50, 197, 201–2
    pre-   103 (see also Kafka, Vorwelt)

representation of   5, 14, 38, 42, 50,
    52, 54–5, 67 n.15, 76, 179–80,
    198, 205
and revolution   85, 111 n.17, 178, 208–9
salvation (Heilsgeschichte)   4, 33,
    36–7, 55, 175
and Schmitt   5, 19 n.17, 82, 87
    (see also katechon)
secular   8, 36, 46 n.36, 61, 199, 204
spatialization of   46 n.36, 53–4, 58
theatre and   54–5, 58
universal   17, 185
victorious   11, 197
world-   111 n.17, 163, 172 n.34
Hitler, Adolf   73, 87
Hobbes, Thomas   43 n.8, 55, 67 n.20, 77
Hofmannsthal, Hugo von   65, 69 n.52,
    225 n.21
Hölderlin, Friedrich   101, 104, 112 n.18,
    161–2, 171 n.16
hope   51, 58, 62, 86, 95–6, 99–100, 105,
    107, 107 n.2, 109 n.9, 113 n.27,
    129, 135, 158, 181, 190 n.25,
    205, see also Bloch
    for the hopeless   112 n.19, 148
    principle of   12, 93, 101
    in reverse   12–13, 93–4, 107
humanity, humankind   12, 15, 29,
    47 n.37, 56, 101, 106, 111 n.17,
    113 n.27, 135, 164, 169, 196,
    205, 217
    Cohen's idea of   174, 180–6,
        189 nn.19–20, 190 n.25,
        191 n.26
    fallen/guilty   8, 28–30, 32, 34, 36, 40,
        44 n.19
    free   98, 158, 204
    good or evil by nature   43 nn.8–9
    and happiness   98, 204
    languages of   40–1, 47 nn.40–2
    position in the order of creation   36–
        7, 40
    and redemption   36–7, 198, 203
    revolutionary work of   203–4
    subjection of   28, 44 n.16
    unimproved   101
    uprightness of   219, 222
"hunchback"   195, 219–20, 222–3,
    225 n.18, see also "dwarf"

back, the   17, 148, 202, 218
disappearing   147–8, 217, 219
"hunchbacked" possibilities   17, 213–14, 223 n.4
"hunchbacked" theology   17–18, 150 n.33, 196, 199, 204, 212–14 (*see also* "dwarf"-like theology)
and Mr. Clumsy   214, 216
and Pulcinella   223

idea   14, 175, 177–80
 regulative   16, 176–8, 180–4, 186, 187 n.8, 190 n.25, 191, 195, 198
idealism   3, 60, 180, 182, 184–5, 188 nn.10 and 13, 190 n.25, 197, 210 n.6, 219
idolatry   35, 143, 150 n.29
image   12, 33, 37, 47 n.37, 78, 85, 98, 162, 169–70, 175, 180, 185, 195, 204, 212
 apocalyptic   205, 207
 of the chess automaton   199–202
 and constellation   177, 197
 dialectical-   16, 28, 34–6, 39, 170, 176, 186, 198
 dream   197
 graven   143
 of history   46 n.36, 54–6, 61, 67 n.16, 87, 175, 178, 182, 197
 Kafka's   138, 142–3, 215, 224 n.5
 of melancholy   58 (*see also* Dürer)
 of sovereignty   7, 27–8, 31, 34–6, 39
 thought- (*Denkbild*)   17, 84, 166, 195–7, 199–200
 of unredeemed world   14, 38
immanence/immanent   37, 53, 56, 82, 96, 104, 145, 162, 166, 175–7, 184–5
 alterity of the self   157, 160
 frame   52
 negation   98–9
 order   5, 29, 40–1, 53
 and transcendence   8, 98
 world   8, 38, 101, 104
immortality   94–103, 110 n.15, 112 n.22, 113 n.27, 145, 159–60, 162, 167, 179–80, 185, 188 n.15, 189 n.18, 197

inattentiveness   213–14, 217, *see also* attentiveness; forgetting; guilt; oblivion
indecision   27–8, 35, 50, 75, 81–2, 86, 128, *see also* decision; decisionism; sovereign
infinite   47 n.42, 78, 102–3, 105, 128, 139–40, 172 n.34, 180–1, 183–6, 189 n.20, 203, 209
 abyss   34, 45 n.26
 aporia   74
 bad   64, 209
 development/progress   175, 178, 180, 189 n.18
 hope   51, 107 n.2, 148
 reflection   60
 task   16, 85, 178, 182, 184, 188 n.15, 189 n.20, 190 n.25, 191 n.26
 universe   53, 56
infinitesimal   182–3
injustice   5, 8–11, 31, 33, 39, 82
innocence   8, 16, 28, 32–3, 39, 44 n.20, 80, 107 n.1, 164, 223

Jerusalem   75–6, 86, 106
Jesus   9, 77–8, *see also* Christ
Jewish/Jews   6–7, 9, 12, 15, 66, 73–84, 86, 88, 94, 109 n.9, 110 n.12, 120, 124, 136, 179, 181, 186, 190 n.21, 202, *see also* messianism, Judaic
 Christian violence against   77–8
 folklore   120, 123
 martyrdom   9, 78–9, 81–2, 87
 messianism   14–18, 93–4, 101, 114 n.30, 174–5, 179, 186
Jonas, Hans   109 n.9
Judaism   12, 14, 16–17, 77, 79, 84, 87, 174–5, 179, 182, 186, 190 n.21, 218, *see also* galut
 chosenness and   75, 78
 denial of Christ and   77
 exilic   9, 76–80, 88 n.5, 120
 political theology and   75, 79–81, 88
 rabbinic   76, 86
judgment   125, 149 n.10, 182, 190 n.23
 Day of   5, 29, 95, 110 n.13, 135–6, 190 n.21 (*see also* Last Judgment)

divine  97, 134
    of good and evil  38–41
    human  8, 39, 121, 130, 135–6
    legal  134 (*see also* Law)
Jupiter  58–9, 62, 65
justice  2, 4–5, 10–12, 14, 16, 36, 40, 59, 96, 100, 134, 136, 142–3, 157–8, 164, 167, 180, 182
    and adjustment  219
    divine  8, 10–12, 30–3, 39, 84, 97, 131
    and happiness  12, 144–5
    historical  5, 30, 186
    lack of  9, 14, 82–3
    and law  12, 62, 79, 134, 143
    and messianism  9, 14, 16, 29, 83, 174–83, 185–6, 218
    and myth  10–11, 142
    and punishment  8, 29–33, 36, 39, 150 n.31, 172 n.36
    and rectification  219
    social  9, 14, 158
    and sovereignty  85, 87
    and study  3, 6, 12–13, 127, 133, 141–8
    and time  11, 13, 133
    and truth  170
    and *Tzedakah*  9, 79

Kabbalah  16, 82, 175–6, 187 n.4, 196, 217–19, 225 n.16
Kafka, Franz
    Agamben's reading of  88 n.4, 136–7, 139–41, 143–4, 224 n.8
    Benjamin's reading of  13, 18, 86, 94, 107 n.2, 118–31, 134–5, 138, 140–3, 146–8, 196–7, 202, 213–17, 219–20, 222 (*see also* Benjamin, writings of)
    concept of law  3, 135–41 (*see also* law, Kafka's concept of)
    and hope  51, 86, 93–4, 107 n.2, 135, 148
    K.  120–2, 139, 143, 147
    Kafkan creatures/figures  148, 215, 220–1
    Kafkan politics  10, 111 n.17
    letter to Felice Bauer (March 3, 1915)  222
    and messianism  3, 18, 88 n.4, 111 n.16, 124, 129, 147–8, 202–3, 216–17, 220 (*see also* messianism, Kafka's)
    Odradek  215, 223
    and reversal [*Umkehr*]  140, 216, 224 n.8
    Sancho Panza  140, 219, 225 n.18
    Scholem's reading of  136–8, 140–2, 147
    and students/study  126–7, 129, 141–2, 146
    "Untrammeled happy journey"  124, 127, 129, 131, 146–7
    *Vorwelt* (prehistoric world)  103, 108 n.8, 111 n.17, 113 n.27, 147, 215
    writings
        "Before the Law"  88 n.4, 141
        "The Bucket Rider"  142, 149 n.20
        "Building the Great Wall of China"  127–9
        "The Cares of a Family Man"  215
        *The Castle*  120–3, 126, 139–40
        "A Crossbreed"  215
        "The Hunter Gracchus"  103, 113 n.27
        *The Metamorphosis*  215
        "The Nature Theatre of Oklahoma"  220–1
        "The New Lawyer"  142, 144, 219, 225 n.18
        "In the Penal Colony"  215–16
        *The Trial*  127, 141–2, 147
*kairos*  160, 209, *see also* time, kairological
Kant, Immanuel  3, 85, 89 n.12, 176–7, 179, 182, 187 n.7, 188 nn.10 and 15, 189 n.18
*Katechon*  5, 19 n.18, 82, 87, 107, 114 n.35
key  140–1, 178, 188 n.14
*khora*  103, 113 n.25
Kierkegaard, Soren  134
kingdom
    of Christ  29
    of David  174, 179
    of freedom  196, 217
    of god (heaven, divine)  30, 52, 82, 83, 94, 181, 188 n.14, 191 n.27, 203, 204

of grace  8
of justice  178–9
messianic  98, 100–1, 177, 196, 202–4, 218, 224 n.12
Satan's  29, 37
two kingdoms  52
worldly  30
Klages, Ludwig  96, 108 n.7
Kojève, Alexandre  101
Korach  84
Kraft, Werner  142–3, 149 n.20, 150 nn.22–3, 25, 190 n.21
Kraus, Karl  12, 224 n.7

Lacan, Jacques  69 n.49, 125, 209 n.4
Lacis, Asja  51
lament  39, 41, 97, 158, 161, see also nature, lament of
Landauer, Gustav  12, 107, 114 n.34
language, see also Benjamin, "On Language"
    Adamic  39–42, 47 nn.40–2 (see also name/naming)
    Benjamin's 1916 essay on  5, 41, 47 nn.39–40 and 42, 134, 158
    fallen  39–42, 47 n.40
    poetic  185
    and writing  61, 140, 143, 150 n.27, 159–62
Last Judgment  5, 29, 95, 110 n.13, 135–6, 190 n.21, see also judgment, day of
law
    Benjamin's critique of  11, 15, 84, 119, 133–47
    Cohen's concept of  15, 20 n.28, 176, 179–80, 183–4
    deactivated  142–5 (see also politics, deactivated)
    of entropy/thermodynamics  104–5, 113 n.29
    and fate  143–4, 164, 167–8
    force of  2, 139, 206–7 (see also Benjamin, "Critique of Violence")
    and guilt  80, 164
    halakhik  86, 136, 141–2
    independence from  133, 137–9 (see also exception)

juridical  1, 4–5, 42, 206
Kafka's concept of  3, 135–41
living  59, 68 n.41
moral  179, 183, 188 n.15, 189 n.18
mythic  134, 150 n.29
natural  59, 62, 167, 179
normative, normal  1, 5, 12, 65, 206–7, 219–21
penal  30, 32 (see also punishment)
positive/customary  15, 32, 43 n.6, 65, 164
rule of  65, 77
Schmitt's concept of  1, 4, 8, 13, 32, 41, 43 n.6, 73–4, 84–5, 87, 134, 141, 206–7
Scholem's concept of  13, 134, 136–7, 139, 141–2
shari'a  136
study and  3, 11, 13, 141–7
subordination of life to  15, 33, 139–40, 164 (see also life, bare)
suspension of  8, 32, 43 n.6, 84, 87, 206, 221 (see also exception)
transgression of  32, 94
and violence  84, 114 n.31, 119, 143, 206–7
legitimacy  1–2, 10, 28, 31, 32, 39, 56, 59, 62, 64, 65, 84, 88, 110 n.12, 136–7, 140, 145, 212
liberalism  1–2, 73, 79, 87, 96
liberation  2, 6, 10, 11, 15, 38, 94, 101, 104–6, 127, 131, 159, 204, 208
life
    bare/mere  2–3, 120, 134, 139–41, 149 n.18, 164, 171 n.24
    creaturely  15, 35, 38, 50, 146, 164, 222, 225 n.25
    distorted  133, 147, 196, 202, 213, 215, 221–2 (see also distortion [Entstellung])
    dream-  60–5
    eternal  30, 36, 38, 94–5, 100–1 (see also immortal)
    of faith  52, 56, 113 n.29
    finite/mortal  109 n.12, 112 n.22, 161
    form of  3, 15–16, 40, 100, 101, 103
    guilty  35–6, 38, 50
    human  13, 35–8, 55, 101, 103, 123, 125, 157, 166, 180, 191 n.30

natural 33, 140, 163, 167, 171 n.24
ordinary/everyday 53, 56, 121, 123, 125, 131, 203, 207
politics of 213, 221 (*see also* biopolitics)
seriousness of 79, 81, 87
theater as 54-5
transience of 109 n.12, 147
living, the 52, 120-1, 123-4, 131-2, 205
guilt-context of 16, 164, 172 n.27
love
Augustine's conception of 29, 34-5, 45 n.26
Christian 36, 38-9, 77
and fate 143-4, 165
free 96, 102, 106
of God 29, 34
and melancholy 37, 52
sexual/orgasmic 102, 113 n.24
Löwith, Karl 109 n.9, 189 n.19
Lukács, Georg 20 n.25, 51, 54, 66 nn.5-6
Luther, Martin 30, 43 n.8, 44 nn.15 and 18, 57-8, 63, 65, 68 nn.33-4
Lutheranism 7, 8, 12, 28-30, 33, 44 n.21, 47 n.37, 50-2, 56-7, 60, 68 nn.26 and 30, 172 n.34

Machiavelli, Niccolò 52, 58-60, 63-5, 68 nn.32, 35 and 42
Maimonides, Moses 76, 218
Mainländer, Philip 105-7, 114 n.34
Marcion of Sinope 95, 97-100, 104, 108 n.5, 113 n.29
martyrdom 9, 37, 47 n.37, 78-9, 81-2, 87, 169-70
Marx, Karl 14, 51, 65, 66, 66 nn.6-7, 93, 96, 108 n.7, 111 n.17, 178, 197-8
Marxism 51, 108 n.7, 111 n.17, 200, *see also* communism; socialism
materialism
historical 14, 16, 51, 87, 89 n.15, 170, 179, 187 n.9, 197, 199-201, 204, 208, 212, 223 n.2, 225 n.21
and theology 83-4, 107 n.2, 200-1, 204, 212, 223 n.2
matter 10, 12, 93-4, 97-8, 100-4, 111 n.17, 112 n.20, 113 n.29
mechanism/mechanical 53, 55, 105, 163, 165, 175, 186, 199

medieval 7, 27-8, 34, 45 n.26, 46 nn.31 and 34, 52, 57-8, *see also* Middle Ages
Meier, Heinrich 75, 79
melancholy 7-8, 27-8, 33, 44 n.21, 50-2, 58, 60, 61, 66, 66 n.2, 169-70, 223 n.4
Melanchthon, Philip 57-8, 63, 68 n.29
memory 87, 112, 215-16, 221, *see also* remembrance
Messiah, the 17-18, 86, 94, 125, 197
and Antichrist 205, 207-8
anticipation of 203-4
arrival/entry of 82, 175, 182, 186, 187 n.3, 196, 202-5, 217-20, 222, 224 n.11
Cohen's idea of 17, 179-81, 183
days of 183, 185, 218
and redemption 82-3
Messianic/messianism 2-3, 13-16, 18, 88 n.4, 94, 96, 106, 125, 129, 133-4
adjustment 17, 147, 195-6, 218 (*see also* Kabbalah; rectification; *Tikkun*)
age 76, 80, 179, 185, 197, 199, 203
apocalyptic 101, 198 (*see also* apocalypse)
Benjamin's concept of 14-16, 18, 82-3, 88 n.10, 98, 130, 174-5, 178, 181-2, 188 n.10, 195, 220
Cohen's concept of 15-17, 178-86, 188 nn.10-11, 189 n.19, 191 n.30
and distortion 216-17, 220-1
figure of 4, 14, 17, 195, 199, 204, 216-17
and historical materialism 199-200
and hope 93, 105, 107 n.2, 109 n.9
intensity 83, 93, 95, 97-8, 100-2, 104-5, 107, 109 n.12, 144, 158
Judaic 14-15, 17, 83, 93, 101, 174, 179
Kafka's concept of 111 n.16, 124, 129, 202-3, 216, 224 n.8
kingdom 29, 36, 98, 100, 177, 196, 202-4
life 140
nature 12, 61, 101, 109 n.10, 134, 145

nihilism   101, 107, 138–9
politics   3, 95, 198, 204, 208–9
quietest approach of the   100–1, 144
relatedness to the profane   95–6, 98, 199, 203–4, 209
revolutionary   82, 111 n.17
romantic   203
Scholem's concept of   16, 146, 174, 196, 218
sparks and splinters   83, 175–6
  (*see also* Kabbalah; Shevirat haKelim*)
and study   146–8
task   139, 197
and *Tikkun*   18, 175–6, 187 n.4
  (*see also* Kabbalah)
time   3, 6, 14, 16, 51, 107, 134–6, 139, 147, 174–5, 177–8, 182–3, 186, 187 n.9, 190 n.22, 198, 202, 204–5, 209, 210 n.6, 224 n.11
tradition   9, 83, 101, 108 n.2
weak power   2, 84, 135, 177, 179, 198, 212
world   218–19
metaphysics, metaphysical   13, 19 n.19, 93–6, 98–100, 104–5, 107, 118–19, 124, 129, 162, 165–6, 175–7, 179, 203, 216
Metz, Johann Baptist   2, 18 n.6
Middle Ages   29, 52, 67 n.23, *see also* medieval
miracle   1, 32, 43 n.6, 50, 53–5, 76, 81, 84, 111 n.17, 127
*mitzvot*   16, 176
Molitor, Franz Joseph   187 n.4
monadology   162, 171 n.19, 166, 186
moral/morality   8, 15, 56–7, 81, 141, 171 nn.12 and 21
  and Cohen   179, 181, 183–5, 190 n.25
  and fate   15, 161–2, 164, 166
  law   179, 183, 188 n.15, 189 n.18
  meaning of suffering   9, 79
  and messianism   175, 181, 183, 186
  and Strauss (Leo)   79–80, 82, 87
mortality   96, 101–2, 112 n.22, 125, 145, 157, 160–2, *see also* death/finitude
Moses   36, 43 n.14, 78

mourning (*Trauer*)   5, 33, 40–1, 45 n.26, 47 n.42, 50–1, 66 n.2, 112 n.22, 168–70
mystery   51, 53, 110 n.13, 138, 158, 169–70, 216
mysticism   17, 140, 195–8, 204–5, 224 n.10
myth
  Benjamin's critique of   4, 6, 10, 13, 82, 112 n.17, 148
  and catastrophe   182
  and the cyclical   105, 114 n.31
  and distortion   148, 220
  and drama   167, 169–70
  and eschatology   190 n.22
  and fate   10, 15, 148, 158, 162–4
  Greek/Pagan   58–9, 167
  and Kafka   108 n.8, 111 n.17, 142
  and law   134, 150 n.29
  and the little "hunchback"   148, 213–14
  and martyrdom   87
  and power   4, 13
  and Schmitt   13, 80, 141, 169–70
  and time   10–11, 180, 190 n.22
  and violence   84, 114 n.31, 118–31, 143, 206

Nachman of Breslov, Rabbi   218–19, *see also* Rabbi
name, naming   5, 40–2, 47 nn.40–2, *see also* Adam; Language
natality   81, *see also* Arendt
Natorp, Paul   178, 183 n.13, *see also* neo-Kantianism
natural   10, 28, 30, 44 n.16, 55, 58–9, 81, 95, 96, 100, 102, 104, 110 n.15, 217
  guilt   16, 44 n.19, 134, 164, 171 n.24
  history   16, 54, 61, 67 n.18, 99, 158, 163, 166, 168
  innocence   16, 33, 44 n.20, 164
  law   43 n.6, 59, 62, 84, 167, 179
  life   33, 140, 163, 167, 171 n.24
  order   29, 57
  world   95, 103, 107
nature   43 nn.8–9, 55–7, 61–2, 98, 104–6, 118–19, 136, 146, 160, 165–6, 184–5, 190 n.25

fallen  32, 40–1, 44 n.19
human  29, 39, 44 nn.17 and 19, 73, 166–7, 169, 180
lament of  5, 39–42
material  12, 15, 99–101
messianic  12, 61, 95–6, 101, 109 n.10, 134, 145
second  20 n.25, 32
state of  52, 54
subjugation of  32, 39, 41
Nazism  1, 7, 12, 18 n.4, 42 n.3, 80, 84, 87
negativity  6, 13, 62, 80, 98, 105–7, 112 n.21, 123, 131–2, 170, 179, 215
neo-Kantianism  15, 174, 178, 180, 182, 187 n.9, 188 n.13, 189 n.20, see also Cohen; Natorp; Stadler; and Vorländer
Neumann, Franz  44 n.21
New Testament  36, 43 n.14, 149 n.10, 205
Nietzsche, Friedrich  96, 125
night/nocturnal  37, 47 n.38, 99, 101, 104–5, 108 n.8, 112 nn.17–18, 113 n.24, 160, 162, 165, 169
nihilism  3–4, 6, 11–13, 93–6, 99, 101, 104, 107, 109 n.10, 111 n.17, 137–9, 145, 179
normal  1, 8, 32, 43 n.6, 81, 141, 147, 206–7, 225 n.25
normalization  18, 85, 213, 219–22, 225 n.19
norm/normativity  1, 5, 12, 87, 147, 206–7, 219–21, 225 n.25
nothing  38, 54, 61, 80, 94–6, 101, 105–7, 109 n.9, 110 n.13, 111 n.17, 113 n.24, 114 n.31, 126, 129, 212
creation out of  85, 182–3
and evil  38
and messianic adjustment  148, 218
and nihilism  95–6, 139
of revelation  137–8, 216
and transience  98–100, 107
now  15, 17, 110 n.13, 159, 167, 175, 183, 205, 208, see also time
here and  82, 102, 160, 203
of knowability/recognizability  170, 186, 187 n.2

-time [*Jetztzeit*]  83, 177, 187 n.9, 198, 209

oblivion  103, 108 n.8, 112 n.22, 159, 182, 214–15, *see also* forgetting; inattentiveness
Old Testament  30, 36
omnipotence  28, 31–2, 38, 43 n.6, 57, 63, 84
oppression  2, 4, 6, 9, 10, 16, 64, 82–3, 87, 100, 147, 164, 186, 205–6, *see also* tradition, of the oppressed
order  9, 53, 86, 94, 98, 125, 163
of creation  4, 28–9, 32, 35, 39–42
of fate  15, 56, 164
immanent  5, 29, 40–1, 53
imposed  4–5, 40–2
legal  1, 4–5, 50, 73, 141, 206–7 (*see also* law)
of nature  29, 57
penal  8, 29–31, 33, 36, 38–9, 41–2 (*see also* punishment)
political  29, 32
priestly  52–3
profane  83, 94, 98–101, 111 n.17, 113 n.24, 144, 203, 224 n.10
remedial  28–9, 95
Schmitt and  4–5, 19 n.16, 133, 141
social  63, 111 n.17
of things  63–4
origin  56, 78, 128, 134, 146, 176, 182, 190 n.23, 225 n.26

pagan, paganism  45 n.29, 52, 57–8, 164, 168
Panofsky, Erwin  46 n.34, 68 n.34
paradise  29–30, 32, 35, 39, 41, 47 n.42, 58, 101, 108 n.7, 113 n.27
parallax  197, 209 n.4, 221, 225 n.20, *see also* Žižek
past  63, 78, 88, 142, 161, 163–4, 167, 172 n.41, 185, 188 n.14, 190 n.22, 205, 208, 214, 221, *see also* remembrance
and Benjamin's messianism  174–5, 177–8, 183, 198
claim of  2, 5, 135, 158, 170, 177
and forgetting  214–15

historical image of 87, 175, 197
redemption of 17, 83, 157, 179, 182, 186, 188 n.14, 198
  secret agreement with 135–6
  struggles 6
  unredeemed 186, 198, 215
Paul, Jean (Johann Paul Friedrich Richter) 190 n.25
Paul, St. 3, 37, 43 n.10, 44 n.18, 46 nn.30 and 32, 78, 98, 100, 102–4, 109 nn.9–10, 110 n.13, 114 n.35, 149 n.10
peace 29–30, 50, 59, 65, 100, 106, 174, 179, 185–6, 191 nn.27 and 30
phantasm/phantasmagoria 37–8, 45 n.26, 119, 122, 125, 126, 128, 130, 150 n.29, see also fantasy
Plato/Platonic 29, 34, 59, 60, 68 nn.33 and 39, 103, 182
play (*Spiel*) 18, 50–1, 54–6, 59–60, 62, 64, 67 n.24, 169, 170, 220–1, see also drama
  deactivated law and 143–4
  of fate 57, 161, 167–9, 172 n.32
  and game 55, 67 n.17, 83–4, 111 n.17, 199, 201–2, 209
  *Hamlet* 12, 50, 55–6, 64, 162, 168–70 (see also Shakespeare)
  *Leo Armenius* 36–8 (see also Gryphius)
  *Life is a Dream* 8, 51–2, 54, 56, 58–65 (see also Calderón)
  mourning 51, 168 (see also trauerspiel)
  within the play 50, 56, 60
pleroma 94–5, 100, 106–7
Poe, Edgar Allan 201–2, see also chess automaton
political philosophy 6, 13–14, 19 n.15, 28–9, 43 n.8, 44 n.21, 51, 59, 75
political theology
  and Agamben 140
  Augustinian 7–8, 28–30, 77–8
  Benjamin and 1–6, 12–14, 17–18, 39, 50, 55, 73, 82–3, 87, 93, 96, 99, 104, 107, 157–8, 166, 195, 212, 223 n.2
  Christian 3, 79–80
  exilic 9, 78–80, 88 n.5 (see also *galut*)

history of the concept 1, 18 n.2
  Jewish 6, 9, 75, 79–81, 88
  Schmittian 1–6, 9, 14, 17, 28, 31–2, 43 n.8, 50, 55, 73–7, 79, 82–5, 88, 157, 160, 212
  and Strauss (Leo) 75–7, 82
  and the trauerspiel 28, 31–2
politics 5, 33, 50, 56, 64, 73, 133, 158
  absolutism 1, 27, 43 n.8
  anarchist 3–4, 6, 10–11, 13, 117–18, 120, 124, 126–7, 129–31, 141, 207
  Aristotelian 29, 98
  astral 8, 52, 57–8, 66, 68 n.26 (*see also* stars)
  authoritarian 1, 9–10, 28, 32, 39–40, 43 n.8
  Benjamin's *Politik* 9–11
  biopolitics 12, 74, 101, 107, 213, 221–3, 225 n.26
  deactivated 144–5
  fallen 40–2
  fascist 9, 84, 118–19, 205–8
  Kafkan 10, 111 n.17
  liberal 1, 73–4, 77, 79, 82, 85, 87–8, 96, 118–19
  Lutheran 12, 30, 44 n.21, 57, 68 n.26
  materialist 83, 197, 201, 208
  messianic 3, 95, 175–6, 208
  nihilism as world- 4, 12, 93–6, 101, 107, 109 n.10, 111 n.17, 145
  profane/secular 2, 28, 39, 43 n.6, 204
  revolutionary 14, 51, 56, 63–4, 82, 85, 111 n.17, 178–9, 182, 195, 197–8, 203–6, 208–9
  of sin 7–8, 28, 30–2, 39–40, 42, 43 n.8
  social-democratic 178, 187 n.9
  and theology 1, 3–4, 6, 10–12, 14, 17, 107, 157, 174, 195, 198, 200, 203, 208
*Ponderación Misteriosa* 52, 64, 67 n.24 (*see also* trauerspiel, redemptive ending of)
Ponticus, Evagrius 45 n.25, 46 n.31
Poussin, Nicolas 147
power 2, 5, 35, 36, 54, 63, 74, 77, 106, 123–6, 133, 141, 143, 145, 161, 164, 178, 188 n.14, 224 n.7

absolute 27, 32, 34, 65
archist 117–20, 127
coercive 30, 37
constituent 59, 65, 68 n.38
divine 108 n.3, 131
expressive 40, 47 n.42
mythic 4, 13, 119
phantasms about 122
secular 29–30, 44 n.16, 51, 56
sovereign 1, 18 n.3, 30–2, 65, 84–5, 87, 128, 140–2
state 9, 207
weak messianic 2, 84, 135, 177, 179, 198, 212
praxis 8, 51–2, 66, 182, 186
prayer 127, 138, 146, 181, 214, 216–17
present 2, 4–5, 46 n.36, 64, 98, 108 n.8, 114 n.31, 165, 170, 197, 208, *see also* now-time
and actuality 181–2, 190 n.25, 218
contemporaneous 73, 88
and eternity 183–4
and fate 163, 171 n.25
and future 2, 63, 161, 180, 183, 185–6
and messianism 224 n.12, 198, 209
moment 119, 158
and now-time 83, 175, 198, 205
and past 63, 83, 88, 158, 161, 165, 170, 180, 183, 185, 186, 197–8, 208
profane, *see also* secular
creation 45 n.26, 84
and happiness 98, 144, 204
and history 172 n.34, 199, 202, 204
and law 136–7, 143
(non-) relation of the messianic to the 83, 94, 96, 144, 199, 203, 209
order 83, 88 n.10, 94, 98–101, 111 n.17, 113 n.24, 144, 203, 224 n.10 (*see also* order)
politics 204, 209
profanation 143–4
and secularization 50
and theocracy 10
and theology 157, 161
transience of the 98–9, 109 n.10
world 61, 168, 203–4

progress 5, 34, 85, 94, 96, 108 n.5, 191 nn.26–7, 196
Benjamin's critique of 175, 177, 179, 187 n.9, 189 n.20, 214
Cohen's idea of 180, 185
and empty, homogeneous time 175, 178, 187 n.9
and history 14, 16–17, 54, 56, 58, 61, 83, 96, 99, 107 n.2, 111 n.17, 198, 204, 214
interruption of 111 n.17, 174, 179
Neo-Kantian idea of 174, 178, 187 n.9, 189 n.20
as a storm blowing from paradise 101, 113 n.27
property 35, 43 n.14, 61, 168
prophecy/prophets/prophetic 16–17, 36, 46 nn.31 and 33, 57–9, 63, 76, 96, 105, 174, 181–2, 184–6, 190 n.25
Protestantism 29, 55, 59, 108 n.5
providence 32, 57, 169
punishment 8, 11, 28–30, 41, 60, 64–5, 69 n.52, 88 n.11, 110 n.13, 134, 216, *see also* law; order
puppet 17, 50, 84, 111 n.17, 195, 199–202, 204
purity/pure 42, 57, 112 n.21, 120, 137, 159, 171 n.8, 176–7, 189 nn.15 and 18
concept of in Cohen 176, 180, 183–4
politics of pure means 111 n.17, 131

Rabbi, rabbinic 76, 101, 148, 217, 220
Israel ben Eliezer (Baal Shem Tov) 203, 218 (*see also* Baal Shem Tov; Hasidism)
Nachman of Breslov 218–19 (*see also* Nachman; *Tikkun*)
Scholem as (*see also* Benjamin, "Franz Kafka") 196, 218
Rang, Florens Christian 104–5
rebus 52, 61, 68 n.45
rectification 17–18, 213, 218–22, *see also* right, rectitude
Redeemer 17, 77, 95, 205, 208
redemption 38, 52, 87, 94–5, 107, 109 n.10, 112 n.19, 146, 157, 160–2, 171 n.15, 176–7, 182,

186, 187 n.5, 222, *see also* salvation
absence of 4, 9, 75–83, 88 n.5 (*see also* exile; *galut*)
and distortion 216, 219–21
and messianism 83, 96, 175–6, 187 nn.2 and 8, 203, 216
of missed possibilities 213–14
and revolution 178, 198, 203
secularized 51, 56
of sins 36, 57, 190 n.24
and time 5, 15, 164, 178, 179
and transformation 198, 218
of the world 16, 93, 100, 105, 191 n.27
reflection 8, 16, 50–1, 54, 56, 60–1, 64, 157, 159, 164, 167, 169
Reformation 3, 8, 29, 52, 57
religion 1, 58, 68 n.31, 94, 117, 120–3, 127, 142, 145, 174, 182, 223 n.2
capitalism as 2, 18 n.8, 82, 207 (*see also* Benjamin, "Capitalism as Religion")
Cohen's philosophy of 174, 176, 178–9, 181, 183, 185–6, 188 n.11, 190 n.21
remembrance 10, 78, 158, 161, 177, 182, 186, 198, 214, 217, 219, *see also* memory
Renaissance, the 8, 45 n.26, 46 nn.31 and 33–4, 52, 58, 61, 68 nn.31–3
renewal 146, 162
repression 63, 97, 215, 225 n.26, *see also* distortion; Freud
restitution/*restitutio in integrum* 94–6, 98–100, 106, 145–6, 158, 182
revelation 32, 43 n.6, 75–6, 104, 106, 108 n.4, 109 n.12, 135–8, 158, 170, 182, 198 n.4, 216
reverence 121, 130
reversal (*Umkehr*) 33, 38, 140, 185, 208, 216, 224 n.8, *see also* hope, in reverse; Kafka; messianism
revolution 51, 59, 63–4, 68 n.35, 85, 87, 111 n.17, 113 n.24, 117, 130, 174, 177–8, 187 n.9, 204, 206, 208–9
astrological 8, 56, 58

French 14, 177–8, 187 n.7, 198
revolutionary 9, 56, 58, 65, 82, 84, 85, 102, 111 n.17, 195, 198, 203–6, 208–9
action 14, 60, 63–4, 179, 182, 197
chance 182
politics 14, 111 n.17
praxis 8, 51
right 187 n.7
correct 63–4, 130
idea of 187 n.7
natural 59, 62
positive 59, 62
and power 65, 84, 119–20
*Recht* 81, 87, 89 n.14, 134, 142, 219
righteousness/rectitude 9, 30, 31, 35, 78–80, 83, 87, 179, 213, 219, 221–3
set-right 18, 124–5 (*see also* adjustment [*Zurechtstellung*])
(up)right 215, 219, 220, 222, 225 nn.19 and 26
-wing 6, 20 n.23, 73, 74, 96
Rilke, Rainer Maria 102, 105, 107
Rome 177–8, 198
Rosenzweig, Franz 76, 78, 109 n.9, 187 n.4, 203–4
Ruge, Arnold 51, 66
ruin 50, 61, 81, 102, 112 n.19

sacrifice 10, 36, 79
salvation 30, 33, 36–7, 47 n.37, 50–2, 54–7, 87, 101, 125, 146, 148, 171 n.15, 176–7, 203, 219, 221, 224 n.12
sanctity 179–83, 186, 188 n.15, 189 n.18
Sappho 161
Satan 29, 37, *see also* angel, fall of; devil
Saturn 27, 46 n.33, 57–63, 65, 68 nn.34 and 40, 169, 223 n.4, *see also* melancholy
Saxl, Fritz 46 n.34, 68 n.34
Scherer, Georg 214
Schlegel, Friedrich 203
Schmitt, Carl
and Benjamin 2–9, 16–17, 19 n.19, 20 n.23, 27–8, 31–2, 42 n.2, 50, 53, 56, 67 n.21, 73, 81–8, 134, 172 nn.39–40, 210 n.7, 212

and Christian triumphalism 6, 9,
  76–7, 80–2
decisionism of 27, 75–6, 81–2, 85–6,
  171 n.12, 206–7
intellectual influence of 73–4, 88
*Katechon*, concept of 5, 19 n.18, 82,
  87, 107, 114 n.35
and liberalism, critique of 73–4, 79,
  86–7
Nazism and 1, 7, 18 n.4, 42 n.3, 87
order, concept of 4–5, 19 n.16, 53,
  134, 141
political theology, concept of 1–3,
  18 n.5, 28, 32, 53, 74–7, 79,
  82–3, 85, 107, 157
sovereignty, concept of 1, 4–5, 7,
  13–14, 27–8, 31–2, 34–5,
  39, 41–2, 43 nn.6–7, 50, 75,
  79, 82–7, 128, 133, 134, 141,
  144
state of exception, concept of 3–5,
  7–9, 18 n.3, 32, 43 n.6, 50, 53,
  55, 82, 87, 148, 206–7
and Strauss 6, 9, 75–7, 79, 81–2, 85,
  87, 88
works of
  *Concept of the Political* 43 n.9, 79
  *Constitutional Theory* 77
  "Der Führer schützt das
    Recht" 87
  *Dictatorship* 7, 18 n.3, 27–8,
    42 n.2, 43 n.8
  *Hamlet or Hecuba: The Interruption
    of Time into Play* 54–6, 64,
    67 nn.22–3, 169–70
  *Leviathan in the State Theory of
    Thomas Hobbes* 67 n.20, 77
  *Political Theology* 1, 7, 18 n.3,
    27–8, 32, 42 n.2, 43 n.8, 50, 55,
    76–7
  *Roman Catholicism and Political
    Form* 76
Scholem, Gershom 75, 94, 109 n.9, 133,
  190 n.21, 204, *see also* Kabbalah
correspondence with
  Benjamin 66 n.5, 85, 166,
  188 n.11, 196, 218
as editor (with Adorno) of Benjamin's
  correspondence 7

"Es gibt ein Geheimnis in der
  Welt." *Tradition und
  Säkularisation* 135
exchange with Benjamin about
  Kafka 136–8, 140–2, 216,
  224 n.8 (*see also* nothing, of
  revelation)
and law, concept of 13, 134,
  136–9, 141–2 (*see also* law,
  fundamental)
and "life in deferral" 95
and Lurianic Kabbalah 16, 187 n.4,
  219, 225 n.16
and messianism 101, 112 n.19, 139,
  146, 174, 187 n.4, 224 n.8
as rabbi in Benjamin's Kafka
  essay 196, 218 (*see also*
  Benjamin, "Franz Kafka";
  Rabbi)
"Theses on the Concept of
  Justice" 134, 218, 224 n.14
Schopenhauer, Arthur 105–7
Scripture 36, 127, 129, 140–1, *see also*
  text, holy
secret 2, 83, 135–6, 170, 198, 201,
  224 n.10
secular 1, 32–3, 36, 47 n.37, 52–3,
  108 n.3, 117–20, 127, 140,
  190 n.21, 204, *see also* profane
  authority/power 8, 28–31, 36, 44 n.16
  order 43 n.12, 98
  politics 2, 28, 39, 43 n.6
  post- 18 n.5, 74, 223 n.2
  secularism 18 n.5, 130–1
  secularization 7–8, 18 n.5, 28, 31–2,
    46 n.36, 50, 61, 74, 174, 178,
    199–200, 204
semblance 8, 15, 102, 134, 141, 164,
  169–70
Shabbat (Sabbath) 107, 120
Shakespeare, William 50, 55–6, 67 n.9,
  162, 168–9, 172 nn.38–9
silence 101, 159, 161
sin 7–8, 15, 18 n.5, 28–40, 42, 43 nn.8–
  10, 44 nn.17 and 19, 46 nn.32
  and 34, 57, 60, 68 n.27, 97, 162,
  190 n.24
singularity 5, 39–40, 113 n.25, 163, 170,
  215

Sloterdijk, Peter  68 n.46, 222, 225 n.23
social democracy  14, 111 n.17, 178,
    187 n.9, 214
socialism  180, 188 n.13, 198
soul  16, 34–8, 45 n.26, 46 nn.33–4,
    47 n.38, 63, 95, 110 n.15,
    159, 179–80, 188 n.15, 189 n.18,
    217
sovereign/sovereignty
  and Agamben  13, 53, 137, 140–1,
    225 n.25
  Benjamin's concept of (aside from in
    the trauerspiel book)  13, 84,
    135, 213, 222–3
  in Calderón's *Life is a Dream*  62–3,
    65, 67 n.8
  ego  16, 160–1, 171 n.12
  God's  38
  and Kafka  127, 143
  Lutheran concept of  44 n.21
  and normalization  18, 213, 221,
    225 nn.19 and 25
  representation of in the trauerspiel
    book  7–8, 27–8, 30–9, 42 n.2,
    47 n.37, 55, 84–7
  Schmitt's concept of  1, 4–7, 13–14,
    18 n.3, 27–8, 31–2, 34–5, 39, 42,
    42 n.2, 43 n.7, 50, 53, 55, 73, 77,
    79, 81–5, 87, 107, 128, 133–4,
    141, 144, 166, 206–7
  and Scholem  140–2
  and Strauss (Leo)  80
space  13, 46 n.36, 53, 66 n.7, 75–6,
    113 n.29, 118, 124, 133, 145,
    164–5, 176, 184, 204, 206, 222
spirit  10, 12, 29, 33, 35–6, 93–4, 98,
    100–5, 110 n.15, 113 n.24
spiritual  12, 29–30, 34, 36–8, 41, 93,
    95–6, 99–103, 107 n.2, 112 n.18,
    145–6, 161, 164–5, 178, 186
Stadler, August  178
standstill  85, 111 n.17, 208
stars  56–60, *see also* astral
State, the  55–6, 64, 84, 106, 118–19, 125,
    207
status quo  83, 85, 205–6, 208–9
Strauss, Leo  3, 6, 9, 73–83, 85–8, 88 n.5
Strauss, Ludwig  188 n.11
strike  51, 111 n.17

striving  28, 34, 39, 47 n.37, 56, 96–9,
    101–2, 106, 109 n.9, 110 n.15,
    111 n.17, 145, 183, 204
study  3, 6, 10–13, 127, 129–30, 133, 138,
    140–8, 159, 224 n.8
subjectivity  32, 38, 47 n.37, 160
suffering  5, 9–11, 29–31, 36–7, 39, 41,
    77–81, 83, 95, 99–101, 103, 106,
    144–5
symbolism  34, 39, 41, 161, 176–7
synagogue  78

Talmud  86, 101, 120, 146, 179, 183
task
  historian's  177, 182, 186, 197–8, 205,
    225 n.21
  infinite  16, 85, 176, 178, 182, 184,
    188 n.15, 189 n.20, 190 n.25,
    191 n.26
  messianic  15–17, 139, 197
  of theology  203–4
  of world politics  95, 99, 145, 203–4
Taubes, Jacob  3, 7, 12, 19 nn.15 and
    21, 20 n.23, 98, 104–5, 107,
    109 nn.9–10, 113 n.29, 135,
    149 n.11
Taylor, Charles  52–3
teaching (*Lehre*)  6, 9, 86, 142, 166, 218
teleology, telos  14, 83, 93–6, 98, 101,
    166, 203
  without goal  163
temporal  10, 15, 16, 28–32, 46 n.36, 54,
    67 n.16, 85, 95, 103, 110 n.13,
    117, 136, 145, 158–61, 163–5,
    170, 171 n.16, 183, 185, 186,
    187 n.2, 209, 214
text (*Schrift*)  127, 136–40, 142, 171 n.9,
    *see also* Scripture
  historical  197, 205
  holy  127, 136–8, 143, 146
theater  54–5, 58, 64, 108 n.4, 220–1
theism, theistic  13, 117–18, 123, 125,
    130–2
theocracy, theocratic  9–13, 93–4,
    108 n.3, 109 n.9, 179, 204
theology  52, 58, 61, 68 n.33, 101, 142,
    157, 167–9
  antinomian  94, 101, 146
  Augustinian  7, 28, 33, 47 n.37

Barthian 97, 109 n.9
Christian 18 n.5, 58, 78, 80, 188 n.14
Gnostic 94-5, 97-100, 104-7, 108 n.5, 110 n.14, 111 n.17, 113 n.29
"hunchbacked" 17-18, 150 n.33, 202, 204, 212-14 (*see also* "dwarf"-like)
liberation 2
Lutheran 33, 47 n.37, 52
and materialism 107 n.2, 199-201
messianic 174, 204
negative 123
and politics 1, 4, 10, 14, 17, 18 nn.5 and 14, 203, 208
of sin 33, 38
voluntarist 4, 5, 7, 43 n.6
*Tikkun* 16, 20 n.30, 175, 187 n.4, 218, 225 n.16, *see also* Kabbalah
haKlali 218-19 (*see also* Nachman; Rabbi)
and rectification 17-18, 219
time
chronological 15, 158, 160, 163, 166, 170, 209, 210 n.6, 215
chronophilia 102, 112 n.22
chronophobia 102, 112 n.22
clock- 55, 159
empty 53, 56, 58, 85, 107, 175, 177, 186, 187 n.9, 198, 202
end of 52, 82, 190 n.22, 202, 205, 207, 210 n.6
fulfilled, fulfillment of 174-5, 178, 183, 186, 187 n.9
homogeneous 14, 16, 85, 178, 182, 202, 204
immortal 159, 160, 162, 167
justice of 13, 133
kairological 160, 209 (*see also* Kairos)
linear 14, 16, 159, 224 n.11
messianic 3, 6, 13-14, 16, 51, 107, 134-6, 139, 147, 174-5, 178, 182, 187 n.9, 190 n.22, 198, 202, 205, 209, 210 n.6, 224 n.11
now- (Jetztzeit) 83, 175, 177-9, 182-3, 186, 187 n.9, 198, 209
passage of 14, 110 n.13
redemptive quality of 15, 178, 179
and space 58, 66 n.7, 76, 118, 124, 133, 145, 164, 165, 176

youthful 159
timelessness 32, 110 n.13, 159
Torah 127, 136, 138-9, 141, 150 n.21
totality 61, 95, 105, 145, 163, 177, 179, 184, 186, 191 n.26
tradition 28, 34, 94, 107 n.2, 127, 136-9, 146, 166, 179, 188 n.10, 203
Jewish 76, 80, 82, 84, 86, 101, 142
messianic 9, 17, 83, 101, 107 n.2, 195, 204
of the oppressed 6, 9, 82, 205-6
tragedy, tragic 15, 54-6, 97, 164, 167-9, 172 n.36
transcendence 1, 4, 8, 10, 17, 47 n.37, 52-4, 56, 62, 98, 107, 118-19, 121, 125, 142, 158, 183, 190 n.25, 195, 202, 207
transience 4, 5, 11-13, 15, 19 n.18, 30, 35-8, 61, 93-107, 109 nn.10 and 12, 112 nn.18 and 22, 135, 142, 144-7, 160, 162, 167, 197
trauerspiel 31, 35-7, 41-2, 44 n.19, 52, 53, 58, 61, 67 nn.16 and 18, *see also* Benjamin, *Origin of the German Trauerspiel*
Baroque 7, 8, 18 n.5, 29, 39, 47 n.37, 51, 55, 57, 168-70
German 8, 33, 50, 54, 56, 67 n.24
hero/heroine of 7, 27, 32, 42 n.2, 50
redemptive ending of 36, 38, 64, 67 n.24 (*see also* Ponderación Misteriosa)
Spanish 8, 56, 67 n.8
sovereignty in 28, 33, 34, 42, 85-6
truth 34, 37-8, 46 n.34, 60, 99, 101, 119, 122, 127-9, 131, 136, 158, 164, 166-7, 170, 177, 184, 187 n.2, 189 n.19, 190 n.21, 200-2, 215, 219, 221
tyrant 30-2, 35-8, 44 n.18, 58, 60, 62, 64
tyrannicide 59
tyranny 31, 37
*tzedakah* 9, 79, 81

utopia 12, 93, 96, 101, 146, 175, 179, 190 n.25, 196, *see also* Bloch, *Spirit of Utopia*

validity   10, 13, 51, 76, 134, 137, 139, 141, 187 n.2
vanity   38, 99, 109 n.12
verdict   95, 134
vice   31, 38
victory   64, 67 n.23, 83, 113 n.22, 146, 202
violence   3, 19 n.15, 53, 54, 65, 77, 127, 203, 207, 223 n.2,
   see also Benjamin, "Critique of Violence"
  divine   64, 84–5, 88 n.11, 119–21, 123–5, 128, 131, 206
  law-creating   84, 114 n.31
  law-preserving   84, 114 n.31
  mythic   84, 119–26, 129–31, 143, 206
Vorländer, Karl   178, 188 n.13, see also neo-Kantianism

Warburg, Aby   8, 51–2, 57–8, 60–1, 63, 67 n.9, 68 nn.26, 30–1 and 34
weak messianic power   2, 84, 135, 177, 179, 198, 212
Weber, Max   12, 50, 85, 96, 105
Weimar   97, 110 n.14
  Constitution of   1, 18 n.3, 207
  intellectual history of   7
  period   7, 20 n.23, 104, 107, 108 n.5, 109 n.9, 158
  Republic   12, 81, 207
World, see also Earth

beyond   175, 179–81 (see also Heaven)
to come   15, 17, 108 nn.3–4, 148, 196, 217
empty   27, 57, 169
-politics   4, 12, 93–6, 98–9, 101, 107, 109 n.10, 111 n.17, 113 n.24
profane   61, 168, 199, 203–4
temporal   28–32–32, 35, 38–9
this   16–17, 35, 43 n.14, 60, 96, 98–9, 102, 108 n.3, 109 n.10, 196, 203, 215, 217–18
worldly   28, 30, 36, 38, 47 n.38, 52–3, 56, 60, 83–4, 98, 107, 203, see also earthly; profane; temporal
condition   97, 145
existence   61, 95, 166
restitution   94–6, 99, 145–6, 158
things   35, 37
Wyneken, Gustav   187 n.1

youth
  metaphysics of   159, 161–2, 165–6, 169 (see also Benjamin, "Metaphysics of Youth")
  movement [Jugendbewegung]   160

Zionism   79–80, 174
Žižek, Slavoj   3, 73, 125, 200, 209 n.4, 221, 223 n.2, see also parallax